HERITAGE PLANNING

Heritage Planning: Principles and Process provides a comprehensive overview of heritage planning as an area of professional practice. The book first addresses the context and principles of heritage planning, including land-use law, planning practice, and international heritage doctrine, all set within the framework of larger societal issues such as sustainability and ethics. The book then takes readers through the pragmatic processes of heritage practice, including collecting data, identifying community opinion, determining heritage significance, the best practices and methods of creating a conservation plan, and managing change.

Heritage Planning recognizes changing approaches to heritage conservation, particularly the shift from the conservation of physical fabric to the present emphasis on retaining values, associations, and stories that historic places hold for their communities. The transition has affected the practice of heritage planning and is important for those in the field.

This book is essential reading for both professionals that manage change within the built environment and students of heritage conservation and historic preservation.

Harold Kalman earned a PhD in architectural history from Princeton University, did conservation studies at the University of York and Cornell University, and teaches heritage conservation at the Universities of Victoria and Hong Kong. Kalman managed a Canadian-based international practice in conservation for 35 years. He is the author of *A History of Canadian Architecture* and many books and articles on conservation.

HERITAGE PLANNING

Principles and Process

Harold Kalman

Routledge
Taylor & Francis Group

LONDON AND NEW YORK

First published 2014
by Routledge
711 Third Avenue, New York, NY 10017

and by Routledge
2 Park Square, Milton Park, Abingdon, Oxon OX14 4RN

Routledge is an imprint of the Taylor & Francis Group, an informa business

Library of Congress Cataloging in Publication Data
Kalman, Harold, 1943-
Heritage planning : principles and process / by Harold Kalman.
pages cm
Includes bibliographical references and index.
1. Historic preservation--Planning. 2. Historic buildings--Conservation and restoration--Planning. 3. Historic sites--Conservation and restoration--Planning. 4. Cultural property--Protection--Planning. 5. Cultural policy. I. Title.
CC135.K36 2014
363.6'9--dc23
2014007761

ISBN: 978-1-138-01791-7 (hbk)
ISBN: 978-1-138-01792-4 (pbk)
ISBN: 978-1-315-77985-0 (ebk)

Typeset in 10/12 Palatino
by Fakenham Prepress Solutions, Fakenham, Norfolk NR21 8NN

Printed in Great Britain by Bell & Bain Ltd, Glasgow

Contents

Figures and Tables

Figures

Tables

Preface and Acknowledgments

I recently withdrew from practice after 35 years as a consultant in heritage conservation ('historic preservation' in the US). The business began by working from home and grew to become a partnership with multiple offices and an international clientele. We once boasted enough staff to field two softball (or cricket) teams. The business offered services in various aspects of heritage conservation, my own area of specialty being heritage planning. As consultants, we would generally start with a client's idea—perhaps a nation wanting to showcase historic places in its tourism development, a local government wanting a conservation plan for a neighborhood or park, or a building owner needing a statement of significance—and would work towards finding good solutions.

Stepping back from active practice has provided an opportunity for reflection. I began to realize that heritage planning is rarely defined and poorly understood. Even many of my colleagues are not sure what the term means. Little literature treats it comprehensively as a discipline and few planning schools teach it. Moreover, many public-sector planners with a responsibility for heritage, as well as heritage specialists in a variety of disciplines, have no formal education in either conservation doctrine or the application of best practices.

This book is intended to contribute to filling that vacuum. My objective is to help 'professionalize the profession.' The book is international in scope, fully relevant in all countries whose legal and planning systems are based on English common law. Readers from elsewhere will certainly find the book of interest, although perhaps less pertinent to the details of their work. The primary audiences are heritage specialists, planners, and postgraduate students in the United States, Great Britain, Australia, and my own Canada, as well as other nations that were once under the British sphere of influence. Readers will notice the many examples from Canada, the City of Vancouver, and projects in which I have participated. In my defence, it seemed only appropriate to highlight historic places with which I am particularly familiar.

The text has been written from a practical point of view, but without sacrificing theory. My enthusiasm for heritage doctrine and law is relatively recent. It stems from my having agreed in a weak moment to teach a course on 'Charters and Legislation of Conservation' in the Architectural Conservation Programmes at the University of Hong

Kong. What began as a challenge grew into a delight, as I learned more and more about the efforts of our predecessors and current colleagues to establish a firm foundation for practice. If this book helps pass on those underpinnings to practitioners and students, it will have succeeded.

A few words about technical details: words and phrases that represent important concepts are in **bold** type and defined when introduced. The organization moves from heritage planning principles to the processes of the discipline, and while this might make the subject matter appear to be linear, it most decidedly is not. Consequently the text is full of cross references to help the reader with navigation. Historic places are assigned dates and designers only where they are of particular interest.

Many people contributed to the book. In alphabetical order, Joy Davis, Christin Döinghaus, Michael Duckworth, Sean Fraser, Nancy Green, Ned Kaufman, Jacqueline Mason, Hugh Miller, Laurajane Smith, and Diana Waite provided overall direction and comments that helped make this a better product. Others assisted with specific topics, including Steve Barber, Susan Buggey, Katie Cummer, Marc Denhez, Lynne DiStefano, Vanessa Drysdale, Alastair Gentleman, Sharif Shams Imon, Zlatan Jankovic, Hoyin Lee, Tania Martin, Ken Nicolson, Judy Oberlander, and Erik Watson-Hurthig. Among the many photographers and curators who kindly donated the use of their photographs, I single out John Roaf, who generously provided nearly a dozen superb images and improved some of my own photos. Susan Medville creatively and tirelessly identified and procured the images. The dedicated editors at Routledge's New York and Oxfordshire offices were a pleasure to work with; in particular I am grateful to Nicole Solano, Fritz Routley, Kim Guinta, Alanna Donaldson, and Liz Dawn. Most of all I want to thank my wife, Linda Kalman, who lovingly gave up all that time we could have spent together. To all of them, and to those I have inadvertently omitted, I express my warm gratitude.

Part 1
Principles

1
Heritage Planning

1.1 The Setting of Heritage Planning
Heritage advocacy and heritage planning

Figures 1.1, 1.2 Demonstrators in Greenwich Village, New York, are heritage advocates; the facilitator of the community workshop in Campbell River, British Columbia, Canada, is a heritage planner. (Greenwich Village Society for Historic Preservation; Harold Kalman)

'Preserve our heritage!' This is the traditional—and clichéd—battle cry from those who object to the proposed demolition of a valued historic building, removal of a beloved old tree, or development on top of an archaeological site. Losing the historic place would destroy both the thing and many of the powerful cultural associations that go with it. Concerned citizens will go to considerable lengths to preserve the place they treasure. They might demonstrate at the site, pressure the politicians, communicate in the public media, negotiate with the developer, even lie down in front of the proverbial bulldozer (yet another cliché!).

The visceral reaction to threats to destroy or deface a treasured landmark is an act of **heritage advocacy**. Advocacy draws in the community and the government through political and educational action. Advocacy is often emotional and confrontational, although it can also be rational and collaborative.

Heritage conservation (called **historic preservation** in the US) is the broad discipline that addresses all aspects of retaining and enhancing **historic places**—a term that describes buildings, towns, landscapes, archaeological sites, and other places that hold historical, aesthetic, cultural, social, spiritual, and/or scientific meaning to the community—what we call heritage significance.

Heritage conservation began with advocacy. Many respected heritage organizations, such as the National Trust for Historic Preservation in the United States, began as advocacy groups. The National Trust was established by Congress in 1949 'in order to further [federal heritage] policy … and to facilitate public participation in the preservation of sites, buildings, and objects of national significance or interest.' Its early activities involved work 'to inform the nation of the need to preserve its heritage, to arouse opinion and sentiment in favor of preservation and to mobilize the public to form preservation groups' (Mulloy 1976: 12–13). Similarly, across the border in Canada, Heritage Canada pursues a mission 'to encourage Canadians to protect and promote their built, historic and cultural heritage.' This is advocacy.

Heritage advocates often speak of their activity as a 'movement,' a distinctly politicized and ideological term.[1] Advocates may show a zeal that is akin to a faith-based or religious system. Indeed, the popularity of the term 'preservationist' to describe a person who advocates preservation underlines this point.[2]

Heritage planning (also **preservation planning**, **historic preservation planning**, **conservation planning**, or **heritage conservation planning**) is the application of heritage conservation within the context of planning. It too seeks solutions to the proposed loss of a historic place, but does so in a nonconfrontational manner. It is a professional, collaborative process that strives to channel advocates' enthusiasm into rational dialogue among various community interests. It is a subdiscipline of both heritage conservation and urban planning.

Heritage planning begins with the premise that communities possess historic places that are valued, their significance provides reasons to retain them, there are legitimate social and economic pressures to change those historic places and their contexts, and international doctrine has been developed to guide those changes. Heritage planning is a professional discipline, whereas heritage advocacy is an ideological movement.[3]

The objective of heritage planning is to **manage change** wisely, not to prevent change. 'The aim of conservation,' we read in the *Burra Charter*, 'is to retain the cultural significance of a [historic] place' (Australia ICOMOS 2013b: Article 2.2). Heritage planning does not aim to freeze a historic place in time. It strives to maintain the significance of a historic place within the real-world context of urban planning and development. This is most successful when the conservation and development sectors work together. Advocates have often perceived a conflict between conservation and development, and at a personal level between the 'preservationist' (i.e., the preservation advocate) and the 'developer.' The optics may suggest that demolition threats are struggles that lead inevitably to an 'either–or' resolution. This, however, need not be the case. As American planner Norman Tyler writes,

> Preservationists are not against development; they are against *bad* development. They are opposed to development that is insensitive to the existing context of a community and its significant resources and heritage. They are in favor of development that blends new and old in a compatible way that strengthens both.
>
> (Tyler et al. 2009: 269)

Heritage planning seeks to find solutions that achieve this and encourage conservation and development to work as partners. Both development planners and heritage planners recognize that every living community must change over time to accommodate emerging social and economic needs and values, that historic places are valued, and that development should be managed in a way that respects those values. Heritage planning requires an understanding of the broad social, economic, and legal contexts and the ability to communicate effectively with the various interested parties and to learn from community values and desires.

The practice of heritage planning is professional and multidisciplinary. Its success depends on cooperation and partnerships with the community at large. The practice of heritage planning requires an alliance of knowledge and skills in subjects as diverse as the law, planning infrastructure, international standards for conservation practice, historical research, site investigation, public consultation, impact assessment, and much more. The heritage planner is partly professional expert and partly community facilitator. Where feasible, (s)he will seek consensus, although broad agreement is not always possible and forging a compromise between conflicting positions is often a good solution. Heritage planners help decision-makers make informed and wise choices that will enhance their communities in a manner consistent with widely held public values and overall planning objectives.

Good development combines the best of the past with the best of the present and future. The integration of old and new creates a dynamism that neither can achieve alone. As British-American geographer and historian David Lowenthal has written, 'Past and present should often be commingled, not separated. Every trace we inherit is a testament not only to the spirit of the past but to our present perspectives' (1981: 236).

This book is a practical manual of heritage planning. It is based on the premise that conservation and development are potential partners in the management of change.

The scope of this book

At the most basic level, the present book explains the principles and process of heritage planning within a broad and primarily Western context. It describes the setting and the infrastructure of heritage conservation, keeping in mind the evolving meanings of 'heritage.' The material is presented in a way that is sufficiently general to hold the interest of a broad, international audience, but at the same time adequately specific to illustrate broad ideas with material that is relevant to all readers.

The primary audiences for this book are practitioners and students of heritage planning and conservation. It will also interest community planners, architects, landscape architects, engineers, archaeologists, cultural geographers, government decision-makers, property managers, members of community heritage organizations, and anyone with an interest in historic places. The book is directed at readers in all English-speaking countries, with a focus on the processes in the US, the UK, Australia, and Canada, all of which share a common British legal tradition. The heritage infrastructure and the law may differ from one country to another and from one state or province to another, but the fundamental principles are constant. Experience from other places formerly within the British sphere of influence is also cited. The text addresses situations faced by all without trying to be comprehensive.

Heritage planners may work in the public sector, for one or another level of government; in the community (or civil) sector for non-governmental or non-profit organizations; or in the private (for-profit) sector, within a professional practice or the development industry. Some may have a strong formal education in heritage conservation. Others may be planners, architects, government officials, or management consultants who are involved with heritage work yet have little or no formal training in the field. This book has been written for their benefit, as well as for students, particularly those in post-secondary conservation and planning studies, and in related programs. The book is also directed at anyone who wants to learn about the discipline of heritage planning specifically and the management of the historic environment generally.

What binds all these readers together is their attitude towards historic places—an approach that respects the identification of values and the retention of those features that contribute to the heritage significance of the place, using rational, information-based, and community-based analysis to arrive at recommendations for the management of those places.

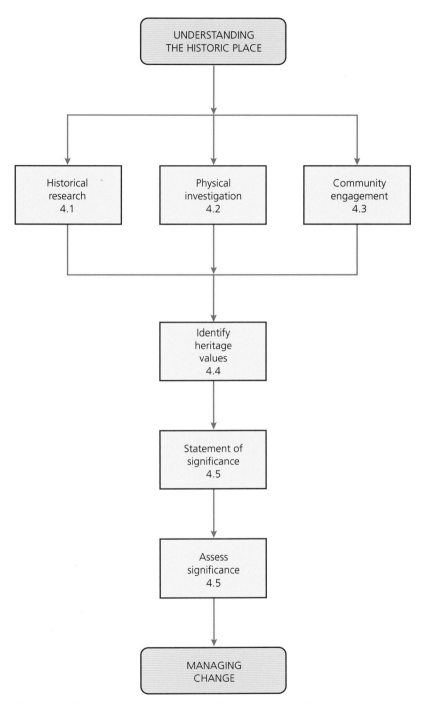

Figure 1.3 Process chart for understanding the historic place.

The outline of the book is straightforward, proceeding from principles to process. Part 1 discusses the principles with which the heritage planner should be familiar. This first chapter introduces heritage planning as a profession and then places it within a larger setting. The final section discusses the organization of the large heritage conservation sector. Chapter 2 discusses the larger real-world context of heritage planning. It begins with the legal basis and planning infrastructure for conservation. Next is a discussion of sustainability, whose emerging values and imperatives pervade all human activity. The final section looks at the ethics of conservation and its practice. Legislation, planning, sustainability, and ethics are essential considerations that reappear throughout the book. Chapter 3 introduces best conservation practices—the formal, international doctrine that defines the most acceptable ways to conserve both the physical fabric and the associated meanings of a historic place. Much is contained in formal, international 'charters' and 'conventions.' These documents define the various 'treatments' that can be applied to a conservation project—the interventions known as 'restoration,' 'preservation,' 'rehabilitation,' and others. The lessons of the charters and the definitions of the treatments, in turn, have been recast as practical advice in 'standards' and 'guidelines.'

Part 2 describes the processes of heritage planning. The procedures described in the text respect those proposed by Australian James Semple Kerr in *Conservation Plan*, the classic manual first published in 1982. Following Kerr's outline, Chapter 4 addresses 'understanding the historic place' and Chapter 5, managing change (Kerr's 'conservation policy').

The process advocated in the present book is illustrated in the two-part chart in Figures 1.3 and 1.4. The chart is intended as a simplified model and not a rigid template. Every heritage planning activity is unique in scope and solution, and the process must be tailored to suit the situation at hand. The actual process is filled with feedback loops—opinions are expressed and ideas reconsidered at every stage—and all bear political uncertainties. These cannot practicably be illustrated. These cautions notwithstanding, the chart will help with the heritage-planning process.

Chapter 4 is 'Understanding the Historic Place.' As Kerr states, prior to embarking on 'any planning process' it is necessary to 'identify and assess the attributes which make a place of value to us and to our society.' Once we have researched the history and associations of the place, investigated and documented its physical nature and setting, and listened to the views of the community, we are prepared to identify its values and assess its significance. Only then can society, in Kerr's words, make 'informed policy decisions … which will enable that significance to be retained, revealed or, at least, impaired as little as possible' (Kerr 2013: 4).

Making those policy decisions is the central activity of heritage planning. Chapter 5, 'Managing Change,' guides the process for developing policy, as well as for interventions to individual historic places and to larger districts and cultural landscapes. Although the actual

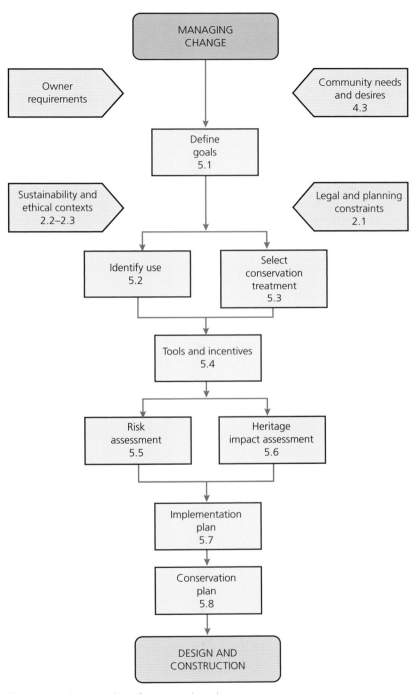

Figure 1.4 Process chart for managing change.

process will vary from one situation to another, the chapter provides a helpful model to use as a point of departure. It begins by talking about how to define goals and objectives, in order to write policy or craft a solution that respects historic places and best practices, and which is acceptable to the community and likely to be approved by decision-makers. The text focuses on change to individual historic places. It goes on to describe how to identify an appropriate use for a place and select one or more suitable conservation treatments. It introduces the many tools (controls) and incentives (inducements) that make conservation work better for property owners, government, and the community at large. Risk assessment and heritage impact assessment, two of those tools, are then treated. The chapter proceeds to discuss implementation. It ends with instruction on how to prepare a conservation plan—in many respects the culmination of the planning process—and outlines the design and construction phases that follow.

The book respects the broadly accepted and also the more innovative ways of thinking about heritage and heritage planning, without attempting to break new conceptual ground. It addresses both theoretical principles and concrete practices, and illustrates ideas with specific experience drawn from a wide range of situations and places.

So much for what this book does. There are also many things that it does not do. The book does not focus on the history, theory, or philosophy of heritage conservation, although it does touch on all three. Nor is it a survey of conservation initiatives by country, a text on urban planning or urban design, or a history of achievements in those areas. It treats in only a cursory manner some subjects that are central to heritage studies, such as heritage tourism and interpretation. And it does not address design or preservation technology. These subjects form a part of conservation architecture, conservation landscape architecture, conservation engineering, and materials conservation. They in turn are subdisciplines of architecture, landscape architecture, engineering, and museology, whose central activities are design, construction, and the pathology and treatment of materials. All are distinct from heritage planning.

Heritage terminology is variable at best, sometimes dictated by national usage, sometimes by choice, and sometimes by ignorance. One person's 'preservation' is another's 'conservation'; what some call 'restoration' others may know as 'renovation.' These and other 'conservation treatments' are defined in Section 3.2. The text adopts what it considers to be the most universal and recent English-language terms, generally guided by the vocabulary of the latest versions of the US *Secretary of the Interior's Standards and Guidelines*, the valuable publications of English Heritage, the *Standards and Guidelines for the Conservation of Historic Places in Canada*, and the writings of respected Australian practitioners and theorists. The principles are based on the international standards for best conservation practice that have been developed over many years by the Paris-based International Council on Monuments and Sites (ICOMOS) and its parent organization, the United Nations Educational,

Scientific and Cultural Organization (UNESCO). Alternative terms and principles are provided where relevant.

Heritage conservation does not exist in a vacuum. Practitioners must give full consideration to the values, opportunities, and constraints provided by their society and its culture, politics, laws, and economics. Only by integrating these disciplines can one ensure a solution that is sustainable and politically acceptable. A subtheme throughout the book addresses the ways in which these concerns are integrated.

What do we conserve?

The heritage sector focuses on the identification and conservation of **cultural heritage**, which comprises the things that are called **cultural heritage resources**, **heritage resources**, or **historic resources**. These include a wide variety of objects, from the temple ruins of antiquity to agricultural landscapes, from paintings by 'old masters' to baskets woven by living craftspeople, from ancient methods of navigation to grandmother's recipes. Cultural heritage is usually divided into three categories, represented by the three pairs of resources cited above: immovable, movable, and intangible cultural heritage.

The word 'heritage' at its simplest denotes what has been inherited.[4] The word has gained in professional and popular usage over the last two generations. 'Heritage conservation' is now the preferred term in much of the English-speaking world. The US will surely continue to use 'historic preservation' because so much has been invested in the term, not least of all the guiding federal legislation (the National *Historic Preservation* Act) and the nation's leading advocacy organization (the National Trust for *Historic Preservation*).

Cultural heritage was defined in 1989 by UNESCO, the United Nations agency responsible for culture. The definition stresses the idea of inheritance:

> The cultural heritage may be defined as the entire corpus of material signs—either artistic or symbolic—handed on by the past to each culture and, therefore, to the whole of humankind. As a constituent part of the affirmation and enrichment of cultural identities, as a legacy belonging to all humankind, the cultural heritage gives each particular place its recognizable features and is the storehouse of human experience. The preservation and the presentation of the cultural heritage are therefore a corner-stone of any cultural policy.
>
> (Jokilehto 2005: 405)

The term 'cultural heritage' has been redefined many times since then—several newer meanings are introduced at the end of this section—and the scope of heritage has been broadened, but the generation-old bureaucratic definition remains a valid guideline, in part because of its dual emphasis on features (tangible heritage) and human experience (intangible heritage).

Three categories of cultural heritage are generally recognized: immovable, movable, and intangible. Descriptions of the three follow.

Historic places: Immovable cultural heritage

Many countries—and this book—use the term **historic place** to describe 'a structure, building, group of buildings, district, landscape, archaeological site or other place … that has been formally recognized for its heritage value' (Parks Canada 2010: Introduction, 2).[5] The present definition is taken from a Canadian government document; the US uses the same terminology in administering the National Register of *Historic Places*. Australians talk about **places** of cultural significance, often keeping the word 'historic' implicit. The UK adopts various terms, including **place** and **historic environment**, the latter prevalent in recent policy documents from England.

Historic places are otherwise known as **immovable cultural heritage** or **immovable cultural property**. They are 'immovable' in that they are integral to the particular site and physical setting (or context) in which they are located. Some exceptions occur, such as a building that has been relocated from its original site.[6]

The historic places that attracted particular attention in centuries past were archaeological remains and uninhabited old buildings—what British law came to define as 'ancient monuments.' Occupied buildings from a previous age came to be recognized as well, first for their historical associations ('the famous so-and-so lived here') and then for their architectural value. They were formerly called 'monuments,'

Figure 1.5 The British have long appreciated their historic places. This is Salisbury Cathedral, which has often been drawn, painted, and photographed. (Andrew Dunn)

but that elitist name has been generally replaced by terms such as 'buildings,' 'structures,' and 'works of engineering.'

This narrow definition has been broadened over time in chronology, social associations, and scope. Historic places constructed ever closer to the present are recognized. Historians retain the idea that the perspective of time is necessary to be able to appreciate what, from the past, has achieved lasting significance. Hence the US National Park Service requires that resources be '*generally* at least 50 years old' to be eligible for nomination to the National Register of Historic Places (National Park Service n.d.-d, italics mine). However, the heritage industry has continually narrowed the window of historical perspective, and most jurisdictions will consider places that were built much closer to the present, often only a decade or two ago.

Attention was once focused mainly on historic places of exceptional design that were linked to the lives and activities of the rich and the powerful—hence the term 'monument.' In recent decades the awareness and appreciation of places associated with the broader reaches and stories of society have increased. Many historic places

Figure 1.6 The Rideau Canal, a 200-kilometer-long waterway that extends from Ottawa on the Ottawa River to Kingston on Lake Ontario, is a designed cultural landscape that has been inscribed as a World Heritage Site. It was built in the early nineteenth century as a military route and is now operated as a recreational facility. (National Capital Commission)

commemorate the working classes, immigrants, slavery, industry, and the lives of ordinary people, and their design qualities may be quite ordinary. This parallels the trend in historical studies towards democratization and popularization, and in architectural studies towards an appreciation of vernacular buildings, all of which in turn reflect the considerable social change of the past generations. Value is assigned to resources that are 'representative' of a particular type of place, and not only to exceptional ones.[7]

Conservation efforts were also directed first at landscapes, and then at collective (or contiguous) historic places—immovable heritage that comprises related groups of individual properties that possess a common character. This frequently comprises groups of buildings and their associated landscapes in a built-up setting. These are usually called **conservation areas** in the UK and **historic districts** in the US; another popular term is **historic areas**. Some US cities began to protect historic districts in the 1930s (the first is considered to be Charleston, South Carolina, in 1931) and English communities pursued the same course with conservation areas some time later (an early initiative was Magdalen Street in Norwich, begun 1975). Today such recognition is popular and is linked to the economic regeneration of urban cores.[8]

Cultural landscapes—extended landscapes with features that have been shaped by human use—comprise another type of collective historic place. They include places as diverse as farms or extended agricultural lands, transportation corridors, urban areas that are made coherent by their use and/or design, and largely undisturbed natural landscapes that have been occupied extensively by, and hold potent cultural meanings for, Aboriginal people.

The term 'cultural landscape' has been used for some time—formerly as part of the rather cumbersome term 'historic and cultural landscape.' The prevalent current definition was accepted internationally with its recognition in 1994 in the *Operational Guidelines* to the UNESCO *World Heritage Convention* (UNESCO World Heritage Centre 1994: Clauses 35–39). The document defined cultural landscapes as 'the combined works of nature and of man [*sic*],' which are 'illustrative of the evolution of human society and settlement over time.' It recognized three categories of cultural landscapes:

- 'The clearly defined landscape designed and created intentionally by man [*sic*],' which has come to be called a **designed landscape**. This category had long been recognized and often described as 'historic gardens and landscapes.'
- 'The **organically evolved landscape** … [which] results from an initial social, economic, administrative, and/or religious imperative and has developed its present form by association with and in response to its natural environment.' These in turn fall into two categories:
  - 'A **relict (or fossil) landscape** … in which an evolutionary process came to an end at some time in the past.'

○ 'A **continuing landscape** … in which the evolutionary process is still in progress.'

● 'The **associative cultural landscape** ... [which has] powerful religious, artistic or cultural associations of the natural element rather than material cultural evidence.'[9]

These typologies have been challenged, but for the most part continue to be respected today.[10]

Landscapes and cultural landscapes are inherently different from other types of immovable heritage because they are organic, and therefore change involves natural renewal as well as human-caused factors. This was recognized in the *Florence Charter* (ICOMOS 1982), a doctrine that addresses designed landscapes, which notes that the constituents of landscapes 'are perishable and renewable.' Moreover landscapes and cultural landscapes should be addressed as systems, since their many components are so interdependent.[11]

Another kind of immovable heritage is represented by a place that has powerful meaning to a particular group of people, even though in some cases it may have been modified little or not at all by humankind. This kind of historic place is known as **traditional cultural property**

Figure 1.7 A temple mound at Ocmulgee Old Fields Traditional Cultural Property, Georgia, listed on the National Register of Historic Places. The mounds were created by ancestors of the Muscogee Creek Nation and the site contains archaeological remains going back 12,000 years. (National Park Service)

(or **traditional use site** or **natural sacred site**), which extends the idea of the associative cultural landscape. The category was added to the kinds of places eligible for listing on the US National Register of Historic Places in 1990. The National Register guidelines define 'traditional cultural significance' as representing:

> those beliefs, customs, and practices of a living community of people that have been passed down through the generations, usually orally or through practice. The traditional cultural significance of a historic property, then, is significance derived from the role the property plays in a community's historically rooted beliefs, customs, and practices.
>
> (Parker and King 1990, rev. 1992, 1998: 1)

Although the category was originally defined primarily to accommodate Native American sites (and by extension Aboriginal sites in any country), places with traditional meaning to non-Aboriginal cultures are equally applicable. Traditional cultural property may or may not have been modified by human use, and may or may not contain physical remains of earlier use. The key characteristic is its cultural meaning to a community.

The management of **archaeological sites** has diverged from that of other historic places. Their protection is specified in different legislation, usually with stricter controls and harsher penalties. Archaeologists are formally accredited in most jurisdictions, a status towards which other heritage professionals are working. Archaeological impact assessments (a kind of heritage impact assessment; see Section 5.6) are usually required in advance of proposed developments. New World archaeology focuses on Aboriginal sites from prehistory, European archaeology on Caucasian sites. Because of the differences in legislation and practice, archaeology is addressed here less thoroughly than other kinds of immovable heritage.[12]

Movable cultural heritage

The term 'movable cultural heritage' is used to define any portable natural or manufactured object of cultural heritage significance (Heritage Branch, New South Wales n.d.).[13] Artifacts that might be included in a museum collection (paintings, sculptures and other objects, as well as the collections themselves) are the prime examples, but everyday objects that have cultural meaning also fall within the category.

Movable cultural heritage is also considered to comprise media (e.g., audiovisual media, books, plays, and scores), as well as consumer and industrial goods (Klamer and Zuidhof 1999: 26).

Movable heritage is often not integral to a place or location, although the association with a specific place—usually the place of origin or long-time use—or with a particular cultural group may be important to its value. Because of this, Indigenous peoples in North America and Australia put great significance on repatriating (returning) artifacts that originated with them.

Figure 1.8 This Kwakwaka'wakw (Kwakiutl) sun mask, produced in coastal British Columbia, Canada, is an example of movable cultural heritage. (Marcel Regimbald)

Another situation in which movable assets are associated with a particular historic place occurs with furniture and furnishings that were used in a historic building. These objects often contribute to the heritage value of the place, and our appreciation and understanding become all the richer when they remain intact and are located within their historical context.

From a legal perspective, movable assets are considered chattels and personal property. They are difficult to regulate except when they are related to international trade in cultural property. Heritage protection legislation can address property and immovable assets, but rarely movable objects.

Intangible cultural heritage

Cultural heritage also includes traditions or living expressions inherited from our ancestors and passed on to our descendants. UNESCO has defined intangible cultural heritage (ICH):

> The 'intangible cultural heritage' means the practices, representations, expressions, knowledge, skills—as well as the instruments, objects, artefacts and cultural spaces associated therewith—that

communities, groups and, in some cases, individuals recognize as part of their cultural heritage. This intangible cultural heritage, transmitted from generation to generation, is constantly recreated by communities and groups in response to their environment, their interaction with nature and their history, and provides them with a sense of identity and continuity, thus promoting respect for cultural diversity and human creativity.

(UNESCO 2003)[14]

Intangible heritage encompasses many things, including oral traditions, performing arts, social practices, rituals, festive events, knowledge and practices concerning nature and the universe, or the knowledge and skills to produce traditional crafts. The traditional skills involved in both the carving and the use of the mask illustrated in Figure 1.8 as movable cultural heritage are intangible cultural heritage.

ICH (also called **traditional knowledge**, **folklife**, **folklore**) emerged as a type of heritage in the 1990s, although its value had long been recognized by anthropologists and described by a variety of names. A number of institutions are devoted to research and conservation of ICH,

Figure 1.9 Flamenco from Spain, which integrates song, dance, and musicianship, has been inscribed by UNESCO on the Representative List of the Intangible Cultural Heritage of Humanity. (Ruggero Poggianella)

among them the Smithsonian Center for Folklife and Cultural Heritage in the US.

The heritage value of traditional knowledge is found not only in the actual practices represented by the genre, but also in the stories and associations of the practitioners. Beyond being a vigorous type of heritage in its own right, ICH also has considerable relevance to planning for tangible places by providing substantive information for interpretation—to enable telling the many stories associated with specific places.[15] As will be seen later in this section, several recent definitions of 'heritage' focus on intangible qualities in preference to material ones.

Why do we conserve our historic places?

Why we conserve the past and for whom we conserve it are fundamental questions that go far beyond the practical, planning-centred scope of this book. Nevertheless they must be addressed, if briefly.

Many factors have motivated people to want to conserve historic places:

- **Cultural factors**. The enthusiasm for wanting to preserve survivors of our past has traditionally focused on the products and symbols of our history and culture. Finnish conservation educator Jukka Jokilehto writes that 'since the eighteenth century, the goal of this protection has been defined as the cultural heritage of humanity,' and that the main motives have been

    > the esteem held for specific qualities of past achievement, the desire to learn from past experiences, as well as … the shock caused by … destruction and demolition of well-known historic structures or pleasing works of art.
    >
    > (Jokilehto 1999: 1)

    'Past achievement,' 'past experiences,' 'well-known historic structures,' and 'pleasing works of art' all assume an appreciation of—as well as a deep-seated need to retain connections with—society's social and cultural heritage and its collective memory. Historic places are understood as being indispensable to our spiritual, social, and cultural well-being. We are threatened by their proposed loss and take appropriate action to neutralize the threat. Reusing historic places also draws on traditional skills and construction principles, contributing to the conservation of the intangible cultural heritage.

    Conservation of heritage assets for their cultural values was long a construct of the social and economic elite. The quest to document and conserve the past began in eighteenth- and nineteenth-century England, initiated by societies of self-named 'antiquaries' and 'dilettantes.' Preservation advocacy in the US was likewise initiated by and for the establishment. Recent generations have seen a broadening of the conservation community and the types of historic places in which they are interested, especially with the rise of the other, non-cultural motivations for heritage conservation.

- **Social factors**. The social dimensions of conservation relate not only to society and its culture, but also to present-day social equity. Heritage conservation done well should provide positive benefits to ordinary people and their daily lives. Conserving historic places can contribute to societal and community utility in many ways, such as by providing job opportunities and affordable housing, helping to keep established communities intact, and developing historical literacy among disadvantaged segments of society.

  Writers and practitioners are interested, among other things, in questions of national identity and personal psychology (Lowenthal and Binney 1981, cited in Delafons 1997: 4). National identity is a polite term for patriotism and nationalism, which have long been motives for conservation.

- **Economic factors**. Since the 1980s the many economic benefits of conservation have been increasingly recognized. This is now often a prime motivator for heritage activity. The paybacks range from the cost savings found in rehabilitation to the economic activity generated by heritage tourism. Conservation is now perceived more as an investment than as a subsidy.

- **Environmental factors**. The energy crisis of the 1970s led to an appreciation of the environmental benefits of heritage conservation. These include rehabilitation's having a smaller carbon footprint than new construction and the opportunity to retain 'embodied energy' found in existing buildings. Many current practitioners emphasize that retained and reused buildings are 'green' buildings, and see conservation as a necessary route to reducing greenhouse gases.

These last three reasons to conserve historic places have received ever-increasing attention beyond the heritage sector, as the need to achieve **sustainability** gains universal momentum. Social (usually combined with cultural), environmental, and economic factors together are widely accepted as the 'pillars' of sustainability, and heritage conservation is generally considered to be a sustainable activity. Sustainability is the subject of Section 2.2.

- **Psychological factors**. Society's regard for preservation also derives to a large extent from **nostalgia**, a wistful yearning for the past. Nostalgia is in turn a feature of Romanticism, the intellectual movement that began in the eighteenth century and which also brought us historicism, the more scientific investigation of the past. Nostalgia is a feeling often savored, a sensation exploited by the marketing industry. The central role of nostalgia in conservation is a key theme posed by David Lowenthal in his inspiring book, *The Past is a Foreign Country* (1985).

Nostalgia is often thought of as an evocative, personal sentiment: as a subjective entity with little or no objective basis, which cannot be quantified. However, nostalgia is also seen as a kind of social memory, which in turn is closely related to historical thought. Like history, memory is socially conditioned and altered from one generation to the next (Samuel 1994).

English archaeologist Jane Grenville (2007) argues that the urge to conserve the past—or alternatively to reject the past—is linked to an understanding of a sense of self, and to the three themes of individual personality, physical surroundings, and political context.[16]

- **Aversion to change**. Call it conservatism (a cognate of 'conservation') or Neo-Luddism, or see it as debunking the modern myth, promoted by the marketing industry, that novelty and change are by their very nature good things. Whatever it may be called, more and more people are recognizing that change in itself is neither good nor bad. Change introduced simply for the sake of change is a wasteful and unsustainable activity. This attitude is highly relevant with respect to historic places. Replacing an old building that works—or which can be made to work with moderate effort—with a new building just to introduce a measure of modernity is inadequate justification for change. The new spirit of sustainability is helping to discourage this kind of inappropriate action.

These factors enable conservation to contribute to a 'sense of place,' the awareness that a place has a special and unique character that sets it apart. A conserved historic place also provides a 'sense of time' in that it illustrates a particular period in past history. Both perceptions contribute to our personal well-being. American planner Kevin Lynch recognized their importance in his provocatively titled book, *What Time Is This Place?* (1972), which addresses environmental images that are both spatial and temporal (cited in Aplin 2002: 5).

Shifting approaches to heritage conservation

Approaches to heritage conservation have undergone a remarkable transformation over the last half-century. While these changes are addressed in their appropriate places within the book, it is helpful to summarize them here.

- The emphasis on what is most important to conserve has shifted from the **physical fabric** of historic places—old sticks and stones—to their **intellectual and social aspects**—the meanings, associations, and stories that historic places hold for their communities. Expressed differently, the focus of heritage awareness has evolved from **tangible and material** to **intangible and nonmaterial** heritage.
- Instead of finding heritage significance only in **outstanding** historic places, there is an equal interest in seeking out **representative** places—those resources that are illustrative or symbolic of broad types or movements.

- Instead of prioritizing only the **universal values** (i.e., Eurocentric values) of heritage, there is an emphasis on **cultural diversity**—on conserving those values and characteristics that have avoided globalization.
- Consistent with the broadening scope of what is conserved, the heritage sector now holds a more **pluralist** and **democratic** view of the people for whom historic places are being conserved. This, and the acceptance of multiple and diverse values, has led to an acceptance of **conflict** over what should be valued and conserved, and how to do it.

These shifting approaches can be seen in part in the changing focus in two 'conventions' produced three decades apart by UNESCO, the United Nations agency that is responsible for culture: the *World Heritage Convention* of 1972, which supports the identification of tangible historic places with 'outstanding universal value'; and the UNESCO *Convention for the Safeguarding of the Intangible Cultural Heritage* of 2003, which is directed towards forming 'a representative list' of intangible heritage. While the two documents are complementary and not at all mutually exclusive, their areas of concentration are notably different.[17]

The changes are also evident in the 'charters' issued by ICOMOS, an international non-governmental organization that operates under UNESCO. The charters define best conservation practices, which in turn are based on international approaches. The seminal *Venice Charter* of 1964, whose authors, mostly from Western Europe, styled themselves 'architects and technicians of historic monuments,' described the ways to conserve and restore historic building fabric. The charter focused on the monuments and archaeological remains of the past, emphasizing 'respect for original material' and validating modern science and technology. The recommendations in the *Venice Charter* encouraged the discipline of conservation architecture and the growth of architectural and scientific expertise in preservation technology.

An outcome of these developments was an impressive array of caringly and professionally conserved buildings. They include the highly praised York Minster in England, where architect Sir Bernard Feilden stabilized a stone cathedral in danger of collapse by underpinning it with massive concrete foundations that represent a *tour de force* of vision and of engineering (completed 1972; more work has been undertaken since).

In the generation that followed, heritage practitioners became increasingly interested in issues that reached more broadly—and less scientifically—into society. Australia's *Burra Charter* (1979–2013) imparted the need to conserve the 'cultural significance' of historic places, which is determined through a broad range of values, including their 'social or spiritual value' and their associations and meanings. The *Burra Charter* (Australia ICOMOS 2013b) also taught that 'places may have a range of values for different individuals or groups.' This reinforced the need to engage the community in order to determine

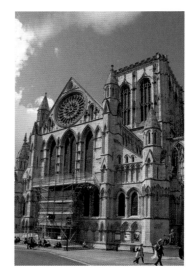

Figure 1.10 Conservation work to York Minster in England began in the 1960s and is ongoing. (Tony Hisgett)

their values, and led to the concept of 'values-centred conservation,' an approach that maintains that values are socially constructed and fluid, and not inherent in historic places. The heritage sector also expanded its focus from the great monuments of mainstream society to include more modest places from both the distant and recent past, and to respect the products—and values—of working-class, minority, and Aboriginal groups. Extended groups of resources, such as historic districts, cultural landscapes, and marine parks, also came to be recognized and protected. This evolution followed changes in society during the 1960s, such as the acknowledgment of civil and indigenous rights, the demise of colonial empires, and the spread of democracy.

Conserving Intangible and Tangible Heritage at Dhimurru

One achievement of the newer approaches to heritage conservation has been the protection and management of Dhimurru Indigenous Protected Area, on the Gulf of Carpentaria in northeast Arnhem Land, in Australia's Northern Territory. The large terrestrial and marine cultural landscape covers about 550,000 hectares. The management approach addresses traditional practices and knowledge as well as using current science to protect wildlife and flora. Dhimurru is a part of the traditional land of the Yolŋu people, who began to be concerned about threats to their land and autonomy with the development of a bauxite mine and alumina refinery in the late 1970s. The objective of the protected area is to conserve Indigenous and Western values and resources, both tangible and intangible. These range from traditional agricultural practices and dance to marine turtles and eucalyptus woodland. Elder Roy Dadaynga Marika articulated the vision for Dhimurru: 'Our country (land and sea) will exist forever. It must be protected so that it will remain the same, so that it can be seen in the same way that the elders saw it in the past. Our vision and hope is that Yolŋu will continue to use our country for all the generations to come' (Hoffmann et al. 2012).[18]

Figure 1.11 Djawulu teaching children the Brolga dance at Dhimurru Indigenous Protected Area. (Vanessa Drysdale, Dhimurru Aboriginal Corporation)

Figure 1.12 The African Burial Ground National Monument, New York, opened in 2007 on part of a five-acre site with no visible historic remains and without the current monument. (Carol M. Highsmith Archive, Library of Congress, Prints and Photographs Division)

In the past generation, heritage theorists have continued to shift the definition of 'heritage' ever more from the tangible to the intangible. Whereas Intangible Cultural Heritage (see above and Section 3.1) had been considered to be a subset of heritage—one of several categories of resources that heritage professionals sought to manage—the overarching concept of 'heritage' has become increasingly intangible in itself.

As an example, the emphasis placed on interpreting stories—including stories with inherent conflicts—has continued to grow relative to that placed on preservation of materials. American teacher and heritage practitioner Ned Kaufman is a voice for this new point of view. He writes about one such place, the African Burial Ground in New York City. The eighteenth-century cemetery may have held 20,000 burials, mostly slaves and free blacks. Planning for a new federal office building in 1989 rediscovered historical evidence of the long-forgotten site, but it was difficult to gather backing for a forgotten African-American site whose preservation would threaten to exploit the economic value of the land. The government proceeded with construction, unearthing many human remains. A coalition of high-profile supporters finally stopped the work in 1992. Most of the site had been excavated, but a portion was excluded from development and planted in grass. It now features the African Burial Ground National Monument (2007) and an indoor visitor centre fitted out nearby, making it look more like a conventional historic site. The larger area (five acres) was declared a municipal historic district and National Historic Landmark. Although nothing historic is visible or tangible, the place is well known and the event has done much to raise awareness of the African-American role in early New York history (Kaufman 2009: 299–302).

A more extreme voice is that of Australian educator Laurajane Smith. She 'starts from the premise that all heritage is intangible,' and that 'places are not *inherently* valuable.' What makes them valuable and meaningful 'are the present-day cultural processes that are undertaken at and around them, and of which they become a part.' Smith acknowledges the traditional Western idea of the 'physicality' of heritage, including the best practices discussed in Chapter 3, and calls it the 'authorized heritage discourse' (AHD), which 'dominates and regulates professional heritage practices.' Alongside this authorized discourse is 'a range of popular discourses and practices ... concerned with the negotiation and regulation of social meanings and practices' (Smith 2006: 3–4). Australian archaeologist and educator Rodney Harrison agrees, writing that 'heritage is not a "thing" or a historical or political movement, but refers to a set of attitudes to, and relationships with, the past.' He refers to Smith's AHD as 'official heritage,' which is 'authorized by legislation or charter' (Harrison 2013: 14, 20).

American cultural geographer Julie Riesenweber (2008: 32) echoes these approaches when she writes that 'landscapes are ... texts that tell stories' and 'preservation is itself a form of memorializing and interpretive activity [whose] meaning and value are socially constructed.' She notes that most people

> are not part of [the professional preservation] community and do not necessarily share the distinct connotations of concepts such as significance and integrity. For most people, a significant place or event is one that has had great impact on their or other people's lives.

A view shared by many current writers on heritage theory is that our understanding of heritage conservation, including values and best practices, is socially constructed and not absolute. Australian archaeologist and cultural resource manager Denis Byrne goes further and suggests that cultural heritage is a field of social action (Byrne et al. 2003: 58, elaborated in Byrne 2008). These positions explain how changes in society have, in turn, altered society's attitudes towards heritage and its conservation. Riesenweber (2008: 32) writes that 'preservation constructs a story of the past through the lens of the present.' She cites David Lowenthal (1985: 214–16), writing 20 years earlier:

> The past we know or experience is always contingent on our own views, our own perspective, and above all on our own present. Just as we are products of the past, so is the known past an artifact of ours.

We may speculate as to the causes of some of these conceptual changes. One is the increasing number of practitioners with links to the social sciences and 'heritage studies' (see Section 1.2). This perspective infuses conservation principles and practice. Consider that Ned Kaufman wrote:

> If preservation were fundamentally a technical discipline, then it would be appropriate to gauge its success by technical measures. But it is not: it is a social practice, part history and part planning. Its ultimate goal is not fixing or saving old things but rather creating places where people can live well and connect to meaningful narratives about history, culture, and identity.
>
> (Kaufman 2009: 1)

How different this is from the preamble to the *Venice Charter* of 1964, adopted less than 50 years earlier, which reads in part:

> The historic monuments of generations of people remain to the present day as living witnesses of their age-old traditions. ... The common responsibility to safeguard them for future generations is recognized. It is our duty to hand them on in the full richness of their authenticity.

Lowenthal's, Smith's, Kaufman's, Harrison's, and other new voices appear to point to the future—if not the present—of heritage conservation. The present book does not engage in the debate. Nevertheless ideas such as these are important since they have an impact on heritage planning. We must ask how heritage planning is affected by the diminishing importance of the materiality of historic places, and how to consider significance as being based on multiple, shifting, and often conflicting values. Heritage planning, after all, is a practical and highly politicized activity that deals with tangible properties ('historic places') and depends on community consensus for its solutions. Obtaining that consensus depends in part on how attuned the community—and the heritage planner—are to these new ideas.

Ironically, just as the philosophy of heritage becomes ever more abstract and intangible, heritage planning may be becoming more pragmatic. While historic places were once conserved mainly for their cultural values, heritage conservation—particularly in an urban heritage planning context—is now concerned with practical and utilitarian (or 'instrumental') benefits. This is consistent with the increasing importance of social outcomes and the financial bottom line in most facets of daily living. Europe, in particular Great Britain, has been a leader in this regard. The *European Charter of the Architectural Heritage*, adopted by the Council of Europe in 1975, articulates the importance of social, economic, and environmental values—what we now call the pillars of sustainability. English Heritage's *Conservation Principles* of a generation later (2008b) places conservation squarely within a framework of sustainability.[19] A few years later, the *National Planning Policy*

Framework for England urges that conservation of historic places should go beyond 'sustaining and enhancing the significance of heritage assets' by 'putting them to viable uses' and providing 'wider social, cultural, economic and environmental benefits' (Department for Communities and Local Government (UK) 2012: para. 126). Conservation is seen as having 'instrumental' values ('the economic, social and environmental benefits of policy and funding') as well as its long-appreciated 'intrinsic' values ('what is important about heritage, why and to whom?') (Mattinson 2006).[20]

English urban planners and educators Ian Strange and David Whitney (2003) write about this trend towards utilitarian/instrumental values. They cite four themes:

- *Conservation-led regeneration*: a shift from conservation as preservation towards conservation as part of urban regeneration (revitalization) and economic development
- *Conservation and sustainability*: the integration of conservation with environmental concerns
- *Conservation and the planning process*: increasing integration of conservation into mainstream planning
- *The governance of conservation*: a shift in conservation-related decision-making from local grassroots interests to local government, and non-governmental organizations.

All four themes are developed in the present book.

Consideration of the economic and community benefits of conservation has been central to programs encouraging the revitalization of historic town centres, seen particularly well in the Main Street Project of the US National Trust for Historic Preservation, which began in 1977 and continues as the National Main Street Network. What is new in the recent English planning policy is in the extension of these principles to the broader concept of sustainability and taking it beyond city centres to the conservation of historic places generally.

The importance of achieving benefits to the wider community is also seen in the considerable emphasis now placed on community engagement and providing stakeholders with a meaningful role in heritage decision-making and ongoing management.

Many formerly radical-sounding approaches to heritage conservation are reflected in legislation and related incentive programs. For example, the prominence of material conservation in the *Venice Charter* was made tangible in the US with the *Tax Reform Act* of 1976, which provides tax credits to property owners who rehabilitate buildings in accordance with federal standards.[21]

The movement towards recognizing that cultural significance is found partly in nonmaterial heritage has been seen in the substitution of nonmaterial language in doctrine, seen best in the UNESCO convention on intangible cultural heritage (2003), and in legislation, such as the Australian *Environment Protection and Biodiversity Conservation Act's* protection against interventions having a 'significant impact on ...

heritage *values*,' rather than on sites (Commonwealth of Australia 1999: s. 15B). And the emphasis on heritage conservation as sustainability is front and centre in the English policy statements of 2008 and 2012, cited previously. As will be seen in Section 3.1, concepts such as sustainability and community involvement are increasingly finding their way into international heritage doctrine.

The present book balances older with newer ideas, synthesizing them into a consolidated set of principles and practices for the heritage professional. Heritage planning must follow Smith's (2006: 29) 'authorized heritage discourse' and Harrison's 'official heritage' since, as Harrison (2013: 20) writes, this approach is 'authorised by legislation or charter.' Heritage planning is practiced in the day-to-day pragmatism of the urban and rural worlds, and so the discipline must respect heritage legislation and heritage charters, the latter being the doctrine that defines best practices.[22]

New heritage theory remains based, for now, in the classroom and the literature. Nevertheless the professional heritage planner must be familiar with the full range of approaches towards heritage. (S)he should infuse her/his work with the most current ideas about heritage, while conforming to the regulations and practices that are in force and balancing the needs of property owners, the community, and decision-makers.

1.2 Organization of the Heritage Sector

Heritage conservation is addressed by organizations at just about every level of government and society. This section looks at the way in which the heritage sector is structured at the international level and within a number of individual countries. The organizations are ordered here as on a pyramid from the top down, although it would be just as valid to list them from the bottom up—from grassroots associations to international institutions.

The heritage professional should be aware of the organizational structure as it relates to her/his jurisdiction, since it helps to understand who makes decisions and which groups may be of help—in other words, it tells where power is held, who makes decisions, where the money is, and where to find technical information. Most organizations have websites that describe their responsibilities, capacities, and resources. Much of the information that follows has been drawn from the sites.

When it is clear which organization holds the power in a given situation, and should that organization be situated higher on the pyramid than others whose priorities may be in conflict with it (i.e., a state or provincial government vs. a local authority or neighborhood group), the decision-making process is clear, even if it is not always fair or just. However, when decisions must be made jointly by two organizations that are located at or near the same level on the pyramid and which hold contrary values, the ensuing conflicts may be difficult to resolve.

Governments and government agencies

All governments have departments (or ministries, bureaus, offices) that are responsible for heritage conservation at the national level, and usually also at the state/provincial and local levels. The primary heritage activities of governments are developing policy, introducing legislation, recognizing and protecting significant historic places, and regulating change to recognized and protected places. The heritage regimes in the four principal English-speaking countries—the US, the UK, Australia, and Canada—are addressed in Section 2.1, with legal infrastructure. The application of heritage laws is discussed in Section 5.4, with heritage tools and incentives.

The shifting relationships between heritage conservation and other disciplines—and the priority given to heritage by a particular government—are revealed in the various departments to which governments have assigned and reassigned the heritage file. It has been placed within ministries responsible for culture (e.g., England), the environment (Australia), parks (US), planning (formerly in British Columbia), and development (Hong Kong). In some cases government has set up an arm's-length heritage agency that remains responsible to the minister (or secretary). An example is the Parks Canada Agency, which operates outside the bureaucratic structure but reports to the Minister of the Environment.

The trend appears to be to move the heritage file from cultural to planning departments. This follows the tendency to view heritage conservation as a revitalization activity. It also enables local governments to use planning tools and incentives to achieve conservation ends. In this way conservation and development can cooperate and heritage planning will thrive.

International quasi-governmental organizations

The primary international quasi-governmental organizations (sometimes referred to by the acronym 'quango') involved in heritage

Figure 1.13 UNESCO headquarters in Paris, home also of the World Heritage Centre and (until 2014) ICOMOS. (Omar Bárcena)

conservation are organizations within the United Nations. The most important ones fall under the umbrella of UNESCO.

UNESCO

The United Nations Educational, Scientific and Cultural Organization (UNESCO) is the Paris-based UN agency mandated with furthering cultural objectives, including responsibility for natural and cultural heritage. From time to time it issues high-level documents called 'conventions,' which are similar to treaties in that individual nations ('states parties') are invited to ratify them and make them official national doctrine.

Several UNESCO **conventions** are concerned with cultural heritage and historic places: the *Hague Convention* of 1954, the *World Heritage Convention* of 1972, and the *Convention for the Safeguarding of Intangible Cultural Heritage* of 2003. These are described with heritage doctrine, in Section 3.1. The conventions are the international equivalent of national policy and carry a level of obligatory value if states sign them in their sovereign capacity.

UNESCO also issues **recommendations** to governments for programs it feels they should adopt in the development of their own effective heritage conservation systems. These are stated at the policy level, intended for individual governments to implement in their own manner. Two, for example, are that 'all official plans must provide for heritage conservation' and 'every government should empower an entity to advise it on endangered heritage property.' These and some other UNESCO recommendations are considered in Section 2.1.

Several organizations that focus on heritage conservation report to UNESCO:

World Heritage Centre

Established in 1992 and based in Paris, the World Heritage Centre manages the *World Heritage Convention* (1972) and processes nominations to the **World Heritage List**. The **World Heritage Fund** provides some assistance to member states to protect the places.

Intergovernmental Committee for the Safeguarding of Intangible Cultural Heritage

Members of the Intergovernmental Committee are elected by the states parties. They meet annually to evaluate nominations to the **List of Intangible Cultural Heritage in Need of Urgent Safeguarding**. Support is provided by the UNESCO office.

ICOMOS

The International Council on Monuments and Sites (ICOMOS) is 'a non-governmental international organisation dedicated to the conservation of the world's monuments and sites.' It was organized in 1965, one year after the adoption of the *Venice Charter*, as an association of conservation specialists that would be independent of the already existing associations of museologists. The central office of ICOMOS is in Paris, and UNESCO provides the organization with support. Many states parties have organized their own national chapters of ICOMOS. The organization is best known for developing conservation doctrine and for its many publications.

ICCROM

The International Centre for the Study of the Preservation and Restoration of Cultural Property (ICCROM) is a Rome-based international governmental organization established by UNESCO in 1959. It has a worldwide mandate to promote the conservation of all types of cultural heritage, both movable and immovable. The institution works to improve the quality of conservation practice and raise awareness about the importance of preserving cultural heritage through training, research, advocacy, and other activities.

In addition, UNESCO itself operates conservation programs. As one example, the Asia and Pacific regional bureau of UNESCO, in Bangkok, honors the best projects in the region with its annual Asia-Pacific Heritage Awards for Heritage Conservation.

The non-government and non-profit sectors

Many **non-governmental organizations** (NGOs) and **non-profit organizations** (NPOs, also called **amenity societies**, **volunteer societies**, and **social enterprises**) are deeply involved in heritage conservation.[23] These range from large, well-funded organizations with a global reach to small, local volunteer advocacy groups that care for the well-being of historic places in their community. The heritage sector would grind to a halt without their devoted participation. NGOs and NPOs collectively are often referred to as **civil society** or the **civil sector**.

This section provides a very selective overview to provide an idea of the mandates and work of such groups, and to suggest the ways in which they make their services accessible to their communities.

International non-governmental organizations

Some heritage NGOs run programs and/or provide significant funding for worthy projects at the international level. To name only a few:

Getty Conservation Institute

Funded by the J. Paul Getty Trust, the Getty Conservation Institute is dedicated to advancing conservation practice through 'the creation and delivery of knowledge'—i.e., research and dissemination. Based in Los Angeles, it promotes high-quality and sustainable conservation work and develops innovative approaches and model conservation strategies. The Institute funds and administers many ongoing projects around the world. Its many valuable publications are mostly available without charge at the Institute's website.

Aga Khan Development Network

The Aga Khan Development Network (AKDN) is a group of development agencies with mandates that include architecture, culture, and the revitalization of historic cities. Many of these initiatives are managed through the Aga Khan Trust for Culture and the Aga Khan Foundation, two of its agencies. Among its many programs, the Trust for Culture administers the prestigious Aga Khan Award for Architecture and the Aga Khan Historic Cities Program.

World Monuments Fund

The World Monuments Fund (WMF) is a New-York-based organization whose mission is to preserve the world's architectural heritage of significant monuments, buildings, and sites. It does this with programs of advocacy, financial and technical support, education, capacity building, and disaster recovery. Every year it produces the World Monuments Watch, a list of highly significant threatened places, and provides generous funding for the conservation of some of them.

National, state, provincial, and local non-profit organizations

Countless organizations have been formed to advance heritage interests. Most maintain broad membership bases. The national groups are often broadly mandated, well staffed, and reasonably secure financially. Local groups, in contrast, may have small budgets and be mostly or entirely voluntary (in which case they may be called 'volunteer societies'). Some are organized for advocacy with respect to a single issue. All have their places in the activities of the heritage sector.

The primary activities in which heritage NPOs engage are:

- *Heritage advocacy*: influencing government, businesses, and the community to adopt policies and take actions that respect heritage values
- *Public awareness and education*: raising the level of awareness of the values and techniques of heritage conservation among the public
- *Ownership, development, and management of historic properties*: acting as 'national trusts,' accepting donations of (or purchasing) historic places; usually making them available for public visitation
- *Funding support*: providing funding assistance for projects, usually in a range of genres, including communication and physical conservation
- *Awards*: confering awards on meritorious projects; sometimes these are tangibly recognized with signs or plaques.

The following is a selection of heritage organizations in Britain and the US, provided to illustrate the high amount of organization and the range of activities, and to introduce some of the more influential groups. Other countries have formed societies with similar objectives and achievements.

Great Britain

The National Trust and other preservation trusts

The National Trust was conceived in 1884 and incorporated in 1895, with a mandate to 'promote the permanent preservation, for the benefit of the nation, of lands and tenements (including buildings) of natural beauty or historic interest.' Its initial priority was to protect landscapes as common land for recreational use. The Trust was given its first place, five acres of clifftop at Dinas Oleu in Wales, a few weeks after incorporation; a year later it purchased (for £10) a clergy house in Sussex. The protection of country houses, for which it is best known today, was a later initiative.

The organization describes itself as 'a charity that works to preserve and protect historic places and spaces.' It serves as the model for other national trusts around the world. The statistics are impressive: the National Trust has 3.8 million members and 61,000 volunteers. It owns more than 350 historic houses, 73,000 archaeological sites, many gardens, hundreds of thousands of acres of countryside, and 700 miles of coastal land. Each year more than 17 million people visit pay-for-entry properties and about 50 million visit open-air properties. The annual budget is more than £400 million, not including capital projects and acquisitions. It is the second largest property owner in the UK, after the Crown.

The National Trust for Scotland was established in 1931, with similar powers. The English National Trust retains its properties in Wales and Ireland.

Many cities and regions have formed trusts to hold and protect historic places. The first was the Bath Preservation Trust, created in

Figure 1.14 The estuary at Barmouth, Wales, from Panorama Walks on Dinas Oleu. The 'photocrom' image was taken in the 1890s, when Dinas Oleu became the National Trust's first acquisition. (Library of Congress, Prints and Photographs Division)

Figure 1.15 The Royal Crescent at Bath, a masterpiece of Georgian urban planning and design. The Bath Preservation Trust owns and operates a museum at No. 1 Royal Crescent, the unit at the far right. (Harry Wood)

1934 'to preserve for the benefit of the public the historic character and amenities of the city of Bath and its surroundings.' It advocates for conservation, reviews planning applications in the conservation area and listed building consent applications, provides grants to owners of listed buildings, and operates museums and educational activities.

More than 250 building preservation trusts with similar objectives are members of the United Kingdom Association for Preservation Trusts, formed in 1989 as an umbrella organization to coordinate local efforts. Some trusts have a narrowly defined area of interest. One is the Friends of Friendless Churches, which owns 40 former houses of worship in England and Wales. The Landmark Trust acquires interesting historic places and converts them for use as holiday rental accommodation.

The Society for the Protection of Ancient Buildings (SPAB) and other amenity societies

One of the world's oldest and continuously operating heritage organizations, the SPAB was founded in 1877 under the leadership of designer William Morris to improve the standards of conservation practice in Britain. Its primary interest remains the nature of the 'restoration' and 'repair' of old buildings. The SPAB offers advice and training for property owners and practitioners. The SPAB has a semi-autonomous branch in Scotland.[24]

Many other volunteer societies developed over the years. At the national level, the three best known may be the Ancient Monuments Society, formed in 1924 to promote both study and conservation; the Georgian Group, established in 1937 as an offspring of SPAB; and SAVE Britain's Heritage, a 'strong, independent voice in conservation' founded in 1975. Other groups focus on the historic environment of a particular era; these include the Victorian Society and the Twentieth Century

Society. The objects of interest to the Council for British Archaeology and the Garden History Society are self-evident. All the above are members of the Joint Committee of the National Amenity Societies, and as such they participate in the review of applications to change or demolish listed buildings or registered gardens.

Countless parallel organizations occur at the regional and local levels, whether long-time historical societies or short-lived single-interest groups. These are the organizations that undertake advocacy at an immediate, hands-on level.

The Civic Trust and other civic amenity societies

The Civic Trust was founded by Duncan Sandys in 1957 to coordinate the activities of urban advocacy groups striving to improve heritage awareness and achievement in historic communities. More than 900 organizations belonged to the Trust at its peak. Among its best-known achievements was the promotion of the Norwich Plan, an innovative scheme to conserve and revitalize the centre of that city.[25] The Civic Trust ceased operations in 2009. Its legacy lives on in the Scottish Civic Trust, which works with more than 100 civic groups to improve and conserve buildings and areas of historic interest.[26]

United States

Early preservation advocacy

Grassroots organizations and private initiatives played a key role in the development of the preservation 'movement' in the US. One of the earliest achievements in advocacy was the petition ('memorial') of 1813 put forth by a group of Philadelphia residents to prevent the demolition of that city's Old State House—the place where the Declaration of Independence had been signed in 1776. Three years later, although not before the State of Pennsylvania demolished two major components,

Figure 1.16 Independence Hall, Philadelphia, the former Old State House, seen in a postcard. (www.historyimages.com)

the City of Philadelphia responded by purchasing the building and its adjacent public square for posterity. The historic place is now revered by all Americans as Independence Hall (Hosmer 1965: 29–31).

Many other populist activities set examples for the nation. The most frequently cited is the purchase in 1858 of Mount Vernon, the threatened Virginia home and burial place of George Washington, the first American president, by Ann Pamela Cunningham and the Mount Vernon Ladies' Association. The organization continues to operate the property.

A number of well-connected and well-funded preservation societies were organized in the subsequent decades. The first statewide organization was the Association for the Preservation of Virginia Antiquities (APVA, renamed Preservation Virginia), founded in 1889. A member of APVA, Boston antiquary William Sumner Appleton Jr., went on to found the Society for the Preservation of New England Antiquities (SPNEA, renamed Historic New England) in 1910. The two organizations set the tone for later preservation organizations in the US, focusing on acquiring old churches and homes and restoring or reconstructing them to their early appearance—often with more than a soupçon of imagination and fancy (Lindgren 2004).

An influential charter member of APVA was the Reverend William A.R. Goodwin, to whom the valued past provided 'a spirit that stirs the memory and fires the imagination' (Lindgren 2004: 107). Goodwin advocated for the restoration and reconstruction of Williamsburg, the former capital of Virginia, which he considered to be the birthplace of the US. In 1926 Goodwin convinced the wealthy industrialist, John D. Rockefeller Jr., to finance the ambitious project, called Colonial Williamsburg. Rockefeller found the opportunity to restore an entire town 'irresistible.' A central objective of the project, which went on for decades, was to maintain rigorous standards of professionalism in

Figure 1.17 The Reverend William A.R. Goodwin (*left*) and John D. Rockefeller Jr., at Colonial Williamsburg in 1926. (The Colonial Williamsburg Foundation)

preservation. The restoration of Williamsburg, which is now operated by the non-profit Colonial Williamsburg Foundation, fostered important developments in conservation theory and practice, including launching the field of historical archaeology and expanding the interest in preserving groups of buildings and landscapes as ensembles. Many Williamsburg innovations have come to be incorporated into international heritage doctrine (Hosmer 1981: chapter 1; Stubbs and Makaš 2011: 433).

Goodwin also approached Henry Ford for financial support. Ford declined to help with Williamsburg, but in the 1930s he developed his own ambitious historic place: Greenfield Village (now called 'The Henry Ford') in Dearborn, Michigan, an outdoor museum that comprises more than 80 moved buildings and which became the automotive magnate's obsession in his later years.

Ford's and Rockefeller's projects established the central role of private philanthropy in American historic preservation. This reflects the long-time American practice of wealthy industrialists funding projects that, in other countries, might be undertaken by government.[27] Preservation Virginia, Historic New England, Colonial Williamsburg, and The Henry Ford remain as flourishing non-profit organizations, as do hundreds of other early groups not cited here, reinforcing the particular importance of private initiative in preservation in the US.

Figure 1.18 A street scene in Greenfield Village, a privately developed outdoor museum that forms part of The Henry Ford. The white building is the former house and bicycle shop of the Wright Brothers, moved here from Dayton, Ohio. (Andrew Balet)

The National Trust for Historic Preservation

By the end of World War II, heritage advocates and professionals alike recognized the need for a national, non-profit organization that could supplement government programs, particularly with regard to ownership of historic places. Another role that was foreseen was to coordinate and provide support to the many state and local groups active across the country. The National Trust in England was studied as a model.

The National Trust for Historic Preservation was created in 1949 by an Act of Congress. Government and the Department of the Interior were supportive of the Trust (Finley 1963). The first director, Frederick Rath, had been a National Park Service historian who worked at the Home of Franklin D. Roosevelt National Historic Site. The National Trust has grown to become a large and effective organization, with 750,000 members, 300 staff, a portfolio of 27 properties, and a wide range of programming in education, professionalism, and advocacy. A number of its activities, including the Main Street Program, are described elsewhere in this book.

The private sector

Wealthy individuals such as John J. Rockefeller and William Sumner Appleton Jr., were important as funders of activities described above. Participation in the conservation sector by private interests now usually occurs in corporate and professional environments.

The development industry

The private sector (the for-profit sector) continues to play an important role in heritage. Today's leaders are property owners and developers, whether they be individuals or corporations. These are the people and organizations that undertake many conservation projects. The products—buildings, landscapes, communities—have a direct impact on our experience and understanding of the continued use of historic places.

Private-sector activity does not occur within a vacuum. It is enabled by laws and planning regulations put in place by the public sector, resources provided by the financial sector, and input from the community at large. Private enterprise forms one important sector that combines with others to create the built environment.

The majority of private-sector conservation work comprises projects that involve the reuse and rehabilitation of tiring, older urban buildings, whether for residential, commercial, or institutional use. The conserved building may be self-standing, or it may be integrated into a larger, new development. The development industry recognized some time ago that old buildings can often be rehabilitated for less than the cost of demolition and new construction and, therefore, the initiative makes good business sense, as well as presenting a more sustainable course. This approach may be encouraged by constraints on demolishing a listed building or by incentives, such as rehabilitation tax credits, which reduce the net cost of the work.[28] Nevertheless, the venture generally must show the potential to realize a profit on investment or it would not be undertaken.

Developer-driven projects represent the future of heritage conservation in a society that values the economic bottom line above all else. The outcome is a dynamic partnership between development and conservation.

The professional sector

The success or failure of a development is nominally the responsibility of the professional sector, which comprises the architects, heritage professionals, planners, engineers, landscape architects, archaeologists, contractors, and trades who plan, design, and carry out the work. The quality of the finished product depends on their expertise and vision. Nevertheless their initiatives can succeed only within a conservation context that demands quality, community and local government support, and a property owner or developer who has the vision and the means to commission and pay for the work.

Skill and expertise depend on education and professional development. An effective heritage professional requires formal knowledge of the discipline. Fortunately an ever-increasing number of educational institutions offer classroom and distance courses, programs, and academic degrees in conservation. Another way to upgrade expertise in practice is through professional associations and societies, which are increasing in numbers and strength. Conservation education, professional associations, and their contribution to heritage professionalism are introduced next.

Education and professional recognition

Formal education serves both students and current practitioners. The former are prepared for practice and the latter benefit with improvement to the quality and consistency of their work, with good outcomes that include professional recognition for practitioners.

Conservation education

Skill and expertise depend on education and professional development. An effective heritage professional requires formal knowledge of the discipline, in the same way as does an architect, planner, lawyer, or accountant. Fortunately an ever-increasing number of educational institutions offer courses, programs, and academic degrees in heritage studies.

Heritage conservation and planning are taught at many postsecondary schools under a variety of names. Some of the differences in nomenclature are national (as already noted, what is called 'historic preservation' in the US is called 'heritage conservation' in other Englishspeaking countries), others are pedagogical. It is not the name that counts—what matter are substance and approach.

Figure 1.19 The author works with graduate students at the University of Hong Kong. (Architectural Conservation Programmes, The University of Hong Kong)

Heritage practice (as distinct from heritage advocacy) began with architectural conservation. The first professionals to care for historic places were architects, who tended to look at individual buildings and sites; and planners, who focused more broadly on communities. The authors of the first widely accepted international conservation doctrine, the *Venice Charter* of 1964, were self-styled as 'architects and technicians.'[29] It follows that most post-secondary conservation education began in schools of architecture. Two of the leading programs were at Columbia University in New York, where the Historic Preservation Program—which began to offer degrees in 1973—resided in the Graduate School of Architecture and Planning, and at York University in England, in the Institute of Advanced Architectural Studies.

Urban planners also took an interest in heritage and recognized the affinity between the two disciplines. Cornell University in New York State was one of the first universities to teach heritage within the rubric of planning, although also with ties to architecture. The Department of City and Regional Planning began to offer courses in historic preservation in 1962, and Historic Preservation Planning became a formal degree program in 1975 (Forsyth and Kudva 2010: 40).[30]

Despite the precedent of Cornell, heritage planning/historic preservation planning is taught in relatively few planning schools today and is recognized as a discipline by few professional planning organizations. Many excellent conservation programs continue to be based in architectural schools, while ever more are affiliated with university departments of cultural geography, history, anthropology, and other social sciences, as well as with multidisciplinary arts and social science programs. This has led to a distinct academic discipline called 'heritage studies,' whose teachers and graduates have been the main contributors to the new critical literature on heritage (e.g., Lowenthal 1985, Smith 2006, Harrison 2013; see also Carman and Sorensen 2009). Gone is the dominance that the 'architects and technicians' who drafted the *Venice Charter* had on heritage conservation theory and practice. Their proportion among heritage practitioners declines as those from the social sciences increase. Nevertheless the objective is, in the words of Canadian educator Herb Stovel, 'a common discipline of conservation, whatever the members' profession of origin' (1994: xxxv).

Archaeology was once taught primarily within departments of art history and classics, when it was associated mostly with the ruins of antiquity. With the growth of Aboriginal archaeology in the New World and the interest in early European civilization in the Old World, many archaeologists are now trained in departments of anthropology, ethnography, and history. Once again, the tendency has been to move from arts and design disciplines to the social sciences.

It would be helpful if heritage education were a prerequisite not only for practicing planners, but also for their supervisors (e.g., senior municipal planners and elected and appointed decision-makers), not to mention the many others whose professional work (sometimes unknowingly) affects conservation outcomes, such as lawyers who practice property law and government officials who draft taxation legislation. In an admirably forthright article, Canadian heritage planners Robert Shipley and Nicole McKernan (2011: 90) document the ignorance of many officials of this kind and conclude:

> Good decision-making concerning the planning, management, and conservation of our built environment depends on adequate and accurate knowledge. ... If current decision-makers are the problem, then teaching future decision-makers is the solution.

They describe a number of successful public educational programs in elementary and secondary schools and beyond the classroom that can serve as universal models.

The US National Parks Service, which maintains qualification standards for its historic preservation staff, notes:

> When decision makers lack the expertise required to make informed decisions, historic and cultural resources can be overlooked, mis-identified, mis-evaluated, damaged, or lost. Partial expertise can be just as harmful, whether a person is well-grounded in historic preservation, but lacks professional discipline skills, or, alternatively, is an expert in a professional discipline, but fails to understand its important connection to historic preservation.
> (Prism Economics and Analysis and Barry Padolsky
> Associates n.d.: 29)

Another aspect of education is capacity building—assisting governments and organizations in developing the resources for heritage management. As an example, the UNESCO World Heritage Centre has developed a capacity building strategy that addresses the needs of clients 'whose well-being and sustainable development are linked to heritage protection.' Efforts are directed at entire organizations and institutions, a paradigm shift from the previous practice of training individual professionals and managers. The initiative includes sharing knowledge and best practices, and operates in partnership with ICCROM, ICOMOS, and IUCN (International Union for Conservation of Nature). The program also presents awards for best practices in sustainable site management (Cave 2013: 414).[31]

Professional recognition

A generation or two ago, membership in ICOMOS or a large heritage NPO was considered to be sufficient to be recognized as a heritage professional. Most were government employees. They made their qualifications known when they were hired and did not require public recognition. Things have changed. With the increase of heritage practitioners in the private sector, it is difficult to distinguish the qualified from the unqualified.

Heritage practitioners now have an opportunity to achieve formal recognition by organizing themselves into professional associations and institutes. Many new groups have emerged, and more will appear with time. These organizations serve several purposes. The most important are to encourage good practice, further professional development, encourage ethical conduct (disciplining malpractice), and give formal recognition to qualified practitioners. The associations operate similarly to architectural and planning institutes, law societies, and medical associations. Their ultimate objective is to achieve professional licensing (or certification) and registration by means of dedicated legislation.

At present the best-structured of the heritage disciplines is archaeology. Professional associations have been organized in most countries, states, and provinces. Their many roles usually include promoting and regulating practice, setting professional standards, providing ethical and legal guidance, debating technical issues, and publishing journals. In many jurisdictions archaeology is controlled by legislation, requiring practitioners to obtain a license before undertaking excavation work.

Practitioners in the conservation of buildings, landscapes, and the broader historic environment are often less well organized, although numerous professional associations do exist. One well-established group is the Institute of Historic Building Conservation (IHBC) in Britain, which describes itself as:

> the professional body for building conservation practitioners and historic environment experts. ... The Institute exists to establish, develop and maintain the highest standards of conservation practice, to support the effective protection and enhancement of the historic environment, and to promote heritage-led regeneration and access to the historic environment for all.
>
> (IHBC n.d.)[32]

IHBC's members include 'a range of professional disciplines in the public, private and voluntary sectors, including conservation officers, planners, architects, regeneration practitioners and academics.' The Institute maintains a robust publication program, including a bimonthly journal (called *Context*), an annual yearbook, and occasional books and booklets. Its publications inform members and also explain to the public the value of heritage professionals and qualifications. A portion of its website is dedicated to 'Why planning authorities must have conservation skills!' Perhaps of most importance to the profession, it recognizes service providers who 'seek to operate in accordance with the IHBC's guiding principles and standards of historic environment conservation, principally our Code of Conduct.' The list of those professionals who have received Historic Environment Service Providers Recognition (HESPR) is posted, and their skills promoted.

Membership in the Hong Kong Institute of Architectural Conservationists (HKICON) is limited to applicants in 'architectural conservation practice.' While the actual disciplines are not identified, practice is clearly restricted to professionals who work with the historic built environment, particularly architects, engineers, surveyors, and heritage planners. Professional members must undertake continuing professional development (CPD). In order to retain their status, members must accumulate a minimum number of annual credits for attending conferences, field visits, lectures, workshops, or other events sponsored or approved by the Institute. HKICON has earned respect for its close, if unofficial, ties to the Architectural Conservation Programmes at the University of Hong Kong. Given these strengths, the executive is actively working towards statutory recognition of the profession.

2
Context

Heritage planning is very much a real-life activity, affected by and involved with the values and concerns of the community, nation, and world. External matters do, and should, influence the process and outcomes of heritage activity. This chapter provides an overview of the most important contextual issues that affect the good practice of heritage conservation: the legal and planning infrastructure, sustainability, and ethics. Together they form a holistic framework for conservation.

2.1. Legal and Planning Infrastructure

Heritage planning and management operate within the context of statutes, ordinances, and regulations. The present discussion of heritage conservation law provides an overview of the principal legal powers and responsibilities current in English-speaking nations. Although laws and regulations differ from one place to another, the principles are quite constant because of their shared roots in English common law.

In all democratic nations the community and the bureaucrats make recommendations and the elected officials make decisions. An inherent problem is that elected decision-makers rarely have the knowledge base that their staff and constituents may have. Their ignorance may lead to poor decisions or indecision, which in turn can promote rather than resolve conflict.[1] But such is democracy.

Since heritage legislation is based largely on land-use law, and land use is controlled by planning statutes and regulations, the next segment addresses the planning infrastructure. As will be seen, the practice of planning—which includes heritage planning—is usually enabled by the national or state/provincial government and carried out on a daily basis by local government. The practical application of specific aspects of heritage and planning legislation is addressed in Section 5.4, in the discussion of the tools and incentives that are used to manage change to historic places.

Heritage legislation

Legislation consists of **statutes** (also called **acts** or **laws**; at the municipal level they are often called **bylaws** or **ordinances**), which are enacted by the elected legislature of the country, state, or local government; and **administrative regulations** (or **guidelines**), which are often prepared to explain procedures in more detail and tell how to comply with the statutes. A third kind of government declaration is **policy**, which indicates directions that a government intends to follow (usually with future legislation) but does not have the force of law. And all legislation is guided by a constitution in those countries that possess one.

Statutes must be written with clarity. They can only control actions that are relatively straightforward to interpret and enforce, so that the courts may address enforcement. Since best conservation practices (the subject of Chapter 3) are often matters of judgment and their interpretation rarely allows a fully objective determination as to whether an action is 'right' or 'wrong,' statutes cannot enforce best conservation practices directly.

Laws can, however, enforce best practices indirectly. A statute may require that any proposed change to a protected historic place

Figure 2.1 Tr'ochëk is a former First Nation settlement located on a bench (at the right) at the confluence of the Klondike and Yukon Rivers, across the Klondike from Dawson City, Yukon. The site has been protected by a formal agreement. (Michael Edwards)

must receive prior consent from a specified public entity, with the accompanying regulations stating that consent is conditional on the owner's following best practices (e.g., the ICOMOS charters or national standards). Alternatively, the statutes can make a property owner's acceptance of financial incentives conditional on following best practices. As an example, in the US the owner of a building listed on the National Register of Historic Places can qualify for tax credits if alterations to the building comply with the *Secretary of the Interior's Standards for Rehabilitation*—a document that describes best practices, and which is introduced in Section 3.3. Best practices can also be encouraged by means of conditions placed on the acceptance of heritage incentives.

Treaties and **formal agreements** comprise another kind of legal obligation. International treaties are made between two or more separate countries. The UNESCO conventions, introduced in Section 3.1, are similar to treaties, in that member states ('states parties') are expected to ratify them, in which case they become national policy.

Treaties may also occur between two 'nations' within a single country. This is seen, for example, in the many treaties and formal agreements that Canada has concluded with its Aboriginal peoples, known as 'First Nations.' While concerned first and foremost with land and land claims, the treaties address many other topics as well, including cultural heritage.

As an example, the *Tr'ondëk Hwëch'in Final Agreement* (Aboriginal Affairs and Northern Development Canada 1998), a formal agreement signed by the Government of Canada and the Tr'ondëk Hwëch'in, provides for self-government by the Yukon First Nation, which is based in Dawson City, formerly the hub of the Klondike gold rush. Protection of Aboriginal culture and heritage comprise an important component of the agreement, with generous funding for conservation provided by the federal government. A swift outcome has been the start of development of Tr'ochëk National Historic Site, a former summering place located just across the Klondike River from Dawson, which the *Final Agreement* protected and for which it provided overall heritage objectives.[2]

The legal basis for heritage conservation

Legislation protecting historic places is not a modern invention. Its roots go back at least to Roman antiquity, if not earlier.[3] The Romans enacted a law of treasure (addressing movable heritage) around AD 200, and this became a part of the basis for European law on the protection of antiquities (Boer and Wiffen 2006: 8–9, citing Hill 1936: 3). A century and a half later, between the 350s and 370s, a number of emperors decried the damage being wreaked on ancient monuments. The Emperors Valentinian, Valens, and Gratian declared their intention to 'restore the condition of the Eternal City and to provide for the dignity of the public buildings' and to prevent builders from 'quarrying out of old buildings, digging up the foundations of noble buildings … or tearing away pieces of marble by the mutilation of despoiled buildings' (Pharr 1952: 412, cited in Jokilehto 1999: 5; Glendinning 2013: 18).

The Emperor Majorian made an effort to conserve ancient historic places in the mid-fifth century. As Edward Gibbon recounts in *Decline and Fall of the Roman Empire*:

> The monuments of consular or Imperial greatness were no longer revered as the immortal glory of the capital: They were only esteemed as an inexhaustible mine of materials, cheaper, and more convenient, than the distant quarry. ... Majorian, who had often sighed over the desolation of the City, applied a severe remedy to the growing evil. He reserved to the senate the sole cognisance of the extreme cases which might justify the destruction of an ancient edifice; imposed a fine of fifty pounds of gold (two thousand pounds sterling) on every magistrate who should presume to grant such illegal and scandalous license; and threatened to chastise the criminal obedience of their subordinate officers by a severe whipping and the amputation of both their hands. ... Majorian was anxious to protect the monuments of those ages in which he would have desired and deserved to live.
>
> (cited in Morrison 1965: 1)

The actual preservation order to the Prefect of Rome declared: 'All the buildings that have been founded by the ancients as temples and as other monuments, and that were constructed for the public use or pleasure, shall not be destroyed by any person' (Pharr 1952, cited in Jokilehto 1999: 5).[4]

The builders of Renaissance Rome, popes included, were no different from those of antiquity, scavenging building materials from the city's abundant ruins. Pope Nicholas V is alleged to have removed two thousand cartloads of marble from the Colosseum in a single year (1450), and Pope Alexander VI reportedly leased the place for exploitation as a commercial quarry (Kennet 1972: 12).

Figure 2.2 Protective decrees were issued many centuries ago in reaction to stones being stolen from the Colosseum and other ancient Roman antiquities. (Andreas Tille)

In reaction to this kind of destruction, Popes Martin V (in 1425) and Pius II (1462) both issued directives opposing construction that damaged ancient monuments. In 1534 Pope Paul III established an Antiquities Commission and gave it powers to protect historic remains. This was taken a step further in 1624, when Cardinal Aldobrandini issued an edict forbidding excavation without a permit and requiring immediate reporting of all archaeological discoveries (Denhez 1997: 31, 33–4). These Roman and Vatican statutes were precedents for the heritage laws of today, as was the idea of an appointed citizen 'commission' advising decision-makers on heritage matters.

The legal origins of other current practices can be traced to seventeenth-century Sweden. In addition to enacting protective legislation, the Baltic kingdom introduced a responsible government official, a heritage inventory, and a research institution. King Gustav II Adolph appointed the first Director General of Antiquities in 1630, charging him with responsibility for recording and collecting inscriptions and ancient stones from prehistoric sites. In 1666 King Charles XI decreed the protection of ruins and prehistoric sites, and a year later the College of Antiquities was founded in Uppsala to research Sweden's ancient cultural heritage and manage its historic sites (Selling 1964, cited in Stubbs and Makaš 2011: 147).

The primary constituents of this European-derived heritage legislative system are:

- A list (often called a register or an inventory) that **recognizes** historic places considered to have merit:
  - For the earliest lists, age alone was sufficient to merit listing. Since the twentieth century, historic places must be shown to possess sufficient heritage significance to qualify for the list; this in turn requires the articulation and application of criteria of excellence.[5]
  - By the 1960s, places eligible for listing were extended to include conservation areas as well as buildings and ruins. This has since been extended to landscapes, cultural landscapes, and other kinds of historic places.
- Legislation that **protects** historic places considered special from defacement, destruction, or unapproved changes.
- The requirement to report **archaeological discoveries**, usually placing a chronological limit on the remains that qualify and conferring immediate protection of them.
- The availability of **funding assistance** for conservation work on recognized and/or protected historic places.
- Creation of an **administrative body**—usually a government agency, sometimes advised by an appointed citizen commission (or other group)—to oversee the heritage program.[6]

In many countries, government agencies also hold and manage historic properties, fulfilling the role of a national trust. In other places, this is the responsibility of a non-profit organization.

These precedents form the building blocks of today's heritage legislation systems throughout much of the world. Many of the heritage statutes in place today were products of the 1960s and 1970s. The time frame is likely a consequence of the social and political transformations of the 1960s.[7] Both heritage and environmental conservation participated in that period of change.

The Curatorial Management of Historic Places

The general structure of heritage legislation for historic places—recognition, protection, funding for conservation, and administration—follows the methods used by museums for the collection of movable heritage. A museum curator identifies a valued artifact, and, if it meets criteria expressed in a museum's accessions policy, (s)he may place it in the museum's collection, whereupon the museum assumes responsibility for protecting and conserving it. Seen this way, the body of protected immovable heritage would become the state's collection of buildings, areas, landscapes, and sites, whether or not the places are owned and cared for by government.

This is a curatorial approach, and indeed the process is referred to as the 'curatorial management' of the historic environment.[8] A literal application of this approach is seen in the 'architectural museum,' which collects fragments and casts of buildings. Examples are Sir John Soane's Museum (early nineteenth century) and the Victoria and Albert Museum (present building opened 1909), both in London. A related institution is the 'outdoor museum,' to which entire buildings are transported, transplanted, and displayed. The earliest is acknowledged to be Skansen in Stockholm, 1891; the genre subsequently became popular in North America (Kaufman 2009: 140 and Chapter 5). Newer attitudes towards heritage conservation support a more holistic and sustainable approach, in which material value comprises only part of the object's significance.

Figure 2.3 Part of the architectural collection in Sir John Soane's Museum. (By courtesy of the Trustees of Sir John Soane's Museum, photographer Derry Moore)

Heritage legislation and British common law

The UK, US, Australia, and Canada were all constituted under British common law, and therefore have a shared legal heritage. For this reason the underlying bases for current law in all four countries (as well as others that were once part of the British Empire) can be discussed collectively, despite the many differences in detail.

Heritage legislation addresses the management of property and, as such, is based on traditional English land-use law.[9] The basic premise is that a property owner has the right to do as (s)he wishes with her/his home, as long as the use of the property is not harmful or a nuisance to the community. This is epitomized in the often-repeated statement 'a man's home is his castle.' The expression originated with famed English jurist Sir Edward Coke (1552–1634), who used several variants of the clause in his judgments. It was canonized in *Coke's Institutes of the Laws of England*, published in 1794, long after his death.

A man's home is his castle.

The present usage of this 'Castle Doctrine' is a slight misinterpretation. Coke wrote in the context of protecting one's home from invasion: 'A man's house is his castle ... and where shall a man be safe if it be not in his own house?' The present interpretation of this centuries-old principle relates more to use than to protection. Nevertheless the Castle Doctrine remains valid, although its application has been modified by jurisprudence (New World Encyclopedia n.d.).

Britain and other Commonwealth countries have increasingly regulated private property for heritage (and other) reasons, contending that regulation is in the interest of the broader community. Most people have been reasonably sanguine about this and quite accepting of heritage legislation, although not without disputes that have found their way to court. The prevalent attitude is summed up by Australian historian Graeme Davison: 'Heritage is, above all, a political concept. It asserts a public or national interest in things traditionally regarded as private' (Davison and McConville 1991: 7, cited in Boer and Wiffen 2006: 12).

Not so in the US, a particularly litigious society. The American belief in personal liberty led to these rights being carried further. The Fifth Amendment to the Constitution establishes the principle that 'private property [cannot] be taken for public use, without just compensation.' The Fourteenth Amendment states that a person cannot be deprived of property 'without due process of law.' A 'taking' of property by the state for public use traditionally requires the government to purchase the property by means of its power of **eminent domain** (called **compulsory purchase** in the UK, **expropriation** in Canada, and **resumption** or

compulsory acquisition in Australia). In the US exercising the power of eminent domain is called **condemnation**.

Despite this libertarian ideology, successive American litigation provided government with powers to regulate private property without acquiring it. It was established early in the twentieth century that the state can establish zoning laws to regulate land use, since this is in the public interest.[10] The courts subsequently ruled that government can not only protect citizens from negative actions, but that it can also ensure positive outcomes. As US Supreme Court Justice William Douglas wrote in a 1954 decision: 'It is within the power of the legislature to determine that the community should be beautiful as well as healthy, spacious as well as clean.'[11]

American community conservation efforts intensified with rulings of this kind. The New York City Landmarks Preservation Commission was created in 1965 (one year before the passing of the *National*

Figure 2.4 Litigation over New York's Grand Central Station supported the right to protect historic places. (Eric Baetscher)

Historic Preservation Act) as a regulator and not simply an advisor, empowered to protect significant historic places ('landmarks'). The Commission waded into treacherous waters when it designated (i.e., protected) Grand Central Station, a local landmark, then denied its owner, the Penn Central Railroad, approval for a proposed 55-story tower atop the station. Penn Central claimed a 'taking' and argued that it should receive compensation for not being able to develop its property. The Landmarks Preservation Commission's ruling was supported by the New York Court of Appeals (1977) and upheld by the US Supreme Court (1978), marking the first Supreme Court decision directly addressing—and upholding the legitimacy of—historic preservation. The court said, however, that whether or not a taking has occurred under the provisions of the Fifth Amendment (which would require compensation) must be determined on a case-by-case basis.

In his opinion, Justice William Brennan remarked on the significance of the case:

> The question presented is whether a city may, as part of a compre-hensive program to preserve historic landmarks and historic districts, place restrictions on the development of individual historic landmarks—in addition to those imposed by applicable zoning ordinances—without effecting a 'taking' requiring the payment of 'just compensation.'[12]

With this background, we turn to an overview of heritage legislation and related programs in the four countries on which the text focuses.[13]

United Kingdom

The first legislation in Great Britain to address the protection of historic places was the *Ancient Monuments Protection Act* of 1882. It provided for the 'guardianship' of some 50 prehistoric sites and (in 1893) appointed an Inspector of Ancient Monuments to oversee the program. The statute was revised several times over the years to extend its coverage, but for more than a half-century it protected only unoccupied structures. Occupied historic buildings came to be protected with the passing of the *Town and Country Planning Act* in 1947. The latter Act also introduced Building Preservation Orders, to be issued when a building of architectural or historical interest was endangered. In order to identify buildings of interest before a threat occurred, the *Town and Country Planning Act* was amended in 1962 to require the minister to prepare lists of buildings to be afforded protection against demolition, damage, or alteration.

Similar powers were extended to historic areas, called 'conservation areas,' with the *Civic Amenities Act* of 1967. This differed from the earlier legislation in that the primary responsibility for defining and designating conservation areas lay with local planning authorities, rather than the central government.[14]

The current governing legislation is shared between the *Ancient Monuments and Archaeological Areas Act* of 1979 and the *Listed Buildings and Conservation Areas Act* of 1990. The acts provide the means for identifying places of special archaeological, architectural, or historical interest, regulating proposed changes to them, and protecting the most significant ones. The 1979 Act even enables the designation of areas of archaeological importance (AAIs), where enhanced provision is made for rescue archaeology during development (Rydin 2003: 295). Some particulars of the management process for listing are provided in Section 5.4.

Other statutes introduced over the years enable the government to provide funding assistance for the conservation of monuments and buildings, which comprises an integral component of a heritage program.

Each of the various countries that make up the UK has its own heritage agency. England, Scotland, Wales, and Northern Ireland all possess distinct government heritage organizations and policies. Generally, heritage matters are administered by a quasi-non-governmental organization ('quango') that ultimately reports to a particular department—an entity midway between a government agency and a non-profit society.

England

English Heritage—its formal name is the Historic Buildings and Monuments Commission—is the government's statutory advisor on the 'historic environment.' Commissioners are appointed by the Department of Culture, Media and Sport. Previously the agency responsible for heritage conservation (variously named) reported to the Ministry of Works and the Department of the Environment. The responsibility therefore shifted within only a few decades from the department responsible for construction, to the one for environment, to the one for culture. The first reflects that building is a major activity of conservation; the latter two show an uncertainty whether conservation belongs with environment or culture—a widespread ambivalence.

The many programs administered by English Heritage focus on identifying and protecting significant places, advocacy ('championing' heritage), dispensing financial and technical support, and increasing awareness. English Heritage manages more than 400 historic properties that are visited by the public, and it has a public membership base. Three-quarters of its funding is by government appropriation, including the Heritage Lottery Fund.

To fulfill the first responsibility, English Heritage maintains the National Heritage List for England (NHLE). It includes all buildings built before 1700 which survive in anything like their original condition, and most that were built between 1700 and 1840. The criteria have become tighter with time, so that post-1945 buildings have to be exceptionally important to be listed. A building normally must be more than 30 years old to be eligible for listing. About 375,000 buildings (or groups of buildings) and nearly 11,000 other kinds of historic places had been listed (recognized) or scheduled (protected) by 2012, the latter representing:

- 1,601 registered historic parks and gardens
- 9,080 conservation areas
- 43 registered historic battlefields
- 46 designated wrecks
- 17 World Heritage Sites.[15]

Places can be nominated for listing by the central government, local authorities, amenity societies, or individuals.

English Heritage devotes considerable resources as well to its other programs. Undertaking advocacy, providing technical support, and increasing awareness all involve research, publication, awards, and more. Financial support has been quite substantial, particularly in the years around the millennium.

Most public intervention in the historic environment occurs at the local level, which comprises towns, cities, and counties. Local authorities play a direct role in planning and managing change to specific historic places. They consider applications for proposed changes to listed buildings and grant (or deny) 'listed building consent.' They are also responsible for designating conservation areas, which include historic districts and cultural landscapes.

Scotland, Wales, and Northern Ireland

In the United Kingdom, heritage planning and management are decentralized. Each constituent jurisdiction has its own agency that is responsible to its elected authorities and reflects the cultures of its people. While their overall responsibilities are generally similar to those of English Heritage, the actual programs are distinctive.

Historic Scotland (Alba Aosmhor) is an executive agency responsible to the Scottish government's Department of Arts, Culture & Sport. It is particularly active in listing and scheduling historic places and in producing a highly respected series of publications. As in England, local authorities are responsible for direct heritage management. Historic Scotland has long focused on the conservation of vernacular buildings, in particular with its Little Houses Improvement Scheme, launched in 1960.

Cadw (a Welsh word meaning 'keep' or 'protect') is the heritage agency for Wales. It is part of the Welsh government's Housing, Regeneration and Heritage Department. Some recent initiatives have been innovative, such as producing the All-Wales Interpretation Plan.

Heritage in Northern Ireland is the responsibility of the Northern Ireland Environment Agency, which resides in the Department of Environment. It is responsible for protecting, conserving, and promoting both the natural environment and built heritage—an integration of disciplines with considerable potential. The vision of the agency 'is that we will have a healthy and well protected environment and heritage in Northern Ireland which contributes to the social and economic wellbeing of the whole community.'

United States

In the United States, the development of heritage legislation followed a similar progression to that in England, from the protection of antiquities to additional place-types of more recent vintage. The *Antiquities Act* of 1906 provided a means for setting aside and protecting important places with historic, prehistoric, and commemorative value, and also established a permitting system for the excavation of sites and removal of objects. The legislation responded to the destruction of archaeological sites that resulted from the settlement of the American Southwest in the late nineteenth century.[16]

Historic preservation in the US became the responsibility of the National Park Service (NPS) upon its founding in 1916 as a bureau of the Department of the Interior. The mandate of the Department of the Interior is to manage both natural and cultural resources; NPS is the designated manager. Within a year of its formation, NPS was operating 14 national parks and 21 national monuments.

A significant step occurred with the founding of the Historic American Buildings Survey (HABS) in 1933. Created as a New Deal emergency measure to create work during the Depression, HABS immediately employed about one thousand unemployed architects, sending them around the country in teams to document historic buildings. HABS was subsequently made a full program of NPS and continues its valuable work today alongside more recent companion programs, the Historic American Engineering Record (HAER) and the Historic American Landscape Survey (HALS). The New Deal also saw the formation of the Civilian Conservation Corps (CCC) which developed national park sites, including providing labor for the conservation of many historic places. This and more were formalized in legislation with the *Historic Sites Act* of 1935, which addressed the preservation of buildings. It empowered the Secretary of the Interior to survey, acquire, restore, and operate buildings and sites of national significance, and to develop educational programs.

An effective and coordinated federal/state system was initiated with the *National Historic Preservation Act* of 1966. The statute established the Advisory Council on Historic Preservation, an independent federal agency; the National Register of Historic Places, a list of recognized historic resources; and State Historic Preservation Offices (SHPOs).

The states are the primary administrators of historic preservation programs enabled by federal legislation. SHPOs are responsible for conducting surveys of historic places within the state, processing nominations to the National Register, administering grants, and providing various technical services. SHPOs are represented nationally by the National Conference of State Historic Preservation Officers.

Most states have created agencies to carry out historic preservation programs. New York was first, with its Office of Parks and Recreation. Several states have also formed historic preservation review boards, which advise the SHPO on register nominations. Native American tribes can form a Tribal Historic Preservation Office (THPO), which can assume the functions of a SHPO. Listing on the National Register recognizes historic places but does not protect or otherwise restrict the use of private property.

Section 106 of the *National Historic Preservation Act* requires review and comment on federal and federally supported projects that affect historic places, whether they are included in, or simply eligible for, the National Register. The federal agency that is the proponent or the funder is intended to consult with interested parties, identify historic places, determine whether the proposed action will have adverse effects on the properties, and try to resolve any adverse effects. Critics note that the system is flawed, not least of all because the agency is placed into a situation of conflict whereby the same party proposes and reviews the project (King 2009).

The regulation and management of proposed change to privately owned historic property (other than projects reviewed by Section 106) and the day-to-day administration of planning and preservation-planning regulations take place at the local level. Protection (or 'designation') is a municipal responsibility, separate from listing on the National Register. Municipal preservation review agencies are enabled by the *National Historic Preservation Act*, but several predate the 1966 legislation. Each local process is specified in a historic preservation ordinance (Roddewig 1983).

The earliest municipal efforts focused on historic districts by using zoning legislation, with the designation of individual buildings emerging later. Charleston, South Carolina, used a zoning ordinance to

Figure 2.5 The historic core of Charleston, South Carolina, was protected in 1931. (Khanrak, Wikimedia Commons)

create an 'Old and Historic' District in 1931 (Weyeneth 2004), and some other cities followed in the same decade. New York City established a Landmarks Preservation Commission in 1965, in the aftermath of the demolition of Pennsylvania Station and just prior to the Grand Central Station controversy. The *National Historic Preservation Act* formally enabled cities to establish preservation review agencies.

Other countries protected areas before Great Britain and the US. One was Poland, which adopted a comprehensive conservation statute in 1928, reported to have been the first modern law to enable the protection of an entire historic neighborhood (Tung 2001: 75; Stubbs and Makaš 2011: 260; Hosmer 1981: 238–42).

Australia

Heritage was first addressed at the Commonwealth (federal) level under the *Australian Heritage Commission Act*, 1975, which set up the now-defunct commission of that name. The Commonwealth government is responsible for maintaining lists of places of national heritage value. The Australian Heritage Council, an independent appointed body of experts (which succeeded the commission), advises the minister on nominations and assessments.[17]

In the current structure, the Australian system is similar to those in Britain and the US, but with an important difference: heritage and environmental protection are addressed in the same statute: *The Environment Protection and Biodiversity Conservation Act (EPBC Act)*, 1999, and its amendments, particularly the *Environment and Heritage Legislation Amendment Act (No. 1)*, 2006. Administration of the act rests with the Department of the Environment (formerly the Department of Sustainability, Environment, Water, Population and Communities), which places heritage conservation squarely within a framework of sustainability.[18]

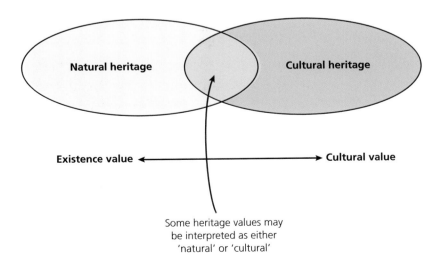

Figure 2.6 The relationship between natural and cultural heritage, as considered by the *Australian Natural Heritage Charter*. (© Copyright Commonwealth of Australia, 2002)

The *Australian Natural Heritage Charter* (Australian Heritage Commission 2002: 4) takes an integrated approach: 'Places may have both natural and cultural heritage values. These values may be related and are sometimes difficult to separate. Some people, including many Indigenous people, do not see them as being separate.'[19]

The *EPBC Act* enforces Australia's international environmental and heritage obligations, including adherence to the World Heritage Convention. It requires that the Commonwealth prepare and implement management plans for all properties on the World Heritage List, and provides principles for their management.

The *EPBC Act* provides for identifying historic places to include in the National Heritage and Commonwealth Heritage lists. Regardless of whether listed places have been protected internationally or nationally, the *EPBC Act* protects the heritage values of a place, rather than the site itself. This is an Australian innovation, following the emphasis on cultural values that dominates Australia ICOMOS's important *Burra Charter* (1999).[20] The Act also abolished the Australian Heritage Commission and replaced it with the Australian Heritage Council.

Recognition and protection of Indigenous cultural heritage has been addressed by legislation since the enactment of the *Australian Heritage Commission Act*, 1975, and the legal connection between heritage protection and land rights since the *Aboriginal Land Rights (Northern Territory) Act*, 1976. Even though these have been followed by numerous statutes at the Commonwealth, state, and territorial level, the heritage of Aboriginals and Torres Strait Islanders is not considered as rigorously or consistently as the heritage of the settler communities. Indigenous customary laws, some of which address cultural heritage, are not recognized by the Anglo-Australian legal system other than where the two systems may coincide (Boer and Wiffen 2006: chapter 9).

The Commonwealth's power is limited. It can enforce its statutes only on federal land or within states at the request of a state government. Management of heritage therefore occurs primarily at the state level, and the states in turn have passed on some responsibilities to local government. Each of the six states and two self-governing territories has enacted its individual heritage act. Each act establishes the state's own list ('register') of historic places and advisory heritage council. All address natural, Indigenous, and non-Indigenous cultural heritage, often combined in a single register. A recent trend among the states and territories has been to increasingly integrate heritage concerns in the wider context of land-use planning (Aplin 2002: chapter 10; Boer and Wiffen 2006: 220).

Canada

Canada is a federation of provinces. The nation's founders clearly separated responsibilities between the federal government and the provinces. This was defined by Section 92 of the *British North America Act* (1867) and has continued with relatively few changes in current law, which is represented by the *Constitution Act* (1982).[21] Land use, the regulation of property, and local works are clearly responsibilities of the provinces (see Stubbs and Makaš 2011; Fulton 1999; Denhez 1978a, 1978b). The federal government has the power to overrule provincial decisions, but it chooses not to exercise this authority with respect to land use or heritage. The most effective leverage that the federal government can use to influence provincial and territorial control of heritage is by means of cost-sharing agreements: 'he who pays the piper calls the tune.'

Since the federal government does not have the authority to regulate privately owned land, there is no need for overarching federal heritage legislation. A proposal (c. 2000) to introduce a federal *Historic Places Act*, which would have protected federally owned heritage property and Aboriginal heritage property, and administered various federal heritage programs, never reached Parliament.

Two statutes enable the federal government to protect particular building-types: the *Heritage Railway Stations Protection Act* (1990) and the *Heritage Lighthouse Protection Act* (2008). Both plug gaps in the present constitutional system. Since railways and lighthouses are controlled by federal legislation and/or federal agencies, the provinces have no jurisdiction over them. Therefore only the federal government can protect them.

The federal government identifies and commemorates (but does not protect) places, persons, and events of national historical significance. The Historic Sites and Monuments Board of Canada, created in 1919, advises the federal government on their recognition.[22] Commemoration (also called 'designation,' which is misleading since it does not offer protection) leads to the erection of a plaque and enables some federal funding for conserving privately owned national historic sites.

Despite its limited powers, the federal government has had immense influence on the practice and awareness of heritage. Canada's federal heritage program is administered by the Parks Canada Agency, paralleling (and preceding) the American model, although the Canadian park service is an arm's-length agency rather than a line department. Established in 1911 as the Dominion Parks Branch of the Department of the Interior, it was the first national parks agency in the world. At present Parks Canada reports to the Department of the Environment. Within the past generation, it has been overseen by the Department of Indian and Northern Affairs (which descended from the Department of the Interior) and the Department of Canadian Heritage (which is responsible for cultural policy), and had another stint with Environment between those two. These frequent transfers show ambivalence (as in other places) with respect to the relationship of heritage conservation to environment and culture.

Parks Canada's most influential heritage activities have been the management of national historic parks and federally owned national historic sites, and the development of heritage policy and standards (Taylor 1990). The *Cultural Resources Management Policy*, introduced in 1994 and 'renewed' in 2013 (Parks Canada 2013), provides a highly admired national and international model for the management of historic places. In 2001 the agency introduced the Historic Places Initiative (HPI). While several aspects of the program, not least the intended overarching legislation, were never implemented, the legacy of HPI includes the Canadian Register of Historic Places, which lists places already recognized or protected by the provinces and territories, and the authoritative *Standards and Guidelines for the Conservation of Historic Places in Canada* (Parks Canada 2010). The federal government provided funding to the provinces and territories to encourage their contribution to the Canadian Register, persuading many also to adopt the *Standards and Guidelines* as their official doctrine.

The regulation of privately owned land—the activity most closely associated with heritage conservation—is, as mentioned above, a provincial responsibility. The listing, protection, and administration of heritage property—other than places owned by the federal government and First Nations (whose welfare is technically a federal responsibility)—are the responsibility of the ten provinces and three territories. Most passed heritage conservation acts in the 1970s. Each provincial and territorial government has created an entity that holds responsibility for heritage management under authority of a provincial (or territorial) statute.[23] Provincial heritage agencies often reside within the ministries responsible for culture; some have found a different home. Their responsibilities focus on the identification and recognition of historic places, the regulation of change to designated places, and the provision of funding assistance for conservation.

Some provinces have created an entity that commemorates places and people of provincial significance, and many municipalities also place plaques on recognized property. Some also operate a heritage trust that owns and manages historic places.

Archaeology is addressed by either the same or a different provincial agency as built heritage. The provincial statutes usually include the licensing and accreditation of archaeologists and the protection of sites. The laws that require archaeological impact assessments prior to development tend to be stronger and better honored than those calling for heritage assessments, in part because those who work with the built heritage are not licensed or regulated (Pokotylo and Mason 2010).

The provinces have passed on many responsibilities to local government. The 'heavy lifting' occurs there. Municipalities select historic places to be listed on a heritage register and to be protected by designation. They are responsible for day-to-day administration and enforcement, including the consideration of applications to alter or demolish a listed or protected place and the application of incentives. The work is usually done by the municipal planning or development department, often advised by a heritage committee or commission. Provinces also pass planning statutes that enable municipalities to undertake community plans, which often address heritage matters.

Code compliance

Building codes and related regulations have a significant effect on the planning and design of conservation and development work. Sometimes they serve as an incentive, sometimes as a disincentive (see Section 5.4). It is important to determine at an early stage whether compliance with codes will be an issue. If it will, then the matter must be given careful attention. Code officials should be involved early in the project to discuss alternative interpretations of the regulations and whether exemptions to the more onerous restrictions may be available.

Codes have been developed in most nations to ensure the safety of buildings, particularly from fire and structural failure, as well as the health and welfare of users and the general public. More recently, specialized codes have been drawn up to improve accessibility, reduce greenhouse gas consumption, and meet other sustainability objectives.

Building laws that promote safety have existed since antiquity. As an example, the Old Testament orders: 'When you build a new house, you shall make a parapet for your roof, that you may not bring the guilt of blood upon your house, if any one fall from it' (Deuteronomy, R.S.V., 22: 8). The City of London regulated building construction as early as around 1200, issued its first *Building Act* in 1667, following the Great Fire, and has addressed health hazards in structures since the first *Public Health Act* of 1848 (Manco 2009). The government of New France (now Québec) introduced an 'Ordinance with regulations for the construction of houses in incombustible materials' in 1727, forbidding frame houses, external wood trim, and roofs with excessive internal wood structural members (Kalman 1994: I, 58).

Building codes have traditionally been 'prescriptive,' in that the regulations describe the specific requirements for construction. This straightforward approach works well for new construction. The rules are clear and easy to follow, although the approach is inflexible and discourages innovation. In contrast, prescriptive codes can pose unreasonable constraints on the renovation or rehabilitation of old buildings, whether or not they have heritage significance, since contemporary building systems cited in the codes often differ from those used in the past. Old buildings usually must be upgraded to comply with current codes if they undergo a 'substantial alteration,' which is usually defined as a change in use or work whose cost exceeds an established threshold.

As an example, most prescriptive codes stipulate that partition walls be built of wood or metal studs covered with gypsum wallboard. The required thickness of the wallboard is determined by the 'fire-rating,' which is the length of time that the wall must resist fire. In the early twentieth century, wood-stud walls were covered with wood lath and 'wet' plaster. Most modern codes do not recognize lath-and-plaster construction. As a consequence, that archaic wall system has been prohibited in code upgrades, forcing a renovator to demolish and rebuild the partitions with what in essence is less fire- and sound-resistant construction.[24] Another obstacle can be meeting the requirements for egress in the event of fire. Many old buildings have sufficient exit capacity but do not meet the prescribed number or width of staircases and exit doors.

A recent solution to this dilemma has been to supplement the building codes with special provisions for old buildings that provide the means for 'alternative compliance' (or 'equivalences'). These provisions are in effect incentives for rehabilitation, since they reduce inherent biases against conservation. Sometimes the old-building provision is a prescribed alternative building system; in other cases the renovated building may be permitted to meet a lower standard or at least be no more hazardous than its pre-rehabilitation condition, although this is a subjective call that is interpreted by the responsible building official (Swanke Hayden Connell Architects 2000: 75).[25]

A new kind of code has begun to replace the prescriptive code. Called a 'performance-based' (or 'objective-based') code, it establishes the required performance that a building system must meet. For example, it will stipulate the fire-rating of a partition or the egress requirements in terms of volume of people and time to exit, without dictating the method of construction or precise number of doors. In the latter situation, computer-based egress modeling allows quantification of the level of safety. In all such cases, the proponent must demonstrate that the minimum level of performance (the objective) is met.

A performance-based code is equally and indiscriminately applicable to both new and old construction. It is not an incentive, but it does reduce the anti-heritage biases of prescriptive codes. The strengths of performance-based codes include their encouragement of innovation and the frequent reduction of building costs; weaknesses include the sometimes broad articulation of performance-based requirements in ways that are not readily measurable, and which are difficult to administer and enforce.[26]

Energy codes, a product of the drive for achieving sustainability in the building industry, may discriminate against old buildings because they often prescribe new products with high thermal efficiency without taking into consideration their appearance or their lack of heritage authenticity. Windows—which are so important to the heritage character of a building—are a prime example. Most codes require double- or even triple-glazed windows and sashes with thermal-breaks. The typical wood-sash window on a historic building may or may not be capable of supporting a new, heavier glazing unit, a problem that is made worse in old windows with mullion and muntin bars that divide the glass into multiple small panes. Once again a performance-based code (stipulating the level of thermal insulation) is better than a prescriptive code. Wood (the sash) is a naturally good insulator and upgrading weather-stripping helps, as do storm windows, but sometimes the energy goals remain unattainable.

Some places have succeeded in negotiating exemptions for historic places. As an example, in British Columbia advocates and bureaucrats together successfully urged the provincial government to exempt recognized historic buildings from the strict window-replacement requirements for residential conversions under the *Homeowner Protection Act* (Heritage BC 2010b).

Energy-efficiency regulators seem to be unaware that many old buildings have inherent energy-saving features not found in typical new buildings and can achieve a level of human comfort with little if any energy-consuming mechanical ventilation or air conditioning. The characteristics include high ceilings, natural cross-ventilation, large windows, and masonry walls with a high thermal capacity. In many situations the only retrofitting required may be the addition of thermal insulation above the ceiling and weather-stripping around the windows and doors.

Accessibility standards for disabled persons can also pose hurdles for heritage conservation. In the US, the *Americans with Disabilities Act* ('ADA,' 1990) sets prescriptive provisions for establishing unimpaired access to new and existing buildings that accommodate the public, without exempting historic properties. Parallel regulations in other jurisdictions do much the same. Barriers to access may be created by entrances, ramps and stairs, surface textures, parking, size of doorways, interior corridors, toilets, signage, and more. The recommended upgrades can have a serious negative impact on historic places (Swanke Hayden Connell Architects 2000: 79–92).

A rational approach to planning accessibility modifications to buildings and landscapes is to review the heritage significance of the property and identify its character-defining elements, assess the existing and required level of accessibility, and evaluate accessibility options within a conservation context. Recognizing the national interest in conserving historic properties, the US has established alternative requirements for properties that cannot be made accessible by following ADA guidelines without 'threatening or destroying' the properties' significance. Some alternatives, such as home delivery and audiovisual programs, provide access to program content without requiring a change (or access) to the subject building (Jester and Park 1993).

Heritage conservation law is a reflection of the shared values of society. Most countries now recognize conservation as a legitimate goal of government, whereas this was not the case a half-century ago. Nevertheless that goal remains overshadowed by other rights and protections, which society considers as being more fundamental and compelling (Mayes 2003: 159). Perhaps these values will change as society continues to evolve; only time will tell.

Planning

Heritage planning can be considered a subdiscipline of both heritage conservation and planning. Alternatively, heritage conservation can be seen as a tool of planning. Seen either way, the two professions are closely entwined. British planner John Delafons emphasizes the link: 'Indeed "planning" and "conservation" are sometimes portrayed as antagonists. It has become important to reassert that conservation is part of planning and that planning must incorporate conservation objectives' (1997: 2).

The planning framework

At the most general level, **planning** (also called **community planning, town and country planning, urban and regional planning, community development**) is concerned with planning for and administration of land-use law. Planners endeavor to produce a vigorous community with a high quality of life. Its well-being is seen holistically as deriving from a balance among physical, social, and economic factors. The physical aspects address features such as layout, circulation, aesthetics and attractiveness, and environmental and public health; the social qualities include equity, cultural diversity, and community amenities; and the economic issues include robust development and commercial vitality. These are the components of sustainability.[27]

Good planning balances conceptual models with pragmatic regulations. Countless architects and planners, from Vitruvius in ancient Rome to Ebenezer Howard and Le Corbusier in the last century and the computer modelers of today, have promoted their concepts of 'ideal cities.' The realities of land and life, however, require that these models be implementable and have community support. This requires modifying the ideal with the practical, which in turn requires that planners be able to work with people, politics, and the law.

The broad basis for planning is usually defined in an overarching **planning statute** enacted by the government authority responsible for land use and property ownership. Planning statutes enable state, provincial, and territorial governments to produce large-scale land-use plans, which, in turn, allow local governments to prepare region-wide, city, or rural **development plans** (called **comprehensive plans** in the US, **official plans** and **official community plans** in Canada, and by various other names elsewhere). Many local planning authorities also issue **neighborhood plans** (or **area/sub-area plans**) for individual neighborhoods or districts, and **site plans** for specific properties.

Development plans are statements of municipal or rural land-use policy, primarily as the policy relates to future growth and development. Any development controls that are introduced as a consequence of the plans will put those policies into effect. For example, as will be seen below in the discussion of incentive zoning, if a municipal policy encourages the creation of public open space in a densely developed commercial area then passing an ordinance that permits additional floor space as a reward for creating a public open space validates the policy by linking it with regulations.

The components of a development plan vary from one place to another, but topics that are usually addressed include some or all of:

- Land use (urban and rural/transitional)
- Housing
- Economic development
- Social progress
- Heritage conservation
- Environment and natural resources

- Energy
- Sustainability
- Transportation
- Growth management
- Design.

The planning process involves a number of distinct phases: research, community goals and objectives, drafting the plan, and extensive community engagement. The last is particularly important. Virtually all planning documents generate conflict, and every reasonable effort should be made to listen to the community's desires and resolve any differences.

Authorities may also develop specific plans based on one or more of the topics in the list, such as a housing plan, a transportation plan, an environmental protection plan, or a heritage conservation plan. The recent past has seen the growth as well of community sustainability plans. While these dedicated plans are useful, it is desirable that they elaborate policies articulated within the community plan and not be self-standing documents. If such plans are intended to be considered alone, they may well go disregarded.

The local government level is where day-to-day planning occurs and the majority of public-sector planners (planning officers) are employed. Planners' responsibilities are often divided into long-range planning (or forward planning), which is concerned with the preparation of policy and high-level plans for the region, the municipality, or a neighborhood; and current planning, which responds to specific proposals for development and addresses the short-range administration of land-use law.

Development control and zoning

The policies expressed in development plans are implemented by means of regulations called **development controls** (or **zoning** in the US and Canada, and both in Australia). These procedures provide detailed guidance for land use and development within an individual community, and follow the rationale for land use stated in the community plan. Development control and zoning are intended to regulate the use of private land for the common good, ensuring that the interests of private property owners are balanced against the interests of the public (Tyler and Ward 2011: 188). This includes public health, which was a primary motivation for development controls in generations past.

'Zoning' is so-named because zoning plans divide a community into a series of 'zones,' usually identified by their land use (e.g., residential zones and commercial zones). In the UK, these are called 'use classes' and the regulations that control them are 'use classes orders' and 'general development orders.'

In North America, zoning is usually enacted at the local government level as **bylaws** or **ordinances**. The first zoning regulations in the

Figure 2.7 The former Point Grey Fire Hall. Point Grey, now part of the City of Vancouver, adopted the first zoning bylaw in Canada in 1922 (two years before the photo was taken) to protect its elitist values, seen here in the use of the Tudor Revival style to evoke associations with Britain. (City of Vancouver Archives, CVA 677–697, Philip T. Timms)

US are acknowledged to have been in New York City in 1916, and the legal right of a municipality to use zoning was supported by the US Supreme Court in 1926.[28] The first in Canada was in the professional Municipality of Point Grey, now part of the City of Vancouver, in 1922. Zoning was first used as a tool of heritage conservation with the protection of part of Charleston, South Carolina, as a historic district in 1931. Today heritage legislation, rather than zoning, is generally used to achieve this end.

Zoning began with a focus on regulating land use, but it typically controls numerous other aspects of development and design. These usually include site coverage, **floor area ratio** (or **floor space ratio**, **plot ratio**, which measures the ratio of the total area of all floors to the ground area of the property), height limits, building envelopes, distances to property lines, relationships to adjacent buildings, and requirements for providing parking. Signs are frequently controlled by zoning, or by a separate bylaw or ordinance. Sign regulations control acceptable sizes, materials, and illumination, and sometimes also the design, colors, and fonts. Landscaping can also be mandated or otherwise controlled.

The UK, where development control has acquired a largely negative reputation, has experimented with, and generally rejected, the concept of zoning. Instead, these kinds of measures are regulated within overall development control. The British system is **discretionary**, allowing officials considerable flexibility. The *Town and Country Planning Act* requires local planning authorities to 'have regard to the provisions of the development plan, so far as material to the application,' but also to 'any other considerations.' In other words, the local authority can approve a proposal that is not in accordance with the provisions of the plan (Cullingworth and Nadin 2002: 120). The American system, in contrast, is **regulatory**, based on the desire for certainty and the need to define rights (as provided by the Constitution), and therefore prescribes measurable limits to the development that is acceptable on any given property (Booth 1996: 6–7). Canada has generally followed the American approach, although the country had no constitution until the late twentieth century. The Australian system is closer to the regulatory model.

The original purpose of zoning in America was to separate uses that were seen as being incompatible with each other. While this may have succeeded in locating factories at a distance from housing, thereby removing noxious smells and unwanted noise from residential areas, it also created a divided city with single-use neighborhoods—commercial city cores and residential suburbs—which ensured lifeless city centres after offices and businesses closed. In *The Death and Life of Great American Cities* (1961), American-Canadian planner Jane Jacobs argued passionately for restoring diversity to the city: a diversity of functions and a diversity of building-types (including mingling old and new buildings), as well as short streets and dense populations.

Jacobs's reasoning was widely heard, and the last two generations have reintroduced these features into urban planning. The current focus is on encouraging innovative approaches to creating mixed-use and diverse neighborhoods, rather than simply separating uses and preventing bad development. To help achieve this, many local governments have adopted a negotiated approach to zoning and development control. In some cases certain plots (or larger assembled properties) are designated **comprehensive zones** (or **contract zones**, or in the US for large assemblies, **planned unit development**). These usually

Figure 2.8 Jane Jacobs admired Boston's North End for its small blocks, concentration of residential units, old buildings, and friendly street atmosphere. These features were planning anathema in 1960, but are highly valued today. (Tim Grafft/ MOTT)

encourage the developer to propose the land uses, floor area ratios, building forms, and other factors, and local authorities determine through negotiation whether they meet the overall planning objectives of the development plan and would otherwise provide a good development.

A particular negotiated method that is often used is **incentive zoning**, whereby development that meets established policy objectives is encouraged with a system of rewards. Incentive zoning was introduced with the New York Zoning Resolution of 1961 (Cullingworth and Caves 2009: 115–16). Incentives, often in the form of additional height and/or density (floor area), are offered to induce developers or property owners to provide public amenities that are regarded as benefiting the community at large. The 1961 regulation bonused the creation of open space ('plazas'), which it called privately owned public spaces, in the midst of a development boom. The concept was inspired by the plaza of the Seagram Building (1958), designed without any municipal requirements by architects Ludwig Mies van der Rohe and Philip Johnson, and which proved to be a popular gathering place. As a result, many office buildings in midtown Manhattan from that era feature point towers set back from the street to create at-grade open space, which was deemed to be a public amenity.[29]

Today the range of public amenities that are rewarded has been broadened to include the provision of things as diverse as cultural

Figure 2.9 The open plaza in front of the Seagram Building, New York, created a precedent that was subsequently encouraged by incentive zoning. (Alex Schwab)

facilities, day-care centres, affordable and/or accessible housing, and parks, as well as the protection of environmental attributes and historic places. Incentive zoning is applied at the local government level.

The value of incentive zoning was described a decade after its introduction by American law professor John Costonis. He wrote:

> By modifying the economics of downtown development, these programs encourage development decisions that would normally be precluded by the harsh realities of the marketplace. Where successful, they have enabled cities to channel development in accordance with municipally selected urban design policies.
>
> (Costonis 1972: 575–6)

The rewards usually consist of regulatory relaxations and bonuses (called **amenity bonuses**). Relaxations, which override zoning regulations, may involve items such as land use, lot coverage, height, or parking, but not human safety. Bonuses can be provided in the form of additional floor area (also called floor area ratio, floor space ratio, plot ratio, and density). Incentives are given on a discretionary basis according to local criteria. Amenity bonuses are a key instrument in urban conservation, and they are discussed further with heritage conservation tools and incentives, in Section 5.4.

Another planning innovation in early 1960s America was **advocacy planning**, the approach that invited the affected public—in particular disadvantaged groups—to participate in the planning process. Advocacy planning is described in Section 4.3, with the discussion of community engagement.

Zoning and development control form the basis of a permitting system. Potential developments must comply with zoning regulations or else present a successful case for varying or changing the guidelines. Authorities may approve a planning proposal, give approval subject to certain conditions, or refuse it. The regulations include provisions for enforcement, which can be as drastic as requiring the demolition of an unapproved structure.

Development controls often address design, despite the difficulty in defining or regulating 'good design.' Design is considered to be more subjective and judgmental than objective, and a literal application of precise constraints may be impossible. **Design guidelines** are often set out in the planning documents, usually with illustrative examples. Municipal officials and/or an appointed design committee are charged with responsibility for ensuring that the proposals follow those guidelines. This is a challenging task that relies on the design skills of the officials and committee members, and their sense of 'good design' may differ from that of the proponent. If guidelines are made to be followed very closely, the outcome may be a boring sameness to everything that is built; whereas a looser interpretation will enable stronger and bolder design, but may also permit bad design.

Strong Design Controls Discourage both Poor and Distinguished Architecture

The City of Vancouver, BC, has recently loosened its grip on design control. In the 1990s and early 2000s, under the leadership of Associate Director of Planning Larry Beasley, the City controlled design in the downtown core closely. Beasley abhorred 'bad design' and ensured that none would occur on his watch. Incentive zoning encouraged developers to provide community amenities. The result was excellent urban design, producing a formula that has been widely praised as 'Vancouverism,' as well as uniformly good architectural design, but with few buildings of exceptional quality. Since Beasley's departure, the city's planners have been willing to take chances. This has led to some stellar signature buildings by international 'starchitects,' who were discouraged under the previous regime, but has also produced some mediocrity.

English planner John Punter has summed up the Beasley years this way:

> The guidelines and processes are deemed to be good at producing safe 'background' buildings but cut out the truly innovative risk-taking design that might break the mould and/or provide those highlights of townscape so valued by postmodern urban designers and architectural photographers.
> (Punter 2003: 345)

Figure 2.10 QuayWest Resort Residences (2002), facing Vancouver's False Creek, typify the prescribed mixed-use, pedestrian-friendly, podium-and-tower approach praised as 'Vancouverism.' (John Roaf)

Celebrated Swiss architect Harry Gugger, whose first Vancouver office tower is scheduled to be completed in 2017, says of the city's downtown: 'The recent [residential towers] seem to be a bit off the shelf, I would say' (Gold 2013: S8).

Design guidelines are commonly applied in historic districts and conservation areas, and not only in developing neighborhoods. Most such areas contain non-conforming buildings and vacant lots that provide development opportunities, and local authorities want to ensure that new construction will be compatible with the dominant character. Good guidelines will encourage harmonious design and avoid unwanted intrusions, but will also prohibit brilliant one-off solutions that might inject a spark of inspiration. Bad guidelines, such as those that encourage reproducing historical details and ignore larger design issues, such as form and massing, can have a deleterious effect.[30]

Heritage planning

Many local authorities retain one or more planners responsible for heritage (often called a **heritage planner**, **preservation planner**, or **heritage officer**). At best this position is held by a person who is both a professional heritage specialist and a professional planner. In actuality, however, many municipal heritage planners have only one of these skill sets, often the latter. Regardless of formal training, all heritage planners must be familiar with the relevant planning infrastructure and with heritage legislation, which was discussed in the previous section. Heritage planners participate in administering heritage statutes, regulations, and programs. Their work usually includes maintaining inventories, registers and lists of historic places, processing applications to modify listed or protected historic places and, when time permits, long-range planning.

Heritage policy is most effective when the conservation plan for a community is a component of the comprehensive community plan. UNESCO has recommended that 'all official plans must provide for heritage conservation' (Denhez 1997: 21). England is following this suggestion: the *National Planning Policy Framework* (2012) states that 'local planning authorities should set out in their Local Plan a positive strategy for the conservation and enjoyment of the historic environment' (Department for Communities and Local Government (UK) 2012: para. 126).[31] However, the integration of planning and heritage planning is only beginning to be the norm. International guidelines take time to implement and most community plans still do not address heritage conservation. American planners Robert Ward and Norman Tyler identify a disconnect between the two, noting that 'historic preservation has been viewed by many city planners as ancillary to the process of master planning.' They report that a survey of State Historic Preservation Offices undertaken in 2005 revealed that only a few states (4 of the 28 that responded to the survey) mandate a historic preservation element in local comprehensive plans and that the level of compliance by local governments varies significantly from one community to another (Tyler and Ward 2011; Ward and Tyler 2005: 117).[32]

More frequently, heritage policy is contained not in the comprehensive community plan, but rather in a separate document, often called a **conservation plan** (or **[historic] preservation plan**, **heritage management plan**), whether at the national, state/provincial, regional, local, or neighborhood level. The separation of the conservation plan from the community plan is less effective than integration of the two, because a stand-alone conservation plan is sometimes overlooked and only the community plan consulted. Moreover, many jurisdictions have no conservation plan at all. And where some conservation planning has taken place, it is sometimes marginalized. This is seen in the US and

Canada, for example, where historic districts are often referred to in plans as 'overlay zones' (i.e., overlays to the underlying zones, which are primary), a term that indicates their diminished priority. The integration of heritage into mainstream planning may be gaining traction, but it still awaits universal widespread acceptance.

The relationship between planning and conservation is better integrated in England than the US, particularly with respect to conservation areas. The *Planning (Listed Buildings and Conservation Areas) Act 1990* instructs local planning authorities to give special attention to the desirability of preserving and enhancing the character of conservation areas. The government has also emphasized the importance of integrating conservation into the preparation of development plans. Planning guidance emphasizes the need to control the management of change with respect to demolition and alterations of buildings, including unlisted ones (Pendlebury 2001: 304; Pickard 1996: 230).

Turning again to the US, the American Planning Association, which advocates preservation planning, has suggested that a community's historic preservation plan should contain at least ten essential components:

1   Statement of the goals of preservation in the community, and the purpose of the preservation plan.
2   Definitions of the historic character of the state, region, community, or neighborhood.
3   Summary of past and current efforts to preserve the community's or neighborhood's character.
4   A survey of historic resources in the community or neighborhood, or a definition of the type of survey that should be conducted in communities that have not yet completed a survey.
5   Explanation of the legal basis for protection of historic resources in the state and community.
6   Statement of the relationship between historic preservation and other local land-use and growth management authority, such as the zoning ordinance.
7   Statement of the public sector's responsibilities towards city-owned historic resources, such as public buildings, parks, streets, etc., and for ensuring that public actions do not adversely affect historic resources.
8   Statement of incentives that are, or should be, available to assist in the preservation of the community's historic resources.
9   Statement of the relationship between historic preservation and the community's educational system and program.
10 A precise statement of goals and policies, including a specific agenda for future action to accomplish those goals.

(White and Roddewig 1994: 4)

These components are relevant whether the conservation plan (historic preservation plan) is freestanding or integrated into the development plan. Similar components make up the structure of a conservation plan whose scope is limited to a single historic place. The scope and contents of both kinds of conservation plan will be presented in Section 5.8. In that discussion, the community-scale plan is called a 'macro' conservation plan and the historic-place-specific plan a 'micro' conservation plan.

The preparation of a conservation plan, at either scale, is the product of the most restrictive definition of 'heritage planning.' The present book addresses heritage planning at a much more comprehensive level, addressing the many principles and processes that should be considered in writing conservation plans and managing change to historic places.

2.2 Sustainability

The Brundtland Report and the pillars of sustainable development

The concept of sustainability has been around for a long time, but only since 1987 has it taken on the particular meaning and terminology used today. Credit for this is given to the definition of 'sustainable development' contained in 'The Brundtland Report,' the common name for the publication, *Our Common Future*, produced by the World Commission on Environment and Development (WCED), a United Nations agency chaired by Gro Harlem Brundtland, at the time Prime Minister of Norway. The much-quoted passage from the report reads: 'Sustainable development is development that meets the needs of the present without compromising the ability of future generations to meet their own needs' (WCED 1987: chapter 2, para. 1).[33]

The Brundtland Report spawned a series of important international events. It was a primary stimulus for the U.N. Conference on Environment and Development in 1992, otherwise known as the Rio Summit or the Earth Summit. The Rio Summit produced *Agenda 21*, an action plan for sustainable development, which was intended for voluntary compliance at all levels of government. *Agenda 21* focused mainly on environmental issues. Other progeny of Rio included the Kyoto Protocol and subsequent environmental summits in 1997, 2002, and 2012.

In the years following the Rio Summit, sustainability came to be generally accepted as requiring the resolution of three interrelated areas: the social, environmental, and economic dimensions. This is usually expressed with the metaphor of sustainability being supported by three 'pillars.' Sustainable development is said to be achieved when the goals of social equity, economic development, and environmental quality are met in a coordinated manner (Levy 2011: 294).

In this model, culture (and heritage, when considered to be a cultural endeavor, as has been traditional) is considered to be part of the social dimension. Some authorities argued for culture as a fourth, independent pillar of sustainability. This concept was promoted in *Agenda 21 for Culture* (a document distinct from *Agenda 21*), drawn up in Porto Alegre, Brazil, in 2002, and approved in its final state two

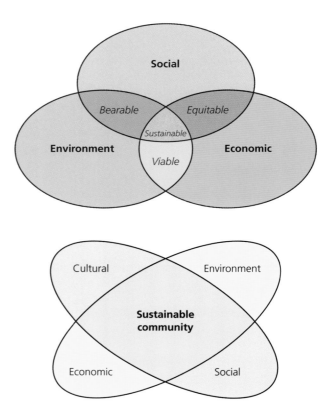

Figures 2.11 and 2.12 Models of sustainable development comprising three pillars or dimensions (social, economic, and environmental) and four pillars (with the addition of cultural).

years later in Barcelona, under the leadership of the United Cities and Local Governments (UCLG), an organization dubbed the U.N. of the cities. The goal of *Agenda 21 for Culture* is that cities and local governments should develop strong cultural policies based on a commitment to a number of factors, including human rights, cultural diversity, and sustainability. While the principles and recommended undertakings do not identify heritage conservation directly, they include the need 'to consider cultural parameters in all urban and regional planning ... to ensure protection of local cultural heritage and the legacy of previous generations' and to recognize public spaces as 'collective goods that belong to all citizens' (UCLG n.d.: paras. 16, 26).

As was noted in Section 1.1 and will be explored throughout this section, heritage conservation began somewhat one-dimensionally as the preservation of our past culture. UNESCO and other international agencies continue to use the term 'cultural heritage' to describe historic places. In the past generation, however, the environmental and economic dimensions of sustainability have become increasingly essential components of conservation. As Turkish-Dutch conservation specialist Silvio Mutal expressed it, 'conservation is not sustainable if it is only carried out for cultural reasons' (Rodwell 2011: 45). Heritage conservation has its important economic and environmental dimensions, as well as the long-familiar sociocultural one. Indeed, heritage is increasingly thought of as a social activity that addresses issues such as housing and quality of life; an economic activity allied with planning and urban development; and an environmental activity with the potential to play a meaningful part in the drive to conserve resources and reduce greenhouse gases. However one may choose to classify heritage, and whichever of the two sustainability models (three or four pillars) is preferred, authorities and the general population have come to recognize the close ties between heritage conservation and sustainable development.

As an example, the *National Planning Policy Framework* for England, issued by the UK government in 2012, places heritage squarely within an environmental, and not a social, context. (As was seen previously, England describes historic places as components of the 'historic environment.') The *Policy Framework* sets all planning within the rubric of 'sustainable development,' which is defined simply in the Minister for Planning's foreword (Department for Communities and Local Government (UK) 2012: i) as: '*Sustainable* means ensuring that better lives for ourselves don't mean worse lives for future generations.' Minister Greg Clark continues:

> *Development* means growth. ... Sustainable development is about change for the better, and not only in our built environment. ... Our historic environment—buildings, landscapes, towns and villages— can better be cherished if their spirit of place thrives, rather than withers. ... Sustainable development is about positive growth— making economic, environmental and social progress for this and future generations.

Scotland takes this approach a step further, asserting:

> The protection and enhancement of the historic environment contributes to the Scottish Government's central purpose, which is 'to focus government and public services on creating a more sustainable country, with opportunities for all of Scotland to flourish, through increasing sustainable economic growth.' To support that, the Scottish Government has identified as a national outcome that 'We value and enjoy our built and natural environment and protect and enhance it for future generations.' Scottish Ministers will therefore take account of the wider sustainability agenda in all their decisions on matters relating to the historic environment.
>
> (Historic Scotland 2009: 1.11, p. 7)

In this spirit, the Council for British Archaeology has modified the Brundtland statement to appropriate it for heritage, defining sustainable development as: 'Development which meets the needs of today without compromising the ability of future generations to understand, appreciate and benefit from Britain's historic environment' (cited in Historic Scotland 2002: 7).

Not all countries have embraced sustainable development as core policy as enthusiastically as England and Scotland, but all indications point to this as an ongoing process. The challenge that confronts policy-makers and planners is not whether, but rather how, to incorporate sustainability objectives into heritage conservation, as well as the converse: how to incorporate heritage conservation into planning for sustainability.

The first task requires planning for heritage in a manner that will not decrease the value of social equity, environmental quality, and/or economic development. The second involves mitigating negative impacts on historic places that might be caused by too literal an imposition of sustainability standards. Yet a third challenge is the integration of sustainable heritage planning with sustainable urban planning. Many communities have prepared sustainability plans, but these are often distinct from their comprehensive plans and heritage plans—yet all contain parallel objectives. Evidently there are no easy solutions, but it is important that heritage planners and urban planners think holistically and keep these broad, integrative objectives in mind.

One pillar—the environmental dimension—has captured more attention than the others. It is common to read that places are sustainable if they reduce their energy consumption and carbon emissions. While these are undeniably important objectives, they alone do not comprise sustainability. The sociocultural and economic dimensions must also be taken into consideration.

UBC Renew: A Program in Heritage Sustainability

The University of British Columbia (UBC) in Vancouver introduced UBC Renew in 2004 to preserve and upgrade its aging building stock. The program places a strong emphasis on sustainability. The choice to renew rather than replace existing structures retained familiar places and patterns of campus use. Interior spaces were reconfigured as needed to meet contemporary teaching needs and current seismic and life-safety standards, while retaining heritage character-defining elements. These efforts attained sociocultural sustainability. Environmental sustainability was addressed by bringing the buildings up to a high level of energy efficiency, in most cases upgrading rather than replacing windows, wall and roof assemblies, and mechanical systems; by reducing the construction energy footprint; and (in Phase 1, to 2010) by diverting 1,500 metric tonnes of construction waste from the landfill. The economic dimension benefited as well: in Phase 1 the program avoided $89 million in construction costs, leading UBC to boast that 'every third building is free'; and it eliminated $77.4 million from UBC's accumulated deferred maintenance debt.

The Chemistry Centre was the first project undertaken, completed in 2008. Originally known as the Science Building, it was the first structure on the UBC campus (built 1914–25). Campus architects Sharp and Thompson adopted the popular Collegiate Gothic style for this and other early buildings. Conservation measures included preserving the stone exterior walls, the metal casement windows, and an exceptional tiled corridor. Other buildings that have benefited from UBC Renew include early modernist gems, including the Buchanan Building and its landscaped courtyard (1956–60). Eleven buildings had been renovated as of 2012, some achieving LEED® (Leadership in Energy and Environmental Design) gold certification (University of British Columbia n.d.).

Figure 2.13 Chemistry Centre, University of British Columbia. (John Roaf)

Pocantico Proclamation on Sustainability and Historic Preservation

In order to encourage heritage professionals to acknowledge these challenges, the National Trust for Historic Preservation and the Friends of the Center for Preservation Technology and Training, the latter the supporters of an agency of the US National Park Service, convened a symposium on 'Sustainability and Historic Preservation—Making Policy.' The meeting was held at the Pocantico Center, north of New York City, in November 2008. It produced the *Pocantico Proclamation on Sustainability and Historic Preservation* (2009), which contains a set of fundamental premises and principles linking the two sectors (National Trust for Historic Preservation and National Center for Preservation Technology and Training 2009).

The premises, with abridged descriptive text, are:

1 *The climate change imperative*
   ○ We must immediately and significantly reduce greenhouse gas emissions.
2 *The economic imperative*
   ○ A new green economy must rest upon a conservation-based foundation.

3 *The equity imperative*
   ○ Our consumption patterns must be altered to foster social equity, cultural diversity, and survival of all species.

The principles are:

1 Foster a culture of reuse
2 Reinvest at a community scale
3 Value heritage
4 Capitalize on the potential of the green economy
5 Realign historic preservation policies with sustainability.

A companion document, *Actions to Further the Pocantico Principles on Sustainability and Historic Preservation*, provides recommendations for advocacy, education, public policy, and techniques (National Trust for Historic Preservation 2008). The actions are mostly pragmatic and reasonable. All are quite general (e.g., 'incorporate sustainability into preservation curricula at all levels of education'; 'develop performance based energy codes, so that historic properties can find non-standard methods for improved energy performance'; 'explore the use of urban growth boundaries and promote sustainable planning as seen in historic districts'). Emphasis is placed on measures that would achieve energy conservation and reduce greenhouse gases, as well as other environmental benefits. The Pocantico Proclamation and its actions may not break new ground, but they provide a succinct, useful overview of the ways to integrate heritage conservation with sustainable objectives.[34]

Sustainability was defined in the Brundtland Report in terms of 'sustainable development.' Building new structures and rehabilitating old ones involve 'sustainable design,' an approach to design that respects social, environmental, and economic considerations. The remainder of this section discusses separately the sociocultural, environmental, and economic dimensions of sustainable heritage development and design. Because the commitment to enhance the relationship between heritage conservation and sustainable development is so current, the thinking and the literature are evolving quickly and many of the thoughts that follow may be outdated by the time they are read.

Social and cultural considerations

The first pillar of sustainability is the 'social' dimension; the 'cultural' dimension is either subsumed within this or treated separately, depending on whether one counts three or four pillars. This section considers the two aspects separately.

Cultural factors

Heritage conservation began as a culturally driven (or 'curatorial') activity whose mission was to identify and retain places that have aesthetic and historical significance. The temples of antiquity, the cathedrals of the Middle Ages, and the mansions of the industrial age were seen as great works of art to be studied, treasured, and preserved. In past generations, heritage conservation served mainly the interests of the mainstream establishment. Even recently, historic houses were of interest only when they had accommodated the social or political elite (often scorned as 'dead white men'), and rehabilitated historic districts were usually 'gentrified' (or 'white-painted')—marketed to well-to-do owners or occupants—when the properties were upgraded. Although the heritage sector has broadened its interests far beyond the products of elite society and mainstream ethnicity, these remain its roots.

The cultural dimension of conservation is summed up neatly in Australia's *Burra Charter*, a compendium of best conservation practices. The Charter, which is discussed in Section 3.1, focuses on the retention of 'cultural significance,' which it defines as 'aesthetic, historic, scientific, social or spiritual value for past, present or future generations' (Australia ICOMOS 2013b: Article 1.2). 'Culture' in this broad sense refers to the many attributes and values that distinguish one group, society, or nation from another. Historic places are felt to be indispensable to our spiritual, social, and cultural well-being. We are threatened by their proposed loss and therefore take appropriate action to neutralize the threat.

Protecting historic places is also motivated in part by patriotism, which is an aspect of devotion to history. It was seen in Section 1.2 that two of the earliest buildings in the US to benefit from preservation activism were Independence Hall and Mount Vernon, both places that participated in the birth of the American republic. A government-produced book that contributed to convincing US legislators to adopt the *National Historic Preservation Act* began:

> What we want to conserve ... is the evidence of individual talent *and* tradition, of liberty *and* union among successive generations of Americans. We want signs of where we came from and how we got to where we are, the thoughts we had along the way and what we did to express the thoughts in action. We want to know the trails that were walked, the battles that were fought, the tools that were made. We want to know the beautiful or useful things that were built and the originality that was shown.
>
> (United States Conference of Mayors 1966: 1)

The spirit of using heritage as a tool of patriotism is also evident when a decision is made to conserve a historic place—or to reconstruct one that has been lost—when it represents a valued way of life, or as a symbol of power, authority, and community.

Social factors

Article 3.1 of the *Burra Charter*, cited previously, includes 'social or spiritual value' as a component of cultural significance. In this context, 'social' is simply an adjective that refers to 'society.' This is further explained in the guidelines to an earlier, 1988, version of the *Burra*

Charter: 'Social value embraces the qualities for which a place has become a focus of spiritual, national, political or other cultural sentiment to a majority or minority group' (cited in Australia ICOMOS 2000: 12).

'Social' may also have a more complex meaning, referring to the organization and nature of society, with particular reference to one or another level of society. Attention has turned to conservation that serves the needs of minorities and the less advantaged components of society. Heritage work is often intended to achieve social equity or social utility. This is seen, for example, when conservation provides job opportunities, affordable housing, or political empowerment—in short, when its benefits are accessible to all and it contributes to community sustainability. Conservation done well should bring about positive social benefits.[35]

A number of arguments are commonly made with respect to social benefits of conservation. They include:

- Conservation retains intact, functional neighborhoods and communities, and reduces displacement (resettlement, relocation).
- Older, somewhat rundown neighborhoods provide affordable accommodation that can be repaired at relatively low cost to accommodate groups and individuals with low incomes.
- Traditional residential buildings, with porches and windows facing the street, provide 'eyes on the neighborhood' and increase area security.
- Rehabilitation is labor-intensive and provides local job opportunities (also an economic benefit).
- Conservation protects and celebrates both the intangible and tangible cultural heritage that define us and our communities, producing a stronger social identity.
- The interpretation of heritage resources provides valuable educational opportunities.

Just as Australians embedded social and spiritual values in the *Burra Charter*, English Heritage (n.d.-a) has declared explicit objectives for achieving equality (i.e., social equity) and diversity through heritage policy:

- Provide and encourage opportunities for all to access, understand and enjoy the historic environment.
- Seek to understand the diversity of England's heritage and promote a more inclusive understanding of our past.
- Value and share an inclusive interpretation of England's heritage.
- Demonstrate that the historic environment contributes to positive change in the lives of individuals and communities.
- Promote good practice on equalities issues in the historic environment sector and actively engage with partners to encourage others to do the same.
- Positively promote equality of opportunity as an employer and a service provider.

- Ensure that all our activities as an organization take into account the widest possible range of needs.
- Encourage a more diverse range of people to train for and join the heritage sector workforce in order to secure our shared heritage for future generations.

Authorities in Britain also speak of the 'public value' of retaining historic places. The Institute of Historic Building Conservation asserts that this includes the preservation of local identity and sense of place, the high level of public support, and the contribution to local empowerment (Institute of Historic Building Conservation n.d.: 4).

Other countries and organizations have their own criteria—sometimes stated formally, as in Britain, sometimes implicit—for assuring that heritage conservation achieves social benefits and contributes to sustainable development. The objectives are as diverse as increasing the stock of affordable housing and encouraging historical literacy among racial minorities.

Urban renewal and conservation

Nowhere is the convergence of shaping the built environment and achieving social objectives more evident than in the planning, rebuilding, and conservation of historic urban centres. The large-scale redevelopment of old cities began in the 1940s. The principal cause in Europe was the need for post-war reconstruction and the provision of mass housing for the homeless. In America, on the other hand, urban redevelopment was intended to eliminate substandard housing, reduce de facto racial segregation, and revitalize the urban economy. Both continents saw old, congested areas as symbols of opportunity, and both were inspired by the ambitious visions for 'modern' urban planning and development that envisioned the social solution in widely spaced, high-rise apartment blocks, with freedom of movement at ground level. This urban form was widely promoted by architect Le Corbusier in his *Ville contemporaine* (1922) and by the Congrès international d'architecture moderne (CIAM), a European organization that promoted 'modern' design and whose manifesto (1933) declared architecture to be a 'social art' (Appleyard 1979: 2–49).[36]

European reconstruction after World War II often disregarded traditional street patterns and historic design traditions. This was partly the case, for example, in central London, which suffered extensive bomb damage during the 'blitz.' The largest post-war development was the Barbican, a 40-acre site that had been cleared by bombing, and which the City determined would be replaced with high-density residential construction. Designed in 1956 by Chamberlin, Powell and Bon, the Barbican is dominated by three point towers and a number of slab blocks enclosing squares and linked by elevated walkways. The architecture is uncompromisingly contemporary. Nevertheless connections to the past are maintained by revealing remains of the Roman and

Figure 2.14 The Barbican Estate, London, with the Barbican Centre at the left. (Nevilley, Wikimedia Commons)

medieval city wall as well as the church of St. Giles' Cripplegate, which was restored and reopened (Lloyd 1976: 52–3).

The Barbican succeeded in repopulating central London. However it was criticized because residents were largely from the middle class, thereby not achieving social equity; and also for being cold and dehumanized. This was remediated to some extent with the completion of the Barbican Centre, a large performing arts centre that was part of the original concept but opened only decades later, in 1982. It has made the Barbican a major, accessible destination and enlivened the complex considerably.

In the US, 'urban renewal' was initiated with the *Housing Act* of 1949, which was intended to facilitate the construction of good, new housing. In the next 25 years, some 600,000 inexpensive housing units—often dismissed as 'slums' and 'blight'—were demolished under government programs. Their 2 million residents were forced to move, mostly to other neighborhoods. Urban renewal acquired and cleared great swaths of land, absorbing the residual value of existing structures and undertaking the tedious work of land assembly, then selling or leasing the land to private developers. More often than not, the land was redeveloped with large residential buildings occupying 'superblocks' that ignored the historic street patterns.

Urban renewal had a commendable social purpose—providing poor people with housing that met contemporary standards—but ironically the outcomes were often socially disastrous. More often than not renewal reduced the supply of affordable housing, destroyed functional neighborhoods, and did nothing to improve racial imbalances. The existing urban economic structure was damaged. Intact historic urban districts with well-constructed, if dilapidated, buildings were destroyed. Nothing could have been less sustainable (Levy 2011: 208–16).

The social situation within the 'projects,' as the new public housing complexes ('council flats' in England) came to be called, was often far more dysfunctional than before urban renewal. The poster child for the failure of this form of American urban renewal was the demolition in the 1970s of the 20-year-old Pruitt-Igoe public housing project in St. Louis, Missouri (see text box). The Hulme Crescents in Manchester, England, which opened in 1971, shared many of the same problems and met the same fate. The immense complex was demolished in 1993 and replaced by far more successful brick terraces that look very much like the Victorian housing whose social conditions The Crescents had sought to improve (Hollis 2009: 227–52).

Pruitt-Igoe: Urban Renewal Gone Bad

The Pruitt-Igoe housing development comprised 33 apartment blocks of 11 storys each, containing a total of 2,870 units. It was designed by architect Minoru Yamasaki and completed in 1955. The buildings stood for less than two decades, their failure as housing leading to total

Figure 2.15 Demolition by implosion of the second block of Pruitt-Igoe, St. Louis, in April 1972. (United States Department of Housing and Urban Development, Office of Policy Development and Research)

demolition between 1972 and 1975. The design sowed the seeds of dysfunction, with small units, elevators that stopped only at every third floor, and large communal corridors on those floors. Things got worse when Missouri desegregated public housing and as a consequence the vacancy rates in Pruitt-Igoe soared. The project was vandalized, its condition quickly deteriorated, and it became infested with crime. All this as adjacent Carr Village, a low-rise development with a similar demographic makeup, remained fully occupied and trouble-free.

State and federal officials considered many solutions, including cutting the buildings down to four storys and removing some to reduce density. But in the end Pruitt-Igoe was entirely demolished, marking a disaster in architecture, sociology, and politics—the ultimate in unsustainable social development (Bristol 2004; Wikipedia n.d.-f).

The socially destructive characteristics of much urban renewal— single-use neighborhoods, demographic and architectural homogeneity, and large superblocks—were targets of the widely admired writings of Jane Jacobs, and her and others' arguments largely succeeded in ending that phase of North American planning, with its failure to achieve its social objectives (Jacobs 1961).

Partly under the spell of Jacobs's way of thinking, many neighborhoods have been rehabilitated rather than redeveloped, often taking old commercial or industrial buildings and renovating them at minimal cost, often to accommodate artists and cultural uses that don't require fancy space. Well-known examples are SoHo ('South of Houston') in New York City; DUMBO ('down under the Manhattan Bridge overpass') across the river in Brooklyn, New York; and the Covent Garden area of London. However, this tends to create a new cycle of gentrification: people in higher economic levels 'discover' the attractive character of these low-rent districts, and before long the buildings have been upgraded yet again, this time for upmarket businesses and expensive residences, displacing the very groups that 'discovered' the neighborhood in the first place. SoHo remains zoned an artists' neighborhood, but property owners ignore the zoning, trendy retail shops now occupy many ground floors, and lofts sell for as much as $8 million (Smechov 2011).

Indeed, conservation areas that have resisted the pressures of gentrification are few and far between. The consequences are the loss of traditional neighborhood populations and economies. It is challenging at best, impossible at worst, to legislate against rising land values in a free-market society. One solution has been the application of financial incentives to encourage local craft businesses to remain in the area (Rodwell 2007: 95–7).

The conservation of historic urban centres can be done in a way that does not destroy the urban fabric or cause gentrification. Some cities have found superb opportunities to integrate conservation with sustainable social equity. The rehabilitation of the medieval city centre of Bologna, in northern Italy, was an early, ambitious, and successful experiment. Undertaken by a Communist municipal government and directed by architect and city councillor Pier Luigi Cervellati, the plan for Bologna, adopted in 1960 and approved by the central government in 1965, was intended to reverse the post-war reconstruction effort, which had proposed clearing and rebuilding the areas affected by wartime bombing, while relocating residents to new suburban high-rise blocks.

The overarching policies included limiting population growth, treating public housing as a public service, decentralizing and democratizing decision-making by creating neighborhood councils, opposing the opportunity for speculative gains in the land and housing markets, and establishing the principle that conservation also means *cultural* conservation, in that the characteristics of the existing population and its culture had to be preserved. Inhabitants were guaranteed that they could remain in the same buildings after rehabilitation and that their rent would be based on income.

Figure 2.16 Arcaded houses, some old and some new, in the rehabilitated city centre of Bologna. (Marika Bortolami)

The new plan focused on improving the housing conditions of the working classes and low-income groups, while protecting the historic environment of the urban centre. The city expropriated (acquired by eminent domain) vacant land in the city centre and introduced a program of rehabilitating buildings that were seen as meriting retention, demolishing and rebuilding those that did not, and building new on vacant land. All construction, old and new, respected the established typological and stylistic characteristics of the neighborhood (including the prevalent arcades) while providing a variety of well-working interior designs that accommodated families, students, and the aged. Areas that had been open space in the historical urban structure were reserved for this traditional public use. Through traffic was excluded from the city centre (Bandarin 1979; Lottman 1976: 169–71, 201–12).

The Bologna experiment has been cited widely as a highly successful model for urban rehabilitation and social sustainability. It contributed significantly to improving the situation of the working class, by providing a large stock of newly built public housing close to the urban centre. However, the communist ideologies and economic assumptions that supported the project—such as considering public housing to be a public service—may make imitation difficult in non-leftist environments.

Environmental considerations

A second pillar of sustainability is the environmental dimension. Sometime around the middle of the twentieth century, it began to be recognized that past and current levels of extraction and use of non-renewable natural resources, as well as the introduction of toxins and pollutants, were inflicting serious harm on the natural environment. Several events, such as the publication of American biologist Rachel Carson's *Silent Spring* (1962) and the energy crisis of 1973, motivated an environmental movement that identified the environmental costs of unmanaged growth and revealed our dependence on fossil fuels. Since that time, scientists have warned of the potentially catastrophic outcomes of continuing current levels of greenhouse gas emissions and thereby worsening ongoing climate change. The global initiative to reduce and put limits on the use of resources is at the core of the quest for environmental sustainability.

Heritage and environmental conservation

A symbiotic relationship between degradation of the natural and built environments was acknowledged at the time. Indeed, heritage advocates recognized that they shared many objectives with advocates for environmental conservation. Leaders of several organizations in the two arenas found opportunities for cooperation. As examples, the president of the National Trust for Historic Preservation in the US wrote in 1981 that 'the same ethic [exists] behind protecting wildlife, guarding the beauty of fragile natural areas and saving gasoline, fuel oil and electricity' (Gunn 2001: 5). And a decade later the National

Figure 2.17 People cross a flooded Piazza San Marco, Venice, on a raised boardwalk. (Roberto Trombetta)

Audubon Society, an American organization devoted to conserving and restoring natural ecosystems, moved its offices into a rehabilitated old office building as a reflection of its conservation mandate, asserting that 'hundreds of thousands of buildings renovated or constructed along the same lines could make an indelible difference in the economy and the environment' (Gunn 2001: 5).

While these common goals are still recognized, the two causes have diverged, with environmental advocates succeeding in achieving much greater public recognition and support. Nevertheless some precious links endure and the shared interests remain vital. As examples, Australia combines environmental and heritage conservation in the same legislation; the methodology for heritage impact assessments was borrowed directly from that for environmental impact assessments; and the discussion of 'green' architecture, introduced just below, combines the two.

As an illustration of the relationship between environmental and cultural disasters, a massive flood in 1966 brought international attention to the problems of Venice. The historic city was sinking into the sea because of a host of environmental issues—particularly increasing tidal surges and the city's descending into the lagoon as a result of too much water having been drawn from the aquifer—as well as from a myriad of social and economic causes. Innumerable architectural and artistic treasures were damaged and countless more threatened. The intervention of UNESCO, the formation of charities such as Venice in Peril, the response of donors around the world, and the actions of local and national government have helped to stabilize Venice (Tung 2001: 318–42). Nevertheless floods continue to inundate the city. Venice was (and is) not sustainable.

The events brought to the fore the risks of unchecked development and rising sea levels on low-lying historic communities around the globe. They also began a dialogue on the need to plan ahead for climate change. 'Superstorm Sandy,' which struck New York City and the north-eastern US in December 2012, vividly demonstrated the vulnerability of New York and, by extension, all waterfront settlements. The recurring wildfires in Australia have reminded the world that the principal characteristic of climate change is global warming.

Defending existing historic places from the forces of nature is one thing; ensuring that historic places contribute to easing the environmental crisis is quite another. The latter may be achieved in two ways: by appreciating the inherent environmental advantages of rehabilitation over new construction, and thereby encouraging the reuse of old buildings; and by retrofitting old buildings to reduce energy consumption and greenhouse gas emissions.

Figure 2.18 A poster promoting the energy savings attributable to preservation (1980). (National Trust for Historic Preservation)

The recognition that conservation provides environmental benefits over new construction was stimulated by the oil crisis of 1973. A number of organizations, chief among them the National Trust for Historic Preservation, undertook studies that demonstrated this. The benefits of rehabilitation, rather than building new, include among others:

- New construction brings about high energy consumption (today we describe this as its 'carbon footprint') when compared to rehabilitation. The additional energy is spent on demolishing an existing old building, fabricating new building products (including extracting the raw materials), hauling the products to the construction site, and erecting the new building 'from scratch.'
- Conservation reduces solid waste and the demand on landfills. Demolishing an existing building creates a considerable amount of debris.[37]
- The 'embodied energy' in an existing building—i.e., the total energy consumed in the original fabrication of building products and construction—is considerable, and therefore demolishing an old building is wasteful of energy already spent. Stated otherwise, the investment of energy in the construction of historic buildings has already been made (Institute of Historic Building Conservation n.d.: 3; Jackson 2005: 47–52).[38]
- Historic masonry buildings have inherent passive energy-conserving characteristics. These include the high 'thermal capacity' of the exterior walls, which keep the interior relatively cool by day and warm by night; the high ceilings, which allow heat to rise; and the presence of natural cross-ventilation.
- Older buildings were often constructed with durable, long-lived materials and building systems with low maintenance requirements. Also, many existing building components are readily repairable. Lowering maintenance costs has the added benefit of reducing the energy required to maintain, repair, and restore materials. As American building scientist Peter Yost has said, 'If you double the life of a building, you halve the environmental impacts [of its construction]' (cited in Carroon 2010: 8).
- Older urban buildings are usually located in areas that already have well-developed infrastructure, including transit, which reduces the need for new infrastructure.
- Many older buildings relied on shade trees and landscape features to cool them in summer, and these features have grown to maturity.

At a more visceral and less technical level, Clem Labine, co-publisher of the *Old-House Journal*, pointed out in 1979 that 'preservationists oppose the conventional American idea of consuming ever more. … We are struggling to reverse the "use it up and move on" mentality. … We are taking individual buildings and whole neighborhoods that have been discarded and trying to make them live again. We are cleaning up after society's litterbugs' (Labine 1979: 18). Today, more than 30 years later, it is generally agreed that demolition is wasteful and waste is bad.

These arguments, while valid, received little attention beyond the heritage industry until early in the present century, when the imperative to achieve environmental sustainability and low carbon footprints finally encouraged a wider audience to pay attention.

'Green' buildings

The inherent energy-saving characteristics of many old buildings notwithstanding, concern is shown over their perceived high energy consumption when compared to new, 'green' buildings. Many old building systems may indeed have relatively low insulating qualities and are therefore comparatively inefficient to heat and cool. Much of this can be improved by an energy retrofit, which usually focuses on improving the insulation of exterior walls and roofs (or ceilings), upgrading the thermal qualities of windows and doors, and increasing air tightness.[39] Well-insulated building envelopes are, of course, a principal focus of green architecture.

The heritage values of historic places should be respected in the process. While retrofitting initiatives can be effective in terms of energy savings, they also pose the threat of compromising the very attributes that give old buildings their heritage value. Windows and interior finishes are particularly at risk in this respect, but every aspect is potentially vulnerable. Whether the change is as seemingly modest as adding a second pane or sash to single-glazed windows in an old

Figure 2.19 This 1890s brick cottage in Hawthorn, Victoria, recognized municipally for its heritage significance, was extensively retrofitted to achieve a high level of energy efficiency, while sensitively retaining and restoring the street-facing exterior and interior features.[40] (Peter Campbell)

house, or as extensive as the proposal (not carried out) to cover the heat-absorbent black exterior of the modernist, 108-story Sears (now Willis) Tower in Chicago with a coat of heat-reflecting silver paint, the impact on heritage character can be significant. The potential conflict between the objectives of energy conservation and heritage conservation—which, as we have seen, began as close allies—can create 'a tension between historic preservation and green architecture' (Kamin 2010).

The incorporation of energy-conserving design into new construction is regulated in many places with energy-efficiency statutes and codes. These same regulations are often applied to rehabilitation work, which often imposes severe constraints on conservation practice. As an example of this kind of conflict, the province of British Columbia, Canada, introduced the *Homeowner Protection Act*, which asserted that doors and windows in all houses, old and new, meet a certain level of thermal performance. The act placed severe limitations on the replacement options that were available. It also required that the building envelope be renewed as a condition of converting a multiple dwelling to strata title (condominium ownership). These regulations would force significant changes to the character-defining elements of historic buildings, to which windows in particular often make a conspicuous contribution. Fortunately, cooler heads prevailed. The provincial government's own Heritage Branch and the advocacy group Heritage BC succeeded in obtaining an amendment that exempted recognized historic buildings from these provisions of the Act (Heritage BC 2010a, 2010b: 3).

The lesson to be derived from this is the need to reach compromises in clashes between heritage and environmental values. Practitioners in both disciplines must learn to talk, negotiate, and reach common ground. Compromise is necessary on both sides.

English Heritage has also made efforts to insert common sense into the sometimes overly zealous debate on energy retrofitting. It has developed a series of 'sensible guidelines' in an accessible website 'designed to help you understand more about the potential impacts of climate change and ways to save energy if you own or manage an older home' (English Heritage 2008a).

This tension between conservation and green architecture was aggravated with the promotion of rating systems for green buildings. The best-known system, but only one of many, is the Green Building Council's (GBC) LEED® (Leadership in Energy and Environmental Design), also a professional accreditation program.[41] In 2010 more than 25 different rating systems were being used in North America and England. Most began as tools for new construction, and the transfer of their prescriptive measures to rehabilitation projects generally undervalued building reuse. The development of the LEED® Existing Buildings system has helped somewhat, as has the emergence of systems designed specifically for retrofitting old buildings, such as the Regreen program, produced by the American Society of Interior Designers Foundation and USGBC (Jackson 2010: 13–18).

However, a physical retrofit is not necessarily the most effective intervention that can be made to reduce energy consumption. Historic Scotland, which gives guidance to the owners of countless old buildings, has compiled extensive research into quantifying the actual U-values[42] of the materials and systems used in traditional stone building. Perhaps surprisingly, they found the measured thermal performance generally to be better than had been estimated with calculated values. With these data in hand, the organization has developed a pragmatic hierarchy for addressing energy-efficiency improvements:

1 Address occupant behaviors
2 Improve heating and lighting efficiencies
3 Make improvements to the building fabric.

The first two interventions have no impact on the appearance of the building (perhaps other than new lighting fixtures or radiators). With respect to changes to the fabric, Historic Scotland made recommendations for particular retrofitting techniques that minimize visual impacts, avoid potential damage from condensation, and improve thermal comfort. The organization 'has identified a range of ways by which traditional fabric can be upgraded to nearly modern thermal standards while retaining original fabric and without compromising the essential passive vapor dynamic that characterizes traditional construction' (Curtis 2012: 13, 19).[43]

Historic Scotland has produced a climate change action plan whose recommendations include improving energy efficiency in traditional buildings. The plan acknowledges that old buildings may not achieve the same level of efficiency as new ones, but it makes the case for their

Figure 2.20 An early nineteenth-century Georgian tenement in Tollcross, Edinburgh, located in a conservation area and within a World Heritage Site. The exterior wall systems of this building were measured for U-value by Heritage Scotland. (© Crown Copyright reproduced courtesy of Historic Scotland)

providing alternative sociocultural and economic benefits—i.e., for their overall sustainability:

> The repair, maintenance and adaptation of existing buildings currently accounts for approximately 46% of the total construction industry output in Scotland. Improving knowledge and skills in this sector will directly support and encourage economic activity. In some cases it may be unrealistic to expect older buildings to achieve the energy efficiency of a new building; however this must be balanced against the contribution made in other ways such as their cultural value, urban identity, life cycle and longevity, and importance and significance to communities.
>
> (Historic Scotland 2012: 14)[44]

The recognition by Historic Scotland that a physical retrofit is not the sole answer to improving energy efficiency is important. Moreover the energy-consumption issue must be seen in the larger context of the intrinsic environmental benefits of older buildings, already noted. American preservation economist Donovan Rypkema (2011: 473) has pointed out the need to appreciate the balance between the two:

> The total carbon footprint of a historic building, including both the embodied energy in the existing place and ongoing energy consumption—is usually far lower than that of a new building. To define the scale of the problem, it has been said that a 100-year-old building could use 25 percent more energy each year than a new building and still have less lifetime energy consumption than the new one that lasts only four or five decades.

Since older buildings generally have a longer life expectancy than new ones, the most accurate way to assess the relative value of rehabilitating or demolishing and replacing a historic building is to factor in both the capital costs and the energy (and other operating) costs. If, for example, a historic building is slightly less energy-efficient in its operating energy but reuses 70 percent of its embodied energy, the two numbers should be considered holistically. It can take more than 30 years before any cumulative energy savings are achieved when a building is demolished and replaced, yet the life expectancy of many new buildings is no more than this, and so there may be no net savings at all (Jackson 2005: 51).

Calculations should therefore estimate both capital and operating costs over the expected life of the building. This is done by means of **life-cycle costing** (or 'life-cycle assessment' or 'whole-life costing'). The method has traditionally been used to calculate the total capital and operating costs of acquiring, building/improving, and using a building over its full estimated lifespan. It is now also used regularly to assess and compare the costs of energy consumption (e.g., Iyer-Raniga and Wong 2012).

It is in this spirit of assessing both the environmental assets of reused buildings and energy consumption that American architect

Carl Elefante declares the widely cited mantra for which he has been credited: 'The greenest building is one that is already built.'

Green architecture has come to dominate the discussion of heritage sustainability somewhat disproportionately. It must be remembered that sustainability has three (or four) pillars and not only the environmental one. Green building rating systems tend to address improving building performance in the natural environment by means of design and technology, primarily by reducing the consumption of energy, water, and materials and the production of greenhouse gases. True sustainable design looks holistically at environmental, social, and economic aspects in order to achieve sustainable communities. As Canadian conservation architects Andrew Powter and Susan Ross write, 'Sustainable building requires balancing economic, social, cultural, and financial demands with the need to responsibly manage human interaction with the natural environment so its carrying capacity is not exceeded' (2005: 5).

American architect and planner Jeffrey Chusid (2010: 44) makes this same point clearly with respect to finding 'sustainable approaches to community and urban-scale development': 'Renewable energy and energy conservation, of course, have taken center stage today, even somewhat to the exclusion of a more holistic view of the environment.'

He suggests that the theme of sustainability in preservation education should address five overlapping themes:

- Environment and energy
- Stewardship and management
- Social equity and economics
- Planning and design
- Better preservation practice.[45]

Even within a discussion of conservation and the environment, environmental guidelines and regulations beyond energy efficiency affect historic places as well. As an example, many countries regulate development along river courses and the ocean foreshore in order to protect water quality and fisheries. Replacing an old building or an old wharf with new construction may lead to innumerable complications and constraints, whereas retaining an existing waterfront structure usually does not require environmental permitting. A similar situation may also exist in situations where agricultural land is protected from a change in use.

The environmental dimension of sustainability is likely to become increasingly important over the years as the threats posed by climate change are taken more seriously, and so heritage planners would be wise to make its consideration a high priority in their professional work.

Economic considerations

The third pillar of sustainability is the economy. The importance of considering economics in planning for conservation cannot be overstated. As American Robert E. Stipe writes,

Preservation always has been, presently is, and always will be primarily a matter of market economics . … Whatever one attempts to save or preserve must always fulfil the basic investment expectations of the owner or owners of the property or the area. If they do not, they will inevitably be lost.

(Stipe 2003: 32)

The economic argument for conservation became particularly compelling in the 1970s and 1980s, with the imperative to make every sector of the economy financially self-sufficient. This approach is often associated with the supply-side economic policies of Prime Minister Margaret Thatcher in the UK and President Ronald Reagan in the US, and it remains an objective with most Western economies today. Heritage advocates, who until then had relied largely on the cultural argument, were forced to defend conservation by demonstrating that it benefits the economy, and showing that funding conservation should be regarded as an investment rather than a subsidy.

What began in the 1970s as a somewhat defensive stance has now become accepted wisdom. Some of the more persuasive high-level economic arguments for preservation include:

- Heritage recognition and protection often increase property values.
- Repairing and upgrading ('rehabilitating') an old building is often less expensive than comparable new construction.
- The life expectancy of rehabilitated historic buildings may exceed that of new structures, particularly those built in the last 50 years, allowing capital costs to be amortized over a longer period and deferring future capital costs. (This is also an environmental argument for conservation.)
- Rehabilitation tends to be more labor-intensive and less material-intensive than new construction, and building materials are often brought in from distant places; therefore rehabilitation stimulates the local economy more than new construction. (This too is also an environmental argument, since the less fabrication and shipping of materials involved in a construction project, the less energy is consumed.)
- Downtown revitalization, of which conservation forms an important component, is key to regenerating the economies of cities and towns.
- Rehabilitated old buildings and neighborhoods often provide affordable commercial and residential accommodation that new ones cannot.
- Old buildings and neighborhoods often attract innovation-, knowledge-, and creativity-based employment, all recognized as yielding high economic paybacks.
- Heritage tourism has become a leading economic generator, as historic places gain in popularity and tourism grows as an industry.
- Conservation is often counter-cyclical; it is active when the economy is otherwise slow, in part because rehabilitation projects are usually modest in scale, stabilizing the local economy during hard times.

The first three items in the list identify **financial**, and the remainder **economic**, advantages of conservation. The terms 'financial' and 'economic' are often confused. 'Financial' considerations refer to the resources of a company or an individual, whereas 'economic' aspects pertain to the wealth of a community or a nation and include both market and non-market effects. An individual investor looks for a financial benefit; a society seeks economic benefits. Financial profits or losses are relatively easy to determine, by recording (or estimating) market-based revenues and expenditures and calculating the difference. Economic benefits are far more challenging to determine, as anyone who pays attention to the steady stream of economic reports and projections provided by bankers and politicians can testify.

Stating the economic arguments for heritage conservation is relatively easy; gaining popular acceptance of their validity is more challenging. Doing so requires analysis by technical specialists, followed by communicating the outcomes and educating the public. The economics of preservation has generated far more interest (and literature) in the US than elsewhere, in part because conventional wisdom in North America (and Australia) has long maintained that historic places lack economic value. This also reflects those societies' relatively low support for culture when compared to Europe.

The National Trust for Historic Preservation began to promote looking at heritage through an economic lens in the mid-1970s. A

Figure 2.21 Seattle's Pioneer Square Historic District, protected by ordinance in 1970, was featured at the National Trust conference of 1975. (Seattle Municipal Archives, Item No: 131565)

groundbreaking conference on the economic benefits of preserving old buildings (in Seattle, 1975) and the consequent proceedings referred to specific redevelopment projects in a number of American cities. The intention of the Seattle conference was to listen to the stories of public officials and private developers. Many made the case that the private and public sectors must work together to preserve historic places, putting government into the position more of enabler than player—although still regarding private capital as 'philanthropic' more than profit-driven. As Washington State official Bruce Chapman (1976: 13) wrote:

> Despite all the tools available to it, government cannot accomplish widespread urban conservation projects alone; indeed, its chief contribution is to provide a hospitable climate and setting. It is important to have government aid for urban conservation activities, but it is also vital that preservation have available private philanthropic capital and talent for generating ideas, hones criticism and information.

Bankers and other financial professionals were less charitable and more pragmatic, indicating the prospect of profit for lenders and developers, but noting that both must overcome established attitudes, learn new techniques, and recognize that money can be made from rehabilitation, albeit with less comfort and often at greater risk. Borrowers, they said, needed to become more engaged in the business side of the development process. Mortgage-provider Richard Crissman (1976: 129) stated:

> Lenders want every loan to have three ingredients: The project should have enough net earnings to insure monthly payments. The borrower should have enough equity to make loan payments worthwhile even if the property fails for a time to meet the projected earnings. And, both the borrower and tenants should have good enough credit to justify the lender's confidence. If a loan request meets these measures, much of the difficulty of finding a loan for an old building will disappear.

The National Trust and other organizations in the US and elsewhere subsequently undertook more detailed financial and anecdotal investigations of individual conservation and development projects, in order to test the high-level assertions of the economic advantages.[46]

Determining the economic value of historic places

Historic places and other heritage assets possess definable and, to an extent, quantifiable economic values. Being able to determine the value is essential to inform responsible decision-making for the management of historic places. Only with reliable data can governments and institutions make sound choices in allocating resources, and thereby develop budgets for heritage programs, determine which historic buildings, landscapes or areas merit protection and/or investment, and decide what cultural heritage assets to develop or interpret.

The value of cultural goods and services cannot be measured solely by traditional market-valuation processes, because a large part of their value is external to markets. Fortunately, economists have recently developed new theoretical frameworks and practical techniques to assess the economic value of non-market goods and services. These theories and techniques are being transferred to the cultural sphere.[47]

One can determine the value of an individual asset—i.e., focus on the micro level—or the value to the community of a related group of assets—i.e., look at the macro level. The discussion that follows begins with the micro level and then continues to the macro level.

Micro-analysis: Valorizing individual assets and situations

A particularly useful concept is that of **cultural capital**, which pertains to all kinds of cultural heritage assets, including historic places, fine art, and theatrical performances. Cultural capital is somewhat equivalent to the notions of human (or social) capital and natural capital, which infer the ideas of accumulated investment and value. Cultural capital differs from the others in that it comprises both **economic value** and **cultural value**.

The problem is that economic value and cultural value represent two separate value systems, and cultural values cannot be captured by conventional economic modeling. As a consequence, cultural value is often overlooked, yet economic value alone is insufficient to determine the value of an asset to the public. One example of this failure to capture full value is the report on historic places by the Australian Government Productivity Commission (2006), which ignored the positive cultural benefits that flow from historic places and other cultural assets. This oversight has vital, negative implications for national policy in the heritage sector (Australian Government Productivity Commission 2006: 47–51; Rappoport 2012).

The challenge, of course, is to reconcile the two value systems, or to ensure that assessments of value take both into account. Thus far no workable solution has been found.

Economic value can itself be considered as having two components. The first is **use value**, which accumulates by means of the direct consumption of heritage goods and the services that flow from those goods. These can be traded and priced in markets. They include the market value of a historic house, the entrance fees collected at a historic site, the wages of workers involved in a rehabilitation project, and the scarcity or rarity of the asset. The values are reflected in market processes and are relatively easy to determine.

Cultural capital also possesses a second kind of economic value, called **non-use value** (or non-market value, or intangible benefits). This is far more difficult—perhaps impossible—to quantify. Non-use value arises from the passive (i.e., 'non-') use of heritage goods and services that are external to markets ('externalities'). These are often called 'public goods' (as distinct from private cultural goods, which usually fall within the market). Economists call this incalculable situation 'market failure.' Non-use values include the enjoyment derived from visiting a historic place—or even from simply knowing that the place exists and has been conserved (called 'existence value'); from recognizing the possibility of consuming the services in the future (called 'option value'); and from the desire to retain the place for the enjoyment of future generations (called 'bequest value'). All are considered to be economic values because people are willing to spend money to use, acquire, or protect the assets in these ways.

Cultural value, in contrast, bears no direct relationship to economics or money. With respect to historic places, cultural value is assessed by identifying aesthetic, historical, scientific, and other qualities that are determinants of heritage value. These values are measured by methods developed by art historians and heritage planners, not by economists. The synthesis of the cultural values of a historic place is called its heritage significance.[48]

Economic value and cultural value are distinct yet related, since the measurement of cultural capital is the product of both. However there is often no correlation between the two—a historic place may have high cultural value and low economic value (e.g., a superb historic house in a neglected neighborhood may have low real estate value) or vice versa (e.g., a mediocre work by a famous artist—'Picasso on a bad day'—may sell for many millions of dollars at auction). The relationship between the two kinds of value may be causal, in that cultural value can be a significant determinant of economic value. For example, a purchaser looking for a fine home may offer a higher price for one with high heritage value than for a newer house with the same physical specifications located in the same neighborhood (Klamer and Zuidhof 1999; Throsby 2001, 2002).[49]

Australian cultural economist David Throsby discusses these issues and draws parallels between cultural capital and natural capital. In doing so, he acknowledges his field's indebtedness to environmental economics—an extension of the connection between cultural and natural heritage discussed previously. He notes particularly that both have been provided to us as an endowment with a duty of care, one from the creative activities of human kind, the other from the beneficence of nature. Throsby applies the concept of sustainable development—a mainstay in discussions of natural heritage—to cultural capital. He defines (2002: 109–10) a set of principles to be considered in evaluating investment decisions relating to cultural heritage. His suggested criteria, all of which are applicable to natural capital as well, are:

- Generation of both tangible and intangible benefits
  - This was addressed above as 'use value' and 'non-use value'
- Intergenerational equity
  - The acknowledgment of the interests of future generations in the cultural capital of today

- Intragenerational equity
  - Providing access to the benefits of cultural capital across social classes, income groups, and location (i.e., social equity)
- Maintenance of diversity
  - The importance of cultural diversity in maintaining cultural systems, parallel to the need for biodiversity in ecological systems
- Precautionary principle
  - Caution about making decisions that may lead to irreversible change
- Recognition of interdependence
  - The realization that no part of any system exists independently of other parts, which requires the examination of the interconnectedness between items of cultural capital and the benefits they bestow.

The discussion that follows offers a highly simplified overview of the principal current approaches to heritage economics. It adopts the technical terms used by economists. The interested reader is encouraged to explore the extensive literature, beginning with the sources cited here.

A useful measure of economic value is the determination of people's **willingness to pay** (WTP) for a cultural asset. Several techniques exist for doing this for non-use values, but all the methods have both strengths and weaknesses, and the discipline remains somewhat tentative and controversial.

WTP can be estimated with practices that are commonly used in environmental, social, and marketing decision-making. One technique considers the consumer's declared preferences (called the

Figure 2.22 The Surrey History Centre in England, whose economic value to local residents was determined by means of a contingent valuation study. (Media Wisdom. Permission of Surrey History Centre)

stated-preference method). Data are obtained by means of surveys, often using what is called the **contingent valuation method** (CV). As an example, a CV study was used to estimate the benefits of retaining the Surrey History Centre, a local archive in England, and to determine how much residents were willing to pay in additional taxes to keep the institution open (Mourato and Mazzanti 2002).[50]

An alternative to contingent valuation is **choice modeling** (CM), which presents survey respondents with various alternative descriptions and asks them to rank or rate the alternatives. This technique has been widely used in market research, but not in in the determination of the non-use values of cultural heritage (Mourato and Mazzanti 2002: 64–5).

A third stated-preference WTP alternative is a referendum, asking voters to approve a public expenditure that a CV or CM study has indicated the community believes is worthwhile. The outcome, of course, is subject to the vagaries of the political process (Klamer and Zuidhof 1999: 34).

Another technique for estimating value analyzes the consumer's past actions rather than her/his explicit preferences (the **revealed preference method**). Again, to use economists' jargon, the most common methods involve calculating the amount of travel expenses that a consumer is willing to pay to visit a historic place (the **travel-cost method**); or determining the extra (marginal) price of a heritage good—such as a historic house—over and above its standard market features, the added value perhaps coming from its distinguished architectural design or its location in a historic area (called the **hedonic-price method**).[51]

Because changes to cultural capital operate largely outside markets, conventional market revenues cannot be depended upon to provide adequate financing for heritage conservation. The solution often requires direct intervention by a government or an institution. The intervention might involve assuming ownership or operation of the place, regulating its protection and management, or offering financial and non-financial incentives to encourage conservation. This is addressed in Section 5.4; protection is also discussed in Section 2.1.

Determining how to estimate the value of cultural capital is much more than a theoretical exercise. It provides a valuable tool to help decision-makers shape public heritage policy and make informed choices on individual issues. The challenge is to provide public officials with sound assessments of both the cultural and the economic value of historic places, as well as an appropriate institutional environment within which to generate effective policy (Rizzo and Throsby 2006).[52]

The text continues with discussions of measuring economic benefits at a macro, rather than micro, scale; then concludes with a look at the outcomes of detailed economic analyses in selected subject areas.

Macro-analysis: Valorizing the benefits to society

Different kinds of analyses are commonly used for determining the broad (macro-) economic benefits of conservation to a community or a geographic entity. The two systems that are most in use for this are cost–benefit analysis and economic impact analysis.

Cost–benefit analysis is a popular tool used by governments and businesses for decision-making. At its simplest, it estimates the economic costs of all components of a proposed project (or policy), predicts the economic value of the benefits, and compares the two to see which is greater and by how much. If the benefits considerably outweigh the costs, then the analysis has produced strong justification for proceeding with the project (or implementing the policy) and indicates that it will be a sound investment. The same method can be used to calculate the costs and benefits of a completed project, and also to compare multiple options.[53]

The result is far more useful than a financial statement that estimates expenditures and revenues, because 'costs' and 'benefits' go well beyond the direct inputs and outputs of the project or policy. For example, in an analysis of the costs and benefits of a protection program for a heritage district, the costs might include an education program to help residents understand what is being proposed, the opportunity cost of forgoing conventional non-heritage development, and a marketing program to attract tourism. The benefits might include the effect on property values, the enjoyment that residents and visitors gain in visiting the area, and the benefits of additional tourism spending.

In order to reflect the values properly, the analysis should identify cultural costs and benefits as well as economic ones. This is entirely feasible, using the methods described above for measuring the value of cultural capital at the micro level. In practice, while methods for determining economic values are well established, much more work needs to be done with respect to quantifying the cultural values (Throsby 2002: 105).

The other common method of macro-analysis is the **economic impact study**. Economists have developed quite reliable methods of measuring the impacts of a proposed action on the larger community. Economists differentiate between **spending** and **impact**. 'Spending' represents the amount of money that is used to acquire goods or services, whereas 'impact' measures the total effect that is generated by spending and re-spending the money. For example, when a property owner pays a fee to a contractor for work done on rehabilitating a house, the transaction represents 'direct' spending (or a direct effect). When the contractor in turn spends part of that fee on wage labor, part on building materials, and part on personal groceries, that is an 'indirect' (or 'secondary') effect. And as that money continues to circulate through the economy, such as when the laborer purchases his/her own groceries, one speaks of an 'induced' (or 'tertiary') effect. The initial direct spending 'multiplies' (or creates 'ripples') as it passes through the

The Value of Heritage to Ballarat

Ballarat, the largest inland city in the state of Victoria, Australia, has an impressive array of Victorian commercial and residential architecture. On the edge of the city is Sovereign Hill, a popular tourism attraction that recreates a goldfields town of the 1850s–1860s.

Two recent studies have estimated the value of heritage to Ballarat. A national willingness-to-pay (WTP) survey estimates that the adult population of Australia would be willing to pay $1.6 billion per year for a modest improvement in heritage protection, which extrapolates to $6.7 million per annum in Ballarat (Allen Consulting Group 2005). A subsequent study focusing on Ballarat identifies the economic, social, and cultural benefits of heritage—three components of sustainability. A central part of the research was a community attitude survey. As an example of the results, some 72 percent of the residents of Ballarat (vs. 56 percent nationally) strongly agree or agree that looking after heritage is important in creating jobs and boosting the economy (Coterill 2007; Sinclair Knight Merz 2007).

The report includes a cost–benefit analysis that identified the costs to the city and community and to individuals, as well as the benefits. The analysis is verbal and not quantitative, with no attempt to estimate monetary value. Nevertheless it indicates a significant potential benefit to Ballarat from its heritage assets, and concludes that maximizing the benefit means protecting, presenting, and promoting history and heritage 'in an innovative and consistent manner'(Sinclair Knight Merz 2007: 3). The findings provide clear direction for policy development.

Figure 2.23 A view of downtown Ballarat and its Victorian architecture, featuring the Mining Exchange (1888). (Mattinbgn, Wikimedia)

economy. Economic impact analysis measures the aggregate effect of the initial direct spending on the economy, through the use of 'multipliers.' Applying the appropriate multipliers can determine how much of that impact is felt within the community, as opposed to how much leaves the region through 'leakage' (e.g., when a contractor purchases a wood window that is produced in a distant city, rather than one that is fabricated locally).

A number of different models are used for economic impact assessment, most of them variants of what economists call the **input–output (I–O) model**. Most are named with acronyms and are distinguished by their particular multipliers. Numerous models have been adopted in the tourism and heritage sectors, including by the National Parks Service in the US and by Parks Canada.[54]

Economic impact analysis focuses on the quantitative effects of spending. It is useful to determine how much money will accrue to the local, regional, or national economy as the outcome of a proposed policy or development. However, the analysis usually fails to capture the qualitative benefits of heritage development—the non-market benefits, discussed previously, which nevertheless can have very positive effects on the sociocultural and environmental dimensions of sustainability.

The remainder of this section looks at four selected types of economic analyses that have been undertaken with respect to cultural heritage goods and services and which frequently comprise a part of the discussion of economics and heritage. They are:

- Construction costs
- Property value
- Downtown revitalization
- Heritage tourism.

Construction costs

Much debate has occurred over the relative costs of new construction vs. rehabilitation. Some early, anecdotal evidence seemed to show rehabilitation costs to be considerably less than comparable new work. As an isolated example, in 1969–72 retail clothier C.J. Feldmann of Des Moines, Iowa, renovated two large, late nineteenth-century houses for use as fashion shops. He reported that he did the work for $22 per square foot (including acquisition), as contrasted to $40 for comparable new construction in the same area (Stella 1978: 41). Other ventures of the day, on the other hand, reported less favorable outcomes. The information was somewhat undependable, but nevertheless publication of these kinds of financial and real estate data, with summaries of the strengths and problems associated with each project, provided useful examples for future analysis.

More recent data, which use more rigorous techniques for measurement, remain somewhat inconclusive. The available information suggests that neither rehabilitation nor new construction is necessarily more expensive. The consensus is rather that the comparative costs depend on additional factors, such as the condition of the building and the experience of the owner and work crew. For work done in the US (Rypkema 2005: 89), it has been found that:

- When complete renovation is required, new construction is usually cheaper, although it is generally of lower quality and shorter life expectancy than the quality rehabilitation of a historic structure.
- When high-quality new construction is compared to high-quality rehabilitation, rehabilitation will generally be less expensive.
- When no demolition is required, major commercial rehabilitation will range from 12 percent less to 9 percent more than the cost of comparable new construction; when the construction costs of a new building include demolition, the cost savings from rehabilitation

usually ranges between 5 percent and 12 percent of total project costs.
- While sometimes more and sometimes less expensive, rehabilitation is usually a cost-competitive alternative.[55]

Because on balance it appears that the costs of rehabilitation vs. new construction are similar, and since the larger economic, sociocultural, and environmental (i.e., sustainability) benefits are greater with rehabilitation, governments have responded with programs of financial incentives (e.g., tax credits) and non-financial incentives (e.g., density transfers) that can tip the scales to make the bottom line of working with old buildings more attractive.

Property value

The market value of a property is generally a reflection of its size, location, age, and condition. Two houses in the same neighborhood that are similar in size, age, and condition will usually sell for about the same price. If the house has heritage significance as well, it can be said to possess cultural capital and cultural value, which may or may not affect the market (economic) value.

Figure 2.24 Port Hope, Ontario, where the property values of 76 percent of designated properties performed better than comparable non-designated properties. (Payton Chung)

A long-held misperception contends that recognizing or protecting a historic place for its cultural value reduces the market value. (Otherwise stated, the cultural value is considered to have a negative effect on economic value.) This view in turn has led some people to conclude that a recognized historic area loses economic value through formal recognition or protection. For this reason, property owners, particularly in North America and Australia, have typically opposed heritage protection vigorously. Another, more general, reason derives from the opinion that land-use regulation infringes on property rights, expressing the belief that 'a man's home is his castle.'[56] Indeed, the notion of heritage protection's decreasing property values is so widely held that it has been entrenched in some law, including statutes in the Canadian provinces of Alberta and British Columbia. Their heritage legislation provides for financial compensation for designated (protected) properties for 'the decrease in economic value' and 'reduction in the market value' respectively.[57]

Data have been collected on property values in order to test the validity of this opinion. As it turns out, detailed research contradicts the perception: If anything, heritage recognition and protection increase both assessed and market values. One comprehensive investigation of the relationship between heritage protection and economic value was carried out in the Canadian province of Ontario in the late 1990s, under the direction of planner Robert Shipley. His team looked at 2,700 properties in 24 communities, reducing this to 208 privately owned properties in 14 communities that met the criteria for analysis (Shipley 2000).

The study compared sale prices before and after heritage designation (protection) with the average property value trend within that community. Shipley (2000: 52) found that 59 percent of individually designated properties performed better than the average and 26 percent performed below average—stated otherwise, 74 percent of properties performed at average or better. The results for properties within designated heritage districts were less conclusive, because only two (of five) communities had sufficient data to be meaningful. In one, 100 percent were average or above; in the other, 50 percent were average or above. The analysis also indicated that designated properties tended to resist downturns in the ambient market, and that the rate of sales among designated properties equalled or exceeded the general rate of sales of properties within their communities. Shipley recognized that a number of external factors with no relationship to heritage also affect values. He also speculated that one factor is the likelihood that the owners of designated properties—who must agree to designation in Ontario—generally maintain their properties to a high standard, which in turn improves the market performance.

Other studies of this kind have produced similar results. In the US, analyses of the impact on property values of location within a National Register historic district had been undertaken in more than ten states by 2002. (Listing on the National Register of Historic Places provides recognition, but not protection.) The results, writes economist Donovan

Rypkema, are remarkably consistent: 'property values in local historic districts appreciate significantly faster than the market as a whole in the vast majority of cases and appreciate at rates equivalent to the market in the worst case' (Rypkema 2002: 6–7). Rypkema also reports on a study that examined the assessed values of mainly residential properties in 18 historic districts and 25 comparable non-historic districts in Florida. It showed that values appreciated more quickly in 15 of the 18 historic districts than in the comparable non-historic districts (Rypkema 2005: 39). Economist Dick Netzer analyzed studies of the relationship between designation and property values. He found that several showed protection to have a positive effect on property values, but overall the results were mixed, reflecting the variation in real estate markets across the US (Netzer 2006: 1246–7). In Australia the conclusions of similar investigations have been similarly inconclusive, revealing both positive and negative impacts on property value (e.g., Armitage 2005; Allom Lovell & Associates and Urban Consulting Group 1995).

Another issue is the determination of the market value of a non-typical, individual historic place. While residences and commercial blocks of heritage significance are sold in the market place frequently enough to determine comparable prices, data on other building-types is not so easy to assess.

Downtown revitalization

Heritage conservation has been a principal driver in the **revitalization** (or **regeneration**) of urban centres. It was seen above how heritage considerations affected urban renewal, particularly in the post-war reconstruction of European cities such as Bologna. Parallel efforts happened across Europe, although usually with less emphasis on social inclusion.

The prototype was the 'redecoration' of Magdalen Street in Norwich, England, 'an experiment never attempted before' that was conceived and coordinated by the Civic Trust between 1957 and 1959. Magdalen was 'dingy and down in the heels.' The Civic Trust and the City Council persuaded 80 businesses to undertake 'a gigantic spring-cleaning operation' that would reintroduce 'good manners' to the street. Property owners, who spent an average of £80 each, stripped away 'unnecessary clutter' from the buildings, undertaking repairs, repainting with coordinated colors, installing colorful new awnings, and redesigning signs. The City made a parallel initiative with the streetscape. The outcomes included increased civic pride and retail trade.[58]

The 'Norwich Plan,' as the scheme became known, was widely publicized and admired, and inspired many organizations to emulate the Civic Trust initiative. However the improvements soon lost their sheen and there was no plan for ongoing protection or maintenance. A new inner ring road was built and a flyover constructed over Magdalen Street, many buildings were demolished, and signs were changed.

Figure 2.25 Magdalen Street, Norwich, in 2011, 50 years after the improvements. (© Stuart McPherson)

What remain of the 1950s improvements look somewhat dated and the scheme has been all but forgotten.

One of many legacies of the Norwich Plan was the US National Trust for Historic Preservation's highly successful Main Street Project, initiated in 1977. Project managers trained by the National Trust were assigned to selected small- and medium-sized towns and cities as facilitators to train and empower local property owners and merchant groups to 'build on downtown's traditional assets' and make depressed main streets viable again, in the face of competition from suburban malls. Economic, preservation, and urban design consultants helped businesses with an ambitious four-part program:

- *Promotion*: marketing downtown as a destination.
- *Organization*: Strengthening local abilities to work together to manage the downtown effectively.
- *Design*: Enhancement of buildings, signs, and public areas.
- *Economic restructuring*: Recruiting new businesses and finding new uses for downtown buildings.

The key to the approach was 'its reliance on local businesses working with government to translate investment opportunities into visible reality,' while keeping 'the variety, diversity and idiosyncrasies that make each town and each building distinctive.' The multidisciplinary nature of the program has been acknowledged to be a huge achievement, with

Figure 2.26 A view of downtown Galesville, Wisconsin, one of three initial pilot projects undertaken by the National Trust's Main Street Project. The area was designated a National Register Historic District in 1984. (Royalbroil, Wikimedia Commons)

dozens of communities working and looking much better than before. In many cases, long-term heritage recognition or protection has been secured. The program continues as the National Main Street Network.[59]

The program differs from earlier urban revitalization projects in Europe (e.g., the renovation of the historic centre of Bologna in the 1960s, discussed previously) in that the American program included historic preservation—albeit with low-intervention changes—as a primary objective. Also, its social program extended only to the business community and had little impact on residents.

The American program has been widely emulated. One effective example was the Heritage Canada Foundation's Main Street program, launched around 1980 with similar objectives (Holdsworth 1985). Similarly oriented multidisciplinary programs have revitalized the centre of communities everywhere, combining heritage conservation, economics, management, and community organization. Revitalization and regeneration have become key objectives for most conservation organizations, as the primary focus of heritage conservation shifts from culture to economics to sustainability.[60] As an example, English Heritage has described itself as a regeneration agency since 1998, although with a caveat that economics alone will not resolve issues. As Chair Sir Jocelyn Stevens writes, 'Let us be clear, the urban problems of our cities, towns and villages will not alone be solved by flinging money at them' (English Heritage 1998, cited in Rodwell 2007: 104–5).

If one thinks holistically as well as historically, it becomes clear that a diversity of uses is necessary to provide a healthy city or town centre. Most important is having a combination of retail uses (usually at street level) and residences (usually above). The harmful effects of the single-use zoning and the demographic factors that drove people out of city cores and into the suburbs after World War II began to be recognized a half-century ago, most notably by the visionary Jane Jacobs. The trend has been reversed with the widespread current policies of encouraging mixed uses, which provide multiple benefits not only for downtown revitalization, but for planning generally (Davis 2012; Jacobs 1961; McKean 1976).

Heritage tourism

Tourism has become, according to many authorities, the world's leading industry. The World Tourism Organization (UNWTO), the United Nations agency that 'promotes tourism as a driver of economic growth, inclusive development and environmental sustainability,' estimates that in 2012 for the first time one billion tourists crossed international borders—more than double the number 20 years earlier—and that another 5 to 6 billion traveled within their own countries. This activity generated 9 percent of the world's gross domestic product, 6 percent of world trade, and 1 of every 12 jobs (World Tourism Organization n.d.).

Cultural tourism (or 'cultural heritage tourism') is a leading component of tourism. Estimates vary, but most agree that at least one-half of all domestic and international tourists are interested in including visits to cultural and/or heritage places and attractions—i.e., museums as well as historic places. This tourism sector has been described in many ways; one useful concise definition is that adopted by the Australian government:

> Cultural tourism embraces the full range of experiences visitors can undertake to learn what makes a destination distinctive—its lifestyle, its heritage, its arts, its people—and the business of providing and interpreting that culture to visitors.
>
> (Australian Government 1994; Australian Policy Online 1994)

Changing world demographics indicate that cultural tourism will become an ever-increasing segment within overall tourism as educational levels increase and the population ages.

Heritage tourism is the name sometimes applied to that part of cultural heritage tourism which involves visits to historic places—and sometimes also natural heritage places—whether the places have been developed expressly as attractions (e.g., interpreted historic sites and historic house museums) or are simply living historic communities that are appreciated for their heritage value. Visitor education was once the primary objective of heritage tourism sites. Today they must also entertain by enabling the visitor to 'experience the past.' Heritage is a part of the new experience economy, in which experience is a marketable commodity (Harrison 2013: 84–6).[61]

The affinities between heritage and tourism, including the economic benefits of heritage tourism, have long been recognized.[62] Because tourism usually helps the economy of the host community, local and regional governments often decide that historic places should be developed as tourism attractions. Another impetus to develop tourism is to provide an opportunity to interpret the resources and the stories of the place and its community to a wider audience.

The statistics are impressive. As an example, a study of the heritage-based tourism sector in the UK carried out in 2009 concluded that: 'Heritage is the mainstay of the UK tourism economy .... Four in 10 leisure visitors cite heritage as the primary motivation for their trip to the UK—more than any other single factor.' The total expend-iture by international and domestic visitors on heritage attractions in the UK was £7.3 billion (£12.4 billion including natural heritage), creating 113,000 jobs (195,000 with natural heritage), including multi-plier impacts, 270,000 (466,000) jobs (Oxford Economics 2009, cited in Heritage Lottery Fund 2010: 6–12).

The economic benefits notwithstanding, if tourism development is allowed to proceed without careful planning and management, it may subject the historic place to considerable risk and the host community to disruption.

Figure 2.27 The Great Wall of China World Heritage Site attracts hordes of tourists, who cause untold damage to the place they are visiting. (Kay Adams)

With respect to the former—risk to the site—these changes often pose threats to the cultural (and natural) significance of the place. Abuses from increased visitor numbers may cause the 'carrying capacity' of the site to be exceeded, resulting in overuse and unacceptable wear and tear to pathways, lawns, floors, and more. Overcrowding detracts from the quality of the experience and the increased difficulty of overseeing visitors leads to vandalism.

Many World Heritage Sites are particularly at risk in this regard. 'World Heritage' is used as a brand, which is marketed aggressively to attract visitors. The Great Wall of China World Heritage Site, for example, attracts a reported 24.2 million visitors a year, who collectively inject US$2.9 trillion into the Chinese economy (2009 numbers). Even though the Wall is 5,000 miles long, the crowds at accessible and repaired portions, such as north of Beijing, are overwhelming and detrimental to the wall and the experience (Global Heritage Fund 2010).

In the rush to attract more visitors and their money, local site managers may make inappropriate 'improvements' to the 'heritage product' that hurt the authenticity of the historic place. These may be as well intended as signs, handrails, and wheelchair ramps, or as poorly conceived as intrusive and inaccurate interpretation or a surfeit of souvenir vendors and other retail opportunities (Cameron 1993; Garrod 2002).

Even the intended benefits to the host community may go awry. The economic benefits can be considerable, but much of the revenue may accrue to international hotel and transit operators, with local residents getting low-paying jobs as tour guides and hotel/restaurant staff. In some places, such as the Historic Centre of Macao, a World Heritage Site, many foreign workers, rather than members of the local community, are engaged in the tourism industry. Increased traffic

Figure 2.28 At the Historic Centre of Macao World Heritage Site, new resorts and casinos that serve tourists' needs have had a negative impact on the visual integrity of the site. (Architectural Conservation Programmes, The University of Hong Kong)

congestion causes pollution, noise, and general inconvenience to the resident community, who may feel overwhelmed by the numbers of visitors. New resorts and casinos have had a negative impact on the visual integrity of the site, forcing UNESCO to demand that the government improve the management system and intended buffer zone 'to protect effectively the very important visual and functional linkages between the inscribed monuments and the wider urban land and seascape of Macao' (UNESCO World Heritage Committee 2009). Another risk at Macao is that economic growth may lead to development pressures that threaten the very same resources that caused the prosperity in the first place (Imon 2013: 258–9).

A solution lies in **visitor management**, a planned approach that maximizes benefits and minimizes negative impacts. These include 'supply-side' techniques that make waiting in queues more bearable, increase site capacity or flexibility, 'harden' the site by reducing its vulnerability, and 'timed' ticketing that stipulates the time of entry and/or length of stay. 'Demand-side' techniques include raising admission prices (which, however, reduce social equality), scaling down marketing, promoting non-peak times, and educating visitors about negative behavior (Garrod 2002: 130–5).

Visitor Management at Hearst Castle

Perched atop a hill at San Simeon, California, is Hearst Castle, a magnificent estate designed by architect Julia Morgan for newspaper magnate William Randolph Hearst. In order to protect the fragile building and grounds from visitor damage, the State of California, operator of 'Hearst San Simeon State Historical Monument,' has instituted a comprehensive visitor management program that controls the number of visitors and where they may go. Tickets, which are expensive, must be purchased in advance and are good only for a particular day and time. Four different tours distribute people around the site. Visitors park at the large visitor centre near the highway and board a bus to reach the 'castle' and its grounds. Museum visitation rules prohibit framed backpacks, skateboards, crayons, and other items that could cause damage. And each tour has two guides, one who leads and one who brings up the rear to prevent stragglers.

Figure 2.29 Hearst Castle. (Victoria Garagliano/© Hearst Castle®/CA State Parks)

In order to speak to these many issues, ICOMOS produced a Cultural Tourism Charter (ICOMOS 2000). The introduction affirms:

> A primary objective for managing heritage is to communicate its significance and need for its conservation to its host community and to visitors. ... Tourism should bring benefits to host communities and provide an important means and motivation for them to care for and maintain their heritage and cultural practices. ... [It] is necessary to achieve a sustainable tourism industry and enhance the protection of heritage resources for future generations.

Six principles, each accompanied by a number of detailed recommendations, cover these important matters.

The current literature invariably links successful heritage tourism to the concept of sustainability. A document issued jointly by the United Nations Environment Program and the World Tourism Organization stresses this and points to constructive directions:

> Making tourism more sustainable is not just about controlling and managing the negative impacts of the industry. Tourism is in a very special position to benefit local communities, economically and socially, and to raise awareness and support for conservation of the environment.

It defines sustainable tourism as: 'Tourism that takes full account of its current and future economic, social and environmental impacts, addressing the needs of visitors, the industry, the environment and host communities' (United Nations Environment Program and World Tourism Organization 2005: 2, 12, cited in Imon 2013: 261).

The need to consider the future as we plan for the present was stated uncompromisingly at a European conference on tourism and conservation back in the early 1970s by Duncan Sandys, long-time British cabinet minister and promoter of heritage conservation: 'Those who are responsible for organising and planning tourism must be careful to ensure that the tourists do not destroy what the tourists come to see' (Dower 1974).[63]

Indeed, as we continue to respect the definition of sustainability in the Brundtland Report of over two decades ago ('Sustainable development is development that meets the needs of the present without compromising the ability of future generations to meet their own needs,' WCED 1987: chapter 2, para. 1) we appreciate its applicability to tourism.

2.3 Ethics

Ethics is the branch of philosophy that is concerned with moral principles. A central topic in ancient Greece, ethics has been relegated to a minor role by the values of today's society. While ethical principles should be applied to all areas of professional and business activity, including heritage conservation, they are infrequently discussed. Cynical observers may say that ethics have been set aside in a world ever more devoted to earning money and to technological advances, but ethics have actually become all the more important as those priorities gain prominence.

This section addresses three aspects of ethics as they apply to heritage practice:

- Conservation ethics as moral practice: acting responsibly to humanity.
- Conservation ethics as best conservation practice: acting responsibly to the historic place.
- Conservation ethics as best professional practice: acting responsibly to clients and colleagues.

Although some documents treat the three together, they are addressed separately here.

Conservation ethics as moral practice

Since ethics concern moral principles, this category addresses decisions that practitioners should make with respect to what actions are in the best interest of the community and society in general. Big matters, indeed!

One discipline that pays particular attention to these kinds of questions is the biomedical sector. This inquiry began 2,500 years ago with the Hippocratic Oath and continues today. However, despite the active debate on ethical issues being carried out by many governments, medical associations, and others, there seems to be disappointingly little agreement.

In an article on the controversial subject of genetic selection, Canadian journalist Carolyn Abraham (2012) wrote:

> We now have the potential to banish the genes that kill us, that make us susceptible to cancer, heart disease, depression, addictions and obesity, and to select those that may make us healthier, stronger, more intelligent. The question is, should we?

This question is a haunting reminder of the ethical conundrum that tormented physicist Robert Oppenheimer and other developers of the A-bomb: 'Should we ...? Is it the right thing to do? Is it ethical?'[64]

American conservation engineer and educator Robert Silman (2007: 3) has asked a similar question with respect to historic preservation:

> I was asked by clients, owners, and contractors on an almost-daily basis as part of my work as a structural engineer, 'Can we do such-and-such a thing?' ... My epiphany came when I realized that ... we can do practically anything nowadays in constructing and preserving the built environment. It suddenly occurred to me that the proper question to ask now was, 'Ought we do such-and-such a thing?' The inquiry had shifted from the technical to the philosophical and the moral.

Figure 2.30 The Cape Hatteras lighthouse is about to be moved along a cleared path to the new site at the bottom right; the keeper's quarters have already been relocated there. (North Carolina Department of Transportation Photogrammetry Unit)

For Silman, the prime example is the Cape Hatteras lighthouse in North Carolina. Built in 1870, and the tallest brick lighthouse in the US, it was originally located 1,500 feet (457m) inland, but because of the effect of storm-driven tides and waves on sands of the barrier island, a century later it was only 300 feet (91m) from shore. The foundations were threatened by the continuing action of the sea. Thirty years of efforts to control erosion had failed, and so the National Park Service determined to move the structure. In 1999, with the help of considerable technological gymnastics and funding, the lighthouse and the principal keeper's quarters (and other structures) were moved to a spot 1,600 feet (488m) from the ocean, where they stand today. Silman questions whether this was the right decision, or whether an alternate solution should have been implemented: 'allowing the lighthouse to become a ruin as a symbol of our occasional inability to defeat the forces of nature and an acknowledgment of the littoral drift of coastal land forms' (4).[65]

As Silman states, the solutions lie in a consideration of philosophical and moral issues. He explains that Aristotle considered politics and philosophy to be the highest purposes of human endeavor—with contemplation the highest form of human activity in the pursuit of politics and philosophy—and technology (i.e., a physical action, or *techne*) to be only a means of achieving that end (*Physics*, Book 2, chapters 1–7, cited in Silman 2007: 7). He suggests that these values are reversed today, with technology considered to be the highest form of human endeavor. This leads to his conclusion that preservation technology is not neutral. Almost every professional decision we make has some moral or ethical significance based on predetermined meanings and values. In developing and using modern technology we must act responsibly by thinking about what we do before we do it. Only when we envision the outcome, Silman concludes, can we decide whether we ought to do it.

The importance of this discussion, of course, goes far beyond abstract philosophy. With respect to heritage planning, it asserts the need to consider a wide variety of possible project outcomes from many perspectives. As an example, Silman suggests the need to apply the values of the sustainability movement in all decision-making, a point of view that is wholeheartedly promoted in this text. The kinds of consequences to be considered may be as wide-ranging as how the project will impact on disadvantaged social groups or whether it will affect the livelihoods of workers in troubled industries.[66]

This broad thinking is appropriate for engineers, since they are obliged to protect 'public health, safety, and welfare.' We are accustomed, perhaps wrongly, to thinking that engineers are retained 'to focus on specific issues and are not normally required to provide a more holistic view,' and so it is encouraging to learn that some in the profession are indeed looking at wider issues (Kelley and Look 2005: 8–9; Salmon 2012).

Another fundamental ethical issue emerges from the conviction that we have a moral obligation to protect our cultural heritage for the benefit and enjoyment of future generations. English conservation advocate and designer William Morris, a founder of the influential Society for the Protection of Ancient Buildings (SPAB) said, more than a century ago, 'We are only trustees for those that come after us' (Morris 1889).

Morris's worthy principles, still current today, are expressed in his manifesto, in which he maintained that the physical fabric of old buildings comprise a record of the past, which must be protected at all costs. Morris reflected the thoughts of critic John Ruskin, who asserted: 'We have no right whatever to touch [ancient buildings]. They are not ours. They belong partly to those that built them, and partly to all the generations of mankind who are to follow us' (cited in Schmitter 1995: 1, 3). To Ruskin and Morris, to disrespect the integrity of old buildings was evil and a breach of moral (i.e., ethical) values.[67]

Australian cultural economist David Throsby says this in a rather different manner, with reference to the concept of sustainability:

> Ensuring that future generations are not denied the cultural underpinnings of their economic, social, and cultural life as a result of our short-sighted or selfish actions now is a matter of fairness for which the present generation must accept a moral responsibility.
>
> (Throsby 2002: 109)

Another ethical dimension is the association of heritage conservation with human rights. This is explicit in the *Declaration of ICOMOS Marking the 50th Anniversary of the Universal Declaration of Human Rights*, known as 'the Stockholm Declaration' (ICOMOS 1998).[68] It is short and provocative. It begins:

> ICOMOS affirms that the right to cultural heritage is an integral part of human rights considering the irreplaceable nature of the tangible and intangible legacy it constitutes, and that it is threatened to in a world which is in constant transformation. This right carries duties and responsibilities for individuals and communities as well as for institutions and states. To protect this right today is to preserve the rights of future generations.

The UNESCO *Intangible Cultural Heritage Convention* of 2003 is another international document that forges this link. Article 2 of the convention declares that 'consideration will be given solely to such intangible heritage as is compatible with existing international human rights instruments.'

Australian law educators Ben Boer and Graeme Wiffen (2006: 15, with reference to Evans 2000) succinctly draw out the associations among ethics, stewardship, human rights, and sustainability:

> The foundation for a coherent ethical basis for environmental law and heritage law may well lie at the interface between a stewardship-based ethic and a human rights-based ethic. The ethical considerations that decide which of these might predominate can perhaps be found in the application of the concept of sustainable development.

Conservation ethics as best conservation practice

Most authors and teachers who have addressed conservation ethics have taken a narrower route, declaring that ethical practice equates to acting responsibly towards the heritage resource and conserving 'correctly.' They consider the effects of actions on the historic place, but not necessarily on society at large.

As an example, English conservation architect and educator, Sir Bernard Feilden (1982: 6), proposed a 'standard of ethics [that] must be rigorously observed in conservation work.' Referring specifically to buildings, he lists his four ethical standards as:

- The condition of the building before any intervention and all methods and materials used during treatment must be fully documented.
- Historic evidence must not be destroyed, falsified or removed.
- Any intervention must be the minimum necessary.
- Any intervention may be governed by an unswerving respect for the aesthetic, historical and physical integrity of cultural property.

These are indeed worthy, overarching principles, whose intellectual source looks back to the manifesto of William Morris. Much as these thoughts dominated English—and Western—conservation theory for more than a century, they are not eternal. Approaches to heritage conservation have changed over time, including since Feilden wrote these words in 1982. As discussed in Section 1.1, many voices now maintain it is the stories and cultural processes associated with historic places that are of greater importance than the physical fabric. This does not in any way negate Feilden's 'unswerving respect for the ... physical integrity of cultural property,' but rather redefines 'respect' to embrace narrative as well as physical fabric.

In a volume commemorating Feilden, English architect John Warren (1996) elaborates on the respected mentor's principles. Warren proposes additional ethical conclusions (which we may think of as standards):

- In any intervention or reuse truthfulness is the paramount virtue.[69]
- Every intervention shall, where possible, be reversible.

And he adds further conclusions that he describes as 'aesthetic' as well as ethical:

- The impact of an intervention should be sympathetic or neutral.
- An intervention should move towards a full appreciation of the building.
- The scale and nature of the intervention must respect the significance of the building and its phases of construction.

A similar approach has been taken by ICOMOS, which has issued an Ethical Commitment Statement (ICOMOS 2002). Its objective 'is to provide a tool to improve and clarify ethical conservation practice and principles useful among [people and communities] who are active in conservation.'

The Ethical Commitment Statement begins:

> It is an ICOMOS member's responsibility to give professional advice and act in accordance with the charters and doctrine of ICOMOS, relevant international conventions, recommendations or UNESCO and other relevant Acts, codes and charters to which ICOMOS is legally committed.

The US National Park Service considers ethics in much the same manner. W. Brown Morton III, a co-author of the *Secretary of the Interior's Standards for Historic Preservation Projects* (1979; considered in Section 3.3), said a quarter of a century later that the *Standards* were 'ethics in action'; they were intended 'to provide a basis for evaluating the quality of preservation work carried out with federal assistance' (Morton 2003: 17). In other words he, like the authors of the ICOMOS statement, saw the compilation of best conservation practices as a guide to conservation ethics.

Another example may be cited of the close relationship between best practices and ethics, as well as sustainability. As a preamble for proposing principles of preservation engineering, American engineer and educator John Ochsendorf justifies the principle of minimal intervention, which is a standard of good practice: 'To maintain historical authenticity [also = good practice], to practice with integrity [= ethics], and to save scarce resources [= sustainability], a preservation engineer should avoid intervening in a historic structure if at all possible' (Ochsendorf 2013: 6).

The first principle of the ICOMOS Ethical Commitment Statement, as just noted, declares that a conservation professional has a responsibility to act in accordance with best practices. The second principle continues in a similar vein:

> The fundamental obligation of an ICOMOS member is to advocate the conservation of monuments, sites and places so that their cultural significance is retained as reliable evidence of the past, doing as much as is necessary to care for them and support their ongoing use and maintenance but adversely affecting them as little as possible. This requires a comprehensive, holistic, dynamic and often multidisciplinary approach.

These directives mean that the heritage specialist on a design team is obliged to act as the advocate for the heritage resource and to speak out if a proposed design solution would threaten the historic place or its cultural significance.[70]

As will be discussed in Chapter 3, the standards proposed by Feilden, Warren, Ochsendorf, and others, as well as the charters and doctrine of ICOMOS, collectively form the basis for best practices in heritage conservation. It is undeniably an ethical responsibility of heritage professionals to respect these practices. However, best practices change with time, often in tandem with larger cultural concepts. Indeed best practices, conservation principles, and conservation ethics may be considered to be more social and cultural constructs than immutable doctrine (Cane 2009).

The Heritage Professional as Advocate for the Historic Place

The author can illustrate the need to speak on behalf of the historic place with an experience from his professional work. Our firm acted as the initial heritage consultant for The Hudson, the rehabilitation of the former Hudson's Bay Co. department store in Victoria, BC, which was repurposed for mixed residential and commercial use. The glazed terra cotta cladding and the original windows were repaired and retained. The planning stage determined that the new residential use would generate a considerable amount of humidity from activities such as cooking and drying clothes, which created the risk of moisture condensing as it migrates through the walls and cools, which in turn would threaten the metal terra cotta fasteners and insulation. The mechanical engineers proposed that the air space between the interior and exterior walls be treated as a 'dynamic buffer zone' (DBZ), with a system of humidistats, fans, and vents that would draw away the excess moisture. The proposed system was quite new, although it had been used and proven to be effective in recent installations. The heritage consultant did not challenge the DBZ technology, but did note that its continued effectiveness over the long term was dependent on rigorous ongoing monitoring and maintenance—something that is sometimes difficult to achieve—because if the automated controls or devices failed to perform properly, damage to the fabric would occur. We argued instead for a passive buffering system that would use convection and/or natural wicking to remove the moisture.[71] In our minds, the debate between a passive and a dynamic system was an ethical one and not a technological one. It was our obligation to 'advocate the conservation' of the historic place and to support its 'ongoing use and maintenance' in a 'holistic' manner, following Article 2 of the ICOMOS Ethical Commitment Statement. Our reasoning fell on deaf ears, the DBZ was installed, and a new heritage consultant was appointed.

Figure 2.31 The Hudson, Victoria, after rehabilitation. (Rafe Grohne—www.ArchitecturalPhotographer.com)

Thinking Long Term: The Restoration of St. George's Church

St. George's Church National Historic Site in Halifax, Nova Scotia, was built in 1800 on a circular plan, leading to its nickname as 'the Round Church.' The chancel and vestibule were added a generation later. The church suffered a major fire in 1994. While common sense might have dictated rebuilding, the congregation was determined to restore the severely damaged building. Our conservation plan noted that the building had stood for nearly 200 years, and consequently proposed that the restoration design should incorporate only proven materials and systems that will withstand another 200 years of use. This was basically an ethical decision, based on retaining the values of the historic place in a morally proper manner, rather than a technical choice.

The 46-foot (14m) diameter dome was rebuilt in heavy timber with mortise-and-tenon joints pegged with oak 'tree nails,' the same technique as the destroyed original dome, although to a modified design.[72] Acorn Timber Frames was able to locate sufficient mature pine within Nova Scotia to produce 90 naturally curved timbers, although no sawmill in the province was large enough to cut the wood. This was a superb application of traditional building methods (intangible cultural heritage). The 44.2-ton dome and roof were fabricated beside the church and raised into place with a crane. The balcony was repaired by the timber framers as well. Repairs to the remainder of the nave and chancel used conventional dimensioned lumber. The vestibule, which had been virtually destroyed by the fire, was rebuilt with new engineered wood products that were not yet tested by time. It will be interesting to see whether the vestibule survives two centuries (Commonwealth Historic Resource Management Ltd. and Fowler Bauld & Mitchell Ltd. 1994; TimberhArt Woodworks n.d.).

Figures 2.32 and 2.33 Left: St. George's Anglican Church, Halifax, Nova Scotia, after restoration. (S.E. Stevenson) Right: The new heavy timber dome being constructed. (TimberhArt/Acorn Timber Frames)

Conservation ethics as best professional practice

A third application of ethics in heritage conservation relates to professional practice, namely adopting the proper 'ethical' behavior towards colleagues and clients. This relates to the interactions among people, rather than those between people and historic places.

Most professions are guided by codes of ethical practice. The Hippocratic Oath contains instructions for professional practice as well as for moral practice, including instructing that a physician should remain 'free of all intentional injustice, of all mischief and in particular of sexual relations with both female and male persons, be they free or slaves' and insisting on patient confidentiality (Edelstein 1943, cited in Wikipedia n.d.-c).

Many heritage organizations have produced codes of practice. One that can be taken to represent many is the Canadian Association of Heritage Professionals. The objectives of its 'Code of Professional Conduct and Ethics' (Canadian Association of Heritage Professionals n.d.) are:

- The establishment of guidelines for members to follow when conducting their professional affairs;
- The establishment of a set of standards to which members must comply;
- Ensuring that the interests of the public in general and the clients in particular will be properly served by members of the Association.

This is treated in five sections:

- Qualifications
- Professionalism
- Responsibility to colleagues, employers, and clients
- Proposals and fees
- Disciplinary procedures.

As an example of the tone, with respect to Professionalism: 'Members shall conduct themselves in such a manner as to uphold the reputation of the Association and of the heritage consulting profession.' Some of the particular points are that members shall:

- Not undertake any duty or task, or carry out any other instruction from a client or employer that involves making statements either in written or verbal form purporting to be their own, but which are contrary to their own bona fide professional opinion;
- Not sign or otherwise associate themselves with any letter, document, report or verbal statement that the member knows to contain false or misleading information;
- Regard as confidential all information gathered as part of an assignment and will not take personal, financial or other advantage of this information as defined in the agreement with the client nor allow others to take advantage of this information;
- Avoid or disclose any conflict of interest which might influence the performance of their work for an employer or client.

The consequence of a breach of this code is a disciplinary procedure which can result in a reprimand, suspension, or termination of membership.

This kind of guidance may seem to be simply a matter of common sense, but in actuality some professionals and organizations openly conduct themselves otherwise. Perhaps the biggest ethical risk is conflict of interest. This happens disturbingly frequently in the heritage business as well as in other sectors. American educator Richard Striner (2003: 2–3) begins an article on professional ethics with seven 'preservation horror stories,' which he labels as 'conflict-of-interest or official malfeasance.' Two are repeated here:

> An attorney serving on the board of a citywide non-profit preservation group takes a case in which he advocates (on behalf of his client) the demolition of a building listed in the National Register of Historic Places. Not one single member of the board of directors of the preservation group appears to see anything amiss in this action, even though the demolition is widely opposed by others in the preservation community. This attorney is subsequently appointed to a commission with major preservation and planning responsibilities. The attorney is appointed as a representative of the preservation movement.

> A historic building is sold by the federal government to a private owner and the sale includes deed restrictions that apply the Secretary of Interior's Standards to any proposed rehabilitation. A developer subsequently proposes a scheme that is grossly at odds with those standards. A hired expert retained by the developer argues that the historic building's integrity is sufficiently compromised that the Secretary of Interior's Standards do not apply. This hired expert turns out to be a full-time employee of the Advisory Council on Historic Preservation and one of the people responsible for creating the initial deed restrictions on the property.

Striner scorns these tales, which he insists are 'completely true,' and argues that if we witness conflicting situations such as these, we should take 'the courageous (and indeed the only honorable) courses of action: blowing the whistle or quitting.' Striner, like Robert Silman, cites Aristotle for justification: 'Those who are not angry at the things that they should be angry at are thought to be fools' (*Nicomachean Ethics*, Book 4, Chapter 5, cited in Striner 2003: 5).

A potential conflict-of-interest situation that may be less flagrant, but which is common in many jurisdictions—indeed, it is often done in accordance with legislation or regulation—occurs when a project proponent is obliged to undertake a heritage (or environmental) impact assessment (HIA or EIA) to identify any adverse effects that the proposed project might have on historic places (or on the natural environment). The inherent problem is that the proponent is usually designated as being the party responsible for retaining the consultant. The consultant has an interest (indeed, an obligation) in serving the client well—(s)he must respect the source of her/his fee—as well as in serving the discipline well. In short, the very appointment of the consultant by the proponent may constitute a conflict of interest.

In the US, for example, Section 106 of the *National Historic Preservation Act* requires Federal agencies to take into account the effects of their

undertakings on historic properties (the equivalent of an environmental or heritage impact assessment, an EIA or HIA), requiring the
proponent to ensure the objectivity of the report: 'Agencies shall insure
the professional integrity, including scientific integrity, of the discussions and analyses in environmental impact statements.'[73] American
consultant Thomas King points out the inherent conflict in this and
other situations in which the analysts/reviewers are also the propo-
nents/advocates. This same situation occurs in many other jurisdictions
as well, indeed whenever the proponent, rather than an independent
professional or reviewing agency, is named as being responsible for the
production of an HIA.

   This in turn leads to the issue of how a practitioner should act when
the interests of the client differ from those of the discipline. Professional
ethics dictate that the interests of the discipline must come first.
Remember that the ICOMOS Ethical Commitment Statement began:
'It is an ICOMOS member's responsibility to give professional advice
and act in accordance with the charters and doctrine of ICOMOS [and
other sources of best practices].' If the client insists that the practitioner
do otherwise, the only honorable choices are the ones posed by Striner:
'blowing the whistle or quitting.'

   It is only appropriate that the reader should now proceed to learn
about best practices.

3
Best Practices

As in any profession—be it medicine, law, or any other—good practice is guided by a body of international and national doctrine that is based on theory, experience, and ethics. If a physician doesn't follow best practices, the patient may die. If an accountant ignores principles of practice, (s)he or the client may end up in jail. If a structural engineer disregards proper practice, the building may collapse. Heritage conservation is much the same, even if the consequences of poor practice are less melodramatic. Without a consensus on overarching principles, there would be nothing to guide the conservation process. The variety of outcomes would be chaotic. Nobody would be able to distinguish good practice from bad, a modified old building from a new one, a skilled conservation architect or planner from an unskilled one.

The underlying principles that define the best in heritage conservation practices are discussed in this chapter. They are contained in a series of formal documents, which are introduced here individually. First are the international **charters** and **conventions**, which dictate the highest-level conservation principles**.** Secondary principles and national charters occupy a second tier. The principles are made clearer and more accessible by **standards**. And standards in turn form the basis for **guidelines**, which provide pragmatic, yet widely applicable, recommendations for hands-on action. This chapter looks at charters, conventions, secondary documents, standards, and guidelines, which collectively describe best conservation practices. It also introduces the alternative **conservation treatments** that are defined by the doctrine.

'Best practices' as defined by the conservation charters and conventions have been formulated and advocated over the years by Western heritage specialists, and have now gained near-universal acceptance by professionals. Best practices have evolved considerably over time, and certainly will continue to do so as society's values change. In this respect best practices and conservation doctrine may be considered to be cultural constructs, rather than absolute truths. Doctrine forms the theoretical basis of heritage planning and distinguishes between good and bad practice. Every conservation professional should become familiar with it.

3.1 Charters and Conventions

Universal codes of practice, called **charters** and **conventions**, have been issued under the authority of UNESCO, the United Nations agency responsible for culture; and by ICOMOS, the International Council on Monuments and Sites, a non-governmental organization that operates under the umbrella of UNESCO. Collectively the charters and conventions provide the core doctrine of the heritage conservation profession.

The ICOMOS charters define best conservation practices in a series of high-level statements that are intended to be respected internationally. UNESCO conventions are similar to treaties—they are top-level decrees issued with the intention that they should be adopted formally by individual nations. Their focus is on providing mechanisms for the protection of cultural heritage.

This section looks first at the charters and other ICOMOS doctrine, called **documents**, **principles**, and by other names. It then examines the UNESCO conventions, which assume the use of best practices in the identification and protection of cultural heritage.

ICOMOS charters

Charters and their sister documents are typically adopted at general assemblies of ICOMOS. Many are named with the city where the meeting occurred and/or with a longer title that explains the scope. Thus we have the *Venice Charter* (*International Charter for the Conservation and Restoration of Monuments and Sites*, 1964), the *Florence Charter* (*Charter on Historic Gardens*, 1982), and the *Nara Document on Authenticity*, 1994 (Nara is a city in Japan). Most were prepared by a committee assigned with the task and were approved by the general assembly of ICOMOS.

The authoritative *Venice Charter* (ICOMOS 1964) distinguishes in the preamble between international and national responsibilities:

> It is essential that the principles guiding the preservation and restoration of ancient buildings should be agreed and be laid down on an international basis, with each country being responsible for applying the plan within the framework of its own culture and traditions.

A number of nations have issued their own charters and guiding documents. Several are intended solely for use within their own jurisdiction, such as *Principles for the Conservation of Heritage Sites in China*, 2004 (known as the 'China Principles') and the *Charter for the Conservation of Unprotected Architectural Heritage and Sites in India*, also 2004. Other national documents have broader application. Supreme among them is *The Burra Charter: The Australia ICOMOS Charter for Places of Cultural Significance* (first published 1979; latest revision 2013). Although ratified only in Australia, the *Burra Charter* has become a primary authority on heritage doctrine and continues to guide practice throughout the English-speaking world. It has been cited several times in the preceding chapters and will be examined below.

The charters build on their predecessors. Each is seen as a step forward, either by addressing place-types or issues not before considered in depth, or else by advancing theory and method. Values and focuses have changed over the years, but the newer charters continue to respect the earlier ones. Thus we find the *Venice Charter* cited in the preambles of many subsequent ICOMOS documents. Nevertheless the progressive modifications to values have been significant, reflecting far larger changes in the societal context.

As was seen in Section 1.1 and is further shown in this section, the focus of conservation has evolved considerably over the past half-century. It has progressed from restoring materials (the *Venice Charter*, 1964), to conserving both immaterial and material heritage (the *Burra Charter*, especially 1999 version), to safeguarding intangible cultural heritage (UNESCO convention, 2003), to encouraging social benefits and sustainability (English Heritage's *Conservation Principles*, 2008b).

Many doctrinal documents have been reproduced frequently and are accessible on the Internet. The ICOMOS website conveniently provides the texts of about 30 charters and other documents adopted by ICOMOS internationally, as well as about a dozen charters adopted by ICOMOS national committees or by other international organizations.

Adherence to the charters is voluntary. They have no intrinsic legal status, but rather are drafted as international models, which individual nations are invited to follow. This is in contrast to UN treaties and UNESCO conventions, which become the obligations of nations that ratify them; and to semi-official UN documents such as declarations (e.g., the *UN Declaration of Human Rights*, 1948), which are intended to be followed when signed but are not enforceable (Denhez 1997: 20).

Conservation educators Ho-Yin Lee and Lynne DiStefano (n.d.) have captured the place of charters:

> While legislation can provide the controls through which consistency and quality in conservation can be maintained, charters ... set the moral ground upon which the good and the bad in conservation can be distinguished. In essence, legislation and charters [together] provide the solid basis for setting policies, standards and guidelines, and thereby help in achieving excellence in conservation.

This section provides an overview of the principal charters and other top-level documents, as well as to the key predecessors to the charters. These summaries, of course, are no substitute for reading the originals. Every heritage professional should be sufficiently familiar with the essential ideas put forth in the core charters to be able to recall where a particular issue is addressed, so that (s)he can consult the document as needed to find the full text and meaning.

Predecessors to the charters: restoration and anti-restoration

Conservation principles have been developed over the past two centuries, with the confluence of the Romantic appreciation of historic places and the development of modern science and technology.[1] The doctrine followed today is a product of the late nineteenth and early twentieth centuries. To a large extent, international consensus on conservation principles stemmed from powerful disagreements that occurred in Europe in the years after 1850, in the extended feud between proponents of 'restoration' and 'anti-restoration.'[2]

Restoration practice of the day is epitomized in the work of French architect Eugène Emmanuel Viollet-le-Duc and English architect Sir George Gilbert Scott. Many of their 'restored' buildings sought a 'unity of style.' This approach advocated that the entire building, regardless of the extent to which it may have been built piecemeal over time and the variety of historic periods represented by its physical fabric, should be transformed so as to recreate the architectural style of a single earlier period. According to Viollet-le-Duc, 'to restore a building is to re-establish it to a completed state which may never have existed at any particular time' (Viollet-le-Duc 1854–68: viii (1866),14, cited in Tschudi-Madsen 1976: 15). Viollet-le-Duc believed in the ability of talented architects to produce an excellent design that did credit to both the past and the present.

Viollet-le-Duc's approach is seen in his restoration of the Château de Pierrefonds, the summer home of Louis-Napoléon Bonaparte (later Napoléon III) north of Paris. Built in the years around 1400, it stood mostly in ruins in the nineteenth century. Viollet-le-Duc rebuilt it completely between the 1850s and 1880s, doing his best to recreate his idea of the style of the original castle. He replaced old stone with new stone and introduced new materials such as metal in the roof structure.

James Wyatt in the eighteenth century, Sir George Gilbert Scott in the nineteenth, and others in England adopted much the same approach. An extreme example is the west front of St. Albans Cathedral and

Figures 3.1 and 3.2 The Château de Pierrefonds, as it appeared in ruins c.1850 and as it looks today, following its 'restoration' by Eugène Emmanuel Viollet-le-Duc. (Chandler 1980, Wikimedia)

 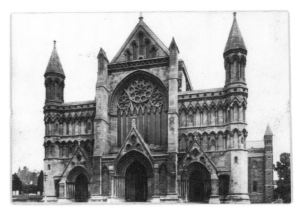

Figures 3.3 and 3.4 The west front of St. Albans Cathedral before and after its 'restoration' by G.G. Scott and Lord Grimthorpe. (Courtesy of The Society for the Protection of Ancient Buildings)

Abbey Church, which had been built in stages between the twelfth and fourteenth centuries. Scott produced the initial designs for the restoration, and after his death the work was continued by the less talented amateur, Sir Edmund Beckett (later Lord Grimthorpe). The west front was entirely rebuilt to an idea of what it might have looked like in the thirteenth century—including destroying the magnificent fifteenth-century window—but entirely unlike what had ever stood before. Little of the old building was retained. Here was the epitome of 'Unity of Style.'

This approach aroused strong reactions. The opposing 'anti-restoration' movement is epitomized in the writings of popular English art critic John Ruskin (1849: 184), who wrote: 'Restoration … means the most total destruction which a building can suffer: a destruction out of which no remnants can be gathered; a destruction accompanied with false description of the thing destroyed.'

Ruskin's vehemence was echoed by designer William Morris, who was largely responsible for the organization, in 1877, of the Society for the Protection of Ancient Buildings (SPAB). Morris wrote the SPAB 'manifesto,' in which he decried restoration as 'a strange and most fatal idea,' a 'forgery,' and 'the reckless stripping a building of some of its most interesting material features,' pleading 'to put Protection in the place of Restoration.'[3]

Morris and the SPAB contended that old material comprised a historic document, a record of the past, which must not be destroyed, and that the architecture of all previous periods is of value and none should be preferred over another—a 'principle of equivalence' that was opposed to the restorers' 'principle of preference' or 'unity of style.' The treatment of historic buildings that they proposed—they called it 'protection,' we would describe it as maintenance and repair—came to be called 'anti-restoration.' Today the approach is called 'preservation.'

Morris, SPAB, and their followers won the battle, in part because a majority of architects and other interested people across Europe considered anti-restoration to be the more correct approach, and in part because the SPAB waged a stellar propaganda campaign. Their theories were read by an influential group of academic architects, particularly in Italy. Camillo Boito, a professor at the Academy of Fine Arts in Milan, began in the 1860s and 1870s as an admirer of Viollet-le-Duc's work at Pierrefonds, but over time he reconciled Viollet-le-Duc's imitation of the original architecture with Morris and the SPAB's respect for all stages of work, writing in 1883 that alterations and additions should be 'scrupulously and religiously respected as documents' so as to avoid giving rise to 'erroneous assumptions' (Boito 1883, discussed in Jokilehto 1999: 200–3).

Admiration for the SPAB approach was taken further by Gustavo Giovannoni, a devotee of Boito who became director of the school of architecture in Rome in 1927. Giovannoni called for a critical, scientific approach ('restauro scientifico') towards historic buildings and urban areas, considering them as documents and advocating the practice of 'philological restoration.' Dismissing Viollet-le-Duc's theory as 'anti-scientific' and causing falsifications, he recommended preserving the authenticity of the structure over its whole 'artistic life,' and not only the first phase (Jokilehto 1999: 219–22; Rodwell 2007: 16).[4] Giovannoni is also credited with having introduced the term 'urban heritage'; he was a planner who appreciated the value of modest, vernacular architecture, and not only recognized monuments, in urban centres (Rodwell 2007: 33–6).

The ideas of the Italian architectural theorists became the core of the twentieth-century conservation charters.

The Athens Charter

The Athens Charter for the Restoration of Historic Monuments (First International Congress of Architects and Technicians of Historic Monuments 1931) was the first international conservation charter, predating the formation of either ICOMOS or the United Nations, making reference instead to the spirit of the Covenant of the League of Nations, which had been organized in 1919 and which created great optimism for international cooperation. The charter was adopted at the First International Congress of Architects and Technicians of Historic Monuments, a predecessor of today's ICOMOS general assemblies.[5] The delegates strove to state in an international framework what had been national—and also to an extent nationalistic—doctrine. Gustavo Giovannoni, now the principal conservation architect of Italy's Superior Council for Antiquities and Fine Arts, attended the congress and his was an influential voice.[6]

The *Athens Charter* proposes seven resolutions:

1 International organizations for Restoration on operational and advisory levels are to be established.
2 Proposed Restoration projects are to be subjected to knowledgeable criticism to prevent mistakes which will cause loss of character and historical values to the structures.

3 Problems of preservation of historic sites are to be solved by legislation at national level for all countries.
4 Excavated sites which are not subject to immediate restoration should be reburied for protection.
5 Modern techniques and materials may be used in restoration work.
6 Historical sites are to be given strict custodial protection.
7 Attention should be given to the protection of areas surrounding historic sites.[7]

The remainder of the *Athens Charter* contains 'general conclusions' that provide informal commentary on the issues. It ends by expressing the 'wish' that all countries develop inventories and document their historic places.

The creators of the *Athens Charter* were evidently strongly influenced by the anti-restoration approach of the SPAB. This is expressed clearly in Article 2, with its insistence that practitioners of restoration accept criticism in order 'to prevent mistakes which will cause loss of character and historical values'—a clear reference to restoration of the day. The voice of the SPAB can be heard elsewhere in the *Charter* as well, as in the general principles on doctrine, which note:

> there predominates in the different countries ... a general tendency to abandon restorations in toto and to avoid the attendant dangers by initiating a system of regular and permanent maintenance calculated to ensure the preservation of the buildings.

In other words, it is better to maintain and preserve the historic fabric than to attempt to restore it. The *Athens Charter* was influenced by the values of its time, which welcomed science and technology (see Article 5) and embraced a positivist attitude that accepted a single truth (Wells 2007: 6–9).

The larger context, and a likely reason for meeting in Greece at that time, was the recognition of the losses to the built heritage suffered in World War I, combined with a widespread enthusiasm for archaeology and the remains of antiquity—which included archaeological work at the Athenian Acropolis and Agora. The fervor was encouraged by the discovery in 1922 of the Egyptian tomb of Tutankhamun ('King Tut') and the realization that not all archaeologists were paying proper respect to the heritage values of the ancient sites. The restoration of historic buildings had also become a preoccupation of the time, the most publicized initiative being the reconstruction of Colonial Williamsburg in the US. Another contributing factor may have been the penchant to convene meetings of leading experts as a response to growing attempts at systematic nationalism (Glendinning 2013: 199–200). The most famous gathering of the time was the Fifth Solvay International Conference on Physics held in 1927, in Brussels. The event brought together such luminaries as Albert Einstein, Max Planck, Marie Skłodowska-Curie, and Niels Bohr.

This was a formidable start! All the resolutions in the *Athens Charter* are repeated—with some variations—in subsequent charters. Many remain respected today. The first three address the need for professional oversight and national legislation, while the rest address protection of the historic place and its larger physical context, as well as the admissibility of contemporary techniques and materials in conservation work.

The Venice Charter

The principal document that defines the universally accepted doctrine of heritage conservation is the *Venice Charter* (ICOMOS 1964), formally titled the *International Charter for the Conservation and Restoration of Monuments and Sites*.[8] Some 600 participants from 61 countries met in Venice for the Second International Congress of Architects and Technicians of Historic Monuments. Their central task was to approve the charter, which was prepared by a committee of 23 people and was explicitly intended to build on the *Athens Charter* by defining basic principles. Buoyed by their success, the professionals founded ICOMOS— and adopted the charter—a year later, in 1965, at a meeting in Poland.[9]

The preamble states the purpose of the charter, namely that 'the principles guiding the preservation and restoration of ancient buildings should be agreed and be laid down on an international basis.' 'Conservation' and 'restoration' make reference to those century-old foes, 'anti-restoration' and 'restoration,' which we now call 'preservation' and 'restoration.'

The *Venice Charter* addresses conservation, restoration, historic sites, excavations, and publication in 16 'articles.' Among its key innovations were the extension of a 'historic monument' to include its urban or rural setting (Article 1); and the definition of 'restoration' as a specialized activity aimed at preserving and revealing the past values of a monument (in contrast to Viollet-le-Duc's approach). Other principles, here abridged, include:

- 'The concept of an historic monument ... applies not only to great works of art but also to more modest works of the past, which have acquired cultural significance with the passing of time.' (Article 1)
- Validation of the use of modern science and technology. (Articles 2 and 10)
- 'The moving of all or part of a monument cannot be allowed' except in extraordinary circumstances. (Article 7)
- Insisting that restoration is 'based on respect for original material and authentic documents [and] must stop at the point where conjecture begins'; and that any new work 'must be distinct from [the old] and must bear a contemporary stamp.' (Article 9)
- 'The valid contributions of all periods to the building of a monument must be respected.' (Article 11)
- 'The decision as to what may be destroyed cannot rest solely on the individual in charge of the work.' (Article 11)
- 'Replacements of missing parts must integrate harmoniously with the whole, but at the same time must be distinguishable from the original.' (Article 12)

- In excavations, 'all reconstruction work should ... be ruled out *a priori.*' (Article 15)
- 'In all works ... there should always be precise documentation in the form of analytical and critical reports, illustrated with drawings and photographs.' (Article 16)

These principles form the foundation on which all subsequent charters were crafted. They have become the basis of good conservation practice today.

The timing of the *Venice Charter* reflects the period of intense reconstruction following the immense destruction from World War II and follows the need expressed by the conservation community to respect damaged historic buildings. Indeed, this provided motivation for a charter. The Italian art historian Cesare Brandi, first director of the Italian Institute of Restoration in Rome, emphasized that the restoration of the work of art is a critical process that requires an appropriate methodology. Brandi's *Theory of Restoration* (1963) influenced considerably the principles of the *Venice Charter* (Jokilehto 2009: 75–7).

The 1960s also saw the growing status of heritage conservation internationally and its acceptance as a discipline that merits official notice. That decade spawned the adoption of important heritage organizations and legislation, such as the launch of ICCROM as an intergovernmental study institute in Rome in 1962 and the enactment of the US *National Historic Preservation Act* of 1966. The *Venice Charter* in turn may have been a catalyst in the proliferation in the 1970s of heritage edicts (e.g., the UNESCO *World Heritage Convention*, the *European Charter of the Architectural Heritage*, heritage statutes in all provinces of Canada, Hong Kong's *Antiquities and Monuments Ordinance*). The 1960s and 1970s also saw universities in Europe and North America begin to teach architectural conservation, and the charter in turn provided them with valuable curriculum material. As with most heritage doctrine, a close relationship existed between its publication and the broader context.

The Florence Charter

The Florence Charter for Historic Gardens (ICOMOS 1982) defines a historic garden as 'an architectural and horticultural composition of interest to the public from the historical or artistic point of view.' The charter states that the unique feature of a landscape is its being a 'living monument,'

> [whose] constituents are primarily vegetal and therefore living, which means that they are perishable and renewable. Thus its appearance reflects the perpetual balance between the cycle of the seasons, the growth and decay of nature and the desire of the artist and craftsman to keep it permanently unchanged. (Article 2)

The text addresses 'Maintenance and Conservation,' 'Restoration and Reconstruction' (following the definitions in the *Venice Charter*), 'Use,' and 'Legal and Administrative Protection.' The primary principles with respect to the first three categories are:

- 'Continuous maintenance of historic gardens is of paramount importance. Since the principal material is vegetal, the preservation of the garden in an unchanged condition requires both prompt replacements when required and a long-term programme of periodic renewal (clear felling and replanting with mature specimens).' (Article 11)
- 'Restoration work must respect the successive stages of evolution of the garden concerned. In principle, no one period should be given precedence over any other, except in exceptional cases where the degree of damage or destruction affecting certain parts of a garden may be such that it is decided to reconstruct it on the basis of the traces that survive or of unimpeachable documentary evidence.' (Article 16)
- 'While any historic garden is designed to be seen and walked about in, access to it must be restricted to the extent demanded by its size and vulnerability, so that its physical fabric and cultural message may be preserved.' (Article 18)

Other articles provide more detailed standards with respect to items such as selecting species, architectural and sculptural features, surroundings, and achieving peace and quiet.

The *Florence Charter* was written before the widespread appreciation of 'cultural landscapes,' and as such addresses only what today we call 'designed landscapes.' It emphasizes physical fabric above the associational aspects of cultural significance. These lacunae reveal it to be a document of the generation that was passing. It is valid as far as it goes, but its authors could not foresee the coming emphasis on the less material aspects of conservation.

The Washington Charter

The 1970s and 1980s brought about a considerable amount of interest in the conservation of historic areas, in part as a reaction to suburban sprawl and to the decline and redevelopment of city centres. This led to the adoption by ICOMOS of a *Charter for the Conservation of Historic Towns and Urban Areas* (The *Washington Charter*) (ICOMOS 1987).

The first three articles ('Principles and Objectives') introduce some very important new ideas that expand the scope of conservation activity beyond that envisioned in the *Venice Charter*:

- The conservation of historic towns and urban areas 'should be an integral part of coherent policies of economic and social development and of urban and regional planning.' (Article 1)
- 'Qualities to be preserved include the historic character of the town or urban area and all those material and spiritual elements that express this character.' (Article 2)

- 'The participation and the involvement of the residents are essential for the success of the conservation programme and should be encouraged.' (Article 3)

We see here for the first time in an ICOMOS document the recognition of links between conservation and urban planning; the value of historic character and spiritual elements, and not only of physical fabric; and the need to include the public in conservation planning. Many of these ideas had, however, been expressed a dozen years earlier in the *European Charter of the Architectural Heritage*, discussed below.

Subsequent principles cited in the charter ('Methods and Instruments') also show an increased awareness of the broader societal and interdisciplinary context, as well as the importance of meeting contemporary urban needs and reaching out to the community:

- 'Conservation plans must address all relevant factors including archaeology, history, architecture, techniques, sociology and economics.' (Article 5)
- 'The improvement of housing should be one of the basic objectives of conservation.' (Article 9)
- 'The introduction of contemporary elements in harmony with the surroundings should not be discouraged since such features can contribute to the enrichment of an area.' (Article 10)
- 'Traffic inside a historic town or urban area must be controlled and parking areas must be planned so that they do not damage the historic fabric or its environment.' (Article 12)
- 'In order to encourage their participation and involvement, a general information programme should be set up for all residents, beginning with children of school age.' (Article 15)

All these recommendations continue to make eminent sense a generation later.

The Burra Charter

Reference has been made several times to the groundbreaking *Burra Charter: The Australia ICOMOS Charter for Places of Cultural Significance*, first issued in 1979, revised in 1981 and 1988, updated with significant changes in 1999 (Australia ICOMOS 1999), and revised again, with the addition of seven practice notes, in 2013 (Australia ICOMOS 2013b).[10] The *Burra Charter* established Australia's leading role in conservation theory and practice. The Charter is one of that nation's many heritage legacies, and is the only charter produced by a national committee of ICOMOS to have gained broad international acceptance.

The most important innovations are evident from the subtitle: the concepts of *place* and *cultural significance*. The 2013 revision begins: 'Place means a geographically defined area. It may include elements, objects, spaces and views. Place may have tangible and intangible dimensions' (Article 1.1).[11]

The term 'place' (what the present book calls 'historic place') replaces the *Venice Charter*'s 'monuments and sites' with a far more inclusive concept. As the integral explanatory notes to the *Burra Charter* explain:

> Place has a broad scope and includes natural and cultural features. Place can be large or small: for example, a memorial, a tree, an individual building or group of buildings, the location of an historical event, an urban area or town, a cultural landscape, a garden, an industrial plant, a shipwreck, a site with in situ remains, a stone arrangement, a road or travel route, a community meeting place, a site with spiritual or religious connections.

'Place' is complemented by the term 'cultural significance':

> Cultural significance means aesthetic, historic, scientific, social or spiritual value for past, present or future generations.

> Cultural significance is embodied in the place itself, its fabric, setting, use, associations, meanings, records, related places and related objects. (Article 1.2)

The *Venice Charter* (ICOMOS 1964: Preamble) focuses on 'principles guiding the preservation and restoration of ancient buildings'—on conserving physical, material fabric. It so took this for granted that its authors never actually felt the need to declare it. Article 2 asserts that: 'The conservation and restoration of monuments must have recourse to all the sciences and techniques which can contribute to the study and safeguarding the architectural heritage.'

The 1979 edition of the *Burra Charter* continues this point of view, declaring that: 'Conservation is based on a respect for the existing fabric, and should involve the least possible physical intervention, and should not falsify the evidence it provides' (Article 3).

The 1999 version of the *Burra Charter* (retained in the 2013 revision), in contrast, modifies Article 3 to include use, associations, and meanings as well as fabric. As a consequence, it is more permissive towards potential change, since the fabric becomes less precious: 'Conservation is based on a respect for the existing fabric, use, associations and meanings. It requires a cautious approach of changing as much as necessary but as little as possible.'

And the present version of the *Burra Charter* contains a statement that may be taken as the key to good conservation—a sentence so important that we emphasize it and urge the reader to commit it to memory:

> *The aim of conservation is to retain the cultural significance of a place.* (Article 2.2)

In the section on 'Conservation Principles' (Articles 2–13), the *Burra Charter* expands on these concepts. Especially relevant is the emphasis on values: 'Conservation of a place should identify and take into consideration all aspects of cultural and natural significance without unwarranted emphasis on any one value at the expense of others' (Article 5.1)[12] and: 'Places may have a range of values for different individuals or groups' (Article 1.2).

Quite a sea change occurred over the space of a generation. Use, association, and meanings—all nonmaterial, intangible characteristics—are now valued equally with physical fabric. This new concept was brought about to some extent by the migration of ways of thinking from Old World Europe to New World Australia. It was further inspired by the importance to Australia of Indigenous culture, whose values are very different from Western principles. This is made explicit in the new practice note, which asserts that 'the Burra Charter's definition of cultural significance is broad and encompasses places that are significant to Indigenous cultures' (Australia ICOMOS 2013a: 1). The *Burra Charter* further reflects the sensitivities of planners as well as architects, and its creators included proportionally more women than did the *Venice Charter*.

Although the *Burra Charter* addresses the matter only implicitly, it is self-evident that consultation with the community—indeed, a diversity of communities—is a necessary step in determining the associations, meanings, and values that are held by 'different individuals or groups.' We have seen that the *Washington Charter*—another New World document—requires 'the participation and the involvement of residents' (although in a more limited context). Here are all the ingredients of community engagement and its outcome, values-centred conservation, which are discussed in Sections 4.3 and 4.4.

The authors of the *Burra Charter* were primarily addressing the divergent and often conflicting values held by Australians of European and Indigenous origin. However the importance of respecting pluralist values is equally applicable to all cultures. A national document was 'catapulted to a leading role within international conservation,' writes Miles Glendinning. He suggests that the *Burra Charter* was

a Trojan horse, projecting the values of postmodern relativism into the heart of the authoritative, Western-dominated organisational structure of the Conservation Movement and undermining the conception of conservation as an Enlightenment narrative of progress.

(Glendinning 2013: 403)[13]

Other ICOMOS documents

ICOMOS has also produced 'documents' and other papers that address specific topics and issues. While not as broad-reaching as the charters, they have made important advances to conservation doctrine. In particular those from the 1990s onwards continue the trend towards emphasizing the immaterial aspects of heritage, further shifting the balance from the narrow materialism of the *Venice Charter*.

The Nara Document on Authenticity

ICOMOS met in the historic Japanese city of Nara shortly after Japan joined the World Heritage Convention in 1992. The outcome was the *Nara Document on Authenticity* (ICOMOS 1994). It reflects Japanese conservation authorities' concerns about global acceptance of their approach to conservation as 'authentic', which periodically dismantles and re-erects significant timber structures with new materials. This contrasts with the Western materials-based preoccupation with retaining and repairing 'original' materials. ICOMOS had long adopted the Eurocentric perspective, as seen in the *Venice Charter*. The *Nara Document* strives to explain authenticity and its relationship to cultural value from a different, multinational, and particularly Asian, point of view.[14]

The preamble establishes the context, emphasizing the importance of authenticity in the quest to temper overly zealous acts of demolition and 'conservation' in the name of nationalism:

> In a world that is increasingly subject to the forces of globalization and homogenization, and in a world in which the search for cultural identity is sometimes pursued through aggressive nationalism and the suppression of the cultures of minorities, the essential contribution made by the consideration of authenticity in conservation practice is to clarify and illuminate the collective memory of humanity. (Article 4)

In this spirit, the *Nara Document* recognizes the prevalence of cultural diversity and the heritage diversity that it produces:

> Cultural heritage diversity exists in time and space, and demands respect for other cultures and all aspects of their belief systems. In cases where cultural values appear to be in conflict, respect for cultural diversity demands acknowledgment of the legitimacy of the cultural values of all parties. (Article 6)

> All cultures and societies are rooted in the particular forms and means of tangible and intangible expression which constitute their heritage, and these should be respected. (Article 7)

The *Nara Document* places cultural diversity first, recognizing that it may involve intangible expression, whereas the *Venice Charter* tacitly accepted a universality of materialist values based on a shared Western European heritage. *Nara* implicitly acknowledges the *Burra Charter*'s emphasis on value, as well as its assertion that 'places may have a range of values for different individuals or groups,' implicitly referencing Asian values. The document takes its relativism a step further in addressing 'Values and Authenticity':

9. Conservation of cultural heritage in all its forms and historical periods is rooted in the values attributed to the heritage. Our ability to understand these values depends, in part, on the degree to which information sources about these values may be understood as credible or truthful. Knowledge and understanding of these sources of information … and their meaning, is a requisite basis for assessing all aspects of authenticity.

10. Authenticity … appears as the essential qualifying factor concerning values …

11. All judgements about values attributed to cultural properties as well as the credibility of related information sources may differ from culture to culture, and even within the same culture …

12. Therefore, it is of the highest importance and urgency that, within each culture, recognition be accorded to the specific nature of its heritage values and the credibility and truthfulness of related information sources.

The *Nara Document* provoked debate among heritage professionals. The national committees representing the Americas countered with the *Declaration of San Antonio* (ICOMOS National Committees of the Americas 1996), which they felt was more suited to their own region. It emphasized three points:

- 'The authenticity of our cultural heritage is directly related to our cultural identity.'
- 'An understanding of the history and significance of a site over time are crucial elements in the identification of its authenticity.'
- 'The material fabric of a cultural site can be a principal component of its authenticity.' (Articles 1–3, lead text)[15]

Jukka Jokilehto (1996: 71) defines authenticity in his discussion of the *Nara Document*: 'Authenticity in the conservation of cultural heritage can be defined as a measure of truthfulness of the internal unity of the creative process and the physical realization of the work, and the effects of its passage through historic time.'

Authenticity is a particularly vital topic in Asia. The Asia-Oceania regional committee of ICOMOS adopted the *Hoi An Protocols for Best Conservation in Asia* at the ICOMOS General Assembly in Xi'an, China, in 2005. It responds to the recognition that 'in Asia, conservation of heritage should and will always be a negotiated solution reconciling the differing values of the various stakeholders,' and the consequent need for region-specific protocols that give practical operational guide-lines for practitioners (Engelhardt and Rogers 2009: 2–5 and passim).[16]

The Stockholm Declaration

The *Declaration of ICOMOS marking the 50th anniversary of the Universal Declaration of Human Rights ('Stockholm Declaration')*[17] is short and provocative (ICOMOS 1998). It begins:

> ICOMOS affirms that the right to cultural heritage is an integral part of human rights considering the irreplaceable nature of the tangible and intangible legacy it constitutes, and that it is threatened to in a world which is in constant transformation. This right carries duties and responsibilities for individuals and communities as well as for institutions and states. To protect this right today is to preserve the rights of future generations.

Because the ICOMOS documents have no official status, the *Stockholm Declaration* is impossible to enforce, other than by moral suasion.

The *Stockholm Declaration* has largely passed unnoticed. Nevertheless, one detects its influence in the conservation policy issued by English Heritage—particularly its first policy on equality and diversity, which says that heritage activity should: 'Provide and encourage opportunities for all to access, understand and enjoy the historic environment' (English Heritage n.d.-a).

The Paris Declaration

One further document may be cited because of the new dimension it adds to the consideration of best practices. This is the *Paris Declaration on Heritage as a Driver of Development* (ICOMOS 2011). Its declared objective is 'to promote a development process that incorporates tangible and intangible cultural heritage as a vital aspect of sustainability, and gives a human face to development.' On the one hand it promotes heritage as a 'crucial aspect of the development process,' rather than as protection against development; on the other it seeks to 'curb the negative effects of globalization' (Preamble). This is done in four sections, considering heritage in the context of regional development; a return to the art of building; tourism and development; and heritage and economics. The Paris Declaration asserts the relevance of cultural heritage to current international priorities.

The 1990s and early 2000s brought about the issuance of several other charters and other documents. They include doctrine devoted to conventional archaeology (*Charter for the Protection and Management of Archaeological Heritage*, Lausanne, 1990) and underwater archaeology (*Charter on the Protection and Management of Underwater Cultural Heritage*, Sofia, 1996). Other charters address cultural tourism (Mexico, 1999), the built vernacular heritage (also Mexico, 1999), and cultural routes (Québec, 2008). Several national committees of ICOMOS, including New Zealand, Canada, and China, also adopted their own guiding documents. The texts of these and other documents are available on the ICOMOS website.

UNESCO conventions

UNESCO, the United Nations agency that acts as an umbrella to ICOMOS, also produces international guidance on heritage conservation by means of 'conventions.' When a member state of the United Nations (a 'state party') signs a convention, it undertakes to observe the conditions.

Several UNESCO conventions address cultural heritage.[18]

Convention for the Protection of Cultural Property in the Event of Armed Conflict

Known as 'The Hague Convention,' this document addresses the protection of historic monuments in the event of armed conflict (UNESCO 1954). In the process it provides the first high-level institutional definition of 'cultural property,' both movable and immovable, as: 'property of great importance to the cultural heritage of every people, such as monuments of architecture, art or history, whether religious or secular; archaeological sites; groups of buildings which, as a whole, are of historical or artistic interest.'

The convention addresses ways of identifying and safeguarding cultural property during conflicts.

Figure 3.5 The damage inflicted on historic buildings in World War II helped to inspire the *Hague Convention*. The photograph shows London during the blitz. (National Archives and Records Administration 541902)

Convention Concerning the Protection of the World Cultural and Natural Heritage

Ever since antiquity, when authorities identified the Seven Wonders of the World, society has craved the creation of lists of places that are 'best.' The 'World Heritage Convention' (UNESCO 1972) identifies and protects both cultural and natural property of 'outstanding universal

value.'[19] It set up the **World Heritage List**, which as of early 2014 contained 981 properties in 160 countries—759 of the places cultural, 193 natural, and 29 mixed. Properties are nominated by states parties and undergo a rigorous assessment process. The World Heritage Centre, established in 1992 and based in Paris, processes nominations and manages the program. Inscription on the World Heritage List obliges the host authority (usually a state government, called a 'state party') to protect the place and manage it in accordance with a formal management plan.[20]

The convention sets out the responsibilities of the states parties to the convention:

> Each State Party to this Convention recognizes that the duty of ensuring the identification, protection, conservation, presentation and transmission to future generations of the cultural and natural heritage ... situated on its territory, belongs primarily to that State. It will do all it can to this end, to the utmost of its own resources and, where appropriate, with any international assistance and cooperation, in particular, financial, artistic, scientific and technical, which it may be able to obtain. (Article 4)

States parties are obliged to establish appropriate conservation policy and set up the administrative structure to manage it. Ongoing monitoring by the World Heritage Office helps to ensure responsible management. The World Heritage Fund provides modest assistance to help protect the places.

The formal convention itself focuses on heritage management. Heritage practice is addressed in some detail in the wide-ranging *Operational Guidelines for the Implementation of the World Heritage Convention*, first issued in 1977 and updated most recently in 2013 (UNESCO World Heritage Centre 2013).[21] For example, they provide criteria for the assessment of outstanding universal value and explain terms such as 'integrity' and 'authenticity,' which are further defined in Section 4.5.

The *Operational Guidelines* are credited with defining the term **cultural landscape** (in 1994) and achieving widespread acceptance of the concept. The current explanation is:

> Cultural landscapes are cultural properties and represent the 'combined works of nature and of man [*sic*]' …. They are illustrative of the evolution of human society and settlement over time, under the influence of the physical constraints and/or opportunities presented by their natural environment and of successive social, economic and cultural forces, both external and internal. (para. 47)

Convention for the Safeguarding of Intangible Cultural Heritage

As a complement to the *World Heritage Convention*, which focuses on tangible heritage, UNESCO addressed the identification and safeguarding of intangible cultural heritage (UNESCO 2003). The convention was driven, in part, by the recognition

> that the processes of globalization and social transformation, alongside the conditions they create for renewed dialogue among communities, also give rise, as does the phenomenon of intolerance, to grave threats of deterioration, disappearance and destruction of the intangible cultural heritage, in particular owing to a lack of resources for safeguarding such heritage. (Preamble)

The convention is consistent with international agreements on human rights and meets requirements of mutual respect among communities and of sustainable development. It establishes two lists: the **Representative List of the Intangible Cultural Heritage of Humanity** and the **List of Intangible Cultural Heritage in Need of Urgent Safeguarding**. The purpose of the first list is 'to ensure better visibility of the intangible cultural heritage and awareness of its significance, and to encourage dialogue which respects cultural diversity' (Article 16), while taking care that this increased attention does not have a harmful effect. As of late 2013, it listed 282 'elements.' The second list, which contained 35 elements as of that date, is envisioned to be more action-oriented. It is intended to lead to appropriate safeguarding measures for those intangible cultural heritage expressions whose continuous re-creation and transmission is threatened.

Nominations to both lists are made by the states parties, but only

Figure 3.7 Okihiki Festival in Ise, Japan, May 2007. A cart carries materials that will be used to build the next shrine. (©Tawashi2006)

with the full participation and consent of the community or group concerned. The two lists are the responsibility of the Intergovernmental Committee for the Safeguarding of Intangible Cultural Heritage. Members of the Committee are elected by the states parties and meet annually to evaluate nominations. Support is provided by the UNESCO office.

Although the convention is now more than a decade old, detailed guidelines for its operation are still being developed. The convention addresses the need for states parties to develop appropriate policy and governance capacity, but it does not address the means for safeguarding. The current operational directives focus on the nomination process and provisions for raising awareness about intangible cultural heritage.

The creation of these two conventions only 30 years apart shows how quickly heritage theory has shifted focus from tangible to intangible cultural heritage. However, to cite scripture, 'there is nothing new under the sun.' Some cultures have long valued passing on building techniques more than the preservation of buildings. In Japan, several Shinto shrines at Naikū and Gekū in Ise, along with their furnishings, are dismantled every 20 years and replaced with faithful replicas by craftsmen trained in the traditional ways. This ritual of continuity follows the Shinto belief in the death and renewal of nature and the impermanence of physical things (Lowenthal 1985: 214; Jokilehto 2009: 80; Wikipedia n.d.-b). The *Nara Document on Authenticity* reinforces this approach as being 'authentic.'

Some heritage professionals have expressed concern that the two UNESCO conventions may create a dichotomy between 'two opposing and mutually exclusive worlds' of the tangible and intangible culture and heritage, including creating regional and geographical separations between 'the west *vs.* the rest.' In order to discuss these and related issues in depth, Canadian heritage educator Christina Cameron convened a 'Round Table' on the two conventions at the University of Montreal in 2007. The distinguished international participants challenged the perceived dichotomy. They acknowledged the need for 'better coordination and further dialogue between those involved in the implementation of the two conventions.' They agreed that the two take different approaches to listing, in that the World Heritage List comprises places of 'outstanding universal value,' whereas the lists of intangible cultural heritage address 'representative' heritage (Cameron and Boucher 2007: 162–93).[22]

If the *Venice Charter* represents the total concentration on built heritage and its setting, and the *Burra Charter* achieves a balance between physical fabric and intangible aspects such as use, associations, and meanings, it seems only a matter of time before ICOMOS will produce a charter on the conservation of intangible heritage. Indeed, the discussions at recent general assemblies have included considerations of intangible cultural heritage, and the term appears prominently in recent ICOMOS documents, such as the *Paris Declaration* (2011) and the 2013 revision of the *Burra Charter*, both cited above.

The Vienna Memorandum

UNESCO also issues heritage-themed documents other than conventions. One that alludes to changing perceptions of heritage is the *Vienna Memorandum on World Heritage and Contemporary Architecture— Managing the Historic Urban Landscape* (UNESCO 2005).[23] The *Vienna Memorandum* was produced in conjunction with the consideration of Vienna as a potential World Heritage Site. It formally introduced the term 'historic urban landscape,' which is less restrictive than 'historic area,' 'conservation area,' 'historic town,' or 'historic landscape.' The memorandum defines 'historic urban landscape' as being 'embedded with current and past social expressions and developments that are place-based,' from overall land uses and patterns to details of construction such as curbs and paving, and including contemporary architecture. The concept is intended to integrate the historic city into the overall dynamics of urban development, to 'break the walls' that separate conservation and development.

The context of the *Vienna Memorandum* is 'the current debate on the sustainable conservation of monuments and sites.' It states that

Figure 3.8 A view of the Historic Centre of Vienna World Heritage Site. (Emmanuel Dyan)

the 'central challenge ... is to respond to development dynamics. ... [f]acilitate socio-economic changes and growth ... while respecting the inherited and its landscape setting.' Management decisions require 'a culturally and historic sensitive approach, stakeholder consultations, and expert know-how.' It serves in part as an update to the ICOMOS *Florence Charter* (1982) and *Washington Charter* (1987), respecting the many new ideas introduced in the intervening generation.

UNESCO recommendations

UNESCO also issues recommendations for heritage management, which states parties are intended to follow if they sign them in their sovereign capacity. Some of the many recommendations that UNESCO has issued over the years advocate heritage policies that are intended to be executed in legislation. These include:

- All official plans must provide for heritage conservation.
- Every government should empower an entity to advise it on endangered heritage property.
- Heritage protection should be binding on government agencies.
- Governments should develop policy to find uses for historic places.
- Public agencies should orient their construction policies to renovating space in old buildings.
- Landscapes should be subject to protection.
- The areas around historic places should be subject to rules ensuring harmonization.
- Groups of modest buildings that are collectively of cultural value should be protected even if no individual one is noteworthy.
- There may be a *quid pro quo* for designation.
- Any policy for protection must be accompanied by a policy for revitalization.

- Owners of historic places should be encouraged by means of tax incentives.
- Governments should establish either special subsidies or a national conservation fund outside the normal budgetary process.
- Governments should make grants, subsidies, or loans available to municipalities, institutions, and owners to bring the use of historic places up to contemporary standards.
- A system should be established with public- and private-sector participation to provide rehabilitation loans with low interest and/or long repayment schedules.
- Rehabilitation projects should observe modern safety standards, but when building and fire codes interfere with conservation, equivalents should be applied.

These and other recommendations comprise a comprehensive heritage strategy. As will be seen throughout this book, many have been adopted in some jurisdictions. However, governments have accepted them only in a piecemeal fashion (Denhez 1997: 17–30).[24]

Regional and national documents

The European Charter

ICOMOS and UNESCO are not the only organizations to establish heritage principles. The Council of Europe, an intergovernmental organization based in Strasbourg, France, whose mission is to ensure respect for fundamental human values, has produced some important heritage conservation policy. The *European Charter of the Architectural Heritage*, adopted in 1975—European Architectural Year—established a set of basic principles (Council of Europe 1975). The first five (of ten) are:

1 The European architectural heritage consists not only of our most important monuments: it also includes the groups of lesser buildings in our old towns and characteristic villages in their natural or manmade settings.
2 The past as embodied in the architectural heritage provides the sort of environment indispensable to a balanced and complete life.
3 The architectural heritage is a capital of irreplaceable spiritual, cultural, social and economic value.
4 The structure of historic centres and sites is conducive to a harmonious social balance.
5 The architectural heritage has an important part to play in education.

The tone differs considerably from the ICOMOS charters of the time, particularly in the attention paid to historic towns and 'groups of lesser buildings' and in the inclusion of social and economic values, with a nod to the environment (as quality of life). These values comprise what we now call the pillars of sustainability, a dozen years before the present meaning of that word was adopted. Only a decade after the

Venice Charter, cultural heritage is declared to be relevant to the general population, extending far beyond the realm of great monuments and architectural technocrats. As the preamble states, 'the future of the architectural heritage depends largely upon its integration into the context of people's lives.'

The Council of Europe produced a number of other documents that guide heritage conservation. These include the *Granada Convention* (*Convention for the Protection of the Architectural Heritage of Europe*) (Council of Europe 1985), the *Valetta Convention* (*European Convention on the Protection of the Archaeological Heritage*) (Council of Europe 1992), and the *European Landscape Convention* (Council of Europe 2000). All three encouraged individual nations to establish policies and laws to protect and manage their historic places.

English Heritage's Conservation Principles

English Heritage is one of the national agencies that have responded to the Council of Europe's lead. After a lengthy period of policy review, it issued an important document, *Conservation Principles, Policies and Guidance for the Sustainable Management of the Historic Environment* (English Heritage 2008b), noting that legislation would follow in time.[25] The new approach to heritage conservation in England and throughout the United Kingdom is significant. The approach conserves historic places for the direct benefit of people and communities, rather than advocating conservation for cultural or aesthetic reasons (Rodwell 2007: 59). In this sense it outdoes even the progressive view of the *Burra Charter*, which values cultural significance over historic fabric.

The document begins with six conservation principles that provide a framework for sustainable management in general policy terms:

1 The historic environment is a shared resource.
2 Everyone should be able to participate in sustaining the historic environment.
3 Understanding the significance of places is vital.
4 Significant places should be managed to sustain their values.
5 Decisions about change must be reasonable, transparent and consistent.
6 Documenting and learning from decisions is essential.

These principles take a rather unique approach to 'best practices.' While the principles are, for the most part, the equivalent of, and traceable to, articles in the ICOMOS charters, the wording (and the explanatory text in the full paper) is quite distinct. The emphasis is on process, sustainability (including social equity), and humanist values, the last in language rather similar to *The European Charter*. This inspiring tone continues throughout the document. An example is a discussion of use:

> The best use for a significant place—its 'optimum viable use'—is one that is both capable of sustaining the place and avoids or minimises

harm to its values in its setting. It is not necessarily the most profitable use if that would entail greater harm than other viable uses. (Clause 87)[26]

The later section on 'conservation policies and guidance' is more directly related to conventional notions of best practices, but even here the methods of addressing interventions is referred to as 'policies' and not 'treatments,' and do not follow the terminology in the *Burra Charter* or other documents that have been considered.

Jukka Jokilehto (2009: 73), an authority on international heritage doctrine, has summarized the evolution of conservation theory over the past half-century:

> The extension of the notion of heritage has come to include the entire living environment with its cultural traditions and changing life styles. As a result, the concept of heritage conservation is thus becoming less static in reference to historical material, and rather more dynamic with reference to culturally sustainable management of heritage resources, taking into account their tangible and intangible dimensions.

3.2 Conservation Treatments

Heritage conservation has long focused on historic places and their material components. While new ideas about heritage may emphasize its nonmaterial aspects, and techniques are being developed for safeguarding and communicating intangible heritage, there remains the need to conserve tangible heritage. This section introduces alternative ways in which to carry out material conservation activity.

The *Venice Charter* differentiated between 'conservation' and 'restoration,' using the former as an umbrella term and the latter to denote revealing the past values of a monument—i.e., returning it to the appearance of an earlier stage of its development. Restoration is one of several kinds of approaches that can be taken to conserve a historic place. The different **conservation treatments (levels of intervention**, **conservation approaches**, or **conservation policies**) were well codified by the 1970s, if not earlier, although some disagreement as to terminology remains in different countries.[27]

Principal treatments

Five terms are in common use and these, as a minimum, must be well understood by the heritage practitioner. The first, 'conservation,' is an umbrella word that refers to all the optional treatments, whereas the other four are distinct. The discussion that follows generally adopts the definitions in Article 1 of the *Burra Charter*, with comments added for clarity and to correlate with usage in other countries. The US and Canada generally agree with Australia, whereas England uses some different terminology. Ideally heritage professionals would agree to a shared universal vocabulary, but given the realities of national and regional preferences, no consensus is likely.

The examples that follow focus on buildings, which demonstrate the treatments most clearly. All are applicable as well to landscapes, cultural landscapes, districts, and some other kinds of historic places. The question of *when* to apply a particular treatment is addressed in Section 5.3.

Conservation

Conservation means all the processes of looking after a place so as to retain its cultural significance (Australia ICOMOS 2013b: 1.4).

- Conservation is an all-inclusive term that refers to any treatment, and is not in itself a treatment. Hence the larger discipline, of which heritage planning is a part, is often called 'heritage conservation' or 'architectural conservation' (or 'historic preservation' in the US[28]).
- 'Conservation' may embrace change, as long as the cultural significance of the historic place is maintained.
- Some doctrines, such as the *China Principles*, retain the inclusive meaning of 'conservation,' but their definitions may be directed not at retaining cultural significance broadly, but rather at the older idea of maintaining physical fabric: 'Conservation refers to *all* measures carried out to preserve the physical remains of sites and their historic settings' (China ICOMOS 2002: Article 2).

Preservation

Preservation means maintaining a place in its existing state and retarding deterioration (Australia ICOMOS 2013b: 1.6).[29]

- Preservation retains a historic place, its form, and its materials 'as is.' Components that originated in different chronological periods are kept in their current appearance. This respects Article 11 of the *Venice Charter*, which declares that 'the valid contributions of all periods to the building of a monument must be respected.' Preservation is the antithesis of Restoration, which is discussed next.
- Preservation is similar to **maintenance** and **repair**. Whereas maintenance and repair are periodic, ongoing activities, preservation is usually a larger, one-time intervention. In financial terms, maintenance and repair are usually treated as operating expenditures and preservation as a capital expenditure.[30]
- The process and objective of preservation are much the same as those of 'anti-restoration' promoted by SPAB nearly a century and a half ago.
- English Heritage does not use the term 'preservation,' but rather **routine management and maintenance** (or **periodic renewal**, **repair**) (English Heritage 2008b: Clauses 111–21).
- Preservation may retain both intangible and tangible cultural heritage. One may preserve a tradition or a use as much as a structure or archaeological remains.

Figures 3.9 and 3.10 Castle Tucker, in Wiscasset, Maine, USA, has been preserved by Historic New England to tell the stories of its residents over two centuries. Built in 1807, the house was repeatedly added to and altered through the nineteenth century but hardly changed since then. The house clearly reveals the modifications over time. Several exterior additions can be distinguished; so too inside the house. The parlor, for example, contains furniture purchased in 1858 and wallpaper from the 1890s. (Historic New England, David Bohl)

A Community Maintains a Treasure: Preserving the Great Mosque at Djenné

The Great Mosque at Djenné, in Mali, is a component of the Old Towns of Djenné, a World Heritage Site that has been inhabited since 250 BC and which was a centre for the diffusion of Islam in the fifteenth and sixteenth centuries. The present mosque was built in the early twentieth century. It is constructed in the traditional technique of using sun-baked mud bricks and a mud-based mortar, all rendered with a coat of smooth mud plaster.

The effects of the weather on the mud finish make annual maintenance essential. This is carried out by the entire community during an annual festival, called le crépissage de la Grande Mosquée. One group prepares the mud plaster in pits, another carries it to the mosque, and a third climbs up the walls

Figure 3.11 Residents of Djenné apply mud plaster to the Great Mosque. (www.visitgaomali.com)

on ladders to apply the plaster. The men and boys undertake the work, carried out partly as races and games, while the women prepare food. The festival not only provides a seasonal social focus, a civic holiday, and a tourist attraction, but it also bestows blessings on the citizens and preserves both the tangible heritage of the mosque and the intangible heritage of the traditional construction technique. In addition, it upholds the spirit of authenticity as defined in the Nara Document.

Even the most loving care can have unforeseen consequences. The accumulated layers of plaster gradually weakened the structure of the mosque. In 2006 the Aga Khan Trust for Culture declared the mosque in danger of collapse and began an extensive restoration. The conservators asked that the crépissage cease until the work was complete. The community lost its festival, with the resulting loss of social and spiritual benefits. The festival finally resumed in 2012, when the conservation was complete, which gave a great boost to local morale (Cotter 2012).

Restoration

Restoration means returning a place to a known earlier state by removing accretions or by reassembling existing elements without the introduction of new material (Australia ICOMOS 2013b: 1.7).[31]

- A historic place is restored to its form at a specific date in the past, which may or may not be the original date of construction.
- The intention of restoration is to reveal the appearance at the period of greatest cultural significance. This is an extraordinary intervention that should be carried out only when the cultural significance of the restoration period is considerably greater than that of the other stages in its history.

Figures 3.12 and 3.13 Casey Farm in Saunderstown, Rhode Island, USA, before and after its restoration. The house was built in the 1750s. Two centuries later, Historic New England attempted to restore it to its original appearance, removing the porch, shutters, dormer, and other nineteenth-century accretions. As a consequence, the house tells the story only of original builder and planter, Daniel Coggeshall Jr., and his wife, Mary Wanton Coggeshall, but not those of their descendants, the Casey family. The remainder of the farm and the outbuildings, however, retain changes made over the years. Today's cultural landscape ensemble never existed in history. (Historic New England, Harry Weir Casey and Dana Salvo)

- Restoration should not juxtapose features from different historical periods in a way that would create an appearance that never existed at any time in the past.
- Restoration is appropriate only if there is sufficient evidence of an earlier state of the fabric (Australia ICOMOS 2013b: Article 19). This respects Article 9 of the *Venice Charter*, which states that restoration 'is a highly specialized operation ... based on respect for original material and authentic documents. It must stop at the point where conjecture begins, and in this case moreover any extra work which is indispensable must be distinct from the architectural composition and must bear a contemporary stamp'—i.e., new work must be distinguishable from historical fabric.
- Restoration may involve the permanent loss (i.e., demolition) of historical fabric that is later in date than the restoration period. If the material proposed to be removed has cultural significance, then restoration would not be good practice and the treatment should be reconsidered. If the restoration period has far greater cultural significance than the period of the material being removed, then restoration may be considered only if the lost material is fully documented before removal.
- A distinction is sometimes made between **period restoration**, in which a place is returned to its appearance at an earlier time (rather like the 'unity of style' of Viollet-le-Duc, although with historical accuracy); and **composite restoration**, in which significant features from all historical periods are left intact, but allowing the removal of material judged to be of little or no cultural significance. Most authorities would consider the latter to be a form of preservation, and not restoration.

Preservation vs. Restoration: The Case of Historic New England

Conservation agencies used to restore historic places to what was considered their 'original' appearance as a matter of course, without considering alternative treatments. The Society for the Preservation of New England Antiquities (SPNEA; now known as Historic New England), an American not-for-profit organization founded in 1910, followed this direction as it built up an impressive portfolio of restored early buildings, converted to museums.

The organization changed its ways in the 1960s, adopting preservation as its preferred treatment. Morgan Phillips, the Supervisor of Properties at the time, provided the rationale for a 'philosophy of total preservation' (Phillips 1971). Preservation was preferred to restoration because:

- The philosophy of restoration is based on the premise that the most important thing about a historic building is its original design, and that later changes that obscure or 'spoil' that design should be removed. However, it is the old material from all periods that matters.
- Restoration obliterates much of the human history of a building.
- Restoration almost inevitably creates a situation that never existed at any time in the past.

Phillips noted that the Society's new philosophy of preservation did admit a few exceptions:

- A building that has already been restored may be restored again to more scholarly standards without suffering damage.
- Restoration is sensible insofar as it is 'unrestoration.'
- Restoration is acceptable in the case of buildings not being preserved as museums: 'we must grant ourselves [the] right to change old buildings today: to modernize or to restore, whichever is our taste. Restoration is necessarily change.'

While newer attitudes to conservation might disagree with the emphasis on material rather than cultural significance, and on the reliance on taste, the arguments remain valid. They mirror the debate between restoration and anti-restoration that occurred a century earlier, although here the debate took place peacefully within a single organization. Phillips did not cite yet another factor that has become increasingly important: preservation usually costs less than restoration.

Figures 3.14 and 3.15 The Amory-Ticknor House in Boston, Massachusetts, built in 1804, enlarged a few years later (left photo) and then again c. 1885 with shopfronts, bay windows, and oriel windows (contemporary photo, at right). Historic New England has chosen to preserve the changes, rather than restore the building to an earlier date. (Library of Congress, American Memory, HABS/HAER/HALS; Mary Beth Mudrick, Federalstyle.com)

Rehabilitation/adaptation

Rehabilitation or **adaptation** means modifying a property to enable an efficient contemporary use, whether this is the existing use or a proposed use. This is done by retaining those components that contribute to its cultural significance and sensitively altering or adding to those that do not (Australia ICOMOS 2013b: 1.9; Parks Canada 2010: 16).

Figure 3.16 The sixteenth-century Rustem Pasha caravanserai in eastern Turkey has been rehabilitated to become a hotel, a variant on the original use. (Emel Yamnturk)

- 'Rehabilitation' is the preferred term in the US, Canada, and some other countries. 'Adaptation' is the preferred term in Australia. English Heritage calls the approach **new work and alteration** (English Heritage 2008b: Sections 138–48). Some jurisdictions (e.g., Hong Kong) prefer the term **revitalization**.
- With a building, this treatment is generally seen as renewing structural, mechanical, and electrical systems as needed, and making upgrades to meet applicable codes and ordinances. With a landscape, the work might include upgrading circulation and security; with historic towns, traffic management.
- The use of the place may be continued or it may be changed (called **adaptive reuse** or **repurposing**). Adaptive reuse may require extensive modifications. Alterations and additions are permissible as long as they do not threaten, remove, or conceal material or immaterial components that provide the place with its cultural significance.
- Debate occurs over whether new work should be contemporary (and compatible) in character or be guided by the historical design. Most recent voices call for the former. In either case, new work must be clearly distinguishable from the original.[32]

Reconstruction

Reconstruction means returning a place to a known earlier state and is distinguished from restoration by the introduction of new material (Australia ICOMOS 2013b: 1.8).

- Reconstruction may involve the total rebuilding of a historic place that has been lost or is unsalvageable; or it may involve rebuilding one or more components of a historic place as part of a restoration project.
- Reconstruction, like restoration, is a highly specialized operation that should be used only in exceptional circumstances. The *Burra Charter* states that 'Reconstruction is appropriate only where a place is incomplete through damage or alteration, and only where there is sufficient evidence to reproduce an earlier state of the fabric.' Moreover, 'Reconstruction should be identifiable [as new work] on close inspection or through additional interpretation'– i.e., it must not be confused with an authentic historic place (Article 20.1–2).
- The *Venice Charter* forbids reconstruction (Article 15, in the context of excavations).

Figure 3.17 The Fortress of Louisbourg National Historic Site of Canada, in Nova Scotia, a fortified French town captured and destroyed by the British in the eighteenth century, was reconstructed by Parks Canada in the 1960s and 1970s, based on original drawings in Paris and elsewhere. (© Parks Canada/ Fortress of Louisbourg National Historic Site)

Reconstructing Old Warsaw

Reconstruction has often been used effectively to rebuild neighborhoods or individual buildings destroyed by war, when the lost historic place holds particular significance to residents. A reconstruction of this kind satisfies strong patriotic and nationalistic sentiments.

Figure 3.18 The Historic Centre of Warsaw World Heritage Site. (Barcex, Wikimedia Commons)

As an example, fully 85 percent of the historic city of Warsaw was destroyed by the German Wehrmacht between 1939 and 1944. Before the war, the faculty of Warsaw Technical University had documented much of the city's architectural heritage. As an act of moral resistance during the German occupation, faculty and students collected images of old Warsaw, developed schemes for rebuilding it, and then hid the documents in a monastery outside the city.

After the war, Polish authorities were determined to reconstruct the city core as an act of devotion to their country. As respected scholar Stanislaw Ossowski stated at the time:

> If the Warsaw community is to be reborn, if its core is to be constituted by former Varsovians, then they have to be given back their old rebuilt Warsaw so that they can see in it the same city and not a different town on the same spot.
>
> (Tung 2001: 84)

Over the course of two decades, Old Warsaw was meticulously reconstructed, requiring an enormous investment of funds and the formation of a government agency dedicated to teaching lost traditional technical skills.

Warsaw's cultural significance was reconstituted along with its city walls, street patterns, land allotments, buildings, and landscapes. The reconstruction of the Historic Centre of Warsaw received formal recognition as an act of conservation by its inscription on the World Heritage List in 1980. The description praises the 26-hectare place as 'an outstanding example of a near-total reconstruction of a span of history covering the 13th to the twentieth century' (Tung 2001: 74–89; UNESCO World Heritage Centre n.d.-a).[33]

The Reconstruction of the Frauenkirche

Figures 3.19 and 3.20 The Frauenkirche in Dresden, destroyed in 1945, is seen before and after its reconstruction, which was completed in 2005. (Courtesy of the Archives of the Evangelical Lutheran Church in America; Matthias Bandemer)

The Frauenkirche (Church of Our Lady) in Dresden, Germany, a treasure from the eighteenth century, was another casualty of World War II, having been destroyed, along with much of the city, during the extensive British and American bombing of Dresden in 1945. Unlike in Warsaw, this time Germany was the victim, rather than the perpetrator. The large church, with its elaborate Rococo interior, was meticulously reconstructed, with surviving fragments embedded in the new work (and distinguishable by color).

The reconstruction was above all an act of reconciliation. A massive international fundraising campaign attracted donations from dozens of countries. Thirty or more societies for the reconstruction of the church were founded in Germany and abroad. In all about €180 million was raised. A poignant instance of a donated component was the new 'Cross of Peace' at the top of the cupola. It was made by English goldsmith Alan Smith, whose father was a RAF bomber pilot who participated in the bombing of Dresden (Stiftung Frauenkirche Dresden n.d.).

One blogger who admires both the Warsaw and Dresden reconstructions writes:

> You could argue that rebuilding the past is nostalgic nonsense, that it falsifies and contradicts history and pretends that significant events from the past did not happen or that it is done only to fool tourists and children. You could make those arguments but who we are is tied up in many different things, including the built environment.
>
> (Hollier 2011)

'Who we are' is, of course, the core of social, cultural, and national identity. Even if it is decried by conservation purists, reconstruction makes total sense when striving to undo an attempt to eradicate that identity.

- A significant risk of reconstruction is that it may damage or destroy the original archaeological record.
- The physical fabric of a reconstruction generally lacks cultural significance and is considered to lack authenticity. For this reason some authorities insist that reconstruction is not a conservation treatment. However, cultural significance is found in the intangible values and stories associated with the place that has been reconstructed, and reconstructed places can be powerful tools for interpretation, as well as for nationalism (see the two text boxes on Warsaw and the Frauenkirche). The debate over the validity of reconstruction is passionate.
- Sometimes historic places have disappeared because of prolonged deterioration, which may have been caused in part by flaws in the original design. It is important that reconstructions not repeat the design errors of the prototype; this will only lead to early failure of the reconstructed place.[34]

Other treatments

Many other conservation treatments have been identified and their definitions generally agreed to. Some are not considered to be conservation by authorities, because they are felt to compromise good conservation practice, but all comprise a conservation component. Most of the terms refer to buildings.

Figure 3.21 This former hardware store in Dawson City, Yukon, was stabilized years ago (note the weathered shoring beneath the bay windows) and then left to continue deteriorating. (Harold Kalman)

- **Stabilization**: Undertaking the minimum amount of work needed to safeguard a historic place from the elements and/or collapse, and to protect the public from danger. One often speaks of **emergency stabilization** when the intervention prevents imminent catastrophic damage.[35]
- **Rescue archaeology**: This is the archaeological equivalent of emergency stabilization. It is applied to remains that are exposed or threatened by active development and is often done under severe pressures of time. If material is removed quickly from the ground as mitigation, the action is called **salvage archaeology**.
- **Consolidation**: Used more with reference to individual components than entire historic places, this refers to the reinforcement of a deteriorated feature, often by the physical application of adhesives or supports within the material, to achieve structural integrity.
- **Replication**: Similar to reconstruction, but usually denotes copying a prototype that still exists; whereas reconstruction refers to something that has been gone for a period of time (whether a few months or a few millennia).[36]
- **Reassembly** (**reconstitution**): A conservation treatment in which the components of a dismantled historic place are put back together again. The *Venice Charter* calls this **anastylosis**, defined as 'the re-assembling of existing but dismembered parts,' as long as 'the [new] material used for integration should always be recognizable' (Article 15, in the context of archaeological excavations).

Figure 3.22 The Rideau Street Convent Chapel in Ottawa, Ontario, was dismantled prior to demolition of the convent and its 3,000+ pieces subsequently reassembled within the National Gallery of Canada. (Michael Bedford Photography)

- **Moving**: Although discouraged by the charters and standards, a building or structure is sometimes relocated to another site, often as a last-resort alternative to demolition. This reduces the cultural significance, and may even destroy it if the significance is based on the association with a particular location. In some situations, areas have been set aside specifically as havens to receive 'rescued' resources. Canada and other countries have established outdoor museums (or 'open-air museums,' 'heritage villages') for buildings threatened by flooding from major infrastructure projects.[37] The Town of Markham, Ontario, created Markham Heritage Estates, 'a subdivision of last resort for heritage buildings in the community that cannot under any circumstances be successfully retained on site' (City of Markham 2012).[38] Ironically this option makes it easier for an owner to declare that demolition of a recognized historic place is unavoidable. Havens exist for landscape resources as well. Indigenous plants from around South Africa that were displaced by urban growth were collected and exhibited at the Johannesburg Empire Exhibition in 1936. When the exhibition closed, the plants were relocated to The Wilds, a tract of parkland between the city and its suburbs (Foster 2012: 42 and note 2).

Figure 3.23 Markham Heritage Estates, near Toronto, Ontario, is instant heritage: a residential subdivision containing threatened historic buildings that were moved here. (Sean Marshall)

- **Fragmentation**: Portions of a historic place are retained and reassembled, either on the original site or elsewhere. The most common application occurs when the façade of a historic building is removed and affixed to a new backing, often a new building but sometimes merely a support. Another variant is the collection of fragments from various historic places within a museum setting, often described an 'architectural museum.'[39] Fragments of historic buildings are sometimes placed in a landscape setting to recreate the idea of a picturesque English garden.

- **Façadism** (or **façadotomy**): A derisive name for a variation of fragmentation, in which the façade of a building is retained and all else rebuilt. English architect-planner Dennis Rodwell calls it 'a form of architectural taxidermy that treats historic cities as theatrical stage sets' and 'the antithesis of a sustainable approach to historic cities' (Rodwell 2007: 207).

Figure 3.24 The 'Tin House' in Ottawa, Ontario, is the metal façade of a demolished house that has been attached to a wall nearby, much like a painting on a gallery wall. (Concierge.2C, Wikimedia Commons)

- **Renovation**: Extensive changes and/or additions are made to a historic place in a process of 'renewal' (etymologically the same). In the case of architecture, the changes may be internal or external. These changes may be made in response to the need to accommodate new uses, where rehabilitation is an inadequate approach. Another motivation may be the desire to assert the process of renewal, usually for social or political reasons. Renovation is another term for **new work**.[40]

Figure 3.26 indicates a hierarchy of treatments, from those that show the greatest respect for cultural significance and historic fabric, to those that show the greatest degree of intervention. As mentioned above, some authorities consider those that demonstrate 'moderate' or 'limited' respect to not be conservation treatments at all; the most doctrinaire

Figure 3.25 Façadism is the name given to projects in which one or two street façades are retained and an entirely new building erected behind (and sometimes above). This residential project in Vancouver boasts that its 36 'heritage homes' have been sold. (Harold Kalman)

recognize only preservation, restoration, and rehabilitation.[41] We prefer to see those in the grey zone as compromise treatments that may occur when best practices cannot be achieved, whether for technical or budgetary reasons, or because decision-makers lack the will to follow best practice. The need to forge compromises in real-life conservation is a recurring theme throughout this book.

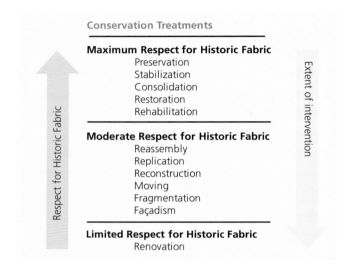

Figure 3.26 Conservation treatments, in order of the extent of intervention.

Combining treatments

In actual practice, more than one conservation treatment is often applied to a historic place. As an example, a historic farm may be preserved (in order to reveal its growth and development over time), while an orchard and a vegetable garden are rehabilitated (to support good new produce) and an ornamental garden restored (because it was created by a significant past owner and is a good example of a garden of its day).

The *Burra Charter* makes it clear that this is acceptable practice:

> Conservation may, according to circumstance, include the processes of: retention or reintroduction of a use; retention of associations and meanings; maintenance, preservation, restoration, reconstruction, adaptation and interpretation; and will commonly include a combination of more than one of these.
>
> (Australia ICOMOS 2013b: Article 14)

The heritage planning process should define the **primary conservation treatment** to the historic place (after having first identified its continued or new use), and then identify what **secondary conservation treatments** may be used for individual components. The techniques used for each component would follow the guidelines for that particular treatment, while retaining a level of consistency within the overall historic place.

As an example, a frequent approach taken in the conservation of urban buildings is to upgrade for contemporary use through rehabilitation (the primary approach), while choosing restoration or preservation as a secondary approach for the main façade.

Guidelines for selecting the appropriate conservation treatment(s) are provided in Section 5.3.

Figure 3.27 Conservation treatments were combined in the former Chinese Freemasons Building in Vancouver's Chinatown. The exterior elevations (one Chinese and one Western in character) were *restored* to their original appearance in 1907. Work included revealing the original painted wall sign ('Pekin Chop Suey House') and *reconstructing* the ground-floor shop fronts and the cornice. The interior was *rehabilitated*, including changing its use from offices to residential units. One may debate whether the primary treatment was the interior rehabilitation or the exterior restoration. (John Roaf)

Combining Conservation Treatments: The Reichstag

The Reichstag in Berlin, built in 1894 to accommodate the parliament of imperial Germany, stands today as a successful integration of old and new. The building was partly destroyed by fire in 1933 and further damaged by war in 1945. It was partially restored and repurposed in the 1960s by architect Paul Baumgarten. Following German reunification, a decision was taken to return the seat of government to Berlin and to restore the building's original use by installing the Bundestag—the modern parliament—here.

Foster and Partners, the firm headed by celebrated English architect Sir Norman Foster, won an international competition to design the changes, carried out between 1995 and 1999. The exterior walls were carefully **restored** to their appearance in 1945, including **preserving** wartime scars and graffiti. As the architects wrote, the renewed Reichstag is

> a living historical museum that frankly shows the scars of its past—pockmarks caused by shells, charred timber, and Russian graffiti from the post-World War II occupation are all left visible.

(Omkar n.d.).

Damaged and missing exterior features were **restored**. The interior, on the other hand, was mostly gutted and **renovated**, including inserting a bright, new chamber for the lawmakers. The large, central dome had not been rebuilt in the 1960s. Foster installed a **new** glass-and-steel hemispherical cupola, different in shape but similar in scale to the original, not dominating or overwhelming the building. The dome offers visitors a superb panoramic prospect of Berlin, as well as a view down into the Bundestag chamber.

The combination of treatments achieves many things. The exterior and the name 'Reichstag' refer to Germany's past, the interior accommodates the needs of the present, and the dome clearly expresses a positive vision for the future of the reunified nation. All is realized in a manner that retains the cultural significance of the historic place.

Figures 3.28 and 3.29 Left: Exterior view of the Reichstag. (Jessica Spengler) Right: Chamber and cupola. (Wolfgang Glock)

3.3 Standards and Guidelines

The heritage professional may understand the key international charters and doctrine, as well as the various conservation treatments, but is (s)he now able to undertake a conservation project with the confidence that the interventions will represent best heritage practice? Not really. The *Burra Charter* declares that 'the aim of conservation is to retain the cultural significance of a place,' but how do we identify the significance? The *Venice Charter* allows the use of modern science and technology, but which new techniques are good and which not so good? The principles contained in the charters are worded far too generally—at too abstract a level—to give the hands-on practitioner clear direction 'on the ground.' Moreover, they do not carry the weight of enforce-ability, as already noted.

To address this dilemma, practitioners resorted to a plethora of manuals of practice that respect the principles embodied in the charters. Some are valuable guides to practice, with titles such as *Conservation of Historic Buildings* (1982; Bernard Feilden, UK), *Conservation Plan* (1982, 2013; James Semple Kerr, Australia), and *Historic Preservation* (1982; James Marston Fitch, US). More detailed have been the countless thinner manuals, often produced by governments or funding agencies, addressing the topics that their work or granting programs promote. They are usually directed at specific audiences, such as the residents of the publishing jurisdiction and grant recipients. Adherence to the manuals can be made a condition of receiving financial support, making the handbooks enforceable to a target group.[42]

Nevertheless there remains a 'disconnect' between the conservation charters and actual conservation work. This has been resolved with the introduction of standards and guidelines. Standards provide more practical direction than the ICOMOS charters, but nevertheless remain rather conceptual. Guidelines are more pragmatic, showing how to follow the standards in specific situations.

Principal documents

Several government agencies have developed sets of principles that are more easily followed by practitioners and property owners than the charters. The US led the way with its *Standards and Guidelines*, and Canada and some other countries have followed the American precedent. As mentioned, the 'standards'—which can also be called 'principles'—remain quite conceptual, whereas the 'guidelines' ('guidance') are more practical.

This section describes the American and Canadian conservation standards and guidelines, as well as their regulatory contexts. The remainder of the section provides several comparative examples to show the interrelationship among charters, standards, and guidelines, and the greater pragmatism at each descending level.

United States

The US National Park Service made a key step towards resolving the issue of the theoretical nature and non-enforceability of best practices in 1976, when it introduced *The Secretary of the Interior's Standards and Guidelines for Rehabilitation*. This landmark document forms a key part of an integrated and innovative national historic preservation system.

The American system for overseeing rehabilitation, in which all levels of government participate, is based on two significant federal laws. The first is the *National Historic Preservation Act* of 1966, which established:

- The **National Register of Historic Places**, a list of places considered worthy of conservation; inclusion on the list does not protect property.
- An administrative system led in effect by **State Historic Preservation Officers** (SHPOs), which required states to set up their own agencies and which in turn encouraged the participation of local governments and Indian tribes.
- Modest grants-in-aid through the **Historic Preservation Fund**.
- **Technical assistance** to owners of historic places, provided by the Technical Preservation Services Division of the National Park Service, including the *Standards and Guidelines*.

The second law is the *Tax Reform Act* of 1976, which provides financial incentives for rehabilitation. Projects wanting to benefit from the tax incentives must follow the *Standards for Rehabilitation* (last major update 1983); the standards are clarified in *Guidelines for Preserving, Rehabilitating, Restoring & Reconstructing Historic Buildings*.[43] For a conservation project to qualify for federal grants-in-aid separate from the incentives for rehabilitation, conservation work must adhere to *The Secretary of the Interior's Standards for the Treatment of Historic Properties* (National Park Service, Technical Preservation Services, 1995).

The *Standards and Guidelines* have been updated and expanded over the years. They are applicable to all types of historic places included in the National Register. Additional standards and guidelines are available for preservation planning, identification of historic properties, evaluation of significance, registration in the National Register of Historic Places, historical documentation, architectural and engineering documentation, archaeological documentation, treatment of historic properties, professional qualification standards, and preservation terminology. These were issued collectively in 1983 as *The Secretary of the Interior's Standards and Guidelines for Archaeology and Historic Preservation* (National Park Service 1983). All are intended to provide technical advice for 'federally mandated' projects and are not regulatory.[44]

One of the original authors of the *Secretary of the Interior's Standards*, W. Brown Morton III, reminisced a generation later about what he and co-author Gary L. Hume had intended: 'The purpose of the Secretary's Standards was to provide a basis for evaluating the quality of preservation work carried out with federal assistance that was not arbitrary.' In other words, federal funds could be dispensed only with objective 'national standards for historic preservation projects' (Morton 2003: 18).[45]

The National Park Service has produced separate guidelines to address the treatment of cultural landscapes (Birnbaum and Peters 1996). While thorough, the guidelines have been adapted from those for buildings and focus on conserving 'the landscape's existing form, features and materials' (p. 20). This has led to criticism that they are too structural, and fail to show an understanding of cultural landscapes, since they do not 'accommodate the more complex systematic relationship of nature' or the basic idea of ecosystems (Hohmann 2008: 109).[46]

Canada

The Canadian government attempted to introduce a similarly comprehensive national conservation system with the launch of the Historic Places Initiative in 2001, as recognition that Canada's historic places 'provide tangible economic, environmental, social and cultural benefits' (Parks Canada 2009: Section 3.1). HPI, as it was called, introduced the Canadian Register of Historic Places, *Standards and Guidelines for the Conservation of Historic Places in Canada*, and a certification program, all following the American model. However, the proposed legislation was never enacted and so the intended tax incentives, certification program, and several other components of HPI did not come into effect.

Nevertheless, the Canadian *Standards and Guidelines* (2003, revised 2010) remain as an important and highly useful document (Parks Canada 2010). While the content is based to some extent on the US *Standards and Guidelines*, the Canadian material is contained within a single document and is clear and easy to follow, making it an outstanding compilation of conservation doctrine that is universally useful.

The core comprises 14 tightly worded standards—9 for preservation, rehabilitation, and restoration; 3 pertaining only to rehabilitation; and 2 to restoration. The standards neatly recap the most important and relevant of the doctrine from the ICOMOS charters, each standard accompanied (in the second edition) by helpful explanatory notes and illustrations.

The document introduces the concept of **character-defining elements**, defined as 'the materials, forms, location, spatial configurations, uses and cultural associations or meanings that contribute to the heritage value of an historic place, which must be retained to preserve its heritage value' (Parks Canada 2010: 5). This follows the idea of 'cultural significance' expressed in the *Burra Charter* and elsewhere, but provides a more specific and usable tool.

To cite the first two standards as examples:

> Standard 1. Conserve the heritage value of a historic place. Do not remove, replace, or substantially alter its intact or repairable

character-defining elements. Do not move a part of a historic place if its current location is a character-defining element.

Standard 2. Conserve changes to a historic place which, over time, have become character-defining elements in their own right.

Lengthy guidelines follow. They refer separately to cultural landscapes (including heritage districts), archaeological sites, buildings, engineering works, and materials. A number of guidelines are cited later in this section.

In Canada the conservation of private property is a provincial responsibility. Most provinces have chosen to adopt the federal *Standards and Guidelines* rather than introduce their own, although some have written policy documents that supplement the federal standards. Because the *Standards and Guidelines* are not backed by legislation, they are enforceable only when projects are supported with federal funding, or with provincial or municipal funding in jurisdictions that have formally approved the document.

The relationship among charters, standards, and guidelines

We may think of the different policy documents as forming a pyramid (Figure 3.30), with the charters at the apex, the standards ('principles' in the UK) next, and below them the guidelines ('guidance' in the UK), which provide practical advice to achieve best practices. There are far more guidelines than standards, because they are more specific in their application.[47] The bottom tier of the pyramid consists of professional advice—usually from conservation architects and engineers or from commercial product representatives—and technical manuals.

Figure 3.30 The policy pyramid: from top to bottom, the layers progress from general principles to practical guidance for applying best practices.

The US National Park Service describes standards as 'common sense historic preservation principles in non-technical language. They promote historic preservation best practices that will help to protect our nation's irreplaceable cultural resources.' They are also called a 'series of concepts' (National Park Service, Technical Preservation Services 1995). Guidelines are more helpful in the real world of practice, in that they address particular situations and materials. Nevertheless they are still sufficiently general in scope so as to be widely applicable. The National Park Service writes:

> The Guidelines have been prepared to assist in applying the Standards to all project work; consequently, they are not meant to give case-specific advice or address exceptions or rare instances. Therefore, it is recommended that the advice of qualified historic preservation professionals be obtained early in the planning stage of the project. Such professionals may include architects, architectural historians, historians, historical engineers, archeologists, and others who have experience in working with historic buildings.
>
> (National Park Service n.d.-a)

The connections between charters, principles, standards, and guidelines can be demonstrated with examples drawing on several specific situations, citing documents at all levels and from various countries. Since the guidelines differ for various place-types and materials, the parameters for the selected examples are identified.

EXAMPLE 1: RETAINING CULTURAL SIGNIFICANCE

Charter:

> The aim of conservation is to retain the cultural significance of a place. (*Burra Charter*, Article 2.2)

Principle:

> Conservation is the process of managing change to a significant place in its setting in ways that will best sustain its heritage values, while recognising opportunities to reveal or reinforce those values for present and future generations. (English Heritage, *Conservation Principles, Policies and Guidance*, Principle 4.2)

Standard:

> The historic character of a property will be retained and preserved. The replacement of intact or repairable historic materials or alteration of features, spaces, and spatial relationships that characterize a property will be avoided. (*Secretary of the Interior's Standards for Preservation*, Standard 2)

Standard:

> Conserve the heritage value of an historic place. Do not remove, replace or substantially alter its intact or repairable character-defining elements. Do not move a part of an historic place if its current location is a character-defining element. (*Standards and Guidelines for the Conservation of Historic Places in Canada,* Standard 1)

Guideline (for visual relationships in cultural landscapes):

- *Recommended:* Protecting and maintaining the features that define the visual relationships by using non-destructive methods in daily, seasonal and cyclical tasks, such as pruning, to retain sight lines. This could also include maintaining the size and massing of vegetation and built features that contribute to the overall scale of the historic place.
- *Not recommended:* Allowing visual relationships to be altered by incompatible development or neglect. Using maintenance methods that alter or obscure the visual relationships in the cultural landscape, such as removing planting that reduces the perceived size of a parking lot to make winter snow removal easier. (*Standards and Guidelines for the Conservation of Historic Places in Canada,* 68)

Guideline (for archaeological sites in urban environments):

- *Recommended:* Preserving archaeological sites in urban environments in situ, through minimal interventions, such as stabilization and consolidation.
- *Not recommended:* Preserving archaeological sites in urban environments in situ, without adequately protecting the site from the potentially harmful effects of contemporary uses. (*Standards and Guidelines for the Conservation of Historic Places in Canada,* 110)

EXAMPLE 2: USING MODERN TECHNIQUES

Charter:

> The conservation and restoration of monuments must have recourse to all the sciences and techniques which can contribute to the study and safeguarding of the architectural heritage.

> When traditional techniques prove inadequate, the consolidation of a monument can be achieved by the use of any modern technique for conservation and construction, the efficacy of which has been shown by scientific data and proved by experience. (*Venice Charter,* Articles 2, 10)

Charter:

> Traditional techniques and materials are preferred for the conservation of significant fabric. In some circumstances modern techniques

and materials which offer substantial conservation benefits may be appropriate. (*Burra Charter*, Article 4.2)

Standard (for restoration of buildings and structures):

Deteriorated features from the restoration period will be repaired rather than replaced. Where the severity of deterioration requires replacement of a distinctive feature, the new feature will match the old in design, color, texture, and, where possible, materials. (US *Standards for Restoration*, Standard 6)

Guidance (for repair of buildings and structures):

The use of materials or techniques with a lifespan that is predictable from past performance, and which are close matches for those being repaired or replaced, tends to carry a low risk of future harm or premature failure. By contrast, the longer term effects of using materials or techniques that are innovative and relatively untested are much less certain. (English Heritage, *Conservation Principles, Policies and Guidance*, Clause 119)

Guideline (for repairing materials and features from the restoration period in buildings and structures):

When the physical condition of restoration period features requires additional work, repairing by stabilizing, consolidating, and conserving is recommended. Restoration guidance focuses upon the preservation of those materials and features that are significant to the period. Consequently, guidance for repairing a historic material, such as masonry, again begins with the least degree of intervention possible, such as strengthening fragile materials through consolidation, when appropriate, and repointing with mortar of an appropriate strength. Repairing masonry as well as wood and architectural metals includes patching, splicing, or otherwise reinforcing them using recognized preservation methods. Similarly, portions of a historic structural system could be reinforced using contemporary material such as steel rods. In Restoration, repair may also include the limited replacement in kind—or with compatible substitute material—of extensively deteriorated or missing parts of existing features when there are surviving prototypes to use as a model. Examples could include terra-cotta brackets, wood balusters, or cast iron fencing. (*The Secretary of the Interior's Guidelines for Restoring Historic Buildings*)

Guidelines (for restoration of architectural and structural metals):

- *Recommended:* Repairing, stabilizing and conserving fragile metal elements from the restoration period, using well-tested consolidants, when appropriate. Repairs should be physically and visually compatible and identifiable on close inspection for future research.

- *Not recommended:* Removing metal elements from the restoration period that could be stabilized and conserved.
- *Recommended:* Replacing in kind a metal element from the restoration period that is too deteriorated to repair, based on documentary and physical evidence. The new work should be well documented and unobtrusively dated to guide future research and treatment.
- *Not recommended:* Removing an irreparable metal element from the restoration period and not replacing it, or replacing it with an inappropriate new element. (*Standards and Guidelines for the Conservation of Historic Places in Canada*, 238)

It is instructive to note that notions about modern materials and techniques have become more cautious over the last half-century. This may be the result of adverse reactions that occurred with the use of some new treatments. As an example, Canadian conservation technologist Martin Weaver warned about the risks of using synthetic resins used to retard deterioration, consolidate materials, and undertake repairs:

> Resins may be irreversible or virtually impossible to remove without causing unacceptable damage; however, at the same time they may also be unstable and may change their nature and appearance, making it necessary to remove them.
>
> (Weaver 1997: 258)[48]

It is for advice like this that the National Park Service recommends seeking the advice of qualified professionals, and not relying solely on charters, standards and guidelines. Best practices are achieved with the appropriate combination of theory and (as the term 'best *practices*' denotes) practical experience.

EXAMPLE 3: NEW WORK

Charter:

The *Venice Charter* addresses this issue, although rather sternly and within the narrow context of restoration:

> Replacements of missing parts must integrate harmoniously with the whole, but at the same time must be distinguishable from the original so that restoration does not falsify the artistic or historic evidence. (Article 12)

> Additions cannot be allowed except in so far as they do not detract from the interesting parts of the building, its traditional setting, the balance of its composition and its relation with its surroundings. (Article 13)

Charter:

The *Burra Charter* is somewhat more lenient with respect to additions, here in the context of rehabilitation:

New work such as additions or other changes to the place may be acceptable where it respects and does not distort or obscure the cultural significance of the place, or detract from its interpretation and appreciation. (Article 22.1)

New work should be readily identifiable as such, but must respect and have minimal impact on the cultural significance of the place. (Article 22.2)

The accompanying explanatory note provides elaboration:

New work should respect the significance of a place through consideration of its siting, bulk, form, scale, character, color, texture and material. Imitation should generally be avoided.[49]

Standard:

The Canadian *Standards and Guidelines* provide more detailed guidance in a standard intended specifically for rehabilitation:

Conserve the heritage value and character-defining elements when creating any new additions to an historic place or any related new construction. Make the new work physically and visually compatible with, subordinate to, and distinguishable from the historic place. (Standard 11)

Figure 3.31 A glass-and-steel entrance pyramid designed by architect I.M. Pei was inserted into the courtyard of the Louvre Museum in Paris in 1989, clearly subordinate to and distinguishable from the centuries-old buildings surrounding it. The feature has been alternatively praised and criticized ever since for its (in)compatibility. (Tallapragada Sriram)

Guidelines:

Two guidelines with respect to the exterior form of building rehabilitation projects address these issues:

- *Recommended:* Designing a new addition in a manner that draws a clear distinction between what is historic and what is new.
- *Not recommended:* Duplicating the exact form, material, style and detailing of the original building in a way that makes the distinction between old and new unclear.
- *Recommended:* Designing an addition that is compatible in terms of materials and massing with the exterior form of the historic building and its setting.
- *Not recommended:* Designing a new addition that has a negative impact on the heritage value of the historic building.

With respect to new work in general, we see continuity in thought. All the cited principles state that new work must be 'harmonious,' 'compatible,' or 'respectful' with respect to the old, and all dictate that the new intervention should be 'distinguishable' or 'readily identifiable.' Where they fall silent is over whether new architectural or landscape work should be designed in a contemporary manner or whether it should have a more timeless, neo-historical character (without being imitative). Both approaches have been adopted with success.

It has been suggested that the introduction of good contemporary new design into restoration work (and subsequently into rehabilitation projects) was validated with the selection in 1951 of architect Basil Spence to design a new Coventry Cathedral. Intended to replace the old cathedral, which had been destroyed by enemy bombs in 1940,

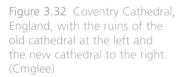

Figure 3.32 Coventry Cathedral, England, with the ruins of the old cathedral at the left and the new cathedral to the right. (Cmglee)

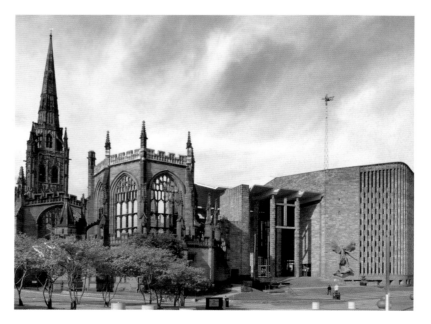

Spence's winning competition design was the only one to retain the ruins and as well as erect a new building. His respectful, much-admired cathedral, completed in 1962, is attached to the stabilized ruins by a raised porch that alludes both to Gothic and contemporary work.

Others see the tipping point towards new design as being more recent, in the reaction to the 1992 fire at Windsor Castle. The historic place has been constructed and modified over the course of a millennium. Many respected observers promoted compatible, contemporary design, but the Royal Household insisted that the three principal spaces be 'restored as [they were] before' (Delafons 1997: 178–80; Nicholson 1997).

The debate will surely continue. Whichever approach is selected, the principle of respect must be dominant.

Two commonly misunderstood principles

In order to understand the level at which principles (or standards) are written, the following two have been selected as examples because they introduce important principles for conservation work not previously discussed in this book, and also because they are often misunderstood. Both are presented by English architects Sir Bernard Feilden and John Warren as ethical standards (see Section 2.3).

The principle of minimal intervention

Figure 3.33 The Mai Po Wetlands, Hong Kong. This area supported a long tradition of fish farming. Nearby development led to many residents leaving and abandoning the annual cycle of dredging. As a consequence, the fish ponds filled with silt. The Hong Kong government and World Wildlife Fund partnered to dredge the wetlands so that remaining residents could continue their farming and demonstrate this important traditional occupation. The conservation treatment is preservation and the approach is one of minimal intervention. However, the maintenance cost is high, a reminder that minimal intervention does not necessarily come cheaply. (Ken Nicolson)

'Conserve heritage value by adopting an approach calling for minimal intervention.' (Canadian *Standards and Guidelines*, Standard 3)

- This is derived from the adage that one should repair rather than replace deteriorated features, and also in reaction to the threat of removing culturally significant material during conservation work.
- The *Burra Charter* makes this recommendation, albeit somewhat indirectly: 'Conservation is based on a respect for the existing fabric, use, associations and meanings. It requires a cautious approach of changing as much as necessary but as little as possible.' (Article 3.1)
- The explanatory notes to the Canadian standards elaborate: 'Minimal intervention in the context of heritage conservation means doing enough, but only enough to meet realistic objectives while protecting heritage values. Minimal does not mean doing little or nothing, or the least possible. In fact, enough intervention to arrest and correct deterioration, meet codes, or introduce new services, can be quite extensive. Determining minimal intervention is a matter of rigorous assessment, options analysis and creativity to identify the intervention that balances technical and programmatic requirements with protecting heritage value' (Parks Canada 2010: 26).

The principle of reversibility

'New additions and adjacent or related new construction will be undertaken in such a manner that, if removed in the future, the essential form and integrity of the historic property and its environment would be unimpaired.' (US *Standards for Rehabilitation*, Standard 10)

- The *Burra Charter* introduced this concept to defend against potentially harmful interventions: 'Changes which reduce cultural significance should be reversible, and be reversed when circumstances permit.' (Article 15.2)
- It is often impracticable to introduce reversible changes, but a concerted attempt should be made to respect this standard.

Figure 3.34 The new entrance to the Selexyz Dominicanen bookstore in Maastricht, repurposed from an old church, has been separated from the historic wall and pavement so that it can be removed without damaging the old materials—i.e., the addition is reversible. A view of the interior—whose alterations are also reversible—is seen in Figure 5.6. and on the cover (© Bence Horvath)

Part 2
Process

4

Understanding the Historic Place

Heritage planning develops policies and management strategies to guide proposed changes to historic places. The proposals may concern individual places or collective groups of places.

The first step in this process is to gain a thorough understanding of the historic place, an activity that forms the foundation of heritage planning.[1] This investigation reveals not only so-called 'objective' and technical data (both socio-historical and physical), but also the stories and the values that are associated with the place. The data and the values together enable us to understand the meaning of the place and to make an assessment of its cultural heritage significance. This in turn provides the basis for making informed decisions as to the management of change to the historic place, a process that is addressed in Chapter 5.

This progression from identification to evaluation to management is the basis for policies in many countries. As an example, the Monuments Protection Programme (MPP) of English Heritage, established in 1986, outlines a three-stage process:

1 To identify the resource: what is there?
2 To evaluate the resource: how relatively important are the sites?
3 To consider what protection should be given to them (Schofield 2000: 78).

The need to understand the historic place and use the information to determine significance before doing anything else is rooted in the international conservation charters. Australia's *Burra Charter* set the standard:

> The cultural significance of a place and other issues affecting its future are best understood by a sequence of collecting and analysing information before making decisions. Understanding cultural significance comes first, then development of policy and finally management of the place in accordance with the policy. (Article 6.1)

Remaining mindful that understanding the historic place is a means to an end—the end is its appropriate management—English heritage consultant Jo Cox writes that the aim of recording is to search for the 'quiddity or essence' of a historic place, which is found by

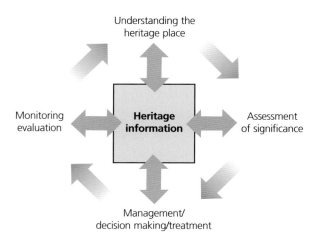

'sorting for sameness'—i.e., discovering the broader context of a place through comparisons to other places—and 'sorting for difference'—i.e., revealing the aspects that make a place unique. She continues: 'Finding quiddity [essence] is simply the act of defining, as clearly as possible, what the building or site actually is, what it means and therefore what there is to conserve' (Cox 1996: 123–5).

The Getty Conservation Institute defines 'heritage information' as 'the integrated activities of recording, documentation, and information management.' It reminds the reader that heritage information is required 'because access to accurate and concise information is the basis for conservation planning.' The use and flow of heritage information is illustrated in Figure 4.1. Heritage information begins with 'understanding the heritage [historic] place' and ends with 'management/decision making/treatment' (Letellier 2007: 11–13).

Heritage information—the data that is collected throughout the conservation process—must be recorded, documented, and made retrievable. A wide variety of digital and manual information systems is available for this purpose.

Understanding the historic place is a process that involves several inquiries:

Research
- Historical research
- Physical investigation
- Community engagement

Evaluation
- Identify heritage values
- Determine significance.

This chapter provides an overview of each of the steps. The steps are indicated in the process chart for understanding the historic place (Figure 4.2, which is repeated here from Figure 1.3). The number within each box indicates the section of the text in which the subject is discussed.

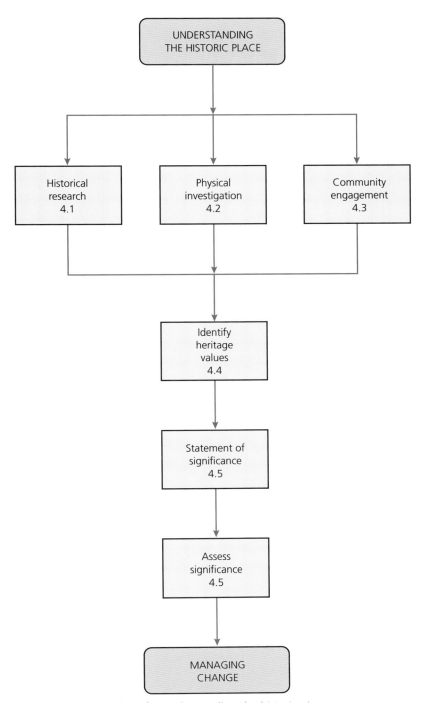

Figure 4.2 Process chart for understanding the historic place.

The importance of proper and careful research and physical investigation in making informed decisions—and the necessity that these practices not be cut out of the budget—have been emphasized by English-Australian heritage administrator and consultant Kate Clark. She has described examples of poor decisions that were based on poor information, and concludes that 'the better you understand a historic building or site, the easier it is to make decisions about it'; and also that good information makes it easier to change a building. She emphasizes that 'understanding is the bedrock of conservation' and 'without understanding, conservation is blind and meaningless' (2001: 8; 2010: 5–10).

4.1 Historical Research

The nature of historical research

Research is the process of investigating sources in order to bring to light the history of a place. Its purpose is to understand the circumstances under which the historic place was built, used, and modified over time, as well as the ways in which people have used and thought of the place. It is not enough simply to describe the appearance and determine the chronology. A history of a place must address the broader physical environment and context. It should make comparisons with other places and include a critical analysis that determines its values.

The history should be sufficiently thorough to convey important material and analyses, but only long enough to serve the purposes of the conservation initiative. It is not intended as an independent publication or a doctoral thesis. A chronology may be added as well, since it is useful for quick reference.

Heritage planners should have easy access to historians—whether the skills reside in themselves, their colleagues, or contracted professionals—and sufficient budget to fund professional-level research to an appropriate level.

History and some of its branches

History is the study of the human past—of its events, its players, its places, and the outcomes of their interactions. History interprets the past in the context of the present day. As an academic discipline, history has a place in both the social sciences and the humanities. It may be further categorized as social, cultural, political, or economic history, but good history generally addresses all sectors of human endeavor. Academic history is analytical and critical in that the historian seeks to identify the causes and effects of human actions. The field has been well established for centuries. It relies to a large extent on documentary sources. History is taught in most universities and is represented by many professional societies. In recent decades its areas of interest have expanded considerably to include labor history, women's history, and many other subjects. **Chronology** is history without the analytical component. A chronology is a sequence of events, which is useful to obtain a basic understanding of the evolution of a historic place. Until the twentieth century, history took a chronological approach, focusing on major events. Historians believed that if they collected enough data, the truth would reveal itself. History now goes well beyond the 'facts' by interpreting the past, attempting to understand the thoughts and motives of the players.

Public history is 'applied history,' practiced in public agencies and private contexts outside the academic arena. It is more pragmatic than academic history, and is often identified with heritage conservation, museums, and archives. A key objective of public history is that the results should be 'accessible and useful to the public.' Public history is a relatively new subdiscipline, which developed largely under the initiative of the US National Park Service. It has been taught in the US since the 1970s and in other countries more recently. Public history has its professional associations, such as the US-based National Council on Public History, whose purpose is 'to promote the utility of history in society through professional practice' and which publishes *The Public Historian* (Howe 1989; Anonymous 2007, cited in Wikipedia n.d.-e).

Archaeology is the study of the human past through the investigation and analysis of its physical remains (what we call 'material culture'). It adds a physical dimension to history. Archaeology is primarily interested in recovering and interpreting human behavior of the past, whereas heritage conservation generally is concerned with the future of historic places (Sprinkle 2003: 253). A key dimension of archaeological analysis is time—understanding *when* the various remains were produced. The remains may include artifacts, vestiges of buildings, cultural landscapes, and other evidence that was created by the culture(s) being studied. In recent decades the examination of environmental and biological evidence has enriched the available sources. In North America and Australia archaeology focuses on Indigenous peoples, particularly before European contact, and is often thought of (and taught) as a subdiscipline of anthropology. Other specializations include historical archaeology, which looks at the early remains of current societies; industrial archaeology, which is interested in the industrial past; and underwater (or maritime) archaeology, which investigates remains preserved beneath the waters (e.g., shipwrecks). In the US, archaeology whose purpose is interpreting the heritage for the general public is often called 'public archaeology' (Little 2009: 29–51). Archaeology is taught widely and is represented by many public associations and periodicals.[2]

Architectural history is a discipline that uses the methods of both historical and architectural investigation to investigate the history of architecture, usually considered to include the history of landscape architecture and urban history. Historical analysis addresses the people, places, and events associated with buildings or communities; architectural analysis looks at the forms, materials, and styles of the buildings. The **history of styles** is one product of architectural history; it satisfies the natural urge to classify things and has been the subject of countless studies. The history of styles is to architectural history as chronology is to history—a somewhat superficial treatment that enables quick comprehension. Education in architectural history involves learning historical methods as well as techniques of architectural analysis. Most English-speaking countries have a journal produced by their national societies of architectural historians, including *Fabrications* in Australia and New Zealand, *Architectural History* in the UK, the *Journal of the Society of Architectural Historians* in the US, and *Architecture in Canada*.

Research sources

The historical researcher (who may or may not be a professional historian) will draw on a variety of sources in libraries, archives, and other repositories. These sources may include some or all of:

- Previous documentation of the historic place
- Books and articles in print and online
- Reports and studies
- Newspapers
- Site descriptions
- Interviews and oral history
- Correspondence
- Directories and gazetteers
- Fire insurance atlases/maps
- Photographs and aerial photographs
- Maps and bird's-eye views
- Drawings and sketches
- Building plans (which may be held by repositories or by the building owner)
- Tax assessments or tax rolls (called 'rate books' in the UK)
- Land title records.

In the past, unpublished materials were called 'primary sources' or 'documents' and published materials or reworked documents were called 'secondary sources.' However the distinction has blurred, particularly since the popularization of the Internet. A word of caution must be given with respect to Internet sources: because articles are infrequently peer-reviewed, their degree of reliability varies considerably.[3] The researcher should always exercise good critical judgment in deciding whether and how to use these sources.

Oral history comprises an important research source that must be properly respected. Formerly reserved by academics for folklore studies, oral history has now become a central component of public history.[4] In the context of heritage planning, oral information, particularly when it addresses community-based meanings of historic places, should be regarded as authoritative statements, subject to that same critical professional judgment. This has been put into law with respect to Aboriginal people, as the US delegates the authority for identifying Indian sacred sites to 'an Indian tribe, or Indian individual determined to be an appropriately authoritative representative of an Indian religion.'[5]

While certain sources may be more 'reliable' than others, no piece of evidence, however reliable, should be treated as an unchallengeable 'fact' or 'truth.' It is normal for various sources to appear to contradict each other. The historical disciplines are interpretive, in that the professional assesses the various sources and their context to make critical judgments that determine what happened in the past, why it happened, and what the impacts were. Sources should be documented, whether by means of footnotes, endnotes, bibliographies, and/or a bibliographical essay.[6]

This book does not provide instruction on how to conduct historical research or write historical reports. Many good introductions to researching historic places are available for consultation. They provide information on the kinds of sources that are available, what to expect to find in various repositories, and often how to interpret the data.[7]

Associations, stories, and interpretation

Research must go well beyond revealing the chronological data surrounding the construction, change, and use of a historic place. It should look at the stories and narratives associated with the place. The *Burra Charter* canonized the importance of this. Article 3.1 states: 'Conservation is based on a respect for the existing fabric, use, associations and meanings.' This is clarified somewhat in Articles 1.15–16:

Associations mean the connections that exist between people and a place.

Meanings denote what a place signifies, indicates, evokes or expresses to people.

The explanatory notes to the latter place it in a decidedly intangible context: 'Meanings generally relate to intangible dimensions such as symbolic qualities and memories.'

The importance of stories to heritage conservation is being increasingly appreciated. Ned Kaufman emphasizes what he calls 'story sites' and larger 'storyscapes.' He notes that places can be experienced in very different ways, including sensory perception—e.g., space, smell, and sound—and memory associations, thoughts, and feelings generated by our and others' previous encounters with the place. His own inclination is to emphasize the contributions of stories, social value, and intangible cultural heritage. He repeats the caution of New York architect Gene Norman that this position risks pushing the buildings out of the picture. Nevertheless, Kaufman writes that, with respect to heritage conservation: 'Its ultimate goal is not fixing or saving old things but rather creating places where people can live well and connect to meaningful narratives about history, culture, and identity' (2009: 1–3, 25–39).

If this perspective points to the future of conservation, then the core priorities of the discipline will have come full circle in little more than a century: from 'saving old things' with historical value (late nineteenth-century advocacy), to saving things with architectural value (early twentieth-century advocacy), to focusing on 'fixing old things' (*Venice Charter*), to valuing places for their social and spiritual associations (*Burra Charter*, 1999), and now once again to creating places with meaningful narratives—in other words, saving places with historical, social, and spiritual value.

The pendulum will never come to rest. For now, we accept that both intangible and tangible features are important to understanding historic places, and that research must investigate both the actualities and the associations. As will be seen in Section 4.5, the significance of the place is determined by synthesis of them. This is just one more case of the integration of streams formerly thought of as separate, as with sustainability.

Identifying stories and associations has a useful secondary outcome: it provides valuable material for interpreting the historic place. 'Interpretation' in this sense is a concept articulated in the mid-twentieth century. Its first champion was naturalist Freeman Tilden of the US National Park Service. He defined interpretation:

> Thousands of naturalists, historians, archeologists and other specialists are engaged in the work of revealing, to such visitors as desire the service, something of the beauty and wonder, the inspiration and spiritual meaning that lie behind what the visitor can with his senses perceive. This function of the custodians of our treasures is called Interpretation.
>
> (Tilden 1977: 3–4)[8]

One of Tilden's six principles of interpretation is that 'Information, as such, is not Interpretation. Interpretation is revelation based upon information' (p. 9). Interpretation is to information as history is to chronology and as architectural history is to the history of styles.

Historic places long provided visitors with information—basic site data such as names, dates, and architectural styles—usually placed on plaques or signboards. Staff would tell people information about the things they were seeing. Only since Tilden's time, however, has communicating broader narratives in captivating ways that enhance the visitor experience been a central consideration of site management.

The *Burra Charter* states the purposes of interpretation: 'The cultural significance of many places is not readily apparent, and should be explained by interpretation. Interpretation should enhance understanding and engagement, and be culturally appropriate' (Article 25).

Most interpreters and interpretive planners describe their work as 'storytelling.' This approach is seen at historic places that have been (re-)interpreted in recent years. At the Tower of London, for example, the online promotion features 'history and stories':

> Explore the wonders of this awesome fortress, and the stories behind them.

Figure 4.3 Interpretation at the Tower of London includes the effective dramatizations of stories. Here the Prince of Wales complains about his treatment as a prisoner in the Tower, while his jailer stands in the background. (Photo: Harold Kalman)

Discover for yourself some of the Tower's sights and stories, whether you're planning your visit or just wanting to learn more about this iconic palace and its history.

(Historic Royal Palaces n.d.)

A visit to the Tower reveals a variety of interpretive media, including conventional panels, interactive electronic stations, and live dramatizations, all of which contribute to understanding the historic place.

The heritage planner must become aware of the interpretive potential of historic places, seeking ways to tell stories and relate associations. Identifying opportunities for interpreting a historic place should be a key consideration in the conservation plan.

4.2 Physical Investigation

Physical investigation complements historical research. Each informs the other. The site investigation looks at, records (or documents), and analyzes the physical characteristics of the historic place.

The depth of investigation should be appropriate to the scale of the historic place, the scope of the intervention, and the available resources. At a minimum the level of detail should be sufficient to understand thoroughly the material evolution of the place.

Physical investigation may involve as-found recording, as-built recording, surveys and inventories of groups of places, archaeological investigation, or a combination. The text that follows provides an overview of the various kinds of investigation, recording methods, and outputs, including their relevance to heritage planning. It also looks at some of the tools that are used. It addresses specific ways of looking at different kinds of historic places, so that the heritage planner may understand the procedures in a general way. A full consideration of investigation methods and techniques belongs with descriptions of conservation architecture, conservation landscape architecture, and archaeology, and is not treated here in detail.

As-found recording

As-found recording, also called **site recording**, **extant recording**, and **surveying**, documents the design, configuration, materials, structure, site, and immediate environment of a historic place before making a conservation intervention. If physical evidence of its previous state(s) is detected, these are recorded as well. The data comprise a key component of the information required to manage change in an informed manner, providing a record of the historic place for posterity and a baseline for measuring change. The act of recording the place becomes a part of the site's history.

The sequel to as-found recording is **as-built recording**, creating a record of the work done in a conservation intervention.

The need for documentation in all phases was stipulated in the *Venice Charter*:

> In all works of preservation, restoration or excavation, there should always be precise documentation in the form of analytical and critical reports, illustrated with drawings and photographs. Every stage of the work … should be included. (Article 16)

The recording is usually undertaken by an architect and/or engineer in North America, and by a chartered building surveyor in the UK and other Commonwealth countries.[9] Other specialists, such as experts in historic materials or landscape, may assist them.

Site recording developed as a skilled profession in the eighteenth century, when Northern European (primarily British) antiquarians and architects visited Italy and Greece and brought back exquisite drawings of classical remains, which were often published as large collectors' folios.

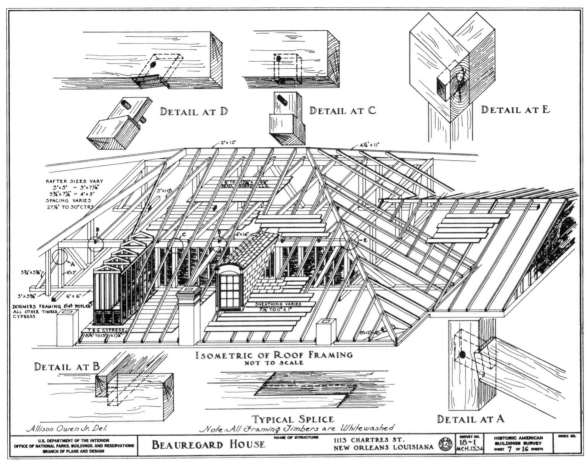

Figure 4.4 A HABS drawing (1934) of the attic of Beauregard House, New Orleans. It explains the structure with a cutaway isometric and details (some 'exploded') of connections. (Historic American Buildings Survey, Library of Congress)

Many countries have developed standards for the documentation of historic places. The US led the way with the Historic American Buildings Survey (HABS), which was founded in 1933 as a job-creation program during the Great Depression and continues today (Burns 2004). HABS was subsequently extended to include engineering structures, with the Historic American Engineering Record (HAER); and landscapes, with the Historic American Landscape Survey (HALS). HABS/HAER standards and guidelines are found in the *Secretary of the Interior's Standards for Architectural and Engineering Documentation* (Burns 2004; National Park Service 1983, revised).[10]

Other organizations have developed standards as well. Examples are the documentation standards for historic buildings, archaeological sites, and cultural objects prepared for the Council of Europe, Getty Information Institute, and European Foundation for Heritage Skills (Thornes and Bold 1998).

The basic method of recording buildings, structures, and landscapes differs little from that used over the centuries, although media and technologies have changed greatly. Recorders produce measured drawings, whether using a tape measure, infrared or laser measuring device, or one of the photogrammetric methods described below. Typical products include formal drawings, sketches, photographs, and field notes. All can be produced digitally or manually.[11] The process for archaeological investigation is somewhat different and involves identifying areas for study, examining the remains, and understanding the meaning of the discoveries. Artifacts may hold more interest for the information they reveal about their creators' culture than for their inherent value. The principal activities are survey, excavation, recording, and recovery (or backfill).

Specialized recording techniques

Many techniques provide information on structures and sites. A selection is described here so that a heritage planner may understand the various methods by which information is gathered and grasp the breadth (and limitations) of the recording discipline.[12]

The first stage of physical investigation should be **non-destructive investigation**, which does not require opening, damaging, or destroying historic fabric or plant materials, nor excavating into the ground. Large-scale, non-destructive investigation, often used in archaeological surveys, is called **remote sensing**. The following methods are all non-destructive.

Survey tools

A number of tools and technologies are used to survey objects and landscapes, supplementing but by no means supplanting the traditional tape measure and camera. Key among them are:

- **Laser measuring device**: Useful for determining the interior dimensions of a building.
- **Theodolite**: Theodolites are key tools for producing site plans, whether for archaeology, architecture, or landscape. They measure angles, allowing positions to be coordinated with the application of trigonometry. Theodolites have been used by surveyors for centuries.

Photography and scanning

- **Photogrammetry**: This comprises various forms of recording, both film-based and digital, which enable taking measurements directly from photographs or, with appropriate software, plotting drawings directly from photographs. Specialized 'metric cameras' virtually eliminate distortion and provide accurate scaling. **Monophotogrammetry** uses a single camera. **Stereophotogrammetry** uses two cameras to take stereo pairs of images (a method that originated in the 1850s). The output can be scaled in three dimensions. Objects concealed by vegetation or fixed objects are not captured and must be recorded separately.

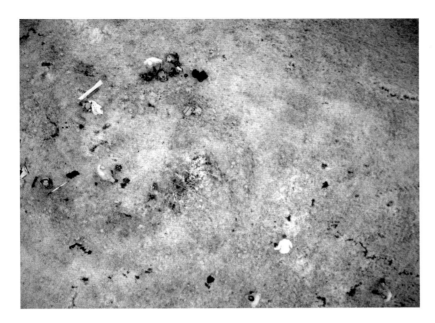

Figure 4.5 An infrared kite thermograph of the site at Ogilface Castle, West Lothian, Scotland, shows features not visible to the naked eye. To get a sense of scale, note the people near the lower right corner. (Dr. John and Rosie Wells)

- **Rectified photography** keeps the picture plane (film or sensors) parallel to the primary surface being recorded. This eliminates (or vastly reduces) perspective distortion and foreshortening. Alternatively, the photographic image can be manipulated in the darkroom or with software. A scale is included on the photograph, enabling dimensions to be measured with reasonable accuracy.[13]
- **Aerial photography**, **aerial photogrammetry**, and **aerial stereophotogrammetry** provide site plans for archaeological surveys, to record large districts, and for mapping. Most aerial photography is taken from airplanes and satellites. At closer range, cameras can be mounted on kites to take low-altitude images of specific sites. When a global positioning system (GPS) is used, locations and distances can be determined with considerable accuracy.
- **Thermography** (or **thermal imaging**, **infrared photography**) records heat distribution within the infrared spectrum across the surface of an object, often a building wall or roof. A common application is in building maintenance, to determine leaks in thermal insulation or accumulations of water. Thermography can detect voids and irregularities in walls, suggesting variations in construction that are not visible to the eye. Aerial thermography is useful in archaeological investigations.
- **Laser scanning** (or **3D scanning**): Objects are scanned with multiple laser pulses, which enable their shapes to be determined accurately in three dimensions. Many different laser technologies are in use. As with photography, concealed objects are not captured.
- **LiDAR** (Light Detection and Ranging) uses a laser beam transmitted from a device carried aloft in an airplane or helicopter. The time that the laser beams take to cover the distance and be reflected

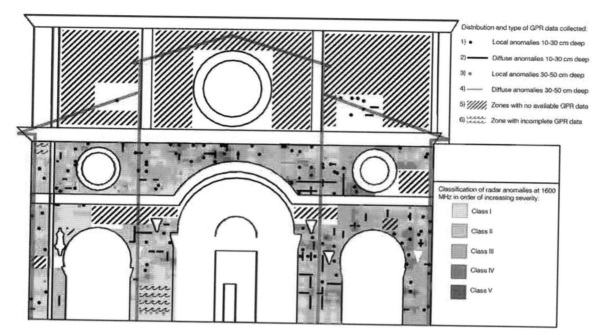

Figure 4.6 A GPR survey of the façade of the Basilica of Santa Maria di Collemaggio in L'Aquila, Italy, reveals multiple anomalies in the wall. Careful interpretation identifies these as voids, cracks, and variations in thickness. This enabled a detailed treatment plan for re-establishing the internal cohesion of the wall. (From Eppich and Chabbi 2007, used with permission of Marco Tallini and the J. Paul Getty Trust)

back is calculated. The product is a detailed three-dimensional topographical map. Enough beams can pass through gaps in trees to detect subtle differences in surface elevation, even in a jungle. The technique was developed in the 1960s and was used to map the moon's surface in 1971 (Evans 2013: 60–3; Otis 2013: F5).

- **Ground-penetrating radar** (**GPR**, or **impulse radar**) sends electromagnetic waves into the ground (or into a structure) and measures changes in wave velocity as the energy pulses pass from one material to another. It reveals subsurface variations to the depth of several feet, deeper than thermography. Archaeologists use GPR to detect buried objects. The technique is useful for architectural investigation as well, revealing structural anomalies, hidden structural features, voids, and metallic components. Since the images do not identify the detected materials, they require careful interpretation.
- **X-ray investigation** (**radiography**) also 'sees' beneath the surface. It is useful in more restricted applications than radar.
- **Impact echo** (**dynamic impedance**, **stress-wave transmission**) calculates the depths and condition of large bodies of homogeneous, solid material, such as concrete. The object is impacted mechanically and the vibrations are measured. An anomalous response may reveal a defect.
- **Ultrasound** (**sonography**) reveals information similar to that of impact echo.

Destructive investigation (intrusive investigation) may be required when non-destructive techniques are insufficient or inconclusive. It is necessary when a knowledge of substrates (whether buildings or archaeological sites) is needed to determine physical properties, condition, and/or the sequence of states. The investigator should disturb or remove as little as is feasible and, with structures, ideally from an area that is not commonly in view.

- Samples of materials in buildings may be removed to be **tested** for strength or otherwise analyzed in the laboratory; or paint may be removed to determine the sequence of colors (**paint analysis** or **chromochronology**).
- Samples may be taken to estimate the age of materials. The methods include **dendrochronology**, which determines the age of wood by analyzing tree rings; and **radiocarbon dating** (or **carbon dating**), which calculates the decay of Carbon 14, an unstable isotope of carbon. The latter can estimate the age of organic remains from ancient archaeological sites.
- Small openings can reveal the nature and condition of wall or floor assemblies. Assemblies are inspected with a **borescope** (or **boroscope**), a fibre-optic cable attached to a light source and inserted through a small hole. The technology was developed for medical examinations.
- **Excavation** of archaeological sites is a destructive technique, since it disturbs the ground and often disturbs buried remains as well.

For individual historic places (e.g., buildings and structures) four other characteristics may be recorded, depending upon the situation:

- **Structure**: The documentation may address the structure and how it behaves. This may be done descriptively, by illustrating the structural members and their connections, and perhaps supplemented by testing the strength of the materials. An engineer can then calculate the loads and capacities, and comment on the performance of the structure. In more complex situations, this may be done analytically, with computer-generated diagrams that model the stresses within structural components. A problem is that few engineers have been trained to analyze preindustrial materials and building systems, such as arches, vaults, domes, and unreinforced masonry, and most current building codes are incapable of assessing their strength or safety.[14]
- **Condition**: A condition report may comprise part of the physical investigation or building survey, or may be undertaken as a separate activity. The work is usually the responsibility of an architect, engineer, surveyor, landscape architect, and/or materials specialist. In the UK a condition report usually comprises the focus of a building survey, which has been defined as 'a comprehensive, critical, detailed and formal inspection of a building to determine its condition, and [financial] value' (Watt and Swallow 1996: 3, citing Nelson 1994: 1). A condition report records the present condition of the historic place—i.e., the state of deterioration of its various components, be they inorganic (i.e., many components of a building or structure) or organic (a landscape). It may also specify what must be done to return the place to a state of stability.

- **Integrity**: The integrity of a historic place refers to its wholeness or intactness. It and the closely related term 'authenticity' are discussed in Section 4.4.
- **Vulnerability**: This is a measure of the degree of risk to the condition and/or the continued existence of the historic place. The risk may emanate from any of a number of sources, such as damage caused by the forces of nature acting to worsen deterioration, threats from armed conflict, intended demolition or inappropriate change, or wear and tear from excessive visitor use. Vulnerability is also a consideration with collective historic places, treated next.

Collective historic places: Cultural landscapes and conservation areas

Because cultural landscapes and conservation areas integrate built features and the land, both should be recorded. Topography, geology, ecology, landscape features, and archaeological remains should all be described (McClelland et al. 1999).[15]

A description of the distinctive **character** of conservation areas and cultural landscapes is helpful. This is a challenging task that is generally presented both verbally and graphically. The British have a long history of character assessment and are particularly skilled at it.[16] Observations should be made as well as to the condition, integrity, and vulnerability of the place (Menuge 2010: 10–13).

Once a cultural landscape or conservation area has been identified and a preliminary survey (see below) undertaken, it becomes necessary to define its boundaries, so as to define precisely what properties will be subject to any controls and eligible for incentives that may ensue. The place should be unified by common historical, social, thematic, or visual characteristics. A consideration will be given to 'edge factors,' such as historic or natural boundaries, constraints such as waterways

Figure 4.7 This agricultural landscape in Swaledale, North Yorkshire, England, shows the importance of considering natural features, land use, field systems, and buildings holistically when recording cultural landscapes. (Freddie Phillips)

and railways, topographical features, concentrations of key resources, potential buffer zones, and political jurisdictions (Wright 1976; Tyler and Ward 2011: 122; Page et al. 1998: 39).

The limits of the area should be mapped. Numerous methods, both manual and digital, are available. Digitization can be enhanced by locating elements by means of a global positioning system (GPS) and/or plotting maps with a geographical information system (GIS) (Box 1999).

Surveys and inventories

The first level of documentation is usually a survey or inventory—two terms that describe an 'organized recording of information.' Some surveys are conducted by or for government and achieve official, perhaps statutory, status, whereas others may be prepared by local historical societies or other volunteer groups wanting to contribute to understanding and conserving places.[17]

The purposes of surveys vary. Some record large numbers of historic places that are considered to have heritage significance, and therefore may be considered for regulatory control. Others collect data on individual resources within a conservation area, cultural landscape, or archaeological site. Still others are intended to document places for public information, future research, and posterity.

The parameters of a survey should be defined at the outset. The factors to be considered include the extent, intended use, information management system, and resources. A survey of the exteriors of a few dozen buildings and their landscapes within a small urban conservation area will occur at a very different scale from an ongoing national register of tens (or even hundreds) of thousands of places. And any particular type of survey may be done at different levels of intensity. The dozens of urban properties, for example, might be surveyed quickly as a step in determining whether or not to proceed with studies to determine whether to protect the proposed conservation area; or it might be done more thoroughly, in order to identify precisely what should be controlled by the legislation.[18]

Depending on the parameters, the effort often proceeds from desk-based research to fieldwork, which in turn may be supplemented by additional documentary research that responds to uncertainties that the fieldwork has revealed.

The data are typically entered on a form that has been designed for that survey. If the field survey is being done manually, the recording sheet will be designed to accommodate the information that is being collected, and no more, with one form used for each place. The same data fields can be used if input is made with a handheld digital device. The quick, relatively superficial survey of buildings in a potential conservation area can often be done on a single page or screen, whereas the statutory survey that supports legislation may require far more data.

The text of the project report will describe the methodology used for the survey. The information collected often includes data under some or all of the following headings:

- Identification
- Location
- Type/use of historic place
- Description
- Historical information: chronology and themes
- Significance
- Heritage recognition, if any
- Illustration(s)
- Sources (supporting documentation)
- Name of recorder and date of the survey record.

Some surveys also include information on the potential for conservation and reuse, but this should more properly be included in a subsequent conservation plan (see Section 5.8). Surveys record the current situation; plans describe a proposal for the future.

The windshield survey

A preliminary survey is often called a **windshield survey** (or **windscreen survey** or **screening** or **cursory screening**). It provides an overview of an area that contains multiple resources, often as seen from the convenience and efficiency of a car. The objective is to compile an initial list of individual places within the area, to compile sufficient data with which to make a preliminary assessment as to whether the area and/or the individual resources deserve more intensive future study. The conventional wisdom is that a skilled pair of eyes will detect the resources that have special merit.

English Heritage calls this an Outline Assessment (Level 1), the least detailed of three levels of historic area assessment. It explains:

> No systematic documentary research will be undertaken, but a limited number of secondary sources may be referred to. Typically an area of several square kilometers will be examined in a day, and a short illustrated report can be quickly produced.

> The guidance notes assert that outline assessments are not superficial and that 'they make heavy demands on the experience and judgment of the assessors.'

> (Menuge 2010: 16–17)

This method may be valid when the purpose of the windshield survey is simply to determine the dominant character(s) of the area, or when time is of the essence because the work responds to an immediate threat. However, the reasoning becomes seriously flawed when the purpose is to select the individual places that will be included in a subsequent, more detailed inventory—a common situation. It is flawed because a windshield survey relies solely on visual evidence—on the external appearance of a building, landscape feature, or other place as seen from the public roadway. The only direct data gleaned from a windshield survey are visual and aesthetic qualities, the character of the larger context, and guesses as to condition and integrity. Anything else is merely inferred. Yet the surveyor implicitly expects this limited perspective to suffice in determining whether or not a place may possess more comprehensive heritage significance. The cursory screening creates an initial list (and rejects all places that don't make the cut) without the benefit of either historical research or community input, both of which are required to collect information about content, meanings, and associations.

For an initial screening to provide useful and reliable data from which to generate a more detailed inventory, it must be compiled from a variety of perspectives. This includes historical research on the area, its residents, and past events, in order to understand the key themes and trends over time and to determine the places where important things happened and which are important to the community. Another key source is interviews with knowledgeable informants who will provide parallel data orally. A third is a more careful look-about *after* the other two have been done, in order to gain a real understanding of a multi-dimensional historic place and the land. Only then can the initial list have any degree of authority. Otherwise the one-dimensional, preliminary, windshield survey will, in effect, have more authority than a future, in-depth inventory.

4.3 Community Engagement

Until the last generation or two, it was 'professional experts' who shaped our knowledge of historic places and told us what to preserve. This now outdated perspective is made patently clear, for example, in the *Venice Charter*. Whereas historical research and physical investigation undertaken by heritage professionals do indeed reveal many characteristics and values associated with a historic place, their inquiries reveal only some of the values—those that emerge from the technical interpretation of documentary records, physical fabric, and environmental context.

Many other values associated with historic places are felt and expressed by the community. We have come to appreciate that the opinions of people who are not experts in the heritage field are essential to gain a full understanding of the historic place. As has been seen, the *Burra Charter* states that 'conservation is based on a respect for the existing fabric, use, associations and meanings' (Article 3), and so we need a way to identify the associations and meanings that society gives to the places from the past.

Going beyond the *Burra Charter*, recent definitions of heritage emphasize the importance of intangible associations, stories, and meanings. Several authors—many of them Australian—even consider them more important than the physical fabric. In the view of Denis Byrne, for example, the values and meanings of historic places are found in communities and individuals, rather than in the places themselves. He further proposes that cultural heritage is a field of social action.

Therefore the full meaning of places and their larger social, cultural, and political context can be learned only by listening to people who are familiar with them (Byrne et al. 2003).

These intangible values are obtained by a process of **community engagement** (also described by many other terms, including **public consultation**, **stakeholder consultation**, **public participation**, **public engagement**, and **community action planning**). An active program of community engagement yields many benefits. Foremost is the opportunity to learn at first hand what people think about a historic place. This usually provides information on beliefs, passions, attachments, experiences, and values. In addition members of the public often have historical data, personal anecdotes, and visual observations made over the years, which supplements the information gleaned through documentary research and physical investigation.

Consultation with the community may serve several distinct purposes. The first is to learn what people value and therefore believe should be preserved. Another is to understand aspects of the historic place that might otherwise go unnoticed. And a third is to hear and assess the public's reactions, concerns, and conflicting opinions with respect to plans for change. While the first two address the meaning of a historic place and the last addresses reactions to an intended management action, the methods for learning the community's thoughts are similar for all. All are therefore treated together.

Stakeholders and techniques

The kinds of stakeholders who are typically consulted include the owner and/or manager of the historic place, elected officials in the local government, historical and community societies, members of the local business association, neighborhood residents, and representatives of the educational, recreational, and tourism sectors. Equally important are the thoughts of people with no formal affiliation, but with an interest in or knowledge of the place and the issues.

Public consultation should occur at various stages of the heritage planning process. It may take several forms, such as individual interviews, group interviews, public meetings and open houses, workshops and 'charrettes,' visioning sessions, focus groups ('citizens' juries'), and participation games. A variety of published and online methods, including responsive publications, places or websites that display detailed information, social media, surveys and other web-based tools, are used as well. For face-to-face consultation to be effective, whether with a large group or one-on-one, it is important that the facilitator communicates well, listen carefully, make it clear that (s)he has heard what has been said, seek agreement, and indicate what will be done with the information (Nissley and King 2014; Sanoff 2000; Sobchak 2012: 15).

The heritage planning team may be able to conduct these sessions, but sometimes it is desirable to obtain specialist assistance from a professional facilitator or communications consultant with well-honed skills in order to ensure productive and constructive sessions. Many professional facilitators belong to dedicated organizations, such as the International Association for Public Participation (IAP2).

At a later stage in the planning process, the public should be invited to attend interim presentations of the proposed actions, in order to elicit comment and feedback. This in turn will reveal additional community values.

The full program of community engagement (often called a **communications plan**) should be designed at the outset of the planning process. Traditionally a municipality would act as a mediator between the public and a proponent (such as a developer) by facilitating participatory activities, but the proponent is now increasingly taking on the engagement process. One must remember that, in addition to being the most direct and open way of hearing community values and concerns, meaningful public consultation represents an important investment in obtaining consensus and acceptance of a conservation proposal. In this regard it is impossible to separate the research aspect from the more political considerations.

At a political level, involvement of the community will alleviate concerns of exclusion and help decision-makers make informed choices. Public participation has long been used by elected officials. Politicians rely on consultation, public hearings, and other kinds of open meetings to supplement the technical advice provided by their professional staff. Heritage planning is now adopting this time-proven democratic approach.

Diverse perspectives

In the 1960s American planner Paul Davidoff shocked his profession by declaring that planners should consult not only members of mainstream society, but also those who are more marginalized. He wrote:

> A planner shall seek to expand choice and opportunity for all persons, recognizing a special responsibility to plan for the needs of disadvantaged groups and persons, and shall urge the alteration of policies, institutions, and decisions which mitigate against such objectives.
>
> (Davidoff 1965: 331–8, cited in Checkoway 1994: 139)

Advocacy planning, as this approach came to be known, took planning out of the exclusive hands of the planning 'experts' and gave a meaningful voice to the people, including those on the edges of society. Social equity, pluralism, and inclusivity were common themes at the time, particularly in the US, where the civil rights movement and its advocacy of equality for African-Americans were reaching their peak. African-Americans were moving to large cities, where they were concentrated in the central ghetto areas, which were threatened with massive urban renewal. Davidoff urged planners to work for social change at a time when leading planners conceded that social and economic problems were beyond their expertise (Checkoway 1994: 139–43).

Davidoff's plea was heard. Advocacy planning achieved widespread support, and far beyond the US It may be remembered from Section 2.2 that the plan to rehabilitate central Bologna for the working classes and low-income groups was adopted in 1960 and approved by the Italian government in 1965. However, as English-American sociologist and planner Peter Marris has observed, over time the practice became more a bridge between professional planning and political engagement than a direct podium for the disadvantaged (Marris 1994: 143–6).

The participation of non-experts and listening to the voices of marginalized groups have become normal practice not only with urban planning, but also with heritage planning. Consultation that seeks out demographics beyond the mainstream community is good conservation practice as well as good politics. The *Burra Charter*, as we have seen, states that 'places may have a range of values for different individuals or groups' and instructs planners to engage with these groups:

> Conservation, interpretation and management of a place should provide for the participation of people for whom the place has significant associations and meanings, or who have social, spiritual or other cultural responsibilities for the place. (Article 12)

Often a number of different cultural, ethnic, or racial groups will hold these 'significant associations and meanings,' and the opinions and feelings of one group may well differ from those of another. The need to identify diverse community values in order to understand a historic place reflects a larger change, by which we understand history by examining the actions of ordinary people and members of cultural or racial minorities, and not only those of the 'leaders' of mainstream society.[19]

Diversity of opinion is respected in site management as well as planning, as the *Burra Charter* recommends. Randall Mason, whom we shall meet in the next section as a key proponent of values-centred conservation, argues for 'values-centred management' of historic places. The primary purpose is protecting the heritage significance of the place, in part by accommodating 'the diversity of interest groups with a stake in their protection' and by 'understanding and acknowledging the different stakeholder interests.' He reports that this has been achieved in the protection and interpretation of the former penal colony of Port Arthur, Tasmania (Mason 2008: 180–96).

In some countries the government has a legislated obligation to consult with Aboriginal peoples. For example, in the US, federal executive departments and agencies 'shall consult, to the greatest extent practicable and to the extent permitted by law, with Tribal governments prior to taking actions that affect Federally recognized Tribal governments.'[20]

Canadian heritage professional Alastair Kerr relates the story of a multi-party conflict that arose when a homeowner unintentionally disturbed a rich archaeological midden (refuse heap) when excavating for a basement addition and found human remains. An archaeologist

Figure 4.8 The ruins and grounds of the former penal colony at Port Arthur in Tasmania, Australia, is recognized as a cultural landscape and operated under principles of values-based management. (Andrew Braithwaite)

confirmed that the remains were prehistoric and recommended a full archaeological assessment. The local First Nation, the traditional owner of the land, wanted the bones reinterred and insisted that the site should not be disturbed, whether by construction or archaeology. Three conflicting sets of values emerged: the property owner (and his neighbors) wanted to enjoy the use of privately owned land, the archaeologists wanted to glean scientific information from the midden, and the Aboriginal people did not want human remains to be disturbed because of their spiritual importance. Insufficient community engagement aggravated the situation. In retrospect Kerr regretted government's inadequate response and suggested that it should have funded a proper dispute-resolution process (Kerr 1999).

4.4 Heritage Values

The previous sections discuss ways of understanding a historic place by means of research, site documentation, and speaking to representatives of the community. However, even after compiling and analyzing the information, many key questions remain unanswered, such as:

- What is the heritage significance of the historic place?
- Is the place significant enough to merit formal recognition and protection?

Determining significance is an essential activity in conservation planning. Methods have been developed for doing this in a way in which the outcome will be respected as authoritative. This is a two-part process:

- Identify the values attached to the historic place.
- Determine the significance of the historic place.

'Value' and 'significance,' although often used interchangeably, have somewhat different meanings:

- **Value** is a characteristic that is valued.
- **Significance** is a synthesis of those values.[21]

This section describes how to identify the values associated with historic places. Section 4.5 explains how to determine significance.

Understanding value

The *Burra Charter* provides a good introduction to understanding the heritage value of a historic place. Article 1.2 defines the values that make up cultural significance:

- Cultural significance means aesthetic, historic, scientific, social or spiritual value for past, present or future generations.
- Cultural significance is embodied in the place itself, its fabric, setting, use, associations, meanings, records, related places and related objects.
- Places may have a range of values for different individuals or groups.[22]

The choice of aesthetic, historic, scientific, and social or spiritual values derives from a long history of identifying the values of historic places. In *The Seven Lamps of Architecture* (1849), English art critic John Ruskin provided seven 'lamps,' or guiding principles—we would call them values—to illuminate the qualities of architecture: sacrifice, truth, power, beauty, life, memory, and obedience. Ruskin's follower, designer and writer William Morris (introduced in Section 3.1), identified five types of 'ancient buildings': artistic, picturesque, historical, antique, and substantial—types that were also implicitly values (1877). Ruskin and Morris both include what we now call **historical values** (Ruskin's 'memory' and Morris's 'historical') and **aesthetic values** ('beauty' and 'artistic,' respectively).

Austrian art historian Alois Riegl (1903, cited in Jokilehto 1999: 215–16) was the first to classify values in a rigorous way. He defined the values of conservation, placing them in two categories: the first group are **intrinsic values** that are inseparable from the place; the second are **temporal values** that relate to the present-day potential for conservation:

Intrinsic (memorial) values	*Temporal (present-day, contemporary) values*
Age	Use[23]
Historical	Art value
Commemorative ('intended memorial value')	Newness
	Relative art value

This was not just a theoretical exercise. Conservation advocates have always justified their actions with values such as these. Some have emphasized historical values: Andrew Green of the American Scenic and Historic Preservation Society insisted in 1895 that it is a 'duty' to preserve historic monuments because they 'quicken a spirit of patriotism.' Others stressed aesthetic values: William Sumner Appleton, a founder of the Society for the Preservation of New England Antiquities (1910; now called Historic New England), emphasized the need to preserve 'houses of superlative architectural interest' (Hosmer 1965: 261–2).

Historical and architectural values appear together in a mid-twentieth-century effort by the National Trust for Historic Preservation (1956: 3) to identify the values of historic buildings:

- Historical
- Architectural or landscape
- Suitability for use
- Educational
- Cost
- Administrative responsibility of sponsoring group.

The list contains both intrinsic/memorial values—historical, architectural or landscape, educational—and temporal/contemporary values—suitability for use, cost, and administrative responsibility. What we now call 'values' were then called 'criteria,' but to the same purpose.[24]

The American Society of Planning Officials (Miner 1969: 19–20) responded in 1969 with a similar list:

- Historic
- Architectural
- Setting
- Use
- Cost.[25]

Variants of these lists remain in use. The *Burra Charter* repeats them, although with minor changes. Its first three values are by now familiar: **aesthetic value** is essentially the same as architectural value, **historic value** remains unchanged,[26] and **scientific value** is another way of describing educational value. The important innovation in the *Burra Charter* is **social or spiritual value**, formerly defined in the Charter's explanatory notes as 'the qualities for which a place has become a focus of spiritual, political, national or other cultural sentiment to a majority or minority group' (Australia ICOMOS 2000: 12).

The *Burra Charter* (Article 1.2) declares the need to assess cultural significance 'for past, present or future generations.' In other words, **values change over time**. Society is constantly in the process of revising what it values. For example, today we recognize racism where earlier generations saw reasonableness. Canada has been preoccupied in recent years with apologizing for previous governments' actions that discriminated against particular cultural groups. These include the 'head tax' imposed on Chinese immigrants through much of the first half of the twentieth century; the mass internment of west-coast Japanese Canadians after the Japanese attack on Pearl Harbor; forcing Aboriginal children to attend church-run residential schools; and refusing to allow the landing of boats filled with immigrants seeking refuge. In some cases, the government has gone beyond apology ('redress') to offer financial compensation. Reconsiderations have resulted in revised interpretive messages that reflect today's changed values, and which have been communicated on historic plaques and interpretive programs.

Changes in value implicitly acknowledge the coexistence of what Alois Riegl called 'present-day' values, which are more societal and change considerably over time, and which are distinguished from 'memorial' values, which are mostly technical and remain relatively constant. The latter are best identified by professional specialists, such as historians, architectural historians, and archaeologists; the former are better expressed by interested, non-professional members of the community. This duality of sources differs totally from the *Venice Charter*, which relied only on Western specialists in architecture,

Figure 4.9 Sikhs from the Punjab aboard the *Komagata Maru* in Vancouver harbor in 1914. Most were denied entry into Canada, revealing the exclusionist values of the day. Those values have changed over time. In 2008 the Canadian government apologized to the Sikh community and provided funds for commemorating the incident. (Vancouver Public Library 121, Canadian Photo Company)

history, and archaeology, emphasizing 'the unity of human values' and declaring that a conservation intervention 'is a highly specialised operation' (Preamble and Article 9).

Considerations such as these increase the scope of where and how to look for values. A simple site visit, paired with research on the place, is clearly insufficient. A sufficient knowledge of the various uses of the place over time is needed. So too is familiarity with related places and objects (and their values), in order to be able to make meaningful comparisons and thereby to determine how effectively particular values are demonstrated in the primary historic place as compared to other places. An appreciation of the **meanings** of the place may be even more elusive: acquiring this certainly requires the insights and awareness of lay people, reinforcing the need for community engagement. Different community groups will likely express different meanings. In order to gain a properly nuanced understanding of a historic place and make management decisions that satisfy more than a single community of interest, the planning team must identify which people and groups value the place and then determine why they value it.

The *Burra Charter* (Article 1.2) also declares that: 'Places may have a range of values for different individuals or groups.' Values are relative, not absolute. Because of the social origins of values, it follows that different parties may hold different sets of values with respect to a historic place, or may assign different weight to the same values. In this respect, **values often conflict with one other**.

Two examples of attempts to resolve conflicting sets of values may be seen at Uluṟu in Australia (see text box) and the Audubon Ballroom in New York (see text box in Section 5.1).

Integrity and authenticity

Two concepts that contribute to understanding the value of historic places are the closely related notions of integrity and authenticity.

Integrity is a term frequently used although infrequently defined. It derives from the Latin 'integer,' which is usually translated as 'whole.' With respect to historic places, 'integrity' is understood to refer to completeness and lack of change from the original and/or a valued subsequent configuration(s).

The *Operational Guidelines* to the *World Heritage Convention* (UNESCO World Heritage Centre 2013: para. 88) define integrity: 'Integrity is a measure of the wholeness and intactness of the natural and/or cultural heritage and its attributes.'[28]

A historic place has integrity if it retains the features that possess cultural significance (i.e., the features that are character-defining elements). If the place has been compromised with changes that reduce or harm the cultural significance, then it has lost integrity. However, if changes made over the years have themselves acquired cultural significance, and those changes remain intact, then the place may still be considered to have integrity, even though it is not in its 'original' state. This is consistent with Article 11 of the *Venice Charter*,

(Do not) Climb Uluru

Uluru, the massive sandstone geological formation in Australia's Northern Territories formerly known as Ayers Rock and now a component of Uluru–Kata Tjuta National Park, a World Heritage Site, is traditionally owned by the Anangu people and managed by Australia's National Park Service. Some 400,000 people visit Uluru every year, despite its remote location.

   The various stakeholders assign it very different values. To the Aboriginal people, Uluru holds great spiritual value. They ask visitors not to climb the rock, partly because of the sacred ground crossed by the trail and partly out of their sense of responsibility for any injuries that might occur. Many international visitors, on the other hand, want to climb to the top, reflecting their recreational and scenic values. Torn between these conflicting sets of values, the owners and the managers agreed to post two signs side by side at the trailhead: one is titled 'We Don't Climb' and explains the Aboriginal point of view; and the other provides climbing instructions, posts climb opening and closing times, and warns of hazards along the trail. The visitor is expected to absorb both perspectives and make an informed decision as to what to do.[27]

Figure 4.10 Sign at the base of Uluru, presenting two conflicting sets of values: 'We Don't Climb' and 'Don't Risk Your Life' in the central panel and 'Climb Open & Closing Times' at the right. Climbers can be seen in the background. (Stefan Krasowski)

which states that 'the valid contributions of all periods to the building of a monument must be respected.' It is also consistent with Standard 10 of the Canadian *Standards and Guidelines*: 'Conserve changes to an historic place that, over time, have become character-defining elements in their own right.' The challenge is to determine which changes are culturally significant.

As has already been seen, Preservation is a conservation treatment that retains the appearance of a historic place as found (including features that may or may not have cultural significance), whereas Restoration returns to a previous (or original) appearance and therefore removes later accretions that may well possess cultural significance. Ironically, Restoration achieves an appearance of integrity while often destroying the integrity of a later configuration.

The US National Register criteria (National Park Service 1997) state that integrity is a necessary condition of listing: 'The quality of significance ... is present in districts, sites, buildings, structures, and

Figure 4.11 The Historic Monuments of Ancient Nara World Heritage Site, Nara, Japan, comprises a number of Buddhist and secular buildings built in the eighth century, when Nara prospered as the capital of Japan. The photograph shows the Kôfuku-ji pagoda and hall, built in the previous capital of Fujiwara and re-erected in Nara in 710. Most shrines and temples at Nara have been restored or reconstructed on many occasions. Since rebuilding of this kind, 'truthful' to the original values and models, is a Japanese cultural tradition, the buildings are considered by UNESCO to have both integrity and authenticity. The *Nara Document on Authenticity* was drafted here in 1994. (636highland, Wikimedia Commons)

objects that possess integrity of location, design, setting, materials, workmanship, feeling, association … '

A second meaning of the word 'integrity' is 'honesty,' which ventures into the realm of ethics.

Authenticity is somewhat more complicated. As has been seen, the *Nara Document on Authenticity* is the defining ICOMOS document. It requires that 'information sources about … values may be understood as credible or truthful' (Article 9). The *Nara Document* further explains 'authenticity' in terms of cultural diversity and consequent heritage diversity.

The *Operational Guidelines* (UNESCO World Heritage Centre 2013: para. 82) base the definition of 'authenticity' on the *Nara Document*, further adding:

> Depending on the type of cultural heritage, and its cultural context, properties may be understood to meet the conditions of authenticity if their cultural values … are truthfully and credibly expressed through a variety of attributes including:
> o Form and design
> o Materials and substance
> o Use and function
> o Traditions, techniques and management systems
> o Location and setting
> o Language, and other forms of intangible heritage
> o Spirit and feeling, and
> o Other internal and external factors.

It may be seen that integrity and authenticity are not in themselves cultural values, but rather lenses through which cultural values can be better understood and appreciated. The degree of integrity and authenticity should be determined as part of understanding the historic place.

English Heritage's *Conservation Principles* state that in managing change to significant historic places, we must 'consider the effects [of change] on authenticity and integrity.' Principle 4 ('Significant places should be managed to sustain their values') continues, in part:

> Conservation is achieved by all concerned with a significant place sharing an understanding of its significance, and using that understanding to … ensure that the place retains its *authenticity*—those attributes and elements which most truthfully reflect and embody the heritage values attached to it.
> (English Heritage 2008b: Principle 4.3 and paras. 91–5).

The Parks Canada definition of 'preservation' says much the same: 'Preservation involves protecting, maintaining and stabilizing the existing form, material and *integrity* of an historic place or individual component, while protecting its heritage value' (Parks Canada 2010: 15).

The National Register criteria, on the other hand, make 'integrity' an essential part of the evaluation process. The overarching criterion that applies to all nominations states:

> The quality of significance in American history, architecture, archeology, engineering, and culture is present in districts, sites, buildings, structures, and objects that possess *integrity* of location, design, setting, materials, workmanship, feeling, and association.
> (National Park Service 1997)

Recognized heritage values are fluid and changing, as are the lists of values to be considered. The traditional emphasis on historical and aesthetic qualities of historic places is now matched by an emphasis on their social, spiritual, and economic characteristics. The new awareness has led to a revised approach to identifying values and assessing significance, an approach called values-centred conservation.

Values-centred conservation

The discussion of values leads to the concepts of American heritage planner and educator Randall Mason who, with colleagues retained by the Getty Conservation Institute, has written extensively and wisely on the subject. Mason uses Riegl's declaration of the 'relative, modern ... art-value of a monument' as the point of departure for introducing the key concept of what he calls **values-centered preservation** (or **values-based preservation**; the present book prefers the equivalent universal term **values-centred conservation**).

Mason begins with the axiom that historic preservation 'reflects ... its society in the choices of what gets preserved, how it is preserved and interpreted, and who makes the decisions,' and uses this as a basis for developing a new model for identifying values in heritage planning. He argues that a tension exists between two 'cultures' in the conservation profession, the older 'pragmatic/technical [mindset, which] relies on preservationists' exclusive knowledge about technical solutions'; and the 'strategic/political mindset [which seeks] to learn the interests of stakeholders ranging outside the realm of experts.'[29] In other words, Mason differentiates between the professional 'experts' and the untrained 'public.' Values-centred conservation relies on both—balancing the technical with the sociopolitical. The traditional reliance on historical and aesthetic values is now countered with an equal, if not greater, emphasis on social, spiritual, and economic values, with which the latter are more in touch (Mason 2006: 21, 28, 37–9).[30]

A central feature of values-based conservation involves listening to the points of view of community stakeholders (see Section 4.3). Other aspects include recognizing the many, and often conflicting, values embodied in a historic place, and understanding that values are fluid and change over time. Mason argues that **values are socially constructed**. They are situational, and not inherent, depending on the memories, ideas, and social motivations of the interested communities.

Mason cites American heritage specialist Howard Green, who wrote that 'what is meaningful about history … is resolved through a broad social process in which historians play only a small role. … Meaning is socially made' (Green 1998: 90, 92).

Mason (2002: 10–13) divides values into two categories—sociocultural and economic. He sees both the categories and the individual values as neither distinct nor exclusive, but rather as overlapping:

Sociocultural values	*Economic values*
Historical	Use (market) value
Cultural/symbolic	Non-use (non-market) value
Social	Existence
Spiritual/religious	Option
Aesthetic	Bequest

The **sociocultural values** (similar to Riegl's **intrinsic values**) resemble those in Australia's *Burra Charter*. The **economic values** (parallel to Riegl's **temporal values** or to what are called **instrumental values**) are related to Cost and Use, seen above in the values promoted in the US by the National Trust and the American Society of Planning Officials.[31] Economic and other instrumental values have gained in relative importance over the past generation, a period during which global society has become increasingly focused on assessing and maximizing the economic and political benefits of virtually every human endeavor.

Mason explains that use values can be assigned a price and are easily analyzed by economists.[32] Non-use values are not captured by markets, but people would be willing to spend money to acquire and protect them:

- *Existence value* is the value placed by individuals for the mere existence of a place.
- *Option value* relates to the option that one might consume the place's services in the future.
- *Bequest value* derives from the wish to bequeath a heritage asset to future generations.

Mason's article appears in the same publication (from the Getty Conservation Institute) as economist David Throsby's paper on cultural capital and sustainability, which was discussed in Section 2.2. It will be remembered that Throsby identified the important concept of **cultural capital**, which comprises both cultural value and economic value. In Mason's construct, sociocultural values are the equivalent of Throsby's cultural values. The economic values cited by both correspond, with Throsby pointing out that 'non-use' values cannot be calculated by conventional means (Throsby 2002: 103).

More extreme is the voice of Australian Denis Byrne, who would remove 'social' from the list of sociocultural values and place those values ('categories') *within* society, rather than alongside it. This has the effect of prioritizing the values held by community groups ahead of 'professional-objective values' (Byrne et al. 2003: 7–8).

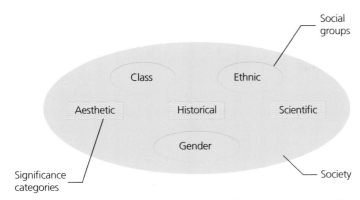

Figure 4.12 Model showing the 'professional-objective' values of a historic place contained by 'society.' (From Byrne et al. 2003, *Social Significance*, with permission from the Office of Environment and Heritage)

Whichever model is preferred, the sociocultural side of values-centred conservation, with its emphasis on the need to consider a wide range of socially constructed, changing values and to listen carefully to what the various stakeholders say they value, is becoming integrated into the conservation policies of many countries. No longer are historic places understood only by the research of technical experts. Wise planners and decision-makers insist on balancing it with—and placing it within the context of—input from the many communities of interest.

The heritage community in England has been particularly effective at introducing these new ideas into policy. A high-level conference in London, held in 2006, explored 'capturing the public value of heritage.' The concept of 'public value' was seen, at its simplest, as the equivalent of shareholder value in the private sector, recognizing that 'heritage is what people value and want to hand on to the future.' It follows that value 'justifies legal protection, funding or regulation; it is what inspires people to get involved with heritage' (Clark 2006: 2–3).

English Heritage followed up on the conference and other initiatives by issuing an overarching framework for conservation philosophy for the early twenty-first century in order to summarize current, best conservation practice. The document, *Conservation Principles, Policies and Guidance for the Sustainable Management of the Historic Environment*, was introduced in Section 3.1. Its principles are applicable far beyond England. As the title states, the vital concept of sustainability also plays a central role.

The document (English Heritage 2008b: para. 5, p. 7) recognizes four groups of heritage values. They are, with concise definitions:

- **Evidential value**: the potential of a [historic] place to yield evidence about past human activity.
- **Historical value**: the ways in which past people, events and aspects of life can be connected through a place to the present—it tends to be illustrative or associative.

- **Aesthetic value**: the ways in which people draw sensory and intellectual stimulation from a place.
- **Communal value**: the meanings of a place for the people who relate to it, or for whom it figures in their collective experience or memory.[33]

These are essentially a repackaging of the values identified in the *Burra Charter*. *Evidential value* is another way of describing *scientific value*; and *communal value* corresponds to *social or spiritual value*—and to the need for broad community consultation, which forms the basis of values-centred conservation.

In Australia, home of the *Burra Charter*, the *Environment Protection and Biodiversity Conservation Act 1999 (EPBC Act)*, which manages cultural heritage, protects heritage values rather than the site itself. The act declares that a person 'must not take an action that has, will have or is likely to have a significant impact on the National Heritage values of a National Heritage place.'

The Heritage Management Principles that accompany the statute state: 'The objective in managing National heritage places is to identify, protect, conserve, present and transmit, to all generations, their National Heritage values.'[34]

These kinds of policies are filtering down into legislation and decision-making in other countries as well. To cite a Canadian example, the *Ontario Heritage Act* was revised in 2006 to eliminate its former dependence on architectural and aesthetic values. The act introduced in its place a system in which heritage protection need be based on any one of three sets of values: design/physical value, historical/associative value, or contextual value (Barrett and Dutil 2012). The new importance of cultural significance, associative values, and contextual values clearly derives from the *Burra Charter* and from values-centred conservation.

One might also talk about 'values-centred demolition.' The term is apt in situations where negative sentiments towards a historic place are so intense that little constructive dialogue can occur. The advocates for demolition appear to come down on the side of moral right and the proponents of conservation have little opportunity to be heard in an unbiased manner.

This is understandable in time of conflict, when feelings run particularly high, as with the Bastille in Paris. Built as a fortress in the fourteenth century, the Bastille had been used by the monarchy as a state prison for centuries and came to symbolize royal tyranny. On July 14, 1789, a group of revolutionaries stormed the Bastille, liberated its few remaining prisoners, and destroyed much of the building. To prevent further acts such as this, UNESCO drew up the *Hague Convention* (UNESCO 1954).

Somewhat different are the situations in which people clamor for the demolition of a historic place that symbolizes a despised event or practice from the more distant past. Such was the case of the Immigration Building in Vancouver, opened in 1915 as a processing centre for would-be immigrants arriving by ship from Asia. Many new

Figure 4.13 The former Immigration Building, Vancouver, photographed in 1920. (W.J. Moore, City of Vancouver Archives, AM54-S4-3-:PAN N233; modified with permission)

Canadians began their successful New World lives in this building, whereas many others were refused entry and sent back to their homelands. When removal of the then-vacant Immigration Building was proposed in 1975, voices that empathized with the rejected travelers from China and South Asia argued convincingly that the place symbolized the racist values of the day—never mind that attitudes towards racism had changed in the intervening 60 years—and therefore it deserved to be destroyed. Very few people spoke for the positive heritage values. Consequently the Immigration Building was demolished and its site used for years as a truck terminal.

By contrast, conservation and interpretation were the chosen approach at several other refugee processing centres, including the Canadian Museum of Immigration at Pier 21 National Historic Site in Halifax, on Canada's Atlantic coast; and the legendary Ellis Island Immigration Museum ('Island of Hope, Island of Tears') in New York harbor, a part of the Statue of Liberty National Monument. Both are celebrated institutions that emphasize the stories of the new arrivals. Significantly, both were conserved in the 1990s, two decades after the Vancouver incident, when attitudes towards heritage had changed as well.

4.5 Significance

As said at the beginning of the previous section:

- **Value** is a characteristic that is valued.
- **Significance** is a synthesis of those values.

Stated differently, the **heritage significance of a historic place** is determined by synthesizing the many values that are attached to it. In theory the process is straightforward; in practice it is fraught with hazards.

English Heritage's *Conservation Principles* (2008b: paras. 61–83, pp. 35–40) define an eight-part process to assess heritage significance:

1   Understand the fabric and evolution of the place
2   Identify who values the place, and why they do so
3   Relate identified heritage values to the fabric of the place
4   Consider the relative importance of those identified values
5   Consider the contribution of associated objects and collections
6   Consider the contribution made by setting and context
7   Compare the place with other places sharing similar values
8   Articulate the significance of the place.

The first step is achieved by means of historical research and physical investigation (Sections 4.1 and 4.2), the second step, with community engagement (Section 4.3). The remaining stages are treated in Section 4.4 and this section. The process culminates in the final step, articulating the significance of the place. As the *Conservation Principles* (Principle 3.4, p. 21) state:

> Understanding and articulating the values and significance of a place is necessary to inform decisions about its future. The degree of significance determines what, if any, protection, including statutory designation, is appropriate under law and policy.

This is often expressed in a formal document called a 'statement of significance.' The text that follows describes how to prepare a statement of significance and identifies some of its limitations. The remainder of the chapter discusses ways to determine the 'degree of significance.'

The statement of significance

Many countries have adopted the statement of significance as the primary document for summarizing the heritage significance of a place. While the details of the document vary from one jurisdiction to another, the primary goal is the same. In the words of the Canadian authorities, 'A Statement of Significance ("SOS") is a declaration of value that briefly explains what a historic place is and why it is important. The SOS identifies key aspects of the place that must be protected in order for the historic place to continue to be important' (Canadian Register of Historic Places 2011).

Canada has the most detailed standards for SOSs, and consequently the Canadian model is encouraged here. The SOS was originally intended for places that have been formally recognized by a government authority, whether federal, provincial, or municipal. It is required for listing a building on the Canadian Register of Historic Places, but it can be used for any place, including as part of the processes of assessment and seeking formal recognition. The declared purposes of the SOS are to increase public awareness (the Canadian Register of Historic Places and its SOSs are available on the Internet) and also as a planning and property management tool, specifically as the first step in developing a conservation plan for the ongoing management of a historic place. The latter use is what makes it essential to heritage conservation planning.

The Canadian SOS is clear and concise, written for a broad audience in simple language. It comprises three sections:

* Description of historic place
* Heritage value
* Character-defining elements.

The *description of historic place* describes the physical character and principal resources of the place as they exist today. It indicates what and where the place is, what is in it, and what its boundaries are.

The *heritage value* section describes the heritage values, in order to identify why the historic place is important to its community. It includes a statement of each principal value, an explanation of the comparative context, and the reason why the historic place is significant within that context. The section is *not* a narrative history.

Character-defining elements (CDEs) are tangible or intangible features that express the heritage values. They are the features that most clearly convey the meanings and importance of the place; if they were removed, it would no longer be possible to understand that importance. This fulfills English Heritage's direction that identified heritage values should be related to the fabric of the place. Heritage value and CDEs depend on each other, as each CDE must relate directly to a value. The inclusion of CDEs makes the SOS a valuable heritage management tool, since it defines what should be protected in order to retain heritage value (Canadian Register of Historic Places 2011).[35]

The SOS guidelines are applicable to buildings, structures, and cultural landscapes. Supplementary guidelines are provided for heritage districts and for archaeological sites and places with an archaeological component.

A sample SOS for a vernacular building, the Wildcat Café in Canada's North, is given in the text box. The primary values of the historic place are social and associative, rather than architectural and historical.

WILDCAT CAFÉ

3509 Wiley Road, Yellowknife, Northwest Territories, Canada

Description of Historic Place
The Wildcat Café is a City of Yellowknife Heritage Site. It is a one-story log building with a gable roof. The designation also applies to portions of surrounding lots. The café is prominently located in the heart of Yellowknife's Old Town, and close to many other municipal heritage sites.

Figure 4.14 The Wildcat Café, Yellowknife, Northwest Territories. (WinterCity296, Wikimedia Commons)

Heritage Value

The Wildcat Café is one of the earliest permanent buildings in the City of Yellowknife. The building's structure and style are an excellent, well-preserved example of its time period. Built in 1937–38 by prominent pioneers Willie Wiley and Smokey Stout, the Wildcat is a reminder of pioneering days for Yellowknifers, and all Canadians alike. A replica of the Wildcat Café is on permanent display at the Canadian Museum of Civilization's Canada Hall, where it serves as an icon of early industrial development in Canada's northwest.

The Wildcat was a gathering place for the founders of Yellowknife: prospectors, miners, and pilots. It was the hub of Yellowknife's social activity. Prospectors wheeled and dealed, community members held meetings and banquets, while visitors came and went by floatplane. Throughout the years, the Wildcat was used as Yellowknife's first ice cream parlor and Chinese restaurant.

The Wildcat is a well-loved community landmark, and a symbol of Yellowknife heritage that nearly every visitor recognizes. From its prominent location in the historic Old Town, the Wildcat creates and encourages a pioneering spirit, which is still alive in Yellowknife today.

Character-Defining Elements

- Log construction
- Massing of the building, including but not limited to low-lying ceilings, and long, narrow profile
- Small, tucked-away entrance
- Simple signage and landscaping, keeping in touch with the building's rustic roots
- Prominent waterfront location, and visibility from the road
- Location next to other heritage sites and float bases
- One-roomed eating area with large, wooden tables and benches
- Use as a café.

Most other countries also rely on a statement of significance to explain the values and significance of a historic place, but they lack the discipline of the Canadian model. In Australia the format is designed by each individual state. As an example, Heritage Victoria, which is the principal heritage agency of the Australian State of Victoria, produces SOSs with three components:

- What is significant?
- How is it significant?
- Why is it significant?

The first heading corresponds to the Canadian 'Description of historic place,' the next two to the Canadian 'Heritage value.' There is no equivalent to 'Character-defining elements.' This fails to relate values to fabric and therefore reduces the importance of the SOS as a management tool.

In the US, nominations to the National Register of Historic Places include a long and comprehensive narrative statement of significance, which is intended to make the case for the property's national historical significance and integrity, and why the nominated place stands out among its peers. Prescribed questions to be addressed in the SOS include (US Department of the Interior 1999: 54–62):

- Applicable National Register criteria (these are touched on below)
- Themes
- Areas of significance
- Period(s) of significance
- Significant person(s)
- Cultural affiliation
- Architect/builder.

Regardless of the template or format, the SOS is a highly useful document that summarizes heritage values and demonstrates heritage significance.

Nevertheless, when looked at in relation to three questions that every decision-maker must address, the SOS falls short:

- Does the historic place have heritage significance?
- Is the place significant enough to merit formal recognition and protection?
- Or, if it lacks sufficient significance, can it be left without formal protection?

The SOS satisfies the first question, but fails to provide an answer to the critical second and third questions: whether or not the historic place warrants formal recognition, and whether recognition should include statutory protection.

Looking at an individual historic place in isolation—even with the introduction of comparable places in the process of assessing values—does not adequately determine the *level* of significance. Therefore it cannot lead to a fully informed decision on how a historic place should be managed.

Evaluation criteria

Strategic decision-making with respect to heritage recognition and protection requires a more rigorous evaluation process to determine the **level** (or **degree**) **of significance** of each historic place under consideration. At its simplest, this consists of establishing **criteria** and assessing whether or not the values meet the criteria—in other words, whether the place is sufficiently significant for recognition. In a more complicated version, grades are assigned to the assessment of each criterion, in order to determine with greater precision the extent to which the criteria are met. The determination of whether to provide formal recognition depends on the outcome of this grading process.

A **criterion** is a standard against which things are judged.[36] With historic places, criteria are usually defined with values having been used as a starting point. For example, if historical value is important, then historical value must be judged against one or more criteria that address history. Three criteria related to historical value might be:

- The historic place is associated with a particular person, group, event, or activity.
- The place contributes to understanding a period, activity, industry, person, or event.
- The place informs about a historic theme, process, or pattern of life.[37]

Notice that the first and second criteria are different: the first addresses historical values and the second, educational/scientific values. Like all values, the two overlap.

Determinations of heritage significance (**heritage evaluations** or **heritage assessments**) are usually undertaken by assessing the values of a historic place against a set list of criteria and determining whether the place has sufficient significance to be formally recognized.

Most jurisdictions have their own lists of criteria for determining significance. As an example, for a historic place to be included on the UNESCO World Heritage List it must have outstanding universal value and meet at least one of the following selection criteria (UNESCO World Heritage Centre n.d.-b):

i   to represent a masterpiece of human creative genius;
ii   to exhibit an important interchange of human values, over a span of time or within a cultural area of the world, on developments in architecture or technology, monumental arts, town-planning or landscape design;
iii to bear a unique or at least exceptional testimony to a cultural tradition or to a civilization which is living or which has disappeared;

Figure 4.15 The Sydney Opera House in Sydney, Australia, is a relatively recent building (1973) that has been listed as a World Heritage Site for its outstanding universal value under Criterion i. (Enoch Lau)

iv to be an outstanding example of a type of building, architectural or technological ensemble or landscape which illustrates (a) significant stage(s) in human history;

v   to be an outstanding example of a traditional human settlement, land-use, or sea-use which is representative of a culture (or cultures), or human interaction with the environment especially when it has become vulnerable under the impact of irreversible change;

vi to be directly or tangibly associated with events or living traditions, with ideas, or with beliefs, with artistic and literary works of outstanding universal significance. (The Committee considers that this criterion should preferably be used in conjunction with other criteria.)

Some lists of evaluation criteria are long and detailed, while others are more succinct. Nevertheless most can be condensed into a few simple, straightforward criteria, with guidance usually provided to help assessors achieve consistency.

The National Register of Historic Places in the US has only a few criteria, but distributes a 60-page booklet explaining how to apply them (National Park Service 1997). The criteria are:

The quality of significance in American history, architecture, archeology, engineering, and culture is present in districts, sites, buildings, structures, and objects that possess integrity of location, design, setting, materials, workmanship, feeling, and association, and:

A. That are associated with events that have made a significant contribution to the broad patterns of our history; or
B. That are associated with the lives of persons significant in our past; or

C. That embody the distinctive characteristics of a type, period, or method of construction, or that represent the work of a master, or that possess high artistic values, or that represent a significant and distinguishable entity whose components may lack individual distinction; or

D. That have yielded, or may be likely to yield, information important in prehistory or history.

Outstanding vs. representative value: a paradox

As was noted in the discussion of the *World Heritage Convention* (1972) in Section 3.1, the world heritage inscription process identifies places with 'outstanding universal value.' The Convention does not, however, actually define 'outstanding universal value.' A definition appeared only in the 2005 revision of the *Operational Guidelines* to the Convention: 'Outstanding Universal Value means cultural and/or natural significance which is so exceptional as to transcend national boundaries and to be of common importance for present and future generations' (UNESCO World Heritage Centre 2013: rev. 2005, 46, para. 49).

The first version of the *Operational Guidelines* (1977) had said that the term 'universal' must be interpreted as referring to a property that is 'highly representative of the culture of which it forms part.' This idea was repeated in Criterion v of the selection criteria for the World Heritage List, just cited. A place is valued for being an 'outstanding' example of its type that is 'representative' of a culture. In other words, value resides in both the extraordinary ('outstanding') and the typical, less-than-extraordinary ('representative'). This parallels the trend towards democratization seen in the acceptance of values-centred conservation.[38]

Figure 4.16 Zollverein Coal Mine Industrial Complex in Essen, Germany, has been designated a World Heritage Site because 'its buildings are **outstanding** examples of the application of the design concepts of the Modern Movement in architecture in a wholly industrial context' (Criterion ii) and also because it is '*representative* of a crucial period in the development of traditional heavy industries in Europe' (Criterion iii). (Rainer Halama)

Therein lies a paradox. As Canadian educator Christina Cameron (2009: 127–42), a former member of the World Heritage Committee, has written, 'outstanding' value implies identifying places that are the 'best of the best,' whereas 'representative' value suggests a lower threshold that is only 'representative of the best.' Cameron suggests that the creators of the convention intended only the former and envisioned a restrictive and exclusive list of outstanding places. However, over the years, as new, non-Western countries with different kinds of heritage joined the World Heritage Convention, the perspective became broader and the list longer. This greater breadth was made unambiguous by the approval of cultural landscapes as an eligible category, and by the 1994 adoption of *A Global Strategy for a Balanced, Representative and Credible World Heritage List*.

The *Intangible Cultural Heritage Convention* (2003) provides for a 'Representative List of the Intangible Cultural Heritage of Humanity.' By the start of the new century, 'representative' had become the norm.

So what does 'representative' signify? The criteria for evaluation for the US National Register for Historic Places state that 'representative' places have significance when they

> embody the distinctive characteristics of a type, period, or method of construction, or that *represent* the work of a master, or that possess high artistic values, or that represent a significant and distinguishable entity *whose components may lack individual distinction*.
>
> (National Park Service 1997: 2)

English Heritage also values 'representativeness,' but contrasts it with 'rarity' (not the same as 'outstanding') in a criterion for evaluating significance: 'Representativeness: is its character or type representative of important historical or architectural trends? Representativeness may be contrasted with [the criterion] rarity' (English Heritage 2010).

Conservation educator Jukka Jokilehto attempts to resolve this apparent paradox between the outstanding and the representative:

> For a cultural heritage resource to have universal value does not—in itself—imply that it is 'the best'; rather it means it shares a particular creative quality, a uniqueness, and the quality of being 'true,' original, authentic, as a constituent part of the common, universal heritage of humanity. Within such a context, it may be possible to identify groups or classes of products with similar characteristics, out of which to select *the most representative or outstanding*. In the essence, *universal value implies that the single item be not only seen for its individual merits but always also as a representation of the common heritage of humanity*.
>
> (Jokilehto 1999: 295–6)

Heritage assessments commonly accept the contrasting criteria of 'rarity/uniqueness' and 'representativeness' without questioning them. Nevertheless this is a philosophical hurdle with which practitioners should come to terms.

Assessing significance

Making value judgments

If a candidate historic place meets one or more of the criteria established by a listing agency (e.g., by the World Heritage List or the National Register of Historic Places), it is generally considered to have sufficient significance to be included on the list. Making this judgment requires a well-researched nomination and thorough consideration. The assessment should involve a group of people (not solely an individual) with a diversity of perspectives and expertise. The group should include some with expertise on the subject, but it should not be a learned discussion among only specialists with a similar knowledge base. The partial reliance on non-experts, which is so important in identifying values, is effective as well in judging significance.

The need to be familiar with comparable places is important, so as to ensure a level of consistency among recognitions of similar kinds of places. The Historic Sites and Monuments Board of Canada, which recognizes places, people, and events of national significance, is provided with comprehensive research papers, prepared by the staff at Parks Canada, which include a discussion of the 'comparable context' for each nomination. Typically this section identifies previous nominations of similar candidates over a span of years and indicates whether or not the nominations were successful. The World Heritage Centre likewise makes an effort to understand places that are comparable to those being nominated.

A multilevel hierarchy exists, with the World Heritage List (places with 'universal' significance) at the top, national lists ('national' significance) second, and lower-government lists ('state,' 'provincial,' 'regional,' or 'local' significance) next. This begs the question as to whether places on higher tiers are more significant than the others, or whether this is simply a result of the bureaucratic and statutory separation of responsibilities.

The answer would seem to be some of each. Older systems valued the upper tiers more highly. For example, the exemplary College Hill Demonstration Study carried out in Providence, Rhode Island, in 1958, valued (and scored) national, state, and community significance in that order (Providence City Plan Commission 1967). Newer systems value the different levels more equally. As an example, the Canadian Register of Historic Places accepts provincially and municipally recognized places as well as national ones; it reflects the current trend towards a more egalitarian heritage assessment.

Determining whether a nomination merits inclusion on one or another list may include not simply whether it meets a particular criterion, but rather how fully it meets it. As an example, the Australian Heritage Council advises the Australian government on whether to include natural, Indigenous, and historic places on the National Heritage List. The Council uses two tests to determine whether a place is worthy of inclusion. The first test is whether it meets one or more of nine criteria. The second test applies a '**significance threshold**.' This helps the Council judge the level of significance of a place's heritage value by asking 'just how important are these values?'

To reach the threshold for the National Heritage List, a place must have 'outstanding natural, Indigenous or historic heritage value to the nation' (Australian Government, Department of the Environment n.d.). This means that it must be important to the Australian community as a whole. A second list, the Commonwealth Heritage List (for places on Australian government land or under its control), requires that places have only 'significant' heritage value. The Council is therefore faced with establishing a hierarchy of places that are outstanding, significant, or (one presumes) insignificant. In other words, the judgments are assigned grades.[39]

The level of cultural significance is important to the Australian system, since it determines who will be responsible for managing the historic place. Places with national and world significance are managed by the Australian government and those of state significance by state governments. The latter, in turn, pass on responsibility for places of local significance to local government.

Grades

The reliance on criteria and the proficiency to make competent value judgments—with or without a significance threshold—usually works well when nominations for recognition are considered on a one-off basis. However, this system can fail when many places are being evaluated as a group, such as when looking at all the properties within

Figure 4.17 Île aux Perroquets lighthouse and light station in Québec, which was assessed and designated as part of the Canadian government's heritage lighthouse program. (Parks Canada/Marie Lachance)

a neighborhood, in order to determine which of the group should and which should not achieve formal recognition. Comparisons must be made among numerous candidates, rather than between a single candidate and comparable former nominations.

The most straightforward way to address this situation is to assign **grades** to each judgment. In other words, rather than responding to a criterion (e.g., Is the historic place associated importantly with the lives of persons nationally significant in the history of the United States?[40]) with a 'yes' or a 'no,' we respond by deciding that the association is excellent, very good, good, fair, or poor—terms borrowed from the classroom—or with a different set of adjectives of descending value, such as outstanding, significant, and insignificant, as used by the Australian government. The choice of which grade to apply to a specific criterion should be justified in point-form or narrative ('This place is excellent with respect to that criterion because ...').

As an example of a grading system, we may look at the efforts, begun in 2010, to assess the significance of federally owned lighthouses in Canada, with the intention of designating (and protecting) those that have particular significance. A set of six designation criteria was established for the purpose, after consultation among various interest groups. They include historical, architectural, and community values, and are fully compatible with the intentions of values-based conservation. The criteria are:

Historical values
1 How well does the lighthouse reflect an important theme in Canadian maritime history?
2 How well does the lighthouse (or light station) illustrate the socio-economic development of its associated community?

Architectural values
3 What is the aesthetic/visual quality of the lighthouse, in the context of its design type?
4 What is the quality of the design, structural innovation, craftsmanship, materials, optical or audible technologies, and/or functionality of the lighthouse?

Community values
5 What is the visual influence of the building on the present character of the area with which it is associated?
6 What is the nature of the lighthouse's identity with its associated community?

Each criterion is assigned one of four grades, A to D, which correspond generally to:
A Excellent (i.e., outstanding)
B Very good (very significant, noteworthy)
C Good (somewhat significant, representative)
D Fair or obscure (not significant).

Lighthouses are recommended for designation when they receive:

- Two scores of A; or
- One score of A, plus two scores of B; or
- Four scores of B.

Any one of these three options achieves the significance threshold.

An evaluation system such as this distinguishes between places that merit formal recognition and those that do not; they separate the wheat from the chaff, the cream from the milk.

The question arises as to how to 'calibrate' the scale—for example, why are two scores of 'A' (and not one or three) required? This requires common sense, not rocket science. The method involves testing and feedback. Make an educated guess as to the appropriate threshold and then test it on samples that appear to represent a variety of levels of significance. If some places of limited significance make the cut, then the 'bar' (threshold) has been set too low; if some of obvious high significance fail to make it, then the bar is too high. Reset the bar and try again until the results appear to be appropriate. Choose another batch of samples and try again. And so on, until a comfort level is reached.

All evaluations should be done by a team. Experience shows that the members of the team will rarely deviate from each other by more than one grade. They may be divided over whether a particular place merits 'very good' or 'good' for a particular criterion, but it is highly unusual for one to say 'excellent' and another 'good.' The final grade should be the one chosen by the majority of the evaluation team. Full documentation of the evaluation should be retained, including an indication of the reasons for assigning each grade.

Numerical scores

The designation thresholds used for Canadian lighthouses—two scores of A, one of A plus two of B, or four of B—may be seen as messy and potentially confusing (although it works well!). A tidier way to evaluate significance is to assign numerical values to the various grades. Let us say, for example, that the following numbers were assigned:

- A = 10
- B = 5
- C = 2
- D = 0.

The three thresholds would then all add up to 20. Stated mathematically:

$2A = 2 \times 10 = 20$
$A + 2B = 10 + (2 \times 5) = 20$
$4B = (4 \times 5) = 20$.[41]

This may have no particular advantage for an evaluation with only six criteria, but what if there were ten criteria? It would take many combinations to define the designation threshold, whereas the threshold could be defined with a single numerical score.

Numerical scores have been used in assessing heritage significance for quite some time. The method was pioneered in the College Hill Demonstration Study of 1958, cited previously; the accompanying text box on the Canadian Parliament Buildings refers to one from a century earlier. A numerical scoring system can be used with any set of criteria. Different criteria can be weighted differently. The criteria and the scores can be revised as needed to reflect changing purposes for the evaluation. And (as with all assessments), a place should be reconsidered if new information comes to light.

A Numerical Evaluation from History

Numerical assessment systems, in which the highest score produces the 'winner,' have long been used to judge architectural competitions. More than a century and a half ago, in 1859, the architects for Canada's Parliament Buildings in Ottawa were chosen by this method. Two officials from the Department of Public Works, Samuel Keefer and F.P. Rubidge, selected the winners by setting out ten criteria. They assessed the submitted designs by giving them a score between 0 and 10 (the 'modulus of superiority') for each criterion and ranking them by the sum of the scores.

Figure 4.18 The former Centre Block of the Parliament Buildings, Ottawa, photographed in 1901. (Detroit Photographic Co., collection of the Library of Congress)

The winning design for the Centre Block, by Thomas Fuller and Chilion Jones, received 89 of a possible 100 points from Keefer. Rubidge, the tougher grader, gave it only 62, but their consensus favored Fuller and Jones. Hindsight supports the validity of the choice, not least of all because they awarded the design only 6 and 3 points respectively for safety against fire—and the building burned down a half-century later (Government of Canada 1862; Kalman 1980: 25).

In order to ensure that the process is transparent, it may be appropriate to assign letter or verbal grades first, and then to convert them to numbers. In this way the numerical scoring is kept distinct from the verbal grades, which remain constant unless new information emerges or values change.

If the assessment process requires only a yes-or-no decision—e.g., should a place be protected?—then a threshold is required to determine which places qualify. In our hypothetical numerical scores for Canadian lighthouses, the threshold would be set at 20 out of 60. Sometimes multiple thresholds may be required, as in helping determine whether (a) to protect a place, (b) to recognize a place without protection, or (c) not to recognize a place. The most straightforward way in which to determine the appropriate scores and thresholds is, as with letters or grades, a process of trial and error. Begin with what appears to be a rational, logical set of scores, try evaluating a handful of places, assess the outcome, and adjust the scores as may be appropriate.

To make numerical scoring work well, a few considerations may help:

- *Excellent* (or *superior* or *outstanding*) should receive considerably more points than *very good (noteworthy)*, and *very good* considerably more than *good (representative)*. This helps distinguish the outstanding places. A progression that halves the score at every grade level (e.g., 20–10–5–0) often works well.
- When the individual criteria are scored and added up to yield a score for the collective category (e.g., *aesthetic value*, *historical value*, and *social value*), consideration should be given to assigning a maximum score for each category. Otherwise a place that has a number of very high architectural or historical values but no social value may receive a disproportionately high score that does not reflect its overall value.

The criterion of 'integrity' (i.e., the amount of change that has occurred to the historic place) is often included within an evaluation. The problem here is that integrity is not an intrinsic value, but rather a temporal value (as the terms were used by Riegl); and a conservation intervention (e.g., restoration) may alter the degree of integrity. Any scoring system that considers integrity should first determine the 'basic score' for the intrinsic values, which are a measure of significance, and then treat integrity as supplementary and changeable. A score for lacking integrity can be *subtracted* from, rather than added to, the basic score.

As long as those who design the evaluation system follow common sense as well as professional expertise, the outcomes should be clear and widely acceptable.

The methodology for a system of this kind was introduced by the present author in the 1970s (Kalman 1976, 1980). A number of government agencies in Canada and the US adopted the method. In recent years numerical scoring has been overshadowed by the rise in more explicitly value-based systems and the introduction of statements of significance. Nevertheless, there is nothing mutually exclusive between values-centred conservation and the use of numbers. Moreover, as was noted previously, a statement of significance alone describes value but may not quantify it sufficiently to justify management decisions.

Support for numerical heritage assessment systems has come from various quarters. Cultural economists Ilde Rizzo and David Throsby, who teach in Italy and Australia respectively, puzzle over how to measure cultural value. They write:

> It can be suggested that the only sensible way to evaluate it will be via a disaggregation into its component elements [such as aesthetic value, spiritual value, social value, and others] …. It may be possible to assign cardinal or ordinal scores to these components and aggregate them into a simple index according to given assumptions. If so, the flow of cultural benefits from alternative projects [or different historic places] might be able to be compared.
>
> (Rizzo and Throsby 2006: 998)[42]

Numerical scoring systems have been long used in other disciplines. Readers will be particularly familiar with judges' scoring at international sporting events such as figure skating, gymnastics, and diving, where the winner may earn a score only fractions of a point higher than the second-place finisher. When disputes occur, they usually focus not

Figure 4.19 Five judges hold up their scores at the Red Bull Cliff Diving World Series competition in Dubrovnik, 2009. (Dean Treml)

on the nature of the scoring system but rather on the integrity of the judges who apply it.

Professionals in the New World seem more comfortable with using numerical scores than those in Europe. In the 1970s an editorial in the *Civic Trust News* censured 'the absurdity of adding together scores—or any more sophisticated variant of judging by numbers' (52, November 1975, p. 1). What the Civic Trust missed is that it is the final determination of relative significance, and not the judging of criteria, that is done by numbers.

The identification of values and the determination of significance are only means to a greater end. That end is the management of change to a historic place in a manner that retains the values and respects its cultural significance. Managing change is the subject of the chapter that follows.

5
Managing Change

The steps outlined in the previous chapter lead to a sound understanding of the historic place. With this information in hand, it is time to plan and manage proposed change to a particular place, or to develop broader policy that will guide change to historic places over time.

A central objective of heritage planning is ensuring that change occurs in a way that is consistent with best conservation principles and practice; another is to respect the will of the community. Whether the heritage planner is helping government undertake proactive planning, part of a proponent team working with a property owner to prepare a worthy development scheme (or with a community group to oppose a poor scheme), a public servant whose role is to respond formally to proposals, or a community representative wanting to ensure the best outcome for the general public, the common objective is seeing that conservation work is carried out in a way that respects the significance of the historic place, is supported by the community, meets the proponent's objectives, and follows relevant regulations. If these objectives can be achieved, then decision-makers will likely approve the proposal. If not, then it should be revised or aborted.

One must continually make choices. Convenient as it would be to reduce heritage planning to an exact science—believing, for example, that these particular conditions and that degree of heritage significance must lead to one and only one policy, use, or conservation treatment—is not how the world works. A variety of policies, uses, treatments, planning tools, and designs can usually follow from any given situation. Thoughtful analysis is required to determine the best option to adopt, or to limit the choice to a very few acceptable options. The analysis will take into account not only conservation doctrine, but also the broader, external circumstances of the physical and political contexts.

Heritage conservation today is very different from what it was only a generation or two ago. As discussed in Section 1.1, whereas in the mid-twentieth century heritage conservation was mostly concerned with techniques of safeguarding the material remains of architectural monuments representing 'universal,' Eurocentric values, by the first decade of the present century heritage conservation had become a social practice that accepts varied and conflicting values en route to creating places where people can 'connect to meaningful narratives about history, culture, and identity' (Kaufman 2009: 1).

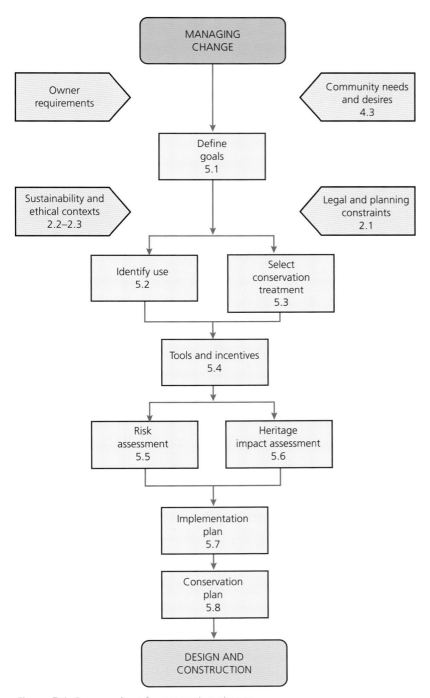

Figure 5.1 Process chart for managing change.

English planners Ian Strange and David Whitney have written parallel thoughts with respect to urban conservation:

> Over the last 30 years conservation activity has been shifting ever more from being characterised as an act of preservation towards being characterised as part of a broader vehicle for urban regeneration and economic development .... Over the course of the 1980s and 1990s, the economic function of conservation became more significant with the rise of a neo-liberal planning agenda intent on easing the restraint of development . ... Conservation has been encouraged to develop its regenerative potential, particularly through the more economically productive use of historic buildings.

and

> The integration of conservation of the historic environment with environmental concerns is now a key feature of the sustainability agenda.
>
> (Strange and Whitney 2003: 220, 222)[1]

To help support their thesis, the authors quote a member of a team that was developing a cultural strategy for Leeds:

> I no longer feel that I have to campaign that conservation is a good thing in itself, but that conservation is part of regeneration and that we're part of the mainstream … not being hard preservationist has given us a seat at the table and allowed us to access regeneration packages.
>
> (Strange and Whitney 2003: 221)

Stated differently, heritage conservation has moved from the margins to the mainstream with the acceptance that the conservation and development sectors should work closely together.

This final chapter discusses the principal tasks that are involved in using heritage planning to manage change in this way. They draw on the principles and on the process of understanding the historic place, addressed in the previous chapter. The process chart for managing change, introduced in Figure 1.4, is repeated here (Figure 5.1). The number within each box indicates the section of the text in which the subject is discussd.

5.1 Defining Goals

This book has, to a considerable extent, addressed 'projects'—specific assignments intended to develop and conserve historic places. Projects have a limited life, made up of a planning stage (the focus of the book), an implementation stage, and a project afterlife. Similar practices are relevant to ongoing conservation processes with no specific time frame and to the development of heritage policy. This is the nature of long-term planning. Unlike the limited life of a specific project, the conservation of a historic place never ends. In theory, heritage protection and conservation are undertaken in perpetuity. Long-term planning may receive less attention than project planning in the present text, but it holds equal priority in heritage planning.

The first, and perhaps most important, task is to define what it is that the planning initiative or project is intended to achieve.

Goals and objectives

Overarching goals should have been in mind since the outset, when the proponent first articulated the concept that has driven the work. If for a specific project, the proponent is usually the owner or manager of the historic place; if for policy development, it may be a government or a community organization. It is essential that these early ideas remain no more than a general guide and that the proponent remains open to a variety of possible directions. The understanding of the historic place and the identification of the legal and planning constraints will help to clarify and elaborate the concept, enabling the goals and objectives to be defined fully at this time.

- **Goals** are high-level statements that describe in a broad manner what the project will accomplish.
- **Objectives** are lower-level and action-oriented statements that describe measurable and achievable outcomes.

As an example, the goal of a project might be:

- To conserve the historic place and repurpose it in a manner that serves the broad community.

The objectives might be:

- To rehabilitate the place, following best conservation practice.
- To adapt the place as a sustainable public recreational facility managed by the municipality.
- To supplement municipal resources with funds provided by the state's infrastructure development program and other sources.
- To complete the work within three years.

The goals and objectives together comprise the core of the strategies (or 'policies') that will enable the project to be achieved, and for this reason they form the heart of what is often termed **strategic planning**.[2] Goals and objectives should be crafted with care, particularly in a publicly supported project, since they will be discussed by the community and will require approval by elected decision-makers. They should be compatible with broader, contextual policies and issues. No less care should go into writing goals and objectives in a privately undertaken project, because they comprise the benchmark against which future

Conflict and Compromise: The Audubon Ballroom

The conservation of the Audubon Ballroom and Theater in New York City provides a paradigm of controversy and compromise. It evoked such passionately argued conflicting values as to require a bold resolution.

The Ballroom was built in New York's Upper West Side, in 1912–15, as the largest dance hall in the city and one of the first purpose-built theatres for film. The developer was film producer William Fox, who built the empire that became Twentieth Century Fox and Fox Broadcasting. The architect was renowned theatre designer Thomas J. Lamb. The facility fell onto hard times during the Depression. After a short stint as a synagogue, it came to be used as a political meeting hall, primarily by trade unions and the African-American community.

On February 21, 1965, Malcolm X, the leader of the Organization of Afro-American Unity and a powerful and divisive figure in New York politics, was assassinated in the ballroom while delivering a speech.

In 1989 Columbia University and the City of New York announced a plan to demolish the building and replace it with a biotech centre. This was opposed by the historic preservation community, mostly middle class and white; and by the African-American community, which was uninterested in conventional heritage values but to whom the place was sacred to the memory of Malcolm X. Columbia students fought the project for environmental reasons. Neighborhood residents, who were largely Dominican, were indifferent to the heritage, political, and environmental values, but wanted the biotech centre for the jobs it would provide.

It was impossible to satisfy these four divergent interests. A compromise resolution was reached, contrived by the Municipal Art Society (part of the preservation lobby) and supported by Manhattan Borough President Ruth Messinger and Malcolm X's widow, Betty Shabazz. The ballroom and its exterior were retained, restored, and reopened in 2005 as the Malcolm X and Dr. Betty Shabazz Memorial and Educational Center. The theatre portion was demolished and replaced by a reduced Audubon Business and Technology Centre and a community health clinic. The solution respected the conflicting values of all communities of interest while pleasing none (Kaufman 2009: 302–5; New York Preservation Archive Project 2010; Wikipedia n.d.-a).

Figure 5.2 The body of Malcolm X being removed from the Audubon Ballroom, seen in the right background. (malcolm-x.org)

progress will be measured and they will be presented to stakeholders and potential investors.

Goals and objectives should be written in simple, unambiguous language. Sometimes they are stated in a more embellished manner and include references to the broader context and future experiences of the place, in which case they are usually called a **vision statement**.

If the proponent is an organization or a government, the goals should be consistent with the entity's **mission** (or **mission statement**), which defines its fundamental purpose.

In crafting the goals and objectives, several key questions must be considered: What is technically feasible? What is politically feasible? What will the community support? What makes the best economic and financial sense? Which is the most sustainable solution? Which is the most ethical alternative? What builds on previous successes? What can be done with available resources? What is achievable? It is important to identify any competing objectives or conflicting values, and to devise ways to resolve or mitigate conflicts. The aim should be to find a way to make every interest group a 'winner.'

In many situations the best practice, as determined solely by conservation doctrine, may have little chance of success. It may have practical or educational value, but lack strategic value and the likelihood of stakeholder acceptance. Rather than insisting blindly on pursuing 'best' practice, it may be necessary at times to identify a solution that represents only 'good' or 'better' practice. This will involve compromises, but it might more likely be achievable within a real-world environment. 'Good,' 'better,' and 'best' practice should all respect conservation principles, although they do so to varying degrees. The strategic objective is to identify the best conservation solution that fits within a pragmatic planning framework and has a reasonable chance of gaining acceptance, even if some compromise is required.[3]

A policy document that provides a good model for identifying strategic planning goals and contextual considerations is the *National Planning Policy Framework* for England, issued by the UK government in 2012. The concise and clearly expressed paper is intended as 'a framework within which local people and their accountable councils can produce their own distinctive local and neighbourhood plans, which reflect the needs of their communities' (Department for Communities and Local Government (UK) 2012: i, para. 1). While intended for local planners, the advice is helpful for property owners and the community as well.

A section on 'Conserving and enhancing the historic environment' (para. 126) begins with guidance that every heritage planner would do well to follow in the management of change:

> Local planning authorities should set out in their Local Plan a positive strategy for the conservation and enjoyment of the historic environment. ... In doing so, they should recognise that heritage assets are an irreplaceable resource and conserve them in a manner appropriate to their significance. In developing this strategy, local planning authorities should take into account:

○ The desirability of sustaining and enhancing the significance of heritage assets and putting them to viable uses consistent with their conservation;
○ The wider social, cultural, economic and environmental benefits that conservation of the historic environment can bring;
○ The desirability of new development making a positive contribution to local character and distinctiveness; and
○ Opportunities to draw on the contribution made by the historic environment to the character of a place.

The responsible management of change requires bringing together all the information related to the historic place and the proposed assignment into a comprehensive document—or a series of discrete, smaller documents—which is usually called a conservation plan. As can be seen in the process chart (Figure 5.1), this includes consideration of the larger context and the matters of sustainability and ethics, as discussed in Chapter 2. The *National Planning Policy Framework* supports this: it states that, in addition to a qualified assessment of significance (part of understanding the historic place), the initiative should be placed within an overall framework of sustainability.

The Medieval City of Rhodes: Integrated, Sustainable Planning

The Medieval City of Rhodes World Heritage Site, located on an island in the Aegean Sea within Greece, provides a superb model for integrated and sustainable heritage planning and management. A much-admired city in Hellenistic times (its Colossus was one of the Seven Wonders of the World), with a gridiron layout that reflects ancient Greek planning, medieval Rhodes features material evidence of the Byzantine, Hospitaller (Crusader), and Ottoman periods and reflects the fusion of Western and Eastern cultures. The city retains its residential and commercial vitality.

Figure 5.3 A street in the Medieval City of Rhodes World Heritage Site. (Friedrich Böhringer, Wikimedia Commons)

The program of conservation and development comprised restoring landmark buildings from all eras as well as the extensive fortifications (built in the seventh century and much modified); upgrading infrastructure, including drainage, electricity, waste management, non-polluting transport, and traffic and parking arrangements; rehabilitating more than two dozen ruined properties into housing for the poor; building facilities for health and the elderly; and developing several museums. Tourism is managed closely, including control of commercial activities and land use. Conservation and management are the responsibility of the Greek government's 4th Ephorate of Byzantine Antiquities (a division of the Ministry of Culture and Sports), in collaboration with the Municipality of Rhodes. Funding comes from the national budget and European Union programs (Gerousi and Brouskari 2013: 30–7).

Opportunities and constraints

In urban settings, the interface between community, property owners, and authorities usually takes place at the municipal level. With defined projects, planners consider an application and make a recommendation that is conveyed to the chief administrative officer, who in turn takes it to the elected decision-makers. In rural settings, the authority might be a municipality, county, or region. When a higher level of government (a state, province, territory, or nation) is involved, either as regulator or as owner/proponent, processing and decision-making may occur at that level.

In order to negotiate this interface in an informed and effective way, it is necessary to determine the legal and planning constraints that may affect the proposal. The regulatory infrastructure was discussed in Section 2.1; now is the time to apply that knowledge to the specific initiative and jurisdiction.

This is best done by compiling a checklist of constraints and opportunities that may affect the proposed work, and then to determine the details of the effects. The conservation plan (Section 5.8) should provide a succinct description of these, perhaps with details provided in an appendix.

An initial checklist might look into the status of the following:

- Planning statutes
- Heritage statutes
- Relevant policies
- Formal agreements with Aboriginal groups or others with an interest in the area
- Heritage recognition or protection status
- Community and neighborhood plans
- Sustainability plans
- Zoning regulations, including allowable uses and applicable constraints
- Procedures for requesting variances
- Design controls or guidelines
- Building codes
- Available incentive programs
- Funding programs
- Other relevant programs.

The remainder of this chapter describes individual aspects of managing change. Much of the text focuses on specific historic places, and so the approach is oriented more towards projects than policy. Nevertheless the same processes are applicable to both short- and long-range heritage planning.

5.2 Identifying a Use

The first priority in planning for conservation is to identify a viable and productive use for the historic place. The present and future uses are fundamental to its conservation and its ongoing management and operation. Often the existing use(s) will be continued. However, the traditional or present use is frequently no longer practicable, perhaps because the place is no longer required for that purpose, its operation is no longer financially viable, demographics or technologies have changed, or because the spatial needs of the traditional use(s) have changed and the place no longer works for that function. The underused or unused place is often described as being 'redundant.'

Figures 5.4 and 5.5 The Tate Modern in London, England, is an art gallery created by rehabilitating the former Bankside Power Station. Much of the exterior and the internal structure remain intact. The former turbine hall (with its turbines removed) is now a spacious entrance atrium. (J.A. Green, Wikimedia Commons; Hans Peter Schaefer)

A choice must be made as to whether to alter ('adapt') a redundant place to accommodate the changed demands of the traditional use, or whether to **repurpose** it for a new use(s) (**adaptive reuse**). An expanded or new use may require revising the configuration and/or constructing an addition, either of which will have an impact on the appearance and likely also on the cultural significance of the place.

The charters provide some guidance. As might be expected, the *Venice Charter* is quite conservative, actually prohibiting physical change:

> The conservation of monuments is always facilitated by making use of them for some socially useful purpose. Such use is therefore desirable but it must not change the lay-out or decoration of the building. It is within these limits only that modifications demanded by a change of function should be envisaged and may be permitted. (Article 5)

The *Burra Charter* is somewhat more permissive with regard to changes in use:

Where the use of a place is of cultural significance it should be retained;

A place should have a compatible use (Articles 7.1–7.2)

and further:

> The policy [conservation plan] should identify a use or combination of uses or constraints on uses that retain the cultural significance of the place. New use of a place should involve minimal change to significant fabric and use; should respect associations and meanings; and where appropriate should provide for continuation of activities and practices which contribute to the cultural significance of the place. (Explanatory notes to Article 7)

The Canadian *Standards and Guidelines* take a similar stand: 'Find a use for an historic place that requires minimal or no change to its character-defining elements' (Standard 5).

The explanation that follows provides more guidance:

> It is important to find the right function for an historic place to ensure a long-term, stable context for conserving heritage value. If the current use is a character-defining element, maintaining this use is in accordance with the standard, as long as growth or technological change does not become destructive to its character-defining elements. If maintaining the original use leads to the removal or significant alteration of character-defining elements, the owners and users may need to consider a compatible new use for the historic place. Finding a new use depends on an analysis of heritage value and physical compatibility with the historic place and its likeliness to provide a lasting, new life for the historic place. Using an old jail as a youth hostel may initially seem like an unusual concept, but it illustrates resourceful, clear-sighted functional analysis as the generator of good reuse: both jails and hostels provide a lot of small rooms for sleeping.

Being resourceful and doing a clear-sighted functional analysis are indeed key to the challenge of repurposing a historic place.

New uses for old buildings

Any type of historic place may be repurposed, although the practice is most often achieved with buildings. Doctrinal guidance alone will never indicate the best use to which a historic place—in this sense a building—might be put. What is required above all is vision tempered by common sense. The proposed use, whether continued or new, should meet one or more of the following conditions:

- If the present use remains viable and continuing to accommodate it (whether or not with alterations or an addition) does not require compromising the cultural value/character-defining elements of the place, then retention of the use would be best.

- If the present use is no longer viable, then the building should be repurposed. The best choice would be one that achieves one or more of the following:
  - The proposed new use differs from, but is thematically related to, the historic use.
  - The proposed new use can be accommodated comfortably within the existing structure and spaces, without major changes or additions being required.
  - Changes and/or additions would be required, but they can be made in a way that does not diminish the cultural significance of the place, require structural gymnastics, incur unaffordable capital or operating costs, or have a negative impact on the surrounding properties or visual context.
  - The proposed new use would make a positive contribution to the social, cultural, or economic context of the neighborhood.

The process of successfully accommodating a new use in an old building may be triggered by one of two situations:

- The property owner (perhaps motivated by community heritage advocates) is looking for a new use for a redundant historic building (i.e., the building needs a use).
- An operator or developer is seeking a building that would be appropriate for a specific use (i.e., the use needs a building).

Sometimes this is a relatively easy choice, as when an unused or underused church or theatre is taken over by a different faith or by an appropriately scaled performing arts organization. On other occasions, however, the match may be more challenging.

Repurposing a historic building is essentially an exercise in match-making. The procedure involves a number of steps; the order in which they are taken may depend on whether it is the building or the use that is driving the process. The key planning and design activities are:

- Consult with the community to identify potential uses or users and/or appropriate redundant buildings.
- Determine the spatial capabilities and structural condition of the building.
- Determine the space needs and technical requirements of the proposed use and potential user organization.
- If the building has been recognized for its heritage qualities, identify its cultural significance.
- Prepare conceptual architectural and structural designs.
- Identify appropriate means of tenure (ownership or lease arrangements).
- Ensure the scheme complies with applicable codes and bylaws.
- Ensure that the location, access, and community context are appropriate for the proposed use.
- Estimate capital costs.

- Prepare a business plan, including a plan for operation and governance, estimates of operating costs and revenues, and sources of funding.
- Incorporate this material into a conservation plan.

If the work to this point demonstrates that the adaptive reuse scheme is feasible, then work may proceed to design development, detailed planning, and approvals. A second round of community engagement would be appropriate, in order to gauge the degree of community support. A common-sense check is essential: would the scheme 'sort-of' work or would it truly meet the needs of the user and the capabilities of the building? A poor decision at this stage can handicap the ongoing operation for the life of the project.[4]

It is essential to determine the end use *before* proceeding with construction. Undertaking rehabilitation work without a firm use in mind would remove any flexibility and quite likely create yet another underused or unused building—but sadly, many enthusiasts do just that. Since the use classification must be identified in order to know which building code regulations to follow—an activity that determines many details of design, from the number and size of exits to the criteria for fire-resistance—the outcome may well be an adapted building that

Figures 5.6 and 5.7 Two repurposed churches: The Selexyz Dominicanen Bookstore in Maastricht, Netherlands, is a former Dominican church, adapted in 2007 by architects Merkx + Girod; The Cornerstone, Vancouver, was the former Mt. Pleasant Presbyterian Church, adapted in 1994 to accommodate 35 residential units. (Bert Kaufmann; John Roaf)

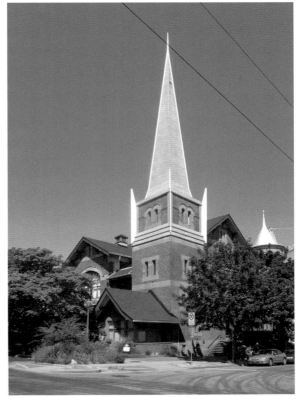

is unsuited to a potential future use that emerges later. Moreover, the burden of maintaining an empty rehabilitated building until a use and user emerge may lead to its demolition before a use is found.

The opportunities provided by adaptive reuse were first appreciated widely in the 1970s, when a flood of books on finding 'new uses for old buildings' appeared.[5] Some addressed all kinds of building-types while others focused on a particular category, such as churches, theatres, railway stations, and factories. This need to find new uses was to a large extent a result of the immense number of buildings that had been made redundant by the social upheaval of the time—by phenomena such as plummeting church attendance,[6] the loss of live theatre audiences to television, the replacement of rail by rubber-tire and air transport, the downturn in manufacturing in Western countries, and emerging new technologies that rendered many places inefficient. The 1970s was also the decade in which heritage conservation emerged as a vital discipline, likewise stimulated by the threats to historic places caused by societal changes.

Most literature from that period provided case studies of successful adaptations. Many were written from a heritage standpoint, others not. Some provided good, practical advice. One of the most pragmatic—and one whose instruction remains relevant—was by American engineer Laurence Reiner (1979: 39), who made his priorities quite clear:

> The final decision to proceed with a recycling project is really a financial one. This book is not about historical preservations as such, although the project may very well be one. ... Architectural preservation is important, but it cannot be the first consideration.

Interestingly, relatively little has been published on repurposing buildings since the 1970s. Perhaps the novelty has worn off and adaptive reuse is now a staple solution in the toolkit of the architect, developer, and heritage planner. Little has been written as well on the challenge of identifying the most appropriate operator (user) and governance to administer the new or continued use.

A most welcome addition to a recent crop of publications on rehabilitation and adaptive reuse is the series produced by English Heritage, showing 'how England's most valued buildings and places can be successfully adapted.' The fifth in this series, and the second to be titled *Constructive Conservation*, presents 44 case studies of buildings and cultural landscapes that exemplify creative uses, economic benefits, and observance to best conservation principles. Author and archaeologist Christopher Catling (2013: 3) neatly sums up the concept of good conservation in the definition of 'constructive conservation':

> 'Constructive conservation' is the broad term adopted by English Heritage for a positive and collaborative approach to conservation that focuses on the active management of change in ways that recognise and reinforce the historic significance of places, while accommodating the changes necessary to ensure their continued use and enjoyment.

The text states the necessity of being guided by English Heritage's *Conservation Principles* and working with the concept of sustainable development contained in the English government's *National Planning Policy Framework* (Department for Communities and Local Government (UK) 2012).

Historic house museums

Before the conservation industry began to focus on identifying innovative new uses for historic places, it adhered to the time-old practice of converting unused old residences into 'historic house museums.' Many heritage trusts and other not-for-profit owners of historic places around the world maintain a portfolio of house museums, most of which interpret the families who lived there and their social context. Some operate at the national level (e.g., the National Trust in England), some at the state or provincial level (e.g., the Historic Houses Trust of New South Wales), and the vast majority at the community level. While some such places flourish, the majority are underfunded and under-maintained, and cannot be sustained over the long term.

While many heritage professionals may consider the repurposing of historic houses as museums to be obsolete, the practice is still encouraged by heritage advocates and governments the world over. This is a knee-jerk reaction that occurs when a house associated with a significant historical figure, event, or movement becomes vulnerable. The outcome is often an undervisited and unsustainable museum that drains the resources of a non-profit organization and/or government.

Historic house museums continue to increase in number, yet are more and more threatened by scarce resources. As Americans Carol Stapp and Ken Turino (2004: 7, cited in Harris 2007: 4) have written,

Figure 5.8 Bethune Memorial House National Historic Site of Canada in Gravenhurst, Ontario, was the birthplace of Dr. Norman Bethune, best known as the physician who served Mao Zedong. Bethune is revered in China and this historic house museum is a 'must-see' for Chinese tourists. (Parks Canada)

The strongest evidence for questioning the value of museumification of a historic property springs from the paradox that the noble objective of interpretation for the public good may in fact be ill served when a building becomes a museum.

In recent years a concerted effort has been made to find creative new uses for old houses, as is common with other building-types. American heritage consultant Donna Ann Harris has analyzed a number of successful reuse and ownership solutions. Many retain the original interpretive mission, while others involve adaptation to an entirely new use. As examples of the latter, the Fairmount Park Historic Trust in Philadelphia, US, has found users for more than 20 properties. The uses include an architectural office, Masonic lodge, art school, professional association, and healthcare facility (Harris 2007: 175–7).

Archaeological sites and landscapes

Practical, sustainable uses may be found for sites and landscapes as well as for buildings. Publicly accessible archaeological sites are typically managed as interpreted places for passive, educational enjoyment. Active uses may be appropriate as long as the use does not threaten the remains or their cultural significance. Likewise rural or urban landscapes can be used for recreational, agricultural, educational, or other uses without diminishing their values. These functions can occur side by side with interpretive programs.

As an example, the thirteenth-century synagogue in Regensburg, Germany, was destroyed long ago and replaced with a Christian chapel, which in turn was demolished. The site and the surrounding

Figure 5.9 'Place of Encounter,' by Dani Karavan (2005), traces the foundations of the medieval synagogue in Regensburg, Germany. The place is used actively as an urban mini-park. (Harold Kalman)

former Jewish Quarter were extensively excavated in the 1990s and the remains backfilled for protection. The footprint of the foundations is depicted in *Place of Encounter*, a monument by Israeli sculptor Dani Karavan (2005), now actively used as an urban park in the heavily trafficked Neupfarrplatz.

5.3 Selecting a Conservation Treatment

The charters and standards define the various conservation treatments (see Section 3.2), but mostly fall silent when it comes to the question of which treatment is best for a particular situation. Nevertheless the choice of treatment (or treatments) is perhaps the most important decision to be made in developing a conservation plan. It guides many subsequent decisions. All operational and budgetary actions will be affected by it, as will the long-term use and appreciation.

The reason for selecting one treatment over another depends on many factors. These include the degree of cultural significance, the proposed use,[7] the objectives of the conservation project (e.g., the commemorative and sustainability objectives), the scale of the place (a grave marker, a building, a farm, a town), the opportunities for interpretation, the quality of documentation and information, the physical condition, the integrity, the context, and the available financial and human resources.[8]

Formal guidance to the reasons to select a particular treatment must be sought in sources other than the charters. Parks Canada and the US National Park Service provide helpful recommendations for the most common treatments with their standards (National Park Service 1992; Parks Canada 2010). The following synthesis draws from them and other sources:

Preservation as a primary treatment should be considered when:
- The continued or new use does not require extensive alterations or additions.
- Materials, features, and spaces of the historic place are essentially intact and convey the cultural significance, without extensive repair or replacement.
- Depiction during a particular period in its history is not appropriate.
- Financial or human resources may be limited.

Restoration should be considered when:
- The cultural significance of a historic place during a particular period in its history highly outweighs the potential loss of existing, non-character-defining materials, features, and spaces from other periods.
- Sufficient physical, documentary, and/or oral evidence exists to carry out the work accurately and without conjecture.
- Contemporary additions or alterations are not planned.
- Ample financial resources and strong professional skills are available.

Rehabilitation/adaptation (with or without a change in use) should be considered when:

- Productive economic use of the place or its neighborhood is particularly important to its continued survival. This may be especially so in urban situations, where historic places should function sustainably within a market economy.
- Extensive alterations or additions to the historic place are planned for a new or continued use.
- Repair or replacement of deteriorated features is necessary.
- A thorough energy refit is desired.
- Depiction during a particular period in its history is not appropriate.
- The cultural significance is moderate or low. If the cultural significance is high, then preservation may be preferable. If rehabilitation is selected, particular care must be taken to conserve character-defining elements.

Reconstruction may be considered when:

- A contemporary depiction is required to understand and interpret a property's cultural significance (including the recreation of missing components in a historic district or site).
- No other property with the same associative value has survived.
- Sufficient historical documentation exists to ensure accuracy.
- Ample financial resources and strong professional skills are available.

Stabilization should be considered when:

- Resources are limited but further deterioration should be stopped until the appropriate time for a more robust intervention.
- It is necessary to avoid catastrophic damage from deterioration while plans are being made and funds accessed.

Moving should be considered when:

- All efforts to conserve the historic place in situ have failed as a result of external economic, political, or social pressures.
- Retention of the historic place in situ would result in a threat to its continued existence (e.g., because of geophysical threats, such as rising water levels) and mitigation is not feasible.
- The siting of the historic place is not a primary reason for its cultural significance.
- The place has been moved in the past.

The decision as to which conservation treatment to apply should be made by a group of informed people (as required by the *Venice Charter*), not an individual. They may well disagree, since conflict is common, but must seek a consensus. The choices—and the ultimate decision and rationale—should be stated clearly in the conservation plan (discussed in Section 5.8).

To Preserve or to Restore? That is Often the Question

A row of shophouses at 60–66 Johnston Road in Hong Kong, built around 1930, formed part of a larger property acquired for residential redevelopment by the Urban Renewal Authority (URA). The historic place had changed over the years—both physically, with the enclosure of the former balconies to yield more floor space; and in its use, as the upper floors had become cramped, unpleasant tenements for residents with minimal incomes. This was the kind of substandard housing unit that the URA is mandated to replace. Public opinion advocated conservation of the building. The URA agreed to retain the old building and concentrate the new residences in a tall tower on the adjacent land.

The issue became one of how to conserve the building—whether to preserve it and retain the later façade elements, or to restore it to its original exterior appearance. Preservation would recognize the cultural significance of the changes over time, illustrating a common solution to overcrowding. Restoration, on the other hand, would reveal the appearance of a 1930s shophouse, a disappearing building-type that was once ubiquitous and representative of Hong Kong's development at the time. Heritage doctrine could support either alternative.

In the end restoration was selected for the exterior and the interiors were rehabilitated for food-and-beverage use. The original features were sufficiently intact (beneath the alterations) or known from photographs to permit an accurate restoration, and the URA was able to meet the cost of the work. The restaurant and building are called 'The Pawn,' a reminder of the familiar pawn shop which used to occupy one storefront, and which relocated nearby. The most compelling argument for restoration was based, however, not in the ICOMOS charters but rather in the subjective sentiments of government officials and the general public. The outcome of preservation, they felt, would have looked too 'messy,' would have been perceived as an injustice to a popular project, and would have been an unwanted reminder of the hardships endured by the hundreds of thousands of Hong Kong residents who occupy substandard housing.

Figures 5.10 and 5.11 The shophouse complex at 60–66 Johnston Road, Hong Kong, as it appeared in 2003 (left) and 2010 (right, with the base of the new tower to the right). (Architectural Conservation Programmes, The University of Hong Kong; Harold Kalman)

Table 5.1 Selecting a conservation treatment. The grades are L = 'low,' M = 'moderate,' and H = 'high.'

	Cultural significance	Need for change	Resources
Preservation	L-M-H	L-M	L-M-H
Restoration	H	L	H
Rehabilitation	L-M	H	M-H
Reconstruction	H	n/a	H
Stabilization	L-M-H	n/a	L
Moving	L-M	L-M-H	M-H

Conservation treatments for cultural landscapes

Heritage landscape specialists have argued that the conservation treatments advocated in international charters were formulated for architecture and are therefore too structural for cultural landscapes. Their criticism applies to the US *Secretary of the Interior's Guidelines for the Treatment of Cultural Landscapes*, which were adapted from those for buildings (National Park Service 1992). Landscape, unlike buildings, must be understood as process as well as product:

> The most important difference between preserving landscapes and preserving structures and objects is the dynamic quality of the land— it continuously changes and grows. Recognizing this quality reveals the fallacy of trying to freeze a landscape at a moment in time.
> (O'Donnell and Melnick 1987: 136, cited in Howett 2000: 190)

Various alternative treatments for cultural landscapes have been proposed, both for conservation and management, which go hand in hand. Several approaches are collected in American educator Richard Longstreth's (2008) anthology on cultural landscapes:

- A 'systems approach' (or 'process-systems approach'), which would add an action called 'intervene' to those already listed in the *Standards and Guidelines* for Rehabilitation (which include 'preserve,' 'protect and maintain,' and 'alterations/additions'). Interventions would require understanding the cultural landscape as a continuum over time.
- 'Ecological restoration,' a treatment that is based on the technical performance of the landscape (e.g., structural replication and species composition) and functions (e.g., wetland filtration) and not only on historic appearance, which is the current overarching gauge of conservation success.
- A 'community-based approach,' which considers social values deriving from cultural processes and cultural memory, and which recognizes the community's knowledge of the natural resources

and ecosystems, including situations that may embody conflicting values.

- A 'values-based approach' to management, which coordinates the operation of a historic place with the primary purpose of protecting its cultural significance. This can be achieved by understanding where the cultural values reside, and managing the site in a way that guards those values.[9]

Pimachiowin Aki: Community-based Protection of a Land and a Way of Life

Pimachiowin Aki, 'the land that gives life' in the Ojibway language, is a 43,300-sq. km intact boreal forest territory that sustains five First Nations who engage in trapping, fishing, and hunting. It spans the Canadian provincial boundaries of Manitoba and Ontario. The innovative approach to management of this immense cultural landscape will be by means of community-based land-use legislation. Enabled by Manitoba's *East Side Traditional Lands Planning and Special Protected Areas Act*, the Poplar River First Nation—one of the five partners—produced the *Asatiwisipe Aki Management Plan*, which aims to sustain landscape and wildlife biodiversity, ecological integrity, and many sacred and cultural spaces, all within the framework of the community's traditional knowledge. The

Figure 5.12 The Poplar River Indigenous Community Conservation Area in winter, the only season in which it is accessible by land. (© A.Pawlowska-Mainville)

land is designated as a park reserve, with a 'wilderness and backcountry' land-use category. This allows recreational development and resource extraction that do not compromise the boreal region or the traditional way of life. It prohibits commercial development, such as logging, mining, and hydroelectric transmission lines, which would permanently alter habitats. The holistic plan protects natural, economic, sociocultural, and political resources. The Aboriginal inhabitants recognize that they must pursue the goal of economic development through biodiversity conservation—activities that are perceived within European values as a contradiction.

An area of 33,400 sq. km has been nominated as a World Heritage Site. The site would be governed by Pimachiowin Aki Corporation, a non-profit organization composed of representatives from each of the five First Nations and two provincial governments. The present Poplar River management plan would be adopted as a model for the larger area, other than for two existing parks (Pawlowska 2012: 91–8; see also Davidson-Hunt et al. 2010; Davidson-Hunt 2012).

Methods for the protection and management of cultural landscapes are not unlike those that have been developed for protected areas, which often combine natural and cultural values. The IUCN (International Union for Conservation of Nature), which has developed a management framework for protected areas, acknowledges that protected areas it has recognized often overlap with World Heritage cultural landscapes. IUCN advises the World Heritage Centre in this regard (Finke 2013).

5.4 Tools and Incentives

It is one thing to determine that a historic place merits conservation for its cultural significance; it is quite another to create a legal, planning, economic, and taxation framework that enables conservation in a way that balances the benefits and costs to property owners, governments, and the general public.

Age-old social attitudes work against conservation. One is the common (mis)belief that novelty and change are by their very nature good things—a conviction firmly entrenched in our cultures, and based on the eighteenth-century Romantic notion of the value of innovation—whereas change is neither good nor bad in itself. Another attitude favoring change involves the concept of planned obsolescence, of designing products with a limited useful life, since it nurtures an ideology of constant change (and ongoing sales of new products). The sustainability ethos is changing these attitudes, but slowly.

Taxation and land-use policies also may work against heritage conservation. In Canada, for example, the federal *Income Tax Act* disallows funds spent on improving revenue properties (e.g., rehabilitation) to be declared as tax-deductible expenses, insisting that they be capitalized (capital expenses are not tax-deductible). Federal tax law has further insisted that depreciation on old buildings be claimed at a rapid rate, thus devaluing them far more quickly than their long, useful lives warrant. It also provides for 'terminal loss,' a significant tax benefit that owners can claim on demolition. Canadian provincial legislation addressing land appraisal assesses real property at its 'highest and best use'—in other words, bases value on the development potential—what a property *could* earn if fully (re)developed. Municipal legislation contributes to this bias, by reducing property assessment when a building is demolished, and frequently taxing parking lots at a lower rate than built-up properties of identical assessment. These and other measures favor new construction over the retention of old buildings and provide *dis*incentives to conservation (Denhez 1997: 8, 1994: 204–5). Fortunately amendments have been introduced to reduce some punitive fiscal disincentives.[10]

The value-added tax (VAT) in England poses parallel problems, as the 'incentives for listed building' actually work against proper repair and maintenance and indirectly give encouragement to the neglect of buildings, so that owners may argue for major repairs, which do get a tax benefit (Pickard 1996: 98).

Established economic forces conflict with conservation as well. As was seen in the discussion of heritage economics in Section 2.2, cultural capital (including historic places) has non-use values that exist outside markets, and therefore one often cannot depend on normal market forces to support cultural assets fully. This may require governments or institutions to intervene, in order 'to correct for market failure.' This may be done with 'direct or indirect intervention and using instruments with monetary or non-monetary content' (Rizzo and Throsby 2006: 999). In lay terms, this refers to the use of incentives.

Many governments have introduced a range of procedures that help to offset anti-conservation biases. The objective is to balance constraints with incentives. These include measures that permit and regulate conservation management (**tools** or **controls**), as well as procedures that facilitate and encourage conservation initiatives by private property owners (**incentives** or **inducements**). Some methods require legislation in order to be enforceable, whereas others need only regulations or procedures. The legislative background and context are provided in Section 2.1; this discussion focuses on the specific tools and incentives that are enabled by those laws.

Governments use tools to enforce conservation policy and make incentives available to property owners to facilitate the work of

Figure 5.13 Carrots, stick, donkey, and enforcer. (Every Woman's Encyclopaedia, 1910–12)

conservation. In both cases, the public sector intervenes in the private sector to assist conservation, and thereby build a more sustainable community. To use the parable of carrots and sticks—you can make the donkey walk by dangling a carrot in front of him or by striking his rump with a stick—tools are sticks and incentives are carrots.

Sometimes it is difficult to distinguish between a tool and an incentive. For example, placing a historic place on a regulatory list is seen by some people as applying a stick, whereas that same listing often enables the property owner to qualify for incentives—definitely a carrot. This discussion therefore does not attempt to make a precise distinction between the two kinds of instruments.

The discussion that follows separates tools and incentives into three categories:

- Planning and protection tools (often sticks)
- Financial incentives (carrots)
- Non-financial incentives (carrots).

Tools are mostly a European creation, whereas incentives are to a large extent an American innovation. New World society has always emphasized that economic growth should be stimulated by novelty and change and, consequently, has been slower than Europe to accept the fundamental cultural and economic (i.e., sustainability) values of heritage conservation. Moreover, preservation in the US has been burdened with the prospect of compensation stipulated by the Fifth Amendment to the Constitution, and so satisfying property owners has been a central concern.[11] For this reason, many examples of incentives cited below have been drawn from the American and, following the American lead, Canadian experiences.

The array of currently available conservation tools and incentives varies widely from one jurisdiction to another. This section describes many that are in widespread use. Each is introduced briefly, generally with some information on the source and/or use of that tool. Some have been introduced in previous chapters, but it is helpful to group them together here. The heritage planner must become familiar with the full range of tools and incentives that are available in her/his jurisdiction, because they broaden the possibilities for resolving conflicts and are often key to the success of a conservation project.[12]

Planning and protection tools

Heritage recognition

The survey and inventory process, described in Section 4.2, produces a **list** of historic places (often called an **inventory** or a **register**) which may or may not have statutory standing (i.e., formal legal status). The list usually resides with one or another level of government, but in some situations it is kept and maintained by a community group, such as a historical society. Listing provides what is usually called 'recognition.'

Non-statutory lists

A list that has no statutory authority is useful for providing information and raising public awareness. It offers informal recognition by identifying historic places that have some heritage significance. The presence of a place on such a list may be preparatory to its future statutory listing or legal protection.

Some lists with official-sounding names may be non-statutory. An example is the Canadian Register of Historic Places (CRHP), an online database of places that have already been listed by a province or a territory, which forwards the data to the federal government. Inclusion on the CRHP provides information, not protection. Whether or not the place is protected depends upon its status with its province or territory, the levels of government that have the power to protect private property. In some provinces, listing on a municipal heritage register (as most are called) requires consent by the elected municipal council.

If a historic place is absent from a list, this does not necessarily mean that the place has no heritage significance. It simply indicates that its values have not been recognized.

Statutory lists

A statutory list is established by law and provides formal recognition of heritage significance. This serves two main purposes: it has regulatory value in that an application to change a historic place will usually trigger a formal reaction process; and it has informational value in that it provides data on historic places, enabling the public to see what has been recognized as having heritage significance. Some statutory lists provide protection (see below), whereas others do not. Some list only buildings; others include landscape features, archaeological sites, and other kinds of historic places.

Listed places must have passed through a formal screening process, and the list may require approval by elected officials.

The National Register of Historic Places in the US lists some 80,000 properties or areas, representing 1.4 million individual historic places, which are significant at the national, state, or community level. Most are nominated to the Register by the states. The Register is supported by a large infrastructure that is headed by the National Park Service and the Department of the Interior, but which includes all levels of government as well as Indian tribes. Numerous *National Register Bulletins* provide technical advice for nominating all kinds of historic places. Listing on the National Register provides recognition but not protection. Private property owners are not required to maintain listed properties or open them to the public, nor do they need federal consent to make changes or demolish listed properties. Any protection or other controls must be imposed at the local level (National Park Service n.d.-d; Shull 2011).

England has been listing 'ancient monuments' (archaeological sites and ruins that are no longer inhabited) since 1882, occupied buildings since 1947, and conservation areas since 1967. The English system grades buildings into three categories:

- Grade I buildings are of exceptional interest, sometimes considered to be internationally important; only 2.5 percent of listed buildings are Grade I.
- Grade II* buildings are particularly important buildings of more than special interest; 5.5 percent of listed buildings are Grade II*.
- Grade II buildings are nationally important and of special interest; 92 percent of all listed buildings are in this class and it is the most likely grade of listing for a homeowner.

In the context of the discussion on grading in Section 4.5 above, Grade I buildings would be considered to have 'excellent' heritage significance, Grade II* buildings, 'very good,' and Grade II, 'good.'

Inclusion on the National Heritage List for England is officially recognition, rather than protection, 'an identification stage where buildings are marked and celebrated as having exceptional architectural or historic special interest, before any planning stage which may decide a building's future.' Listing is technically not a preservation order. Nevertheless it does require that all applications for change or demolition be considered by the authorities. 'Listed building consent' is required to make any changes that may affect cultural significance. Works to listed buildings may also require planning permission for changes of use and building regulation approval for health and safety purposes (English Heritage n.d.-c; Pendlebury 2001: 297–8). The statutory list of buildings compiled by Historic Scotland provides protection, conferring recognition and protection in the same process (Historic Scotland n.d.).

Hong Kong has both a statutory list of 'monuments' declared and protected under the *Antiquities and Monuments Ordinance* and a non-statutory list of graded buildings undertaken as an internal assessment by the Antiquities and Monuments Board. An attempt was made through the court to force a judicial review of a Grade I structure (the Queen's Pier) to force its declaration as a protected monument, but the judge ruled that 'the classification [as a graded building] has no statutory standing' and that there is no automatic linkage between the two lists (Kong 2013; see also Leung 2012).

Australia maintains a profusion of lists: the National Heritage List, the Commonwealth Heritage List, state and territory heritage lists, local government lists, Indigenous site registers, and National Trust lists. All but the last are statutory (Gurran 2011: 102–3).

Heritage protection

Most jurisdictions provide for the protection of selected recognized historic places. The most common way to protect a historic place is to declare it protected, pursuant to the appropriate statute. As was discussed in Section 2.1, several European countries have been protecting individual places for centuries. The process began with archaeological sites and, over the years, evolved to include other kinds of historic places.

Heritage protection legislation was originally derived from statutes that addressed works of cultural and artistic merit, and therefore protected monuments and buildings; whereas the more recent heritage statutes have often evolved from land-use controls, and consequently control (and thereby protect) property. Controlling land use supports the protection of not only buildings, but also historic areas, landscapes, and cultural landscapes. Other laws have evolved from environmental controls: these protect environmental (or heritage) qualities or values, which are more difficult to define but much broader in scope.

Protection is usually intended for the long term, but may apply only for the short term in response to a threat, to allow a 'cooling-off period' in which the parties in dispute can try to negotiate a resolution. Both forms of protection are described below.

Many terms are used to describe protected places. England has adopted the term 'scheduled' for archaeological sites (nearly 20,000 'ancient monuments' had been scheduled by 2012). Canada uses 'designated.' Many American cities choose the word 'landmark.' It is important to know the correct word in your jurisdiction, and to be able to differentiate protected places from those that are simply listed.

Long-term heritage protection

Long-term protection is achieved by statutes or ordinances that prohibit the demolition, removal or alteration of built historic places. Those proposed for designation are usually, but not always, selected from a list of recognized places. The decision to designate a place is generally based on its meeting a set list of evaluation criteria.

Protection usually does not mean preventing change and freezing a historic place in time, but rather managing change to ensure that any modifications are consistent with the protection of heritage values. Change is usually allowed upon the issuance of a permit (or 'consent'), following a process whereby the property owner submits a proposal for change and a duly constituted body determines that the changes are consistent with good conservation practice. In the words of the *Burra Charter*, any changes should 'retain the cultural significance of a place.' Consent is usually given by elected officials, who are often advised by an appointed board; or by staff who have been delegated authority by the elected officials. The particular criteria and procedures for consent vary from one place to another. Some permit appeals while others do not.

Many jurisdictions also allow historic areas to be protected. In the UK the procedure for addressing conservation area consents is identical to that for listed buildings in relation to authorizing works, taking enforcement action, and undertaking urgent works to preserved unoccupied buildings (Rydin 2003: 294). Landscape features, such as trees or gardens, are also protected under many systems. The regulations are usually similar, with the added complication that plant material grows and dies, and natural change cannot be controlled.

The protection and management of cultural landscapes is a product of our generation. Relatively few jurisdictions have yet enacted legislation to protect them as cultural landscapes (they may be protected as conservation areas or designed landscapes), and techniques for their protection and ongoing management are being debated and developed. Protection and management are particularly closely related, since of all place-types, cultural landscapes are the most subject to continual change, and that change often reflects positive actions, namely the evolution of the interaction between people and the land, and the dimension of time. As noted in Section 5.3, protection must therefore accommodate appropriate change in a way that differs from change to buildings or changes to landscapes.

In some situations, more than the listed property can be protected. In the Canadian province of Québec, for example, the government may declare the 'perimeter' of a protected ('classified') or recognized building, which may extend a maximum of 152 meters (500 feet) from the building and may be irregular in shape. Any buildings within that perimeter, even if under different ownership, are protected as well.[13] In the UK, listed property includes not only the subject building, but also its 'curtilage,' which refers to the immediate setting. However, the extent of the features that are included in the curtilage is rarely defined until the owner seeks consent for change.[14]

Penalties for violating protective legislation vary from onerous (such as forcing the perpetrator to rebuild the demolished structure) to a nominal fine that some may see simply as the cost of doing business. The latter—particularly in North America—is representative of the rather weak commitment that some governments show towards heritage conservation. This is seen as well in that many statutes have clauses that enable property owners to evade the full, long-term intent of protective legislation. Generally these provisions enable property owners who apply to alter or demolish a designated historic place to have their way after a specified period of time should attempts to find a resolution fail. Another factor that weakens the effect of protective legislation is the provision of compensation for heritage designation, which is discussed below with financial incentives.

As mentioned above, land-use controls allow the protection of areas larger than a single building, ruin, tree, or small group of buildings. For conservation areas, protection may pertain to all buildings within a defined district, or alternatively only to individually scheduled properties. Alterations and new construction—including those made to unscheduled properties within the conservation area—are usually controlled by design guidelines. Because guidelines are subject to interpretation in the same way as is the appropriateness of proposed alterations to a single building, an appointed review board usually considers applications and makes recommendations to the approving authority.

Archaeological sites and ruins are also frequently protected. Indeed, as seen above, they were the first place-types to be protected under the laws of England and many other countries. Statutes for this purpose often follow the model of protection for their cultural value.[15]

Reservation and dedication

A government may **reserve** or **dedicate** (the two are similar in meaning) public property, including any structures or landscape features on the property, as a long-term commitment to protection. The reservation may be made for park purposes (its most common use) or for any other stated objective.

A 'Reserve' is a term often adopted in the designation of extended cultural landscapes, including places that are not fully in public ownership. Ebey's Landing National Historical Reserve (NHR) on Whidbey Island, Washington, was designated as a 17,400-acre National Historic Reserve in 1978 to 'preserve and protect' a rural agricultural community. Since reservation provides statutory protection only to the publicly owned portion, 2,000 acres of land in private ownership have been protected by the acquisition of scenic easements (described just below). The Trust Board of Ebey's Landing NHR, a unit of local government, is responsible for management of the reserve. Despite the incomplete protection, on balance the outcome of the private–public partnership has been positive (National Park Service n.d.-b; Rottle 2008: 129–49).

Nearby, just across the US–Canada marine border, Parks Canada manages the Gulf Islands National Park Reserve, which comprises 36 sq. km of land and marine area on 15 islands, numerous islets and reefs, as well as 26 sq. km of submerged lands. The reserve has both natural value as habitat for seals and nesting shorebirds, as well as cultural value relating to Aboriginal use and nineteenth-century European settlement.

Figure 5.14 Ebey's Landing National Historical Reserve on Whidbey Island, Washington, USA, a rural agricultural community. (National Park Service)

Short-term heritage protection

Legislation often enables a municipality (or other jurisdiction) to apply interim protection to a threatened property for a limited period of time—usually for several months, and rarely for more than one year. Appeal processes can reverse these actions. A stop order is a similar tool, and likewise must be justified to the courts. This provides a quick response to an immediate threat, and allows time for consideration of various long-term protection options and a resolution of differences between the property owner and the municipality or community.

Enforcement may be effected by withholding a demolition permit or approval, or by a temporary protection order. The tool may be applied to the threatened property, to landscape features, and/or to adjacent or nearby properties.

Easements and covenants

An **easement** or a **covenant** is a contractual agreement that gives one party certain rights to use the property of another party (i.e., acquire 'privileged access' to the property) without possessing or owning it. A common form of easement is one that allows a person to gain access to his/her property by crossing another person's property. The former 'enjoys' the use of the land of the latter.[16] A covenant is similar, but it is usually composed as a promise made by one party to engage or refrain from specified conduct. Easements are registered on the title to the property and are binding on subsequent owners; covenants may also be registered on title, but they do not always pertain to property, in which event their benefits are binding only on the parties to the agreement.

A **heritage easement** (or **scenic easement** or **conservation easement**) is a voluntary agreement made between two parties, whereby a property owner gives the second party—often a government or a trust—the responsibility of imposing certain conditions that ensure conservation of the property. These conditions usually address protection against demolition and inappropriate alterations, by giving the easement-holder the right to approve or reject proposals for change. The property owner may receive a tax credit for donating an easement, or a 'consideration' (usually financial) for agreeing to the conditions. In this way the effect of a heritage easement or covenant is much the same as that of designation and compensation. The advantage is that it is reached through mutual agreement and not through a confrontational process. Unlike designation, the easement or covenant can be tailored to the specific property, as by identifying those elements of a building or a landscape that are intended to be retained in perpetuity and setting out what alterations and development may be permitted without first obtaining permission. And finally the cost of an easement is usually far less than compensation, with essentially the same conservation outcome.

The National Trust for Historic Preservation is one of many organizations that hold easements on historic places. The Trust acquires easements both by donation and as a condition to preservation grants or other financial assistance, while some easements were created to protect properties that the National Trust acquired and then transferred to other owners (National Trust for Historic Preservation n.d.).

In Canada the immense Waldron Ranch in southwestern Alberta, comprising some 30,500 acres (12,350 hectares) with remarkable scenic and historical values, has been protected with an easement between the Nature Conservancy of Canada and the Waldron Grazing Cooperative Ltd. The deal, worth a reported CAD$15 million, allows the 72 ranchers to continue using the land for grazing livestock, but prevents future subdivision, cultivation, and development, including prohibiting new roads, fences, or houses (Cryderman 2013: A4).

Easements are used as well for properties that have natural heritage significance. Land trusts have been established in a number of countries to accept and acquire easements of this kind. Easements and covenants are also used to control the surroundings of historic places, when statutory protection applies only to the immediate place (Brenneman 1971: 416–22).

American real-estate economists Paul Asabere and Forrest Huffman found substantial price increases in Philadelphia associated with historic façade easements as well as those for being in a historic district (1994: 396–401, cited in Netzer 2006: 1246).[17] In economic terms, what an easement does is to introduce a new kind of property right and then create a special market in which these separate rights can be traded and transferred. Separating development rights from property rights is another such device, as is the transfer of density, which is discussed below (Klamer and Zuidhof 1999: 41–2).

Heritage agreements

Other forms of **heritage agreement** (or **conservation agreement**) may be used to protect private property. Similar to a covenant, this is a voluntary agreement between two parties—often a property owner and a municipal government—that outlines the duties, obligations, and benefits negotiated by the parties. The agreement may be registered on title, but this is not a necessary condition.

As an example, in New South Wales the government and the owner of private land (or the lessee of Crown land) may enter into a voluntary conservation agreement to protect either natural or cultural heritage. The agreements may require a management plan. Conservation agreements are registered on the title to the property and 'run with the land,' binding successors to the agreement.

Another instance is the agreement of purchase and sale for New York's Seagram Building drawn up in 1979 between Seagram (the original owner) and the Teachers Insurance and Annuity Association (the subsequent owner). Article 26 of the agreement defines the architectural integrity of the building and its innovative plaza, and prescribes how much (actually how little!) change may occur to the exterior and the first 10 feet (3m) of office space behind the glass façades. This voluntary protection came into force a decade before the Seagram

Building received official landmark designation (Ibelings 2013: 27; Lambert 2013).

Municipalities in the Province of British Columbia often utilize a **Heritage Revitalization Agreement** (HRA) for projects that combine the conservation of a historic place with substantial new development. The HRA is written to describe the specific situation, including the various tools and incentives that are applied. It names the conditions to which the property owner agrees (usually including protection of all or part of a historic place and conservation work to be undertaken); and also the development conditions agreed to by the local government (such as permitted land uses, density, height, and siting requirements). The HRA usually supersedes existing zoning regulations. Although it can be worded to provide statutory protection, some municipalities also require parallel protection by designation, even if it is redundant.

Planning controls

Alternative means of heritage protection

Planning controls, which are based on regulating the permitted use of land, can be used to protect historic places in a number of ways without the need for heritage legislation. These are easiest to implement when heritage conservation is integrated within a regulatory planning environment.

Zoning can be used for protection, although only indirectly. It can effectively protect specified districts by prohibiting uses, building heights, floor area ratios, or other features that are inappropriate to the character of the district, thereby providing a disincentive for demolition and redevelopment. The old city centre of Victoria, British Columbia, escaped redevelopment because the maximum building heights and densities permitted by the zoning bylaw were less than those of most existing older buildings. Elsewhere, a municipal zoning ordinance ratified in 1931 effectively made 'Old and Historic Charleston,' in South Carolina, the first historic district to be protected in the US. A specially appointed Board of Architectural Review saw that all changes to historical buildings were appropriate to their heritage values (Hosmer 1981: I, 238–42).

Another method is **demolition control**, usually a local government power, which is used primarily to retain a particular land use. For example, a city may prevent the removal of housing units in a particular neighborhood, and in doing so will protect historic (as well as new) residential buildings. Another strategy is to withhold a demolition permit until such time as a development permit has been issued for the site, thereby discouraging 'speculative demolition.'

Land-use regulations can help meet conservation objectives directly as well. As was seen in Section 5.3, the Asatiwisipe Aki Management Plan protects the biodiversity of a large Aboriginal cultural landscape by designating it as a park reserve, with a 'wilderness and backcountry' land-use category. This prohibits threatened commercial logging, mining, and hydroelectric transmission lines while permitting recreational development and resource extraction that do not compromise the landscape or the traditional way of life.

Using another type of planning regulation, the City of Halifax, Nova Scotia, introduced **view plane legislation** in 1974 to protect the view of the Halifax waterfront from Citadel Hill and Halifax Citadel National Historic Site (and vice versa). The historical justification is that the fortifications defended the British settlement against maritime attack, and so the visual link between the citadel and the harbor is essential to understanding the historic place.[18]

Design review

Municipalities often require **design review**, usually by an appointed board, for certain applications for development. Design review is usually used as well for proposed work in conservation areas, to determine whether the proposals follow the applicable design guidelines.

An issue with any review board is whether the jury should comprise professional designers, non-specialists, or both. The last is probably the best solution, combining expertise with popular sentiment.

Minimum maintenance standards and mandatory inspection

Owners may choose not to maintain unprofitable historic buildings, which in turn can lead to 'demolition by neglect'—deliberately allowing buildings to deteriorate to the point where their repair may become unfeasible. To combat deliberate neglect, the authorities often have the power to enter a building to inspect its condition, and to force the owner to make urgent repairs—or to do the repairs themselves, at the owner's expense—should the condition warrant it. Because the inspection is tantamount to a hostile search, the inspection ordinance should enable the municipality to obtain a search warrant from the courts if needed.

In England, listed buildings that have been severely neglected—an estimated 7 percent—are declared to be 'at risk.' Nearly twice that many have been found to be 'vulnerable.' The legislation enables a local authority to issue a Repairs Notice on the owners of such structures (Pickard 1996: chapter 4). Many other local governments have comparable regulations to ensure a minimum level of care and maintenance for property. This usually applies to all properties, and not just those with heritage value, although some jurisdictions do have separate regulations for historic places.

Some jurisdictions explicitly make it an offence to allow a protected property to deteriorate. Québec's *Cultural Property Act*, for example, says a person is guilty of an offence if (s)he 'fails to keep classified [protected] cultural property in good condition' (Section 58(3)).

Tax concessions that encourage maintenance also help in this regard. These are discussed below, with financial incentives.

Building codes

Another group of controls on building, development, and heritage conservation are building codes and regulations. These may regulate design to achieve safety, energy conservation, accessibility, or some other benefit. Technically they are building controls and not planning controls, but their effect is similar. Codes are considered with the legal infrastructure in Section 2.1.

Building codes are among the various regulations and statutes that were not enacted for heritage management purposes but can be used to complement the provisions of heritage legislation. They also include, but are not limited to, planning legislation, non-heritage land-use laws, and environmental protection laws.

Financial incentives

The most direct form of financial intervention is for government or an institution to acquire ownership of a historic place and/or to take responsibility for its operation, including assuming responsibility for costs and revenues. This is not an incentive but, rather, direct involvement. It can be justified and effective if the historic place meets the objectives of the potential new owner or operator (i.e., be consistent with government policy or institutional mission), and if that party is willing and able to commit sufficient resources on a long-term basis, which is not always a secure proposition in times of financial restraint. In contrast, financial incentives generally cost less than acquisition or operation. An incentive can also be more effective if the existing owner or operator will commit to effective management of the place after having received the benefits of the incentive.

The incentive system provides a consideration to a property owner in return for a conservation intervention. The principle is one of *quid pro quo*; the owner or developer provides the community with a heritage amenity—deemed a community benefit—and the community gives the owner a benefit in return.

Compensation

In a sense all planning tools and incentives provide compensation to property owners for the constraints (e.g., the requirement to obtain permission to make changes) and obligations (e.g., maintenance in perpetuity) that are imposed by protection. In North America, however, one particular financial tool is termed 'compensation.' The concept is based on the outdated and often erroneous perceptions that heritage protection decreases property values and that the cost (or opportunity cost) of conservation exceeds that of doing the work in a more familiar, non-conservation manner. By these standards, the owner is seen as deserving to be compensated for the work. Indeed this is sometimes the case. However, at times the opposite is true: the cost of preservation or rehabilitation may be significantly less than demolition and new construction.[19]

In the Canadian province of Alberta, for example, if designation (protection) decreases the economic value of a building, structure, or land, the City must provide the owner with 'compensation for the decrease in economic value.'[20] In neighboring British Columbia, the owner of a designated property may demand payment equal to the loss of market value, where designation is proved to cause a reduction.[21] Alternatively the owner may accept a non-financial incentive (described below) as compensation, which is what is nearly universally done by municipalities in British Columbia.

To avoid having to pay compensation, municipalities in British Columbia have adopted a strategy whereby they designate historic places only with the owner's consent, which is usually obtained by the owner's acceptance of incentives in lieu of compensation. An unfortunate precedent was set in 2009, when the City of Victoria designated the interior of the Rogers' Chocolates store, a National Historic Site, to prevent an intended expansion and the loss of century-old interior fixtures. However, designation occurred without the owner's consent. The owner sued for compensation and an appointed arbitrator ruled that the City had to pay CAD$598,000 plus 85 percent of legal costs (Heritage BC 2010c).

Grants

The most common form of financial incentive is a grant (called 'grant-in-aid' in the US). Money is given to the property owner to assist with the costs of conservation work, thereby lessening the financial burden. Grants may be nominal or substantial. Even a small grant can have considerable impact, since it gives the property owner a sense of being valued by society and encourages the activity.

The advantage of a grant is that it is the most direct form of incentive. The disadvantage to the granting agency is that it is a direct and non-reimbursable expense.

Governments and foundations are the most common granting agencies. The agency will want some assurance of a positive outcome— which is usually achieved by insisting that the applicant provide an equal or greater 'matching' contribution and requiring that good conservation practice be followed in the work. The grantor will likely also see the funds as an investment in community development, whether the return on investment is measured by its economic, social, and/or cultural benefits.

European as well as North American governments have long offered grants for conservation, sometimes directly and sometimes through arm's-length trusts or foundations. England has provided improvement grants for housing since 1949 in a series of Housing Acts, which provided for larger grants for listed buildings; and in 1953 the Ministry of Works was authorized to make grants toward the maintenance of buildings of outstanding significance. The program was expanded with the creation of building preservation trusts, which access public funding at the local level and undertake supporting initiatives (Civic Trust

1972: 22–5; Pickard 1996: 122–31; United States Conference of Mayors 1966: 153). The national government enabled local authorities to make grants for historic buildings, pursuant to the *Local Authorities (Historic Buildings) Act 1962*. The granting program has grown exponentially: between 2005 and 2010, English Heritage disbursed an annual average of £33 million in grants to buildings, conservation areas, and the historic environment (English Heritage n.d.-b).[22]

The total amount of grant money available in the UK to historic places, museums, the natural environment, intangible heritage, and more far exceeds the programs of English Heritage. Since its inception in 1993 the Heritage Lottery Fund, which is funded by a portion of the National Lottery, has provided an average of £375 million each year—funding nearly 32,000 projects in its first 18 years (Heritage Lottery Fund n.d.). Other countries also use lottery funds for cultural purposes.

Many foundations and non-governmental organizations offer grants for heritage conservation as well. Programs may fund research, planning, construction, operations, advocacy, and more. The best funded are the large international organizations, such as the World Monuments Fund, the Getty Conservation Institute, and the Aga Khan Development Network. Capital projects make up only a portion of their many activities. Far more numerous are the national, regional, and local foundations and trusts—some large, some small—whose mission is to assist in the conservation of historic places.

Offering Incentives in Lieu of Compensation: Victoria, BC

Municipalities in British Columbia have pursued a broad range of financial incentive programs. The City of Victoria offers an array of programs, using community partners to administer some. The incentive programs comprise:

- House Grants Program: Grants to owners of designated houses.
- Building Incentive Program (BIP) for Commercial & Institutional Buildings: Grants for rehabilitation and structural/seismic upgrades.
- Tax Incentive Program (TIP) for Downtown Heritage Buildings: Ten-year tax exemptions for the provision of new residential units and structural upgrades.

Figure 5.15 Johnson Street in Victoria's 'Old Town,' on which many buildings have been improved with help from voluntary incentive programs. (Bob Matheson)

- Design Assistance Grants: Assistance for rehabilitation design (discontinued).

These programs are seen as worthwhile municipal investments. In addition to implementing several official policies (conservation of historic places, increasing residential units in the downtown core, and seismic upgrade of commercial buildings), they yield a hefty return on investment. Analysis of the benefits (City of Victoria 2013; Victoria Civic Heritage Trust 2012) reveals that:

- The BIP leverages $28.08 in private investment for every $1 in grants.
- The BIP generated more than $123 million in private investment for 196 properties (1990–2012).
- The TIP generated 630 new residential units and seismic upgrades for 25 buildings (1998–2013).
- The house grants helped more than 200 houses and generated $1.8 million in private investment (to 2002).
- The tax base increased faster for assisted properties than for non-supported ones. For TIP-supported projects, the value of property taxes has increased 131 percent vs. an average of 57 percent. This ensures that the property tax revenues forgone over ten years will be recovered over time.
- Tourism increased.[23]

Loans and mortgages

Special loans to property owners for conservation work are another incentive. Although relatively uncommon, government agencies and financial institutions have devised loans and mortgages that are available at a lower interest rate than conventional bank loans, despite the potential for added risk. Moreover, a portion of the loan is sometimes forgivable, making the borrower repay only part of the principal.

A number of US banks have offered historic preservation loans through a high-risk loan pool, sometimes funded by special historic preservation savings accounts that may pay lower interest than conventional accounts, and which are patronized by residents wanting to help improve their neighborhood. As an example, in the 1970s the South Shore National Bank of Chicago established an innovative Neighborhood Development Center (NDC), a profit-oriented division with lower margins than conventional divisions. The NDC's high-risk loan fund was financed by development deposits (minimum deposit of $1,000, paying market interest) from outside the deteriorating neighborhood. The NDC made nearly $3 million in loans in 1976, including home improvement loans and mortgages for rundown properties. The investment stimulated area revitalization and raised commercial confidence (Warner 1978: 160–3).

In a similar and contemporaneous venture, the Bank of America created the City Improvement and Restoration Program (CIRP) to assist community revitalization in California. It began with a program in East Oakland that offered loans at below-market interest rates to high-risk owners of older homes. Loans were secured by a non-interest-bearing deposit account funded by a Federal Community Development Block Grant (Warner 1978: 120–3).

Currently in the US the Department of Housing and Urban Development (HUD) offers preferential-interest lending programs through private lenders. Other advantageous mortgage products sponsored by government and non-profit organizations are available for low- and moderate-income homeowners. While not intended specifically for historic buildings, many of the programs can be used for this purpose (Getty Conservation Institute 2004: 19–21, 26–30). Related incentives include mortgage guarantees, which reduce the risk to the mortgagee.

Revolving funds

A revolving fund for heritage conservation is a particular kind of loan fund, usually administered by a non-profit (volunteer) society, which often expects a modest return on its investments. Typically the fund provides financing for the acquisition and/or rehabilitation of old buildings. In one model it will purchase (or otherwise secure) a threatened building, safeguard it with legal protection, and sell (or lease) it to a buyer who will conserve it. In a second model the fund will undertake the conservation work itself and then sell the improved building. In either case the sale is accompanied by a protective covenant, conservation agreement, or some other protection tool.

When a property has been transferred to a new owner or occupant, the proceeds from the sale or lease are returned to the fund to be reused ('revolved') for the same purpose. Revolving funds are typically managed by a trust or foundation, which may hold title to the buildings or may invest in properties owned by others. The fund is initially built by means of fundraising (Derda and Moriarity 2006).

The revolving fund was one of the earliest financial tools used by the conservation community. It has long been popular in the US, where it is called a (historic) preservation revolving fund. Some of the oldest historic district schemes were funded through revolving funds. In New Orleans, advocate Stanley Arthur proposed in 1937 that a private foundation be set up to provide funds for buying and preserving buildings in the French Quarter, but the scheme was not carried through (Hosmer 1981: I, 296). In South Carolina, the Historic Charleston Foundation (founded in 1947 to help conserve the oldest official historic district in the US, established in 1931) began to operate a revolving fund in 1957. Within 15 years it had 'purchased and restored or caused to be restored' some 63 buildings in Charleston. The Historic Savannah Foundation in adjacent Georgia (incorporated 1954) reportedly facilitated the protection and conservation of more than 800 buildings in its first 20 years of operation (Ziegler et al. 1975: 56–75). The Foundation continues to use the revolving fund today, acquiring marketable endangered buildings with heritage significance through donation, purchase, or options; then selling them with covenants and, if required, rehabilitation agreements requiring the new owner to follow the *Secretary of the Interior's Standards for Rehabilitation*.[24]

Figure 5.16 Dymock's Building (in the centre background), a former warehouse located in a conservation area in Bo'ness, Scotland, was purchased by Historic Scotland in 1997 and rehabilitated under the Little Houses Improvement Scheme. It was then sold to the Castle Rock Housing Association, which manages the eight flats as housing for the elderly. (Alastair Gentleman)

Revolving funds have succeeded in other countries as well. Historic Scotland initiated the Little Houses Improvement Scheme in 1960. Its goal was (and remains) to buy neglected historic buildings, conserve them (or enter into a conservation agreement with a purchaser), and sell them. The objective is to promote the regeneration of the buildings and their communities (National Trust for Scotland n.d.).

Tax concessions

Financial incentives need not put cash into the hands of property owners; they may be just as effective by reducing owners' tax obligations. A wide array of tax concessions is available to encourage conservation work. Because fiscal regimes vary from one jurisdiction to another, there is no consistency among countries, states, provinces, or local authorities.[25]

Tax incentives have proven to be effective in stimulating private-sector investment in conservation. They are attractive to authorities because their implementation is voluntary and not coercive. On the other hand, they tend to benefit higher-income taxpayers more than lower-income ones, which goes against liberal theories of progressive taxation. Benefits aside, fiscal incentive programs come at a real cost to the treasury, whether as expenditures (e.g., government grants) or forgone revenues (e.g., tax credits). The cost can certainly be justified by the social and economic benefits, both of which contribute to community sustainability. Nevertheless the programs can be difficult to maintain in times of fiscal restraint or under certain political agendas. This is particularly so because the concessions are not investments that produce a direct return, but rather yield an indirect economic benefit that is more difficult to attribute to the incentive program.

Property tax exemption or reduction

Tax exemptions eliminate the need to pay tax (usually for a specified period of time); **tax reductions** (or **tax abatements**) reduce the amount of tax payable. The US has been a leader in introducing these concessions. In 1936 an amendment to the Louisiana Constitution empowered the City of New Orleans to create a commission to work towards 'preservation of such buildings in the Vieux Carré section [the French Quarter] ... as ... shall be deemed to have architectural and historical value,' and the legislation gave the proposed commission the power to exempt historic properties from local taxation (Hosmer 1981: 294–5).

This was a wise directive, since the property tax has typically worked contrary to the interests of heritage conservation. As mentioned at the beginning of this section, many jurisdictions require that land be assessed at its 'highest and best use'—i.e., the most intense use permissible under current zoning regulations—and therefore they overtax 'underdeveloped' properties, such as those developed with small-scaled historic buildings. In what seems contradictory policy, some cities also reduce the property tax for parking lots, thereby encouraging speculative demolition. To counteract these biases (*dis*incentives) against conservation, some authorities now allow property owners an exemption or reduction of property tax in return for approved conservation work to a recognized or protected place. At the end of the exemption period, property tax resumes at the then currently assessed amount. The taxing authority forgoes short-term revenues in return for higher long-term property tax revenues, as well as for the economic stimulation of conservation.

In some places, tax reductions are tied to the nature of the property, without requiring conservation work. For example, in the state of Alabama commercial historic properties are assessed at 10 percent of their appraised value, rather than 20 percent for other commercial properties (White and Roddewig 1994: 15).

The City of Victoria, British Columbia, combines three distinct municipal policies in its ambitious property-tax incentive program: heritage conservation of 'Old Town,' increasing residential accommodation in the downtown core, and seismic (i.e., earthquake) upgrading of old buildings (see text box on Victoria).

Income tax credits and deductions

Tax credits lower the amount of tax owed, whereas **tax deductions** for specified actions reduce the owner's taxable income. Tax incentives for historic preservation became established in American practice with the *Tax Reform Act* of 1976. It and subsequent amendments and supplements provide income tax credits for private-sector rehabilitation of historic buildings. The largest credit requires that a building be listed on the National Register of Historic Places or contribute to a registered historic district, and that work be certified as conforming to the *Secretary of the Interior's Standards for Rehabilitation*. The US also provides tax credits for providing housing (in either new or old buildings) for low-income residents, which may be linked to the rehabilitation tax credits (Murtagh 1988: 74–7; National Park Service, Technical Preservation Services n.d.).[26]

The economic impact of these provisions has been immense. In the first quarter-century, more than $55 billion of investment in more than 36,000 projects benefited from rehabilitation tax credits. The social benefits have also been manifold, as much of the work has produced affordable housing and has revitalized historic town centres and neighborhoods, thereby reducing the need to develop new communities and infrastructure.

Many countries in Western Europe (although not the UK) allow the cost of maintenance to recognized or protected property as an income tax deduction. The specific requirements (e.g., conservation standards, public access) and the cost line items that are deductible vary from one jurisdiction to another (Pickard and Pickerill 2007).

Tax deductions are also available in most countries in return for the donation of recognized historic property (buildings or landscapes), or of conservation easements or covenants on those properties, to registered charities (such as heritage trusts and foundations) and to governments. The deduction is usually based on the market value, which can be difficult to determine, particularly with the donation of a partial interest (e.g., an easement). Donations to charitable organizations can often also be used to offset inheritance/estate tax and capital gains tax.

Other tax concessions

Other forms of tax concession include the waiver of fees for building permits and the reduction or elimination of sales or value-added taxes for building materials for recognized historic places. Both reduce the cost of rehabilitation (Getty Conservation Institute 2004: 40). These programs are not used widely, probably because of the difficulty of administering them.

Non-financial incentives

An alternative approach to reducing the cost of conserving a historic place encourages private-sector work by means of non-financial incentives. These generally allow variances to planning regulations in return for a conservation initiative. No direct costs to government are involved other than increased staff time. However, the planning variances provided by non-financial incentives may incur indirect costs, such as increased urban infrastructure (e.g., expanding utilities and transit to serve additional density), and they often have an impact on urban design. Incentives of all kinds are often praised because they can provide a win–win solution, benefiting both the property owner and the general public; and they can also be criticized, since they often compromise good urban design and good conservation practice. As has been said previously, practicable conservation often requires that compromises be made.

Non-financial incentives for conservation are based on the concept of **incentive zoning**, introduced in New York City in 1961 and described in Section 2.1. Proposed development that meets established policy objectives, as stated in the development plan, is encouraged with a system of rewards. Incentives are intended to induce developers or property owners to provide public amenities that are regarded as benefiting the community at large, one of those amenities being the conservation of historic places.

The rewards usually consist of regulatory relaxations and bonuses (called **amenity bonuses**), which may involve items such as land use, lot coverage, height, or parking. Incentives are given on a discretionary basis. For heritage conservation, they usually include the requirement that the subject property be a recognized or protected historic place and that associated conservation work is done to standards of good practice. The detailed conditions may also be influenced by the level of significance of the historic place. Depending on the jurisdiction, the rewards may be combined with financial incentives.

Non-financial incentives shift the cost of conservation from the public sector to the private sector. In some cities, anticipation of the benefits to be derived from incentives encourages property owners to seek recognition or protection in order to qualify for the program. They recognize that development and conservation can be compatible and mutually supportive.

Even more than with financial incentives, non-financial incentives are seen primarily in North America. England has been particularly reluctant to introduce the practice. However, the recent *National Planning Policy Framework* for England (Department for Communities and Local Government (UK) 2012: para. 140) enables local authorities to relax planning restrictions to provide incentives:

> Local planning authorities should assess whether the benefits of a proposal for enabling development, which would otherwise conflict with planning policies but which would secure the future conservation of a heritage asset, outweigh the disbenefits of departing from those policies.

Regulatory relaxations

Municipalities apply a variety of relaxations to zoning regulations in return for a heritage amenity, and often for other kinds of public amenities as well. This section identifies some of the most common types of relaxation. The examples shown are from the Canadian city of Vancouver, to illustrate how a city can deploy an arsenal of non-financial incentives to encourage conservation in a development climate that was previously focused on demolition and replacement.[27]

Lot coverage and setbacks

Zoning typically controls the percentage of the site that can be built upon, minimum setbacks from the four boundaries, and other parameters. Incentives may increase coverage and reduce setbacks, often with the *proviso* that neighbors who may be impacted not object to the changes. The result can provide additional buildable land for new construction that complements the historic building, thereby adding floor space without making major alterations to the heritage resource. Amending coverage and setbacks may also permit moving the historic building within the site (which compromises good conservation practice), again allowing more unencumbered space for new construction.

Figure 5.17 The Thomas Fee House (1904) in Vancouver, British Columbia, was moved to the corner of the property in 1994 and a new addition built behind and beside it in order to increase site density. The angled, brick bay window at the left is part of the addition. The developer received relaxations for site coverage and setbacks. (John Roaf)

Subdivision and infill

Most zoning regulations permit only one 'principal building' on a lot. In residential situations, when space permits, allowing a second house on the property can provide the property owner with revenue with which (s)he can undertake maintenance or conservation work. The second house may be either freehold, in which case the property must be

Figure 5.18 A new infill building (1990, visible at the left rear) was permitted to be built behind the Barber House (1936) in Vancouver to encourage its conservation. (Harold Kalman)

subdivided into two lots; or leasehold, in which case subdivision may not be necessary. In either situation a zoning variance is required and the municipality requires assurance that the added revenue is used for the intended purpose.

Land-use variance

Figure 5.19 Glen Brae (1910), a former private residence in the elite Shaughnessy Heights neighborhood of Vancouver, was awarded a land-use variance as a conservation incentive. It is now Canuck Place, a hospice for terminally ill children. (John Roaf)

Zoning stipulates the use(s) to which a property may be put. As demographic and economic conditions change, it can be challenging to accommodate the prescribed use(s). This is a particular problem in historic urban neighborhoods and rural areas with large properties that were originally developed with large mansions, and which remain zoned for single-family use. A declining number of purchasers will invest in and maintain large, old houses. Many among the wealthy prefer to build new houses designed to their particular specifications, rather than acquire historic houses that they don't see as meeting their needs or tastes.

An effective solution is a land-use relaxation that authorizes multiple-family or institutional use. Another is to permit subdivision and infill. A proposed change of this kind may be opposed by neighbors who have a vested interest in keeping the status quo and who perceive it as a violation of their values and a risk to their investment. However, preventing change poses the threat of reducing market demand and leaving properties vacant, which could ultimately lead to the failure of the neighborhood. A delicate balance must be achieved between conserving the character of the historic building and conserving the character and values of the larger neighborhood. Indeed, this principle lies behind all incentive programs.

Parking relaxation

New urban development or a change in use of a historic building may require the provision of a certain number of on- or adjacent off-site parking spaces. With new buildings, parking is easily (if expensively)

Figure 5.20 The Stanley Theatre, Vancouver, was repurposed from a cinema to live theatre. The City provided an exemption from parking requirements and allowed a density transfer to another site, which together made the project feasible. (John Roaf)

created underground. In rehabilitation projects, it may not be feasible to excavate beneath the existing building to create underground parking. Older commercial buildings often cover most or all of their lots, precluding at-grade parking.

Relaxation of parking requirements can be a very powerful incentive. Of course this has an impact on the neighborhood, increasing competition for scarce curbside parking or space in lots and garages. However, since older commercial and institutional buildings are generally located in neighborhoods that are well served by public transit, demand for parking may be lower than elsewhere in the city.

The Stanley Theatre in Vancouver, a former cinema built in 1930, was rehabilitated in 1998 for live theatre use. The scale of the intervention forced the work to comply with current regulations. The zoning bylaw required the provision of numerous parking spaces; the cinema had none. Underpinning the theatre and excavating for underground parking would have been prohibitively expensive. The non-profit owner successfully argued that since the neighborhood has much retail and office accommodation that is well served by parking garages and lots, and since the theatre is used mostly on nights and weekends, when demand for those parking spaces is low, there is more than sufficient parking within a two-block radius to accommodate the theatre patrons. The exemption from the parking regulation, as well as a transfer of density to another site, made the project feasible.

Sign ordinance relaxation

Figure 5.21 The landmark BowMac sign was conserved and overlaid with a transparent and reversible non-conforming sign for retailer Toys 'R' Us. (John Roaf)

Many cities have ordinances that determine the maximum size, location materials, and sources of illumination for signs. Retailers often install the largest sign permissible, in order to gain exposure. Relaxing the sign ordinance in return for conservation can sometimes serve a useful end.

An instance of this involved the international retail chain Toys 'R' Us. The company leased new retail premises on the site of long-time automobile dealership Bowell McLean Motor Company ('BowMac'). The old BowMac sign (1959), 29 meters high, illuminated with 3,500 incandescent bulbs and neon tubing, and visible for miles, remained standing and had been listed on the Vancouver Heritage Register. The retailer was offered the options of superimposing a new, semi-transparent and 'reversible' (removable) sign—which would not conform to the sign bylaw—in front of the historic sign; or else replacing it with a small new sign as permitted by the ordinance. The toy company chose the former and benefits from its prominence.

Density bonus

Figure 5.22 The large, mixed-use Woodward's redevelopment in Vancouver benefited from an array of density bonuses, justified by the developer's provision of heritage, social, and cultural amenities. (John Roaf)

A density bonus, usually expressed as extra height and/or bulk and resulting in added floor space, remains the non-financial heritage incentive of choice in many cities. It is used when a historic building comprises a part of a larger commercial or residential development. Additional floor space may mean additional profits. The incremental revenue is an incentive to retain, rather than demolish, the historic place and can be applied to the cost of its conservation. The tool is effective when there is strong pressure for new development, and relatively ineffectual when there is little demand for development.

Density bonuses usually reward the provision of public amenities, of which heritage is but one. It may be seen in the Woodward's redevelopment in Vancouver (2010), in which the earliest component of a former department store (1903–08) was rehabilitated and repurposed for commercial and office use, and augmented by three large, new buildings that contain residential, educational, cultural, and retail uses. The project benefited from bonuses for social amenities (including the provision of 200 non-market housing units and public open space), cultural amenities (including Simon Fraser University's School for the Contemporary Arts and offices for the National Film Board), and heritage amenities (including retaining part of the department store and an extensive interpretation program). The overall density increased from a proposed floor-space ratio of 7.57 (already higher than the zoning bylaw enabled) to a final ratio of 9.5. Pundits valued the bonuses at between CAD$25 and $30 million. In return, Vancouver has benefited from a significant social and economic revitalization effort in a distressed neighborhood (Enright 2010; Kalman and Ward 2012: 21–2).

Since, in legal terminology, bonus floor space is created *ex nihilo* (out of nothing), it adds density to a neighborhood over and above what has already been authorized by zoning, leading to the possibility of additional pressure on infrastructure (e.g., public services and facilities, transit, and utilities) and urban design values (through excessive height and/or bulk), and so there may be a negative aspect to the impact on the larger neighborhood environment.

Density transfer

The relaxations and bonuses described above are often used generally as tools in incentive zoning, and are not restricted to historic places. A very useful incentive that was developed specifically to encourage the conservation of historic buildings in downtown urban settings is **density transfer** (or **transfer of density rights**, **transfer of development rights**, **TDR**).

The principle is simple and sophisticated at the same time. Local zoning regulations authorize a certain maximum floor area for a particular lot. Historic buildings often have less floor area than what is permitted. A density transfer allows the owner to sell the **unused floor area** (**unrealized density**) from a historic place (called the **donor site** or **transferor site**) to the owner(s) or developer(s) of one or more other sites (**receiver sites** or **transferee sites**) at a market- or city-determined price.

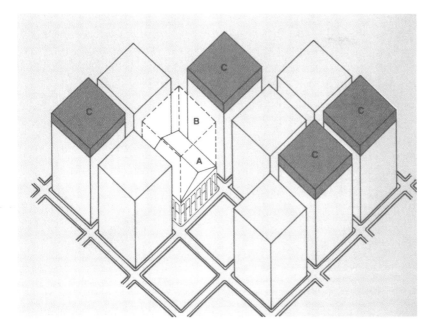

Figure 5.23 The principle of density transfer: Building A is developed to less than its permitted floor area. The unused floor area (B) is transferred to several other buildings (C) to redistribute the density. (John Costonis, *Space Adrift*)

As with a density bonus, the revenue can be used as an incentive not to demolish and/or to assist with conservation work. The tool can be very effective when there is strong developer demand for floor space, but less so when demand weakens. Density transfer does not create new space; it simply redistributes space that has been already authorized, and which is therefore within the capacity of existing infrastructure. From a legal perspective it redefines property rights, by severing all or a portion of development rights from donor site to the receiver site.

New York City once again was the innovator of this tool. It adopted a density transfer program in 1968, but for a host of reasons the regulation proved difficult to use. A serious impediment was that transfers could be made only to an adjacent property, and so there was often no eligible receiver site (Gilbert 1970: 13–15; Costonis 1972: 578).[28]

Lawyer John Costonis took the concept of density transfer a step further with his 'Chicago Plan,' developed for the conditions in that city but applicable generally to urban areas in which historic places are threatened by new development. His plan (somewhat simplified) allows unused density to be transferred to any appropriate site within what he termed a 'transfer district.' (Some cities now permit transfers to other districts.) Costonis proposes the creation of a municipal 'development rights bank' as an intermediary between the parties by holding unassigned rights until a transferee site is identified. The reduced development potential of the transferor site is attached to its land title, reducing the land value and discouraging future redevelopment (Costonis 1972, 1974, 1997).

Density transfers have been adopted, with modifications, by municipalities in several countries. The City of Vancouver was among the

Figure 5.24 The unrealized density from Christ Church Cathedral in downtown Vancouver was transferred to Park Place (left). The substantial financial proceeds enabled the conservation of the cathedral and provide ongoing funds for diocesan programs. The building at the right was erected later. (Harold Kalman)

first to use it. In 1971 Vancouver's Christ Church Cathedral (1895) proposed to raise much-needed funds for its ministry by demolishing its late nineteenth-century downtown church and replacing it with an 18-story office tower and underground sanctuary. A group of citizens and community leaders convinced the City to allow the unused development rights to be transferred to the developer who was intending to build on the property next door. The City rejected the Church's development application, and the outcome saw the adjacent tower, called Park Place (completed in 1984), built taller and bulkier than the zoning would otherwise have permitted. The church received (and continues to receive) a large annual payment from its neighbor.[29]

Technical support

Governments and non-profit organizations may facilitate projects and encourage good conservation practice by offering technical support to owners of historic places. This may comprise practical information delivered by a variety of means, whether in publications describing conservation techniques (such as the US National Park Service's *Preservation Briefs*), by sending a professional to the site to give *pro bono* advice as to how to go about developing a proposal or to provide design assistance, or by a representative of the local authority suggesting the best route to take to achieve approval of a permit application. Some cities offer a 'green-door policy,' whereby applications to change recognized properties are given priority to assure consideration in a timely manner.

Another kind of technical assistance is the provision of training programs for real-estate agents (estate agents) who specialize in heritage properties, helping them become more familiar with historic buildings and with conservation incentives and financing.

5.5 Risk Assessment

Undertaking an assessment of the potential risks that could harm a historic place should be included as part of planning and management. Every risk carries the possibility of bringing about negative effects, and so it is best to anticipate those effects and determine ways to counteract them. As our world grows more complex and people perceive growing risks from an ever-increasing number of sources—sometimes bringing with them the consequent threat of litigation—many large corporations and government entities have made risk management a core activity. Risk management is applied to virtually every discipline, from public health to local government.

Figure 5.25 ChristChurch Cathedral in Christchurch, New Zealand, a Category 1 historic place. The Magnitude 6.3 earthquake in February 2011 toppled the spire and severely damaged the structure. (New Zealand Defence Force)

Potential risks to historic places are far more widespread than the threat of demolition for new development. Risks include the result of damage or destruction through natural forces, such as wildfires, floods, windstorms, and earthquakes. Alternatively risks may be posed by human actions, whether physical (e.g., building fires, vandalism, industrial pollution, or armed conflict), socioeconomic (e.g., loss of external financing, economic recession, or litigation as a consequence of an injury), or human error (e.g., structural inadequacy from a deficient design, permitting excessive visitor use, or management incompetence). In most cases, the outcome can be catastrophic. The term **vulnerability** is often used to describe risk in a heritage context.

The risk-preparedness plan

The outcome of a risk assessment is usually called a **risk-preparedness plan** (or **hazard mitigation plan**). Typically it comprises a number of distinct stages:

- Survey of the historic place
- Risk analysis
- Propose mitigation to offset the risks (before the disaster)
- Determine appropriate responses (during the disaster)
- Plan for recovery (after the disaster).

The text that follows expands on each of the components, without any attempt to be comprehensive.[30]

Survey of the historic place

Some or all of a historic place may be destroyed by disaster, and so it is important to have a reliable record of what was there to assist with insurance claims and repair or reconstruction. The survey should include photographs and record drawings of the place, as well as an inventory of movable artifacts. It should also provide a clear understanding of the heritage values of the place, to help with post-disaster decision-making and so that conservation resources can be focused where they are needed most. Documentation of this kind is recommended as part of good management practice, even without consideration of risk. The documentation should exist in at least two copies, with at least one set kept off-site.

Risk analysis

This stage represents the narrow 'risk assessment,' although the term is better used to describe the entire risk-preparedness process. The analysis identifies the nature of the potential threats that could affect the historic place, determines the likelihood of their occurrence, and estimates the impact of each—how it would affect the project or its setting—should it occur.

The range of potential risks to historic places is enormous. Many common threats were cited just above. The risk analysis should look at the extent of the risks (i.e., how much of the place is vulnerable from a particular threat)[31]; the present impact of the risk, if any; the potential future impact should the risk become reality; and whether the threat is increasing or reducing over time.

Surveys and analyses may be done for large areas as well. As an example, the city of Seattle, US, has been identifying unreinforced masonry buildings (URM buildings), which are particularly vulnerable to earthquakes. Five building attributes based on both risk and historic value have been weighted and scored, providing a prioritization list for retrofits (Chalana and Wiser 2013: 43–51).

Mitigation

Mitigation actions are intended to reduce or eliminate the negative effects of a risk *before* the event happens. As examples, a dike might reduce the risk of flooding; a monitored fire-alarm system and an effective fire-suppression system will lower the risk of fire damage; and seismic upgrading will reduce the risk of earthquake (seismic) damage. Insurance reduces the potential financial loss, as does a backup operating and financial plan in the event of external funding being withdrawn. It is important to identify an acceptable level of risk, and then develop mitigation strategies accordingly.

In risk-management theory, the various types of mitigation—the alternative responses to the risks—are:

- *Risk Transfer* – move the risk to a person or entity able to deal with it.
- *Risk Deferral* – alter the plan to move some activities to a later date when the risk might be lessened.
- *Risk Reduction* – reduce the probability of the risk occurring or lessen the impact.

Figure 5.26 Vancouver, British Columbia, is located in a region with a very high risk of earthquakes. Many masonry buildings are upgraded to increase their resistance to earthquake stresses. An alternative kind of mitigation is seen at St. George's Junior School. Rather than go to the expense of reinforcing the extensive masonry walls, only the floors and structure were reinforced and sheltered exit passages were built to protect students from falling stones as they evacuate the building. (Harold Kalman)

- *Risk Acceptance* – sometimes there is not a lot you can do other than accept the risk and ensure that contingency plans are in place.
- *Risk Avoidance* – eliminate the possibility of the risk occurring, e.g., use alternative resources or technologies (JISC infoNet 2010).

Of course it is one thing to propose mitigation and another to carry it out. An adequate budget should be available to ensure that, at a minimum, the risks that have the highest likelihood of occurrence are mitigated.

Responses

Good risk preparedness includes a response plan for emergencies. This includes aspects such as the organizational structure and chain of command of the response team, the authority to spend emergency funds, and procedures for the initial response. Measures should include training staff to respond to emergencies and determining in advance which movable artifacts should be taken away (if there is an opportunity). The response plan should be rehearsed, reviewed, and updated at regular intervals.

Recovery

Once the emergency has passed, the long, hard job of recovery begins. A checklist for damage assessment should be prepared in advance. Experts who can assist with salvage or conservation rescue operations should be identified. Appropriate conservation standards should be specified to assist with decision-making as to the approach that will be taken—e.g., for buildings, reconstruction, repair, or demolition. Long-term financing (and/or fundraising) provisions will enable undertaking the work.

A risk-preparedness plan is an important, but often overlooked, component of heritage planning. Heritage agencies sometimes (but by no means always) require including a risk analysis as part of a conservation plan. Best practices include one even if it is not formally required.

The Heritage Lottery Fund for England and Wales, for example, does specify that plans include a section on risks and opportunities, which 'should identify all of the risks to the heritage, and how it might be vulnerable. It can also identify opportunities for improving the heritage.' The examples provided by their guidance handbook (2008: 18) are:

- New buildings might put wildlife at risk.
- Proper security measures could make the heritage less accessible to the public.
- An archive might be vulnerable to pests.
- Action to reduce carbon emissions might put the appearance of a historic building at risk.
- Inappropriate development around the site might put its setting at risk.

- Inadequate maintenance could put places and collections at risk.
- Too many visitors may put the heritage at risk; too few visitors may produce insufficient resources to look after the site.
- Extreme weather caused by climate change can put historic buildings at risk and may affect species and landscapes.

5.6 Heritage Impact Assessment

A **heritage impact assessment** (HIA) is a particular kind of risk assessment. It comprises an important component within the heritage planning process. The HIA is a relatively new instrument, one whose methodology is still emerging. An HIA is also known as **cultural heritage impact assessment** (CHIA) and the ensuing report is often called a **(cultural) heritage impact statement**.

An HIA follows the method developed for risk assessment generally, in that it describes and assesses the likely **impacts** (or **effects**)—in this case both positive and negative (**adverse**)—that a proposed development would have on a historic place. The assessment proposes mitigation measures to reduce or eliminate negative effects. It answers three basic questions (Heritage Council of Western Australia n.d.):

- How would the proposed development affect the significance of the historic place(s)? Stated otherwise, what would be the impacts of the proposed development?
- What mitigation measures, if any, are proposed to improve any adverse impacts?
- Would the proposal result in any heritage conservation benefits that might offset adverse impacts?

An HIA enables planners and decision-makers to determine with some objectivity whether it is in the public interest for a proposed development to proceed. If it should proceed, then the HIA determines how best to mitigate any adverse impacts that might ensue. If, however, effective mitigation is not feasible, then the HIA provides a rationale and framework to make major revisions to the proposal or to abort it entirely.

HIAs developed from **environmental impact assessments** (EIAs), which emerged in the 1970s as awareness of environmental degradation and the threats posed by new infrastructure development began to be appreciated. The processes for initiating the two kinds of assessments are similar. In some jurisdictions an HIA is a component of an EIA; in others, they are separate investigations. An HIA may be done as part of an EIA or separately, depending on the circumstances.[32] Both kinds of review contribute towards ensuring that the proposed development meets principles of sustainability. A broad issue with both kinds of assessment however is that, to cite Shakespeare's Hamlet, they are often 'more honour'd in the breach than the observance.'

Generally speaking, the methodology for HIAs follows that established for EIAs. The basic steps are:

- Identify historic places that may be affected by the proposed undertaking.
- Determine the heritage significance of the places.
- Define the nature of the potential impacts (both negative and positive) in terms of quality and magnitude.
- Recommend mitigation measures and their effects.
- Prepare HIA report.

Each of the steps is described below.

The method has been particularly well developed—and enforced—in Europe and Australia. HIAs focus on both archaeological resources and built heritage. In some jurisdictions (e.g., British Columbia in Canada) HIAs are required by law for pre-contact Aboriginal archaeological sites but not for places from the historic period. In the US, review of a proposed undertaking pursuant to Section 106 of the *National Historic Preservation Act* is an HIA, although it is not explicitly called that; the purpose of the review is to determine whether a proposed action will have 'adverse effects' on historic properties (Advisory Council on Historic Preservation (US) 2010: 7).

EIAs and HIAs were initially developed for large infrastructure projects, such as roads and pipelines, which might affect a considerable number of historic places. More recently HIAs have been carried out for more discrete projects, such as a development that might affect a particular archaeological site, landscape, or historic building. While the general approach to impact assessment is the same for both, some aspects differ. For example, a far-reaching infrastructure project requires that a broad inventory of potentially affected places be done first. For this reason, the two categories of HIAs are introduced here separately.

HIA for large infrastructure projects—the 'macro' HIA

Large infrastructure projects typically involve major roads, rail lines, pipelines, and other linear projects; others address comprehensive built developments that affect multiple historic places. An HIA for a major project, particularly rural infrastructure projects, often comprises part of an EIA, although it may also be an independent study. This scale of study is referred to here as a 'macro' HIA.

In many jurisdictions the sequencing of the HIA within the larger project planning process is stipulated in detail by means of a flow chart. In other places the relationship between the various parts is less well defined.

An important consideration—one on which there is little consensus from one authority to the next—is when to undertake the HIA within the overall process.

- If begun early in the planning stage, when the proposed undertaking remains a concept that has not been defined in detail, it is relatively easy for the proponents to modify the project in a way that will avoid potential negative impacts. However, since the proposal has been defined only loosely, the full extent of potential effects cannot yet be understood.

- If done after the project design is developed, identifying the effects is more straightforward. However, by then the proponent will have invested much more time and commitment in the project, and will likely have consulted with the community and authorities and received preliminary approvals. Therefore major changes to the project become unlikely and only relatively minor mitigation is feasible.

The ideal solution is to undertake impact assessment studies at more than one stage in the project. This is done, for example, in Ireland with respect to proposed new national roads. The National Roads Authority guidelines (Manogue Architects and Soltys:Brewster Consulting c. 2006; Margaret Gowen & Co. c. 2006) recommend that the potential heritage impacts for both archaeological and architectural resources be addressed at three times during project development:

1 As part of the Constraints Study, an early stage of the road scheme: this considers a large geographical area and allows for a variety of road alignments. A desk-based research initiative consults readily available sources to identify all known historic places within the study area. The products are a preliminary schedule (or survey, or inventory) of historic places within the study area, including their relative significance and legal status; and a 'constraints map' that uses digital GIS technology to show the places of merit and their attributes. The project planners will select potential routes based in part on these data.

2 As part of the Route Corridor Selection Study, the stage that assesses a number of broad route options. For each possible corridor, the study area will encompass a defined width, often 100m in each direction from the centre line of the route. Desk-based research is supplemented by site visits to verify and photograph the historic places that may be affected. The products are an inventory and larger-scaled base maps. For each place, the potential impacts are described and their levels (see below for this) defined. The relative ranking of route options from a heritage perspective are presented. It is important that archaeological and built heritage data be expressed in a consistent format, even if done by separate firms.

3 As part of the Environmental Impact Statement (or as a discrete Heritage Impact Statement). The statement assesses the potential construction and operational impacts of the road on historic places along the preferred route, building on the information contained in the first two stages.

This is a highly effective sequence for assessing potential impacts. A similar pattern is followed in many places with respect to EIAs. If there is a fault in the Irish model, it is that it pays insufficient attention to public engagement. The community should be involved in the collection and assessment of data, as with other heritage planning activities.

In jurisdictions where the HIA will not extend through multiple phases of project planning, the HIA should be initiated as early as possible in a project's sequence for it to have a meaningful outcome, and reviewed later when more is known about the proposal.

Preparing the inventory

Key to the success of the HIA is the production of an appropriate inventory of historic places that may potentially be affected by the proposed project. The method is similar to that for surveys of conservation areas or cultural landscapes (see Section 4.2). A starting point is the compilation of existing lists and schedules, including both protected and unprotected places. However, it is well appreciated that lists are not—and cannot be—all-inclusive; many resources simply will not have yet been inventoried or even 'discovered.' Current legislation and practice recognize this. In the US, for example, a Section 106 review 'identifies historic properties that may be affected' by the proposed undertaking; and in doing so, must 'determine which properties are listed on, or are eligible for listing on, the National Register' (Tyler et al. 2009: 51). The bigger task lies in identifying historic places that are eligible for listing, but not yet listed. Doing this thoroughly would require a comprehensive and very expensive survey; doing this in a cursory manner would overlook significant places. The challenge is to strike a happy medium.

This raises the conundrum discussed in Section 4.2, whereby the initial screening done in a cursory 'windshield survey' often has a more significant effect on the outcome than the detailed assessment of those places that are captured by the screening. As stated above, it is essential that the initial visual screening be preceded by desk-based research that identifies potential places of significance, whose status must then be verified in the field.

Places on the inventory should be entered into a GIS-linked database, using a standard form that records basic locational data (including distance from project), a succinct description, heritage significance, legal status (e.g., whether protected), and sources that have been consulted. The nature and quality of the impacts and the proposed mitigation measures should be entered on the form as well.

Assessing impacts

The core activity in an HIA is the identification and assessment of potential impacts, both positive and negative, of the proposed undertaking. The process is not unlike that for assessing heritage significance: a series of criteria is established, and each criterion is evaluated according to a scale that determines the level of the impact.

Built environment

The method for addressing heritage impacts on the built environment is more complex than for archaeology, and is discussed here first. Data on the anticipated impact should be collected under several headings. The following list represents a consensus among various systems; the terminology varies from one country to another:

1 *Nature of impact*
   o Succinct verbal description of the impact on primary resource (e.g., negative: visual intrusion through heavy vegetation; positive: reduced nearby truck traffic), contributing resources (e.g., negative: total loss of stand of mature trees; positive: enhancement of setting or access), and associated amenities (e.g., a historic house that is open to the public)
2 *Quality of impact*
   o Positive or negative
3 *Type of impact*
   o Direct (e.g., loss of a structure), indirect (e.g. visual or audible intrusion), cumulative (incremental impact by means of a series of individually minor actions occurring over a period of time, e.g., construction of a road that will likely lead to further infrastructure and development), undetermined, or none; also irreversible or reversible
4 *Duration of impact*
   o Temporary (e.g., during construction only), short term (e.g., until landscape regenerates), or long term/permanent
5 *Magnitude of impact*
   o High, medium, or low (or similar evaluative terms; see Table 5.2)
6 *Significance of impact*
   o The consequence of the change, which is a function of the magnitude of the impact measured against the heritage significance of the historic place.

Several countries, states, and provinces define the levels of significance to be used within their jurisdiction. Table 5.2 is issued by the Irish Environmental Protection Agency and is applicable to architectural heritage impacts (Manogue Architects and Soltys:Brewster Consulting c. 2006: 33).

Archaeological sites

In the case of archaeological resources, the impact assessment methodology differs in some respects. The Irish NRA model continues to conduct the HIA over three stages, but the assessment addresses some other conditions and processes (Margaret Gowen & Co. c. 2006):

● The field work should include a low-level aerial reconnaissance survey that examines areas of known archaeological potential, in addition to identifying known and unknown features.

Table 5.2 Magnitude of architectural heritage impact assessment. (Irish Environmental Protection Agency)

Impacts of Negative Quality	**Profound** An impact that obliterates the architectural heritage of a structure or feature of national or international importance. These effects arise where an architectural structure or feature is completely and irreversibly destroyed by the proposed development. Mitigation is unlikely to remove adverse effects.
	Significant An impact that, by its magnitude, duration or intensity alters the character and/or setting of the architectural heritage. These effects arise where an aspect or aspects of the architectural heritage is/are permanently impacted upon leading to a loss of character and integrity in the architectural structure or feature. Appropriate mitigation is likely to reduce the impact.
	Moderate An impact that results in a change to the architectural heritage which, although noticeable, is not such that alters the integrity of the heritage. The change is likely to be consistent with existing and emerging trends. Impacts are probably reversible and may be of relatively short duration. Appropriate mitigation is very likely to reduce the impact.
	Slight An impact that causes some minor change in the character of architectural heritage of local or regional importance without affecting its integrity or sensitivities. Although noticeable, the effects do not directly impact on the architectural structure or feature. Impacts are reversible and of relatively short duration. Appropriate mitigation will reduce the impact.
	Imperceptible An impact on architectural heritage of local importance that is capable of measurement but without noticeable consequences.
Impacts of Positive Quality	**Significant** A beneficial effect that permanently enhances or restores the character and/or setting of the architectural heritage in a clearly noticeable manner.
	Moderate A beneficial effect that results in partial or temporary enhancement of the character and/or setting of the architectural heritage and which is noticeable and consistent with existing and emerging trends.
	Slight A beneficial effect that causes some minor or temporary enhancement of the character of architectural heritage of local or regional importance which, although positive, is unlikely to be readily noticeable.
	Imperceptible A beneficial effect on architectural heritage of local importance that is capable of measurement but without noticeable consequences.

- The nature, quality, and type of impact are measured as with built heritage. Magnitude and duration will remain relevant for above-ground places and those that are presented to the public, but not for sites having little or no visibility, unless there is likelihood that the site will be developed for public enjoyment.

HIAs and EIAs that address archaeology are far more prevalent than those for the built environment. In many places archaeological assessment is required, whereas assessment of impacts on the built environment is only recommended. The relevant legislation often stipulates the details of how the assessment will be carried out. Practitioners should follow local requirements rather than an ideal international model.

Mitigation

The purpose of an HIA is to identify potential negative impacts that a proposed project would have on historic places, and to make recommendations to mitigate—to eliminate or reduce—the adverse effects. In the case where an HIA (and associated EIA) is evaluating alternative alignments of a linear infrastructure project, it is always hoped that a route can be found that has only few and minor negative impacts. However, a possible outcome of any impact assessment is a conclusion that the adverse effects are unacceptable, with a consequent recommendation that the project be aborted entirely. Whether the decision-makers heed this sage advice is, of course, another matter entirely.

Mitigating the impact on an individual resource is relatively straightforward. Mitigation becomes far more complex when the historic place is a collective resource, such as a cultural landscape or a village. Sometimes the same kinds of measures deployed on a larger scale will do the job, but this can prove difficult.

The most effective form of mitigation is avoidance. However, this option is not always available. In the case of an indirect impact (an intrusion on the site or setting), mitigation will generally focus on reducing the level of the impact while keeping the historic place intact and in its location. This may include some of the following, either individually or in combination:

- Landscape buffers to screen views, light, and/or noise
- Masonry buffers, such as stone or concrete walls
- Adjusting the grading with berms or other screening features
- Relocating access routes to the place
- Adjusting the alignment, grade, and/or design of the proposed work
- Mitigating the noise of a highway with quiet paving materials
- Traffic calming along a road at sensitive locations.

Sometimes the anticipated impact will be direct and unavoidable. In this case a more extreme form of mitigation is required, which may comprise one or more of the following:

- Excavating an archaeological site and removing the remains from their natural environment to a secure place ('salvage archaeology')
- Relocating a building or structure
- Documenting the resource to be lost, excavated, or moved
- Documenting intangible cultural heritage that may be affected
- Interpreting a lost historic resource.

Excavation, relocation, or demolition and documentation must be seen as last resorts and the least preferred options from a conservation

Impact Assessment: The Mackenzie Valley Pipeline Inquiry

A notable—and early—case in which politicians listened to a recommendation to postpone a major infrastructure project was Canada's Mackenzie Valley Pipeline Inquiry. An assessment of the social, environmental, and economic impacts of a natural gas pipeline proposed to traverse Yukon and the Mackenzie River Valley of the Northwest Territories was begun in 1974. The social component included the tangible and intangible cultural heritage of the many Aboriginal groups who would have been affected. The three components together comprise what we now call sustainability—a word that had not been coined at the time. Justice Thomas Berger, who led the inquiry, visited 35 Northern communities and cities across Canada to solicit public opinion, and his team undertook exhaustive research.

Justice Berger's final report, *Northern Frontier, Northern Homeland* (1977), concluded that the Aboriginal cultural heritage had not been considered seriously in the pipeline proposal. With regard to social and economic factors, Berger wrote:

> A strong native society and local renewable resource development can exist side-by-side with large-scale, non-renewable resource development—but only if our priorities are changed, and if renewable resource development is strengthened before the pipeline is built. (p. 6)

Berger recommended a ten-year moratorium on a pipeline through the Northwest Territories and that no pipeline be built through Yukon. The ten-year hiatus was necessary, he wrote, in order to address several critical issues, such as settling Aboriginal land claims and setting aside key conservation areas, before an attempt might be made to build the pipeline. A second pipeline project was initiated in 1999—22 years later—and received approval in 2011 (Berger 1977; Wikipedia n.d.-d).

Figure 5.27 The route of the proposed Mackenzie Valley pipeline (broken line) in northwestern Canada.

perspective. These outcomes should not be recommended simply because project proponents say that there are no technical or financial alternatives (Engelhardt 2011: 4).

And, to repeat what was said previously, if mitigation is not sufficient to retain the cultural value of the historic places along the route, and if avoidance is not possible, then aborting the project may be the only appropriate solution.

The format of the ensuing HIA or EIA report will depend on the relevant provincial, state, or national regulations. It should include all the various components described in this section.

HIA for individual development projects—the 'micro' HIA

Heritage impact assessments are also undertaken to gauge the potential adverse effects that a more limited development may have on one or more historic places. This may be work proposed to be done to the historic place, or a nearby project that would have a direct or indirect impact on that place. The scale and scope of an HIA of this kind are far smaller than with a large infrastructure project, although the methodology is much the same. This kind of study may be called a 'micro' HIA.

Once again the central tasks are identifying the affected historic place and its legal status, stating the heritage significance, determining the nature and magnitude of potential positive and negative impacts of the proposed work, proposing mitigation for the latter, and making a final recommendation. The level of detail usually includes defining the impacts on individual character-defining elements. Declaring the project to be unacceptable and recommending aborting it remains a choice.

Australia has been writing 'Statements of Heritage Impact' (SOHI, also Heritage Impact Statements, or HIS) for projects of this kind since around 1990.[33] They are required in some states and cities and only recommended in others. HIAs have since been adopted in other countries as well. They are now encouraged, if not required, in most countries.

An HIA for a project of this kind may form part of a 'micro' conservation plan (see Section 5.8) or alternatively comprise an independent study. As with HIAs for large infrastructure projects, the sequence within the timeline of the larger project is critical. The earlier in the process that the HIA is done, the more likely it is to be able to affect change that will mitigate adverse effects. The present text recommends taking an initial look at potential impacts (and other risks) at the beginning of the planning process, then undertaking a full HIA as part of—or just prior to—the conservation plan, including recommendations for mitigation.

A Heritage Impact Assessment Postpones Development in Hong Kong

Queen Mary Hospital in Hong Kong, founded in the mid-1930s, developed a large campus on a plateau of limited area in the Pokfulam district. Little space remains for new buildings. When the hospital determined that it required a new trauma and heart centre, the authorities decided to demolish the underused Nurses' Quarters (Block A) and build the new facility on its site.

The Hong Kong government instituted a mandatory heritage impact assessment process for capital works projects in 2007, in reaction to public outrage over the demolition of the Star Ferry Terminal in Wan Chai. The HIA process is defined in detail in a technical circular.[34] This supplements the pre-existing requirement for cultural heritage impact assessments (CHIAs) as part of EIAs for proposed large interventions that would affect a protected historic place.

The HIA for the Nurses' Block at Queen Mary Hospital—a surviving and intact original hospital structure built in 1936—found that the building has very high heritage significance. It concluded that the proposal would adversely affect

Figure 5.28 The Nurses' Quarters (Block A) at Queen Mary Hospital, Hong Kong. (The Oval Partnership)

all the heritage values of the historic place, and therefore the proposal was unacceptable (The Oval Partnership Limited and Commonwealth Historic Resource Management Limited 2008). The report recommended retaining the historic building and constructing the new facility elsewhere, or else building new adjacent or attached to it. The Hospital Authority took the recommendations to heart, stopped the project, and determined to build the new trauma and heart centre elsewhere.

5.7 Implementation Plan

The final stage in the planning process is to lay out clearly the method of implementation so that decision-makers may provide their approval and hands-on work may begin. This usually requires an **implementation plan**.

Table 5.3 A portion of a chart describing an implementation plan. (Commonwealth Historic Resource Management)

PRIORITY: IMPORTANCE

Symbol	Meaning
H	High
L	Low
M	Medium

PRIORITY: PHASE

Symbol	Phase
1	Phase 1
2	Phase 2
3	Phase 3
O	Ongoing

REQUIRED RESOURCES

Symbol	Meaning
$	Low or no cost
$$	Moderate cost
$$$	High cost
($)	External revenue source

STRATEGY		ACTION	IMPORTANCE	PHASE	RESPONSIBILITY	RESOURCES
1.0	**Identify the District's built and natural heritage resources**					
	1.1	Create a Community Heritage Register, including procedures for updating	H	1	Planning	$$$
	1.2	Create an Inventory of significant natural resources of heritage value, and identify mechanisms for conservation	M	2	Parks, Community Services and Local Groups	$$$
2.0	**Preserve and protect significant heritage resources through use of protection tools enabled by the Local Government Act**					
	2.1	Protect publicly owned properties on the Community Heritage Register that have built and/or natural resources with high heritage value, through Heritage Designation	H	1	Council	$
	2.2	Require that resources which benefit from heritage incentives be protected by Heritage Designation and/or Heritage Revitalization Agreement	M	2	Planning	$
	2.3	Seek opportunities to designate private properties listed on the Community Heritage Register that contain built and/or natural resources with high heritage value	M	3	Planning	$
	2.4	Use Heritage Conservation Areas as a means of preserving neighbourhood character, including natural and built heritage resources	M	2	Council	$$
	2.5	Adopt a District-wide bylaw to protect heritage trees	H	3	Council	$$

Tasks, priorities, and timing

The implementation plan takes the various recommendations and indicates some or all of the following for each proposed task (or action):

- Priority (relative importance)
- Timing
- Responsible entity
- Cost or relative cost.

The implementation plan may be presented as a list or, more effectively, as a table, chart, or matrix. The actual format adopted depends on factors such as content, desired simplicity or complexity, and relevant contextual issues. If an emphasis is placed on identifying the responsible entity—i.e., which organization or individual will take responsibility for undertaking each particular task—and the entity is expected to determine its own timing, then a simple list of tasks, organized by the responsible entities, will suffice.

Table 5.3 illustrates an implementation plan for a municipal heritage plan in which the recommendations are divided into high-level 'strategies' and lower-level 'actions.' In this case the identification of all four factors listed above was provided to the client (Commonwealth Historic Resource Management Limited 2006: 20–4).

- 'Importance' is indicated as high, medium, or low. This prioritizes the actions in the event that all cannot be undertaken.
- 'Phase' identifies phase 1, 2, or 3; each phase is expected to take three to five years.
- 'Resources' are shown as having a relatively low cost ($), moderate cost ($$), or high cost ($$$). Actual dollar costs have not been calculated, but this is often required. The high-cost items have been distributed evenly among the three phases.

If the emphasis of implementation is on the sequence and timing of actions, and the other factors are relatively unimportant or addressed elsewhere, the most appropriate solution might be a bar chart (also called a Gantt chart).[35] The chart provides an easy-to-comprehend graphic, although for complex projects the Gantt chart will be far more complicated than is illustrated in Figure 5.29.

Other tools, including the PERT (Program Evaluation and Review Technique) and CPM (Critical Path Method) charts and the AOA (Activity on Arrow) network, are excellent for project management although inappropriate for implementation planning. Several types of computer software effectively develop charts and track project progress and can be used for both planning and management.

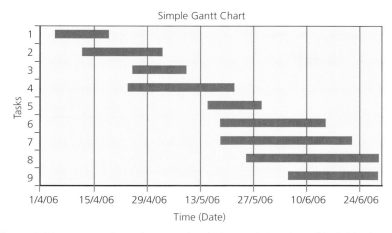

Figure 5.29 A Gantt chart showing the timing and duration of individual tasks. (Wikipedia)

Visitor management and interpretation

Visitor management and interpretation are two principal aspects of operating a publicly accessible historic place. Both may be addressed broadly in the conservation plan, and in more detail in a conservation management plan (see Section 5.8 for the differences between the two), although specifics are best worked out subsequently, after designs, budgets, and governance have been determined.

Visitor management was addressed in Section 2.2 as a consideration in heritage tourism. The intention of planning for this is to maximize the visitor experience, as well as to enhance economic and other benefits, while mitigating the negative impacts of visitation, such as risks to the site and its significance.

Interpretation was discussed in Section 4.1, in the context of its content being one product of research. Interpretive design is a separate task. A detailed interpretation plan, addressing content, design, and visitor experience, should be prepared for every public site sufficiently early in the process to enable proper budgeting. This work is usually done by an interpretive planner. The conservation plan may recommend broad guidelines for interpretation.

5.8 The Conservation Plan

The tasks that comprise the conservation process—understanding the historic place and managing change—are summarized in a conservation plan, which may be thought of as the ultimate product of heritage planning.

Australian James Semple Kerr defines the conservation plan:

At its simplest, a **conservation plan** is a document which sets out what is significant in a place and, consequently, what policies are appropriate to enable that significance to be retained in its future use and development. For most places it deals with the management of change.

(Kerr 2013: 1)[36]

Kerr notes that '"conservation plan" has become a convenient generic term covering a variety of productions.' Other terms in common use include **historic preservation plan** or **preservation plan** (mainly US).

Conservation plans occur at two distinct scales:

- A 'macro' conservation plan looks at a relatively large subject area, perhaps a conservation area, a rural district, or an entire community or municipality. It represents proactive, long-range planning and tries to anticipate the nature of future development proposals. Its conclusions provide broad conservation policies that the community is intended to follow. Plans at this scale are the responsibility of government or local authorities, and may be prepared by them or by consultants.
- A 'micro' conservation plan addresses a proposed intervention to a particular historic place, whether that place be an individual heritage resource (e.g., a building or a landscape) or a contiguous group of heritage resources (e.g., a neighborhood or a cultural landscape). The conclusions provide strategies ('policies') for ensuring that the heritage significance of the place is conserved for the long term. Plans at this scale are usually the responsibility of the proponent.

The 'macro' and the 'micro' conservation plan follow much the same methodology, albeit at different scales.[37] The 'macro' conservation plan is particularly appropriate for long-range planning and policy development, although it is not usually needed for broad, high-level heritage policy. The 'micro' plan is intended for proposed change to a specific historic place. The conservation plan should be drafted throughout the planning process, and then finalized at the end. For clarity it is shown as the last task on the heritage planning process chart (Figure 5.1).

Conservation plans for communities—the 'macro' plan

With respect to the first, 'macro,' scale of plan, it is helpful to recall the American Planning Association's recommended components of a community historic preservation plan, which were introduced in Section 2.1 (White and Roddewig 1994: 4). That publication is two decades old, but remains relevant today.

1 Statement of the goals of preservation in the community, and the purpose of the preservation plan.
2 Definitions of the historic character of the state, region, community, or neighborhood.

3   Summary of past and current efforts to preserve the community's or neighborhood's character.
4   A survey of historic resources in the community or neighborhood, or a definition of the type of survey that should be conducted in communities that have not yet completed a survey.
5   Explanation of the legal basis for protection of historic resources in the state and community.
6   Statement of the relationship between historic preservation and other local land-use and growth management authority, such as the zoning ordinance.
7   Statement of the public sector's responsibilities towards city-owned historic resources, such as public buildings, parks, streets, etc., and for ensuring that public actions do not adversely affect historic resources.
8   Statement of incentives that are, or should be, available to assist in the preservation of the community's historic resources.
9   Statement of the relationship between historic preservation and the community's educational system and program.
10 A precise statement of goals and policies, including a specific agenda for future action to accomplish those goals.

The 'macro' conservation plan is proactive. It develops strategies without reference to specific development proposals. The plan is very much more than documentation of an area's historic resources and their significance. This is made clear in Component 6, which declares 'the relationship between historic preservation and other local land-use and growth management authority, such as the zoning ordinance.' Regrettably, this relationship is infrequently demonstrated, particularly in North America, where mainstream urban planning continues to pay insufficient attention to heritage conservation (Tyler et al. 2009: 271).

Conservation plans are best when integrated as a component of comprehensive development plans. Sometimes they are relegated to being secondary components (or 'overlays'), and often are treated as independent documents. Full integration places heritage considerations within mainstream planning and reduces the risk of their being marginalized. The format of the conservation component should, of course, follow that of the overall plan. The American Planning Association's recommendations provide a good guide to content.

Many community conservation plans address urban areas. They inevitably consider economic issues and downtown revitalization and regeneration, which were introduced in Section 2.2. Many historic districts comprise 'a complete community, with healthy residential, commercial, industrial, recreational, and educational uses' (Tyler et al. 2009: 270). This should be retained and improved, if necessary, with a focus on maintaining the existing infrastructure of buildings, landscape, utilities, and transportation. Conservation plans may look at rural areas as well, a practice more common in Britain than in the US.

Conservation plans for historic places—the 'micro' plan

Depending on local regulations and expectations, a formal conservation plan may or may not be required for approval of a project. Even if a plan is not required, good practice warrants preparing one. The conservation plan provides a sound way to demonstrate that the historic place and its cultural significance are understood and that the proposal meets the objectives of good conservation practice, good planning, and community support.

A conservation plan is similar to—but differs from—a 'management plan,' a 'historic structure report,' and a 'feasibility study.' The differences between the various kinds of plans are discussed later in this section.

The central feature of a conservation plan, according to Kate Clark, is that it 'centres on the significance of the site and how that is to be retained in the long term.' Clark continues (1998: 1–2):

> The advantage of the Conservation Plan is that it should be the first step in the management or design process instead of an afterthought, put in place once most of the major decisions have been made. It provides a model whereby the significance of the site drives the design process instead of limping after it. ... Conservation Plans incorporate a logical development progressing from the understanding of the history and fabric of the site, into an explicit assessment of the significance, and from there, directly into the formulation of policies for retaining that significance. That is all.

Clark notes that a conservation plan is a proactive initiative that uses significance as a basis for planning change, whereas a heritage impact assessment is reactive, beginning with a proposal for change and reconciling it with significance (2000, 2001: 23).

The same approach is applicable to all kinds of historic places, including buildings, landscapes, archaeological sites, large artifacts, and historic towns, or to situations that combine more than one type of heritage resource.

The central messages in the 'micro' conservation plan are a vision for the intended change to the historic place appropriate to its significance, and the path to achieving that outcome. The American Planning Association's recommended components serve as a useful checklist of considerations that should be addressed. Getting there requires applying the processes described in the present book: understanding the heritage significance of the historic place (Chapter 4) and an application of best conservation practices (Chapter 3), all within the framework of heritage conservation infrastructure (Chapter 1) and the contexts of the law, planning, sustainability, and ethics (Chapter 2).

The actual subjects addressed in a conservation plan will vary from one plan to the next. The approach must be flexible. Kerr (2013: 1) cautions against relying on 'standard or model' conservation plans,

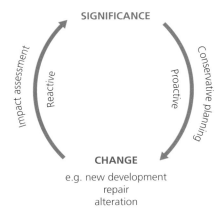

SIGNIFICANCE

Impact assessment

Reactive

Conservative planning

Proactive

CHANGE
e.g. new development
repair
alteration

Figure 5.30 The relationship between conservation planning and heritage impact assessment. (Kate Clark)

and advises using them only as a starting point and checklist. 'The actual structure and scope of the plan,' he concludes, 'has to evolve to suit the particular place and its problems.' He notes that the contents of a specific plan depend on the nature of the project, the scope of work, and the planning budget. The text should be concise and tightly written, with supporting material as needed contained in one or more appendixes. A comprehensive conservation plan covers many bases and a variety of disciplines, and is often best done as a team effort.

With these cautions in mind, a 'long list' of potential topics for the conservation plan, drawn from the heritage planning process, follows:[38]

Introduction
    Executive summary
    Background
        The proposed intervention
        Legal and planning context
    Scope of work for the conservation plan
        Goals and objectives
        Projected outcomes
    Study method

Understanding the historic place
    The place
        History and associations
        Physical investigation
        Community engagement
    Significance
        Identify heritage values
        Statement of significance
        Assess significance

Managing change
   Project context
      Statement of owner's objectives
      Legal and planning (including heritage) framework
      Input from community and authorities
      Sustainability context
      Ethical considerations
   Conservation strategies
      Goals, objectives, vision, policies
      Use(s)
      Conservation treatment(s)
      Applicable tools and incentives
      Potential risks
      Heritage impacts and mitigation
   Implementation
      Tasks, priorities, and timing
      Interpretation
      Maintenance

Each topic is explained in the appropriate section of the book or is self-evident. This outline does not address construction or financial concerns. They are usually treated in a historic structure report and a conservation management plan respectively, which are addressed just below.

   The present book presents a process for conservation planning. A model is illustrated in the chart introduced in Figures 1.3 and 1.4 (and again as Figures 4.2 and 5.1). To repeat, this is a simplified model and not a template, intended within the spirit of J.S. Kerr's advice to remain flexible and not be bound to a specific model. The present process does not take into account the continual process of feedback, whether positive or negative, nor does it consider the unpredictability of political outcomes and other uncertainties.

Related types of plans

The 'micro' conservation plan is a primary product of heritage conservation planning. However, the heritage professional will likely also become involved in other, related, kinds of plans, all of which include components of the conservation plan. This section describes the most common types of these planning documents and indicates their similarities and differences. Defining them categorically is challenging, particularly since names are used differently by the various authorities and some of the other plan-types are themselves called 'conservation plans.'

Historic structure report

A historic structure report (HSR), a term used mainly in the US, is a multidisciplinary document, similar to a conservation plan, but whose focus is to provide specific guidance on the physical treatment of the historic place. The US National Park Service developed the format in the 1930s and continues to recommend it as the primary planning document (Biallas 1990).[39] An HSR differs from a conservation plan in that it is more an architectural study than a planning study. The HSR looks closely at the physical deterioration of the historic place and recommends the design and preservation techniques that are required to conserve the materials and retain the character-defining elements.

Architectural conservator Deborah Slaton (2005: 5) defines an HSR in a reference document issued by the National Park Service:

> A **historic structure report** provides documentary, graphic, and physical information about a property's history and existing condition. Broadly recognized as an effective part of preservation planning, a historic structure report also addresses management or owner goals for the use or reuse of the property. It provides a thoughtfully considered argument for selecting the most appropriate approach to treatment, prior to the commencement of work, and outlines a scope of recommended work. The report serves as an important guide for all changes made to a historic property during the project—repair, rehabilitation, or restoration—and can also provide information for maintenance procedures. Finally, it records the findings of research and investigation, as well as the processes of physical work, for future researchers.[40]

'The ultimate purpose of an HSR,' writes the NPS's Billy Garrett (1990: 5), is 'to maximize retention of historic character and minimize loss of historic fabric.'

An HSR is largely an exercise in conservation architecture and engineering, which are not addressed in the present book. It differs from the conservation plan in the emphasis on the physical investigation, and by focusing on design, technical conservation, and construction considerations. HSRs should also include information on heritage significance and other conservation strategies that are normally developed in the conservation plan. The HSR includes architectural, engineering, and technical drawings, as well as cost estimates. Typical contents are provided in Arbogast (2010).

Conservation management plan

A conservation management plan (CMP) has many variants and comes with many names, including **cultural resource management plan**, **cultural heritage management plan**, and **integrated management plan**.

The Heritage Lottery Fund for England and Wales (2008: 6) defines a CMP:

> A **conservation management plan** is simply a document that helps you to understand why your heritage is important and to whom. It also helps you to use that information to look after it. It includes your management and maintenance plan.

A working definition developed by a multinational European organization states:

> A **cultural heritage integrated management plan** determines and establishes the appropriate strategy, objectives, actions and management structures to safeguard the cultural heritage, to balance the different needs and to use historic [places] as a development asset.
>
> (Scheffler 2009: 4)

Whereas a conservation plan focuses on ways to make change while retaining the significance of the historic place, a CMP goes further. It also addresses management strategies, discussing topics such as governance, operation (administrative management), visitor management, and financial projections.

Feasibility study

Another related type of report is the feasibility study. Its purpose is to test the feasibility of a proposed project, in order to enable decision-makers to choose whether or not to proceed with the proposal.

The feasibility study seeks answers to a number of questions, such as:

- Can the work be done in a manner that is consistent with good conservation practice?
- Is the proposal sound from a technical perspective?
- What will be the capital and ongoing operating costs? What will be the sources of revenue? Can we afford the project over the short and the long terms?
- Does the work meet principles of sustainability?
- Will the work comply with legal, planning, and conservation constraints?
- What are the negative impacts of the work? What will be lost as an outcome?
- What are the principal weaknesses? Can they be mitigated?
- Will the work provide a net benefit to the community?

The study may look at a proposal in isolation or compare the relative feasibility of multiple options. The core of a feasibility study resembles a conservation management plan, but since the feasibility study must precede detailed planning and design, it will make some assumptions about those. Costs will usually be estimated within a broad contingency, perhaps 15 to 25 percent.

Since the stakes are often high, it is important that the author of a feasibility study take the assignment seriously and look hard at both the strengths and weaknesses of the proposal. A feasibility study that warns against a potentially bad intervention is of far more value than the overoptimistic one that emphasizes only its strengths.

A Feasibility Study for a Historic Railway Trestle

The Kinsol Trestle, reportedly North America's largest extant wooden railway bridge, was built by the Canadian National Railways (CNR) on Vancouver Island, British Columbia, in 1920. It was continually maintained and renewed. The last train crossed the trestle in 1979, and the next three decades saw continued deterioration. The local government, the Cowichan Valley Regional District (CVRD), was committed to providing a crossing over the Koksilah River at that location to accommodate the Trans Canada Trail, which follows that part of the CNR right of way. The CVRD decided in 2006 to demolish the old trestle and replace it with a new bridge for pedestrians, cyclists, and equestrians.

An eleventh-hour appeal for reconsideration led the CVRD to commission a feasibility study to evaluate the relative merits of replacement versus conservation. The study demonstrated that rehabilitation of the old trestle was not only feasible, but that it was also superior to the proposed new crossing in several ways. Rehabilitation was *technically feasible* with respect to its structural strength, overall physical condition, and foundation conditions. It was *financially feasible* in that capital costs could be met by existing and anticipated funds and operating costs were within the District's budget allowance. It was *economically feasible* because of the boost it would give to tourism. It was *environmentally feasible* because reuse was more sustainable than replacement, and demolition would have required careful removal of the creosote-soaked timbers. Finally it was *socially feasible* because of the advantages of conserving a significant historic place and providing a superior recreational experience (Commonwealth Historic Resource Management Limited 2008: I:37–39).

On the basis of the feasibility study, the CVRD reversed its decision and proceeded to rehabilitate and reuse the historic structure. The renewed Kinsol Trestle opened in 2011 and has been extremely well received by recreational users and the broader community.

Figure 5.31 The Kinsol Trestle, near Shawnigan Lake, British Columbia, Canada, on opening day, July 28, 2011. (Macdonald & Lawrence Timber Framing Ltd.)

Business plan

A business plan makes a 'business case' for implementing a project that is believed to be feasible. It combines aspects of a concise management plan and feasibility study, one that focuses on the financial and economic aspects of the project.[41] The business plan specifies the goals of the project as well as its costs and benefits, and provides a plan for attaining the goals. It is prepared for the project stakeholders, particularly the decision-makers who will determine whether or not the project proceeds. These are the elected officials in the case of a public venture and the board of directors and investors in the private and non-profit sectors.

Strategic plan

Any of the above plans (except a feasibility study) may be termed a strategic plan if its focus is on the strategies and policies required to achieve the desired objectives. The meanings of 'strategy,' 'plan,' and 'policy' are quite similar; the difference in connotation is that a 'strategy' is perceived as describing a more pointed and direct route towards getting to a particular goal, and therefore implies concerted action. The name 'strategic plan' (be it a strategic conservation, management, or business plan) is often used because its connotations appeal to decision-makers.

Whereas all the above types of plans generally add something to the conservation plan, some other kinds of investigation involve only a portion of the heritage planning process. As examples, heritage professionals are often retained to conduct a **heritage assessment**, which may comprise all or some of the tasks described in Chapter 4, 'Understanding the Historic Place.' Another common study is an independent **heritage impact assessment**, whose method is described in Section 5.6. Other reports may involve anything from an **economic analysis** (part of a larger sustainability analysis) to an **implementation plan** (Section 5.7).

5.9 Design, Construction, and Beyond

Managing change to a historic place is a continuous process that involves a cycle of use, deterioration and maintenance, obsolescence, planning for conservation and/or change, recapitalization and intervention, reuse, deterioration and maintenance, and so on. This holds true whether it is for the long-term stewardship of a historic place or for a defined project. The latter may be seen as a short-term activity with a beginning and an end, but in reality such projects 'are mere nodes on a longer trajectory.'[42] The Ontario Heritage Trust, for example, undertakes conservation plans with 100-year cycles and recognizes that it will have a major project on each site about once every 20 years. Other managers are less proactive, anticipating the need for major recapitalization perhaps every 50 years.

The heritage planning process has proceeded to here without anything having yet been designed, conserved, built, dug, planted, interpreted, or managed. To adopt an old cliché, the shovel is not yet in the ground. At this point the conservation planning initiative has ended and implementation begins. The tasks at hand change from research, planning, and policy to design, construction, and management. The heritage professional may well remain involved in carrying out the project, but it will be in a capacity other than as planner.

Design, construction, and documentation

If the conservation plan leads to construction work, the principal stages that follow are usually:

- Design development
- Preparation of detailed designs and specifications
- Procurement of contractor(s)/trade(s)/artisan(s) to undertake the work
- Construction and project management
- Documentation of the outcome.

Every effort should be made to use the services of professionals who are fully qualified in heritage practice, both at the design phase (e.g., a conservation architect, landscape architect, and/or urban planner, preferably one accredited as a heritage professional) and for construction (e.g., a contractor whose portfolio includes excellent conservation work). This will sometimes be a challenge, particularly when resources are limited and specialists without conservation experience offer to do the work for less money, but it is essential to make every effort to retain qualified heritage professionals.

All work should be fully documented. This is often called 'as-built' documentation. It is useful as a record of work, as a baseline for future maintenance, and as a resource in the event of a catastrophe, as well as being a requirement of good conservation practice. Written records should be kept of all decisions made during the course of construction and retained with the other documentation.

This is stipulated in the *Venice Charter*, and is no less valid today than it was a half-century ago:

> In all works of preservation, restoration or excavation, there should always be precise documentation in the form of analytical and critical reports, illustrated with drawings and photographs. Every stage of the work of clearing, consolidation, rearrangement and integration, as well as technical and formal features identified during the course of the work, should be included. This record should be placed in the archives of a public institution and made available to research workers. It is recommended that the report should be published. (Article 16)

If the conservation plan has focused on community or institutional planning, rather than on a construction project, it may lead to an alternative set of tasks, perhaps including some of:

- Governance and organization
- Capacity building
- Programs of education and public awareness
- Marketing
- Policies for regulating, identifying, and managing historic places
- Implementation of planning tools, including protection and incentives
- Financial planning, including establishing strategic partnerships
- Undertaking pilot projects.

A professional management consultant, working in association with the heritage planner, may be appropriate to do many of these tasks.

Once construction and further work have been completed, the historic place will go into a state of operation—whether as a publicly operated site, a private property, a recognized historic area, an active cemetery, or in some other capacity. Ongoing management must respect the cultural significance that the conservation activity endeavored to protect.

A discussion of these important tasks and responsibilities lies beyond the scope of this book.

Maintenance and monitoring

> From the moment a building is completed, the aging process begins. It is inevitable, unremitting, and progressive.
>
> (Swanke Hayden Connell Architects 2000: 541)

The owner or operator of a historic place must anticipate the inevitable process of deterioration. The causes are both natural processes and human activities. Buildings leak and grow mold, landscapes and archaeological sites become overused and overgrown, both suffer vandalism. Proper maintenance makes the historic place and its materials last as long as possible; but while it retards decay, it does not stop it.

Design for interventions should reduce the need for maintenance by minimizing factors that cause deterioration. Many problems are caused by moisture and humidity, and so preventing the ingress of water from both typical and extreme conditions is critical, usually with proper drainage (of rainwater and groundwater) and careful detailing.[43] Harm to buildings and their contents may be caused by dust (an abrasive) and light (the UV component causes fading and chemical changes). Managing a site so as not to exceed its carrying capacity will reduce landscape deterioration.

'Maintenance' is often used as another word for 'preservation.' As noted in Section 3.2, the main distinction is that maintenance and repair are periodic, ongoing activities, whereas preservation is usually a larger, one-time intervention. In financial terms, maintenance and repair are usually treated as operating expenditures and preservation as a capital expenditure.

Managers of historic places should make every effort to avoid the regrettably common situation in which maintenance is deferred and then addressed only in time of crisis, when there is a risk of catastrophic damage. Easy as this may be to say, the keepers of the purse are often reluctant to spend money on regular maintenance. This is so even if they are constantly reminded not only that maintenance is the best practice, but also that investing in it now reduces the risk of more costly repairs later.[44]

Nevertheless, countless historic places urgently require maintenance. Parks Canada is but one property manager that faces this dilemma. Canada's Auditor General reported in 2003 that 'built heritage is threatened,' noting a high level of deterioration among national historic sites (Office of the Auditor General of Canada 2003). Even though Parks Canada responded by increasing budgets for maintenance, the bulk of it went to roads, bridges, and other 'high-risk' infrastructure rather than to 'cultural assets.' A consultant found in 2013 that some 61 percent of Parks Canada's 2,000 cultural assets are in 'poor' or 'very poor' condition. But given the government's determination to reduce expenditures, no solution is in sight (Beeby 2014). This situation is repeated around the world, exacerbated in a fiscal climate that has many governments reluctant to address spending of this kind.

A **maintenance plan** (**maintenance program**) should form a part of conservation planning, whether within the conservation plan or as a separate document prepared shortly after the work has been completed. The maintenance plan should address issues of sustainable funding as well as technical practice.

The maintenance plan responds to two questions:

- How will the historic place be maintained over the years?
- How can the owner/manager determine whether maintenance is adequate to keep the historic place in proper condition?

A maintenance plan responds to these questions by recommending a number of related activities (Chambers 1976; Sandwith and Stainton 1985):

- **Housekeeping**: Routine maintenance activities to remove dust, soil, and other sources of abrasion from surfaces; clear snow and ice and other sources of risk; ensure proper control of light, heat, and humidity; and similar tasks. The plan may dictate that they are carried out daily, twice weekly, or weekly, usually by staff.
- **Long-term maintenance** (or **cyclical maintenance**): A formal program of minor and major maintenance activities, linked to a timetable. Some tasks might be undertaken seasonally (e.g., pruning trees and shrubs, clearing leaves from storm gutters); some undertaken annually, biennially, or less frequently (e.g., painting, maintaining mechanical systems), often by a contractor.

- **Repair**: Remedial action that returns a damaged or broken component to good condition by fixing or mending it, or by replacing it in kind when fixing is not practicable. Repair is a form of restoration and should follow standards and guidelines for conservation. Repair is done on an as-needed basis.
- **Periodic inspection**: The maintenance program should stipulate regular inspection of the historic place and its components. The objective is to identify anything in need of repair, or maintenance that has been ineffective. In the latter case, the maintenance plan should be amended to reflect the appropriate frequency of maintenance.
- **Documentation**: A full record of all housekeeping, maintenance, repairs, and inspections should be documented in a **maintenance log**. In addition, the manager should prepare a **maintenance manual**, which includes items such as emergency information, a catalogue of relevant documents that relate to the historic place and its components, sources of materials, common treatments, resource personnel, and more. The log forms a supplement to the manual (Chambers 1976: 25–30).

Preparing a full maintenance plan will likely require collaboration with a conservation architect, preservation technologist, and/or others.

Monitoring the historic place is an essential and ongoing process. Periodic inspection is one monitoring activity. The larger task is to set out and implement an ongoing monitoring program to review the effectiveness of heritage management. This may be done from numerous perspectives. With respect to financial management, for example, 'success will be measured in terms of the … overall business outcomes, service delivery obligations and asset portfolio performance requirements' (New South Wales Treasury 2004). In the sustainability context, the ongoing environmental performance and social benefits will be seen as important.

Policy documents should be reviewed regularly as well. The *Burra Charter* states: 'Statements of cultural significance and policy for the place should be periodically reviewed, and actions and their consequences monitored to ensure continuing appropriateness and effectiveness' (Article 26.4).

Most centrally to the present book, success in the heritage conservation context will be measured by the extent to which ongoing operation enables a historic place to retain its cultural significance. Assuming that the conservation intervention followed good practice, then sustaining the heritage values that were identified in the planning phase is perhaps the best test of the maintenance program specifically and of heritage planning generally.

Notes

1. Heritage Planning

1   As an example of this provocative approach, Heritage Canada's magazine ran a lead article whose title advocated 'New Directions for the Movement,' and which began with the lament: 'There is a growing sense in Canada that heritage conservation is losing ground' (Quinn and Weibe 2012).

2   A 'preservationist'—or any other 'ist'—is the follower of a belief system or a dogma—often an 'ism.' Examples are Buddhists and Communists, who adhere to Buddhism and Communism respectively. The term 'preservationist' may be appropriate to describe a heritage advocate, who is a believer of sorts (in 'Preservationism'?)—but not a heritage planner, who is an objective professional. One person may, of course, wear both hats, but preferably at different times.

3   Scottish conservation educator Miles Glendinning (2013) takes a different approach, considering the discipline of heritage planning to be one aspect of the all-encompassing conservation 'movement.'

4   A generation or two ago, 'heritage' was used widely as a marketing term to promote commodities with traditional connotations; for example, the American appliance manufacturer Sunbeam branded a slow-cooker as a 'heritage pot.' 'Heritage' achieved negative undertones in the UK in the late twentieth century with writers who charged—much in the same vein—that heritage is a manufactured commodity presenting a past that never was. See, for example, Hewison (1987).

5   Heritage value will be addressed in Section 4.4.

6   The French cognate 'immeuble' means 'real estate' or 'building.' In legal terms, the immediate setting is called the 'curtilage.'

7   The apparent paradox inherent in seeing significance in both exceptional ('outstanding') and representative historic places is discussed in Section 4.5.

8   This is discussed in Section 2.2.

9   A parallel definition had been posed 20 years earlier: 'Places in nature that have acquired significant associations with human activities and human events become historic and cultural landscapes' (Galbreath 1975: 1). An overview of the consideration of cultural landscapes from an exclusively American perspective is found in Keller and Keller (2003).

10 For recent concepts on the nature and management of cultural landscapes, see K. Taylor and Lennon (2012); Roe and K. Taylor (2014).

11 The *Florence Charter* is introduced in Section 3.1; approaches to cultural landscapes are discussed in Section 5.3.

12 Good introductions to archaeological legislation and policy occur for most countries. See, for example, Hunter and Ralston (1993); Pokotylo and Mason (2010), for the UK and US respectively.

13 'Meuble,' the French cognate of 'movable,' refers to furniture.

14 The convention is discussed in Section 3.1. See also (UNESCO n.d.).

15 Associations, stories, and interpretation are addressed briefly in Section 4.1.

16 Grenville bases her thesis in part on the idea of 'ontological security' discussed by sociologist Anthony Giddens.

17   The two UNESCO conventions and the ICOMOS charters (cited in the next paragraph) are discussed in Section 3.1. The paradoxical association of 'outstanding' and 'representative' is addressed in the discussion of heritage values in Section 4.5. The two conventions are reconciled in Cameron and Boucher 2007.

18   The statement reflects a recent update, kindly provided by Vanessa Drysdale in correspondence, 15 November 2013.

19   Both documents are discussed in Section 3.1. Sustainability is the subject of Section 2.2.

20   Instrumental and intrinsic values are discussed in Section 4.4.

21   Because this and related programs are well entrenched in American practice, the US has been slow to adjust to the emphasis placed on intangible associations.

22   Legislation and charters are addressed in Chapters 2 and 3 respectively.

23   Non-profit organizations are so named because they are incorporated without share capital. Any budget surplus they may accumulate is reinvested in the organization or passed on to charitable organizations, rather than distributed as profit to shareholders. Many, but not all, NGOs and NPOs are themselves charitable organizations, meaning that they can accept donations and issue receipts for tax purposes.

24   For the SPAB's original principles and Morris's 'manifesto' (which is still promoted on the Society's website), see Section 3.1.

25   The Norwich Plan is described in Section 2.2, as part of the discussion of economic considerations.

26   For an overview of the roles and achievements of non-governmental and government organizations, see Saunders (1996). For NGOs in the UK generally, see Rodwell (2007: 65–7).

27   Steel magnate Andrew Carnegie's donating money for the construction of more than 2,500 libraries around the English-speaking world, including 1,689 in the US, is perhaps the best example of this tradition of generosity.

28   Protection and incentives are discussed in Section 5.4. The comparative costs of rehabilitation and new construction are addressed in Section 2.2.

29   Heritage advocates, by contrast, have come from all walks of life.

30   The two pioneers who initiated the Cornell program were planner Barclay G. Jones and architectural historian Stephen W. Jacobs.

31   The program was initiated in 2011 and the first award went to the Historic Town of Vigan, Philippines. See also other articles in the same issue of *World Heritage*, devoted to 'sharing best practices.'

32   The British terms 'historic environment' and 'regeneration' are equivalent to the North American terms 'historic places' and 'revitalization.'

2. Context

1   Specific ways in which this paradox has played out in the Canadian province of Ontario are described in Shipley and McKernan (2011).

2   Objectives and priorities for Tr'ochëk are provided in the *Tr'ondëk Hwëch'in Final Agreement*, chapter 13, schedule B. Three early outcomes of the initiative were its designation as a national historic site in 2002, the publication of Dobrowolsky (2003), and a management plan (Tr'ondëk Hwëch'in 2007).

3   Pre-Roman attitudes towards conservation, which were not expressed in laws that have come down to us, are discussed in Glendinning (2013) and Erder (1986).

4   Pharr attributes the law jointly to the Emperors Leo and Majorian and gives the date as 458. Morrison provides the date 453.

5   Values and significance are discussed in Sections 4.4 and 4.5. Recognition, protection, and other aspects of the legislative system are addressed more fully in Section 5.4.

6   Canadian heritage law specialist Marc Denhez (1997: 7) calls the first, second, and fourth components the 'three pillars' of a national heritage strategy.

7   This has been noted by many authors, including Cotter (2012: 25), citing others, among them Lowenthal (1985).

8   Educator J. M. Fitch used the term 'curatorial management' in the subtitle of his (at the time) ground-breaking book (1982). His introduction talks about the 'curatorial task' of 'preservationists' (xii).

9   In Britain heritage statutes are considered to reside within the context of land-use legislation. As an illustration, the UK Parliament's informational website discusses 'preserving historic sites and buildings' as a part of 'managing and owning the landscape,' which discusses such other legislation as enclosure acts and private acts that enabled landowners to sell parts of their estates. See UK Parliament n.d.

10   In the US, this was established by *Euclid v. Ambler Realty Company*, a 1926 decision of the Supreme Court that supported zoning, since it reduces nuisances and is therefore in the public interest, which overrides the interests of individual property owners.

11   *Berman v. Parker* (1954), cited in Tyler et al. (2009: 122). Portions of this discussion of US law have been adapted from chapter 4 of the book.

12   *Penn Central Transportation Co. v. City of New York (Grand Central Terminal)*; see Costonis (1977); Wolloch (1977); FindLaw (n.d.).

13   For overviews of the systems for regulating built heritage in other countries, see Stubbs and Makaš 2011. For the management of archaeology, see Messenger and Smith (2010).

14   British heritage law is discussed in Pendlebury (2001); Ross (1996); Bigham (1973); and Stubbs and Makaš (2011: 59–60). For the evolution of heritage policy in Britain from a political perspective, see Delafons (1997).

15   The criteria for listing buildings are identified in Pickard (1996: 16–26).

16   The information in this discussion has been drawn from a variety of sources, including official websites and published literature. For the latter, see Tyler et al. (2009): chapter 2; Stubbs and Makaš (2011): chapter 28; Hosmer (1981); Murtagh (1988); Hutt et al. (1999); King (2004).

17   The description of Australian heritage law is drawn largely from Boer and Wiffen (2006) and Kerr (2013). For the legislation, see EDO NSW (Australian Network of Environmental Defenders Offices n.d.).

18   The relationship between cultural and natural heritage in former British colonies is seen in part as retention of core prejudices in the interface between European colonialism and Indigenous people in Deacon (2010).

19   The *World Heritage Convention* (1972), addressed in Section 3.1, set an international precedent for considering natural and cultural heritage together.

20   The difference between the two lists is discussed with 'significance' in Section 4.5. The *Burra Charter* is introduced in Section 3.1.

21   The *Constitution Act* is a Canadian statute; it corresponds to Schedule B of the *Canada Act*, which is a British statute.

22   The Board was created by the *Historic Sites and Monuments Act*, whose predecessor statute dates back to 1919. See <http://www.pc.gc.ca/eng/clmhc-hsmbc/> and Symons 1997.

23   The Territory of Nunavit, created in 1999, has approved Archaeological and Palaeontological Site Regulations, but a formal statute for historic places remains forthcoming.

24   In the early 1970s the author was involved in a project to rehabilitate the early twentieth-century Stanley and New Fountain hotels in Vancouver's Gastown ('skid road') as affordable housing. The local building authority insisted that the original lath-and-plaster partitions be replaced with drywall, an intervention that would have driven the construction cost too high for the project to succeed. The developer objected. Officials from the National Research Council of Canada arrived with blowtorches and stopwatches to test the fire-resistance of the old wall—and determined that it outperformed the code-prescribed wall system. The local authority relented and the plaster walls remained. However the same authority refused to allow the retention of mammoth old sawn timber

beams because the lumber had not been stamped to show that it met current standards. They had to be replaced with new beams about one-quarter their cross section. For the project, see Richardson (1972: 191).

25   The local building official may be personally liable should an approved construction system fail, so officials are understandably conservative.

26   The conclusions are based on an Australian government analysis cited in Pilzer (2005: 19). Canada's National Building Code (2010) is objective-based (performance-based). The British Columbia Building Code (2012), which generally follows the national model, provides for 'alternative compliance' for heritage buildings, intended for the 'protection of heritage character'.

27   This discussion has been drawn from numerous sources, among them Tyler and Ward (2011); Cullingworth and Nadin (2002); Gurran (2011); Levy (2011).

28   The landmark zoning litigation, *Euclid v. Amber Realty Company*, was cited in the previous section as a predecessor of the Grand Central Station decision.

29   Ironically, this urban design form is no longer favored by planners, who now advocate mounting a tower atop a low-rise podium that extends out to the lot line. The 1961 zoning enabled developers to add 10 square feet of office space in return for 1 square foot of plaza. The amount of the bonus was subsequently made discretionary. For the Seagram Building and its plaza, see Lambert (2013).

30   Design guidelines are not addressed in this book because this is the purview of conservation architecture more than conservation planning.

31   It should be pointed out, however, that the section devoted to 'Conserving and enhancing the historic environment' is the twelfth of 13 sections in the document—evidently a low priority. More detail on policy for the historic environment is available in the earlier 'PPS5' (Department for Communities and Local Government (UK) 2010: 14) which has since been repealed. English Heritage (2008b) is a national policy document distinct from the planning policy framework and PPS5.

32   Further evidence of the regrettable gap between mainstream urban planning and heritage planning emerges upon a search through the professional journals of the American Planning Association and the planning institutes of other countries, which reveals very few articles on heritage planning.

33   This is an Annex to U.N. General Assembly, document A/42/427.

34   For a collection of authoritative essays on 'sustainable approaches to the conservation of the built environment,' see Teutonico and Matero (2003).

35   The need to serve disadvantaged communities was introduced into urban planning by American Paul Davidoff in the 1960s. See the discussion of advocacy planning in Section 4.3.

36   The link between social improvements and new housing declared by the CIAM and in the writings of Le Corbusier, including *The Athens Charter* (1933, rev. 1943), Le Corbusier's account of the fourth conference of CIAM (1933), has been widely discussed in the literature.

37   As much as 40 percent of what goes into landfills in the US is construction debris. It has been estimated that demolishing one small masonry commercial structure—two storys high, 25 feet (8m) wide, and 120 feet (37m) deep—negates the environmental benefit of recycling 1,344,000 aluminum cans! (Rypkema 2007) The percentage of construction and demolition waste in other countries is lower.

38   Jackson questions the accuracy of the tools used for estimating embodied energy, but asserts the relevance of considering embodied energy in addressing sustainable design.

39   A 'tight' building (i.e., one that is no longer 'leaky') has lower air-change rates, which combined with the toxins in many building materials, is believed to cause occupants to have adverse health effects. See, for example, Dingle (2009).

40   See Greenlivingpedia 2009; Street 2012.

41   The Green Building Council began in the US and now operates in several other countries.

42   The U-value is a measure of the energy loss of a building component; a low U-value has less

conductivity and therefore better thermal performance than a high one. It differs from the R-value, which is a measure of the thermal resistance of a material; with R-values, higher is better.

43   See also the same team's earlier studies (Baker et al. 2010 and Baker 2011). If water vapor produced within a building cannot disperse, whether through a permeable structure or by mechanical means, moisture caused by condensation becomes a risk to the building and insulating materials.

44   These initiatives have come about in response to the *Climate Change (Scotland) Act 2009*.

45   Tellingly, every other article in this 'special issue on sustainability' of the *APT Bulletin* is devoted to energy- and greenhouse-gas-related issues. So too are the articles in *APT Bulletin*, 36, no. 4 (2005), dedicated to 'sustainability and preservation,' and *Historic Environment*, 24, no. 2 (2012), devoted to 'built heritage and sustainability.' Articles from the three journals are cited in this section.

46   In addition to projects described at the Seattle conference, the National Trust published a number of 'Economic Analyses of Adaptive Use Projects' in 1976 in its series *Information: from the National Trust for Historic Preservation*. The subjects of the analyses included Long Wharf in Boston, Guernsey Hall in Princeton, NJ, Trolley Square in Salt Lake City, and Stanford Court in San Francisco.

47   Two particularly productive conferences, which provide the basis for much of the discussion that follows, were 'Economics and heritage conservation,' hosted in 1998 by the Getty Conservation Institute; and 'The economics of heritage,' hosted in 2007 by Australia's Department of Environment and Water Resources (now the Department of Sustainability, Environment, Water, Population and Communities). Summaries are available in Mason (1999) and Australian Government, Department of the Environment (2007). Some articles from these conferences are cited below. The Getty conference launched an important research initiative on both cultural and economic value, which was communicated in three reports published between 1999 and 2002. See also Bennett 2007.

48   Cultural heritage values and heritage significance are addressed in Sections 4.4 and 4.5.

49   'Qualitative measurements' on heritage assets are also discussed in Rypkema et al. (2011: appendix D). The issue of heritage and property values is discussed later in this section.

50   Mourato and Mazzanti focus on stated-preference methods, including an analysis of the strengths and weaknesses of each. The validity of contingent valuation in environmental assessment was seen in the acceptance by a US court of law of the CV analysis of damage caused by the *Exxon Valdez* oil spill in Alaska; see Arrow et al. 1993, cited in Mourato and Mazzanti 2002.

51   Outcomes of hedonic pricing are addressed in the discussion of property value, below.

52   Rizzo and Throsby suggest the institutional structures and other conditions that will enable informed and effective policy choices.

53   The analysis is, of course, more complex than this brief description suggests. The process of identifying all relevant components is challenging, since assigning economic value is often difficult, as was seen above. All costs and benefits must be expressed as 'net present value,' which requires 'discounting' future costs and benefits.

54   Among the popular models are TEAM, IMPLAN, RSRC PC I–O, MGM2, PEIM, and RIMS II. These are described from a heritage perspective in Gunn 2002: 21–5; and Rypkema et al. 2011: 17–22.

55   The US compiles detailed statistics on rehabilitation projects that participate in the tax credit program; for this and other incentive programs, see Section 5.4.

56   The 'Castle Doctrine' and land-use law are discussed in Section 2.1.

57   *Alberta Historical Resources Act* (RSA 2000), chap. H-9, 28(1) and *B.C. Local Government Act* (RSBC 1996, chap. 323), Part 27, 969(1). See also the discussion of compensation in Section 5.4.

58   Much of the renown came about because of a widely promoted documentary film (Civic Trust c. 1960).

59   The original components of the Main Street Project are captured in, and the quotations taken from, two pamphlets issued early in the program: National Main Street Center (1981, c. 1981).

60   The need to position urban conservation as a determining factor in sustainable development is the thesis of Rodwell 2007.

61 Many have seen the origin of the experience economy in the opening of Disneyland in 1955.

62 The economic benefits of tourism are often measured by using economic impact assessments; see the discussion above. See also Gunn 2002; Rypkema et al. 2011: 19–22, 36.

63 Dower's article is based on the proceedings of the conference organized by the European Travel Commission in collaboration with Europa Nostra and held at Copenhagen on 26 and 27 November 1973. Duncan Sandys (later Lord Duncan-Sandys) was, at the time, president of Europa Nostra, 'the voice of cultural heritage in Europe.' Sandys was also the principal champion of the Civic Trust's Norwich Plan, described above.

64 These questions, often asked of the Manhattan Project, are posed after the surrender of Germany by historian Martin Sherman in a conversation with Oppenheimer in David Grubin's film, *The Trials of J. Robert Oppenheimer*. Oppenheimer replies, 'When you see something that is technically sweet, you go ahead and do it and you argue about what to do about it only after you have had your technical success.' Only later did Oppenheimer substitute remorse for enthusiasm (Grubin 2009).

65 The National Park Service (n.d.-c) asserts that the lighthouse 'should not be threatened by the indomitable ocean waves for another 100 years'—cold comfort when, in theory, conservation is intended for perpetuity.

66 In a thought-provoking essay, European fine art conservator Christabel Blackman (2011) reminds us that ethical decision-making must consider pragmatic constraints, including the limitations of budget.

67 The ideas of Morris, Ruskin, and the SPAB are discussed further in Section 3.1.

68 The *Universal Declaration of Human Rights* (1948) was the first major declaration issued by the United Nations.

69 As an example of truthfulness, Warren said that an intervention to strengthen a historic structure should be visible and not disguised, as the latter would be 'dishonest' and 'deceptive.'

70 Speaking for historic places is much the same as 'speaking for animals,' a motto of the Society for the Prevention of Cruelty to Animals (SPCA), whose name can easily be confused with that of SPAB.

71 For a passive system of wall insulation that disperses water vapor in a newly insulated traditional stone structure, see Curtis 2012: 16.

72 The original dome could not be repaired in part because of the extent of the damage, but also for a technical and bureaucratic reason: building officials declared the original engineering design to be 'indeterminate' and therefore unable to be approved under modern building regulations. The new dome adopts a 'calculable' engineering design. The original design and structure were known because, in a prescient move, Parks Canada had documented the building shortly before the fire.

73 Council on Environmental Quality, NEPA regulations, 40 CFR 1502.24; cited in King 2009: 33.

3. Best Practices

1 See Jokilehto 1999, which discusses the development of conservation theory and introduces the leading practitioners in Europe. The same author focuses on the charters, conventions, and their international context in Jokilehto 1996.

2 The story of restoration vs. anti-restoration has been told many times, including in Jokilehto 1999. The most compelling narrative remains Tschudi-Madsen 1976.

3 Originally published as 'Restoration,' *Athenaeum*, London, 23 June 1877, No. 2591, 807; reprinted in Tschudi-Madsen 1976: 144–6 and available at the SPAB website. Morris most certainly did not seek compromise. The SPAB remains active today and makes compliance with the manifesto a requisite for membership. Great Britain adopted the *Ancient Monuments Act 1882* a mere five years later, demonstrating the influence of the SPAB manifesto on national policy.

4 We may speculate as to what today's best practices would be had the views of Viollet-le-Duc carried the day, and were architects to have license to alter old buildings in the manner of the original

architect, as long as they maintained high standards of design. British architect Edward Hollis (2009: 9) has asked this question, and suggests that only the Slovenian Jože Plečnik and the Italian Carlo Scarpa have seriously (and skillfully) pursued this direction.

5   The document is unrelated to architect Le Corbusier's *The Athens Charter* (1933, rev. 1943), which is referred to in Note 36 above in the discussion of social housing in Section 2.2.

6   After returning from Athens, Giovannoni wrote the *Norms for the Restoration of Monuments* (published 1932), also known as the *Italian Charter for Restoration* (*La Carta Italiana del Restauro*), which provided principles for conservation interventions. See Jokilehto (1996: 76, 2009: 75). Both articles provide skillful analyses of international doctrine.

7   The *Athens Charter* is sometimes called the 'Carta del Restauro' (restoration charter), which is also the name of Giovannoni's subsequent publication (Jokilehto 1999: 222, 288).

8   Available at <http://www.icomos.org/index.php/en/charters-and-texts?id=157:the-venice-charter&catid=179:charters-and-other-standards>

9   Three decades passed between the two charters because Europe had been preoccupied with war and reconstruction.

10 The 2013 version contains the revised charter text, explanatory notes, and Burra Charter Process table. The full 1999 edition (now considered archived) includes guidelines on cultural significance, conservation policy, and procedures for undertaking studies and reports from the 1988 version, as well as a Code on the Ethics of Coexistence in Conserving Significant Places (1998) and notes and conversion tables on the 1999 revisions.

11 This is broader and less precisely defined than the 1999 version, which reads: 'Place means site, area, land, landscape, building or other work, group of buildings or other works, and may include components, contents, spaces and views' (Article 1.1).

12 This principle also makes the connection between cultural heritage and natural heritage. The explanatory notes refer to the *Australian Natural Heritage Charter*.

13 It was, however, the more benign first edition of the *Burra Charter* (1979) that gained the attention of ICOMOS.

14 This is further discussed below with the UNESCO charter on intangible cultural heritage. See also Cameron (2009: 134); Larsen (1994). The *Nara Document* and authenticity are discussed further in Section 4.4.

15 The *Declaration of San Antonio* was the outcome of the InterAmerican Symposium on Authenticity in the Conservation and Management of the Cultural Heritage. Available at <http://www.icomos.org/en/charters-and-texts/179-articles-en-francais/ressources/charters-and-standards/188-the-declaration-of-san-antonio>

16 For a discussion of differences between Western and Asian values, see Chung (2005). Chung argues that East Asian societies are determined more than Western ones by the spiritual and naturalistic qualities of their culture and historic places.

17 The *Universal Declaration of Human Rights* (1948) was the first major declaration issued by the United Nations.

18 Three conventions are not considered here: the UNESCO Convention (on illicit import and export of cultural property) of 1970; the UNIDROIT Convention (on stolen objects) of 1995; and the Underwater Cultural Heritage Convention of 2001.

19 Jukka Jokilehto (1996: 55) points out the analogy with the Seven Wonders of the World. See also Cameron and Rössler (2013), Gensheimer and Guichard (2014).

20 Many countries are under the false impression that UNESCO is responsible for protection. On a recent overseas tour, the author heard numerous informed tour guides declare this at World Heritage Sites. Many journalists have noted the same thing in articles.

21 All versions of the guidelines can be found at <http://whc.unesco.org/en/guidelines/>

22 The paradox of 'outstanding' vs. 'representative' is discussed in Section 4.5.

23   Available at <http://whc.unesco.org/document/6814> This formed the basis for the 'Declaration on the Conservation of Historic Urban Landscapes,' also adopted in 2005; available at <http:// whc.unesco.org/document/6812> The general conference of UNESCO subsequently adopted 'the Recommendation on the Historic Urban Landscape' in 2011. The term forms the title of a book by Francesco Bandarin and Ron Van Oers, both officers with UNESCO, in which they describe the historic urban landscape as 'a tool for the management of change' (Bandarin and Van Oers 2012).

24   The sources of the recommendations are UNESCO, *Recommendation Concerning the Safeguarding of the Beauty and Character of Landscapes and Sites* (Paris, 1962), *Recommendation Concerning the Protection of Cultural Property Endangered by Public and Private Works* (Paris, 1968), *Recommendation Concerning the Protection, at National Level, of the Cultural and Natural Heritage* (Paris, 1972), *Recommendation Concerning the Safeguarding and Contemporary Role of Historic Areas* ('Warsaw Declaration,' Nairobi, 1976); and United Nations, *Agenda 21* (*Earth Summit: The United Nations Program of Action from Rio*, 1992). Agenda 21 is discussed with sustainability in Section 2.2.

25   A key early step in the policy review was the publication of *Power of Place* (English Heritage 2000).

26   The document says, in a similar tone, that: 'Changes which would harm the heritage values of a significant place should be unacceptable' (Clause 15).

27   Conservators of art use similar names for treatments but sometimes with quite different meanings. Their terminology is not addressed here.

28   The US National Park Service does not define 'conservation' with the other treatments, presumably because the US continues to use the traditional term 'historic preservation' as an umbrella descriptor.

29   This is essentially the same as 'protection' (or 'anti-restoration'), as defined by the SPAB.

30   The *Burra Charter* distinguishes between maintenance and repair: 'Maintenance means the continuous protective care of a place, and its setting. Maintenance is to be distinguished from repair which involves restoration or reconstruction' (Australia ICOMOS 2013b: Article 1.5).

31   This meaning differs considerably from the nineteenth-century sense of 'restoration' discussed in Section 3.1.

32   Guidelines for new work are addressed in Section 3.3.

33   The World Heritage Committee discussed at length whether a reconstructed site could be considered to possess authenticity and be inscribed as a World Heritage Site, and determined that no other reconstructed sites would be considered for listing (Cameron 2009: 131).

34   The Fortress of Louisbourg, reconstructed by Parks Canada in the 1960s and 1970s, offers a poignant example. The buildings had been designed by French engineers ignorant of Canadian winters, and were already in poor condition only a few decades after their construction. In the concern for historical accuracy, the design shortcomings were repeated in the twentieth-century reconstruction. Within a generation the new buildings began to show serious signs of deterioration. See Parks Canada (n.d.); Taylor (1990: 176–87). Ironically Parks Canada (2010: 15) does not recognize reconstruction as a conservation treatment despite having engaged in the activity in the past: 'Reconstruction, or reconstitution of a disappeared historic place, is not considered conservation and is therefore not addressed in this document.' The US National Park Service, on the other hand, has been authorized to undertake reconstructions by the *Historic Sites Act* of 1935. The NPS recognizes the controversy and risk, and undertakes reconstruction only after careful consideration of all alternatives; see Mackintosh (2004: 65–74). English archaeologist and educator Nicholas Stanley-Price (2009) proposes principles to determine when reconstruction is permissible.

35   The US National Park Service incorporates stabilization (and 'protection') into preservation.

36   The Shinto shrines at Ise, Japan, for example, are demolished and replicated every 20 years (see the discussion of intangible cultural heritage in Section 3.1). Michelangelo's sculpture of *David*, which stood outdoors in the Piazza della Signoria, Florence, was taken into the Accademia di Belle Arti for protection and a replica placed in the original, exposed location.

37   Construction of the St. Lawrence Seaway led to the creation of Upper Canada Village in Ontario; a hydroelectric dam brought about the formation of King's Landing in New Brunswick. What heritage significance is lost in moving a building to a museum may increase its museological significance as an artifact. The first outdoor museum in the world, Skansen in Stockholm (opened 1891), was created to demonstrate Swedish traditional life and folklore, an act of intangible conservation (as well as tangible conservation, since buildings were preserved).

38   This was a compromise when the subdivision was formed, since before 2005 Markham did not have the legal authority to preserve buildings in situ. For a description and critique of Markham Heritage Estates, which concludes that it is 'a distinctly postmodern heritage landscape' that 'commodifies and manipulates heritage,' see Hall 1999.

39   Architectural museums are introduced in the text box on Sir John Soane's Museum in Section 2.1.

40   These and other interventions are cited in Oberlander et al. (1989: 9–17). 'Consolidation' is defined at length in Feilden (1982: 9).

41   This is the position advocated in Parks Canada 2010.

42   Citing two Canadian examples in which the author was involved, one (Oberlander et al. 1989) was one of three manuals intended to guide recipients of conservation funding from the British Columbia Heritage Trust; the other (Kalman 1979) directed at recipients of funds from the Canadian government's Residential Rehabilitation Assistance Program, as well as at program supervisors and inspectors, with the objective that the quality of conservation work would improve.

43   For details on the American historic preservation system, see Stubbs and Makaš (2011: 442–5). Tax incentives are addressed in Section 5.4.

44   The full set of standards and guidelines was temporarily unavailable on the Internet at the time this book was completed, as the National Park Service website was being revised. The abundance of individual web pages previously available was quite confusing.

45   Brown goes on to say that they were first drafted as 'Guidelines for Rehabilitating Old Buildings,' published by the Department of Housing and Urban Development (HUD) in 1976, and recast as 'The Secretary of the Interior's Standards for Historic Preservation Projects with Guidelines for Applying the Standards' upon the passing of the *Tax Reform Act* of 1976, which enabled the federal tax incentive program. It was seen in Section 2.1 that the law can only enforce actions that are relatively straightforward to interpret.

46   This issue is discussed further in Section 5.3.

47   The Canadian *Standards and Guidelines*, for example, devotes 27 pages to standards (pertaining to all types of historic places and including commentary and elaborations) and 209 pages to guidelines (with a separate set for each category of historic place).

48   The application of silanes (penetrating polyester resins) to consolidate deteriorating stone carvings on English churches in the 1970s, before extensive testing had been done, caused the stone to darken in color, with no practicable method to reverse the damage.

49   Australia ICOMOS provides detailed guidance to the introduction of new work in a Practice Note to the *Burra Charter* (Australia ICOMOS 2013c).

4. Understanding the Historic Place

1   The term 'understanding the historic place' was popularized in 1982 by J.S. Kerr in the first edition of *Conservation Plan*; it has since been widely accepted.

2   For a rich anthology of previously published writings on archaeology, see Sullivan and Mackay (2013).

3   *Wikipedia* (http://en.wikipedia.org/wiki/Wikipedia:Introduction) is a prime example of a non-peer-reviewed resource that is extremely widely used. The policy of collaborative open editing by readers, which has many strong advantages, causes quality to vary immensely. Some articles have been

meticulously researched and are highly reliable, whereas others have not and may contain multiple errors.

4   See, for example, Smith (n.d.) Methods for obtaining oral history have been formalized and promoted by dedicated organizations, such as the International Oral History Association. Many guides to undertaking oral history are available: an example is Robertson (1996).

5   Executive Order 13007, May 24, 1996, 1(b)(iii). Cited in Kaufman (2009: 56).

6   The term 'documentation' is often used to describe historical research (i.e., the search for documents), the physical investigation (i.e., creating documents that describe the place), or both. The compilation of both written and graphic records, contemporary and historical, is the preferred meaning.

7   See, for example, Carter (1983); Clark (2001: chapter 7).

8   Tilden's book was first published in 1957. Some trace the beginnings of interpretation in the modern sense to nineteenth-century Scottish-American naturalist and conservation advocate, John Muir. See Brochu and Merriman (2002: 11–12).

9   In North America, the term 'surveyor' usually denotes a land surveyor or a quantity surveyor.

10   The HABS/HAER records are deposited in the Library of Congress.

11   See, for example, Foxe (2010: 39–45). This issue of *APT Bulletin* is devoted to documentation; many of its articles originated with papers delivered at 'Capturing the Past for Future Use,' a symposium held in Los Angeles on November 2–3, 2009, as part of the annual conference of the Association for Preservation Technology.

12   Many sources expand on this discussion, including Swanke Hayden Connell Architects (2000: 32–40); Eppich and Chabbi (2007: 105–8); Burns (2004: 109–15); Bryan (2010: 25–9).

13   The use of large-format cameras with shifting (perspective-correcting) lenses and rigid glass plates in the second half of the nineteenth century produced rectified photographs that allowed reasonable accuracy in scaling.

14   The bibliography is large; for an overview, see Yeomans (1996: 214–38). For the problem of engineers' inexperience, see Ochsendorf 2013: 6 and other articles in that issue of the *APT Bulletin* (44:1, 2013), which is devoted to preservation-engineering education.

15   Other useful sources, also American, are Page et al. (1998) and Stokes et al. (1997).

16   See, for example, Swanwick (2002). The method was developed well in the classic study of townscapes (Cullen c. 1961).

17   This book uses the words 'survey' and 'inventory' interchangeably, although preferring to describe the process as a 'survey' and the product as an 'inventory.' Some sources describe a 'survey' as being a more superficial overview and an 'inventory' as being more comprehensive. Most formally created lists have been named one of the two (others are called a 'register' or simply a 'list'), and those names are respected as part of their formal titles. Much of the following discussion is from a comprehensive study made some years ago (Sykes 1984: 21–31, 136–9). The phrase 'organized recording of information' (above) is from p. 13. See also Letellier 2007: appendix G. For information management systems, see Letellier (2007: 45–56 and appendix F).

18   Surveys and inventories are also used in research for a heritage impact assessment (HIA); see Section 5.6.

19   The *Washington Charter* of 1987, which addressed the conservation of historic towns and urban areas, also advocated community engagement: 'The participation and the involvement of the residents are essential for the success of the conservation programme and should be encouraged' (Article 3).

20   'Memorandum on Government-to-Government Relations with Native American Tribal Governments' (1994), clause (b).

21   Americans Marta de la Torre and Randall Mason define 'value' as 'a set of positive characteristics perceived in cultural objects or sites by certain individuals or groups,' and 'cultural significance' as 'the importance of a site as determined by the aggregate of values attributed to it' (de la Torre and Mason 2002: 3–4). Elsewhere, Mason defines significance as 'the synthetic statement of a site's value and the

reason why it should be preserved' (Mason 2006: 32–3). Mason's theories of value will be introduced later in this chapter. English Heritage defines significance as 'a collective term for the sum of all the heritage values attached to a place'; see the online discussion of *Conservation Principles* at <http://www.english-heritage.org.uk/professional/advice/conservation-principles/ConservationPrinciples/>

22   An explanatory note states that, in the Charter, 'the term cultural significance is synonymous with heritage significance and cultural heritage value,' not differentiating between 'significance' and 'value'—as does the present book.

23   It was seen in Section 2.2 that 'use value' may be equated with economic value.

24   The difference between values and criteria in today's usage will be discussed in Section 4.5.

25   Miner calls them 'considerations' and 'criteria.' These and other lists of 'criteria' current at the time can be found in Kalman (1976: 3–27; appendix B).

26   Strictly speaking, 'historical' means having a history and 'historic' means having an extraordinary history.

27   A management plan has determined that the climb will be phased out over time (Australian Government, Director of National Parks and Uluṟu–Kata Tjuṯa Board of Management 2010: 92).

28   The definition of 'integrity' poses a challenge with respect to cultural landscapes. American landscape architect Catherine Howett (2000: 207) suggests that their quality and importance 'are determined not by the integrity of the site, but by the quality of what is made of the site through interpretation of its history.'

29   As recently as 1996 the US Heritage Preservation Service insisted that 'certain decisions [concerning the protection and preservation of historic places] must be made by individuals who meet nationally accepted professional standards,' overlooking stakeholders as part of the process (Pannekoek 1998: 29).

30   The *Bulletin of the Association for Preservation Technology* has devoted an entire issue to values-based preservation (vol. 45, no. 2–3, not yet published).

31   Mason cites the values identified by Riegl. A similar dichotomy was adopted in a recent community engagement exercise in the UK, which differentiated between intrinsic values ('what is important about heritage, why and to whom?') and instrumental values ('the economic, social and environmental benefits of policy and funding') (Mattinson 2006).

32   John Logan and Harvey Molotch further divide these into 'use value' (e.g., an apartment building provides a 'home' for residents) and 'exchange value' (e.g., the rent generated for the owners) (Logan and Molotch 1987: 1–2, cited in Kaufman 2009: 27).

33   'Understanding heritage values' is treated in detail in paras. 30–60, pp. 27–32. Economic value is not included.

34   *EPBC Act 1999* (as amended to 2011), s. 15B; *Heritage Management Principles*, Principle 1. The *Australian Heritage Commission Act 1975*, which was the first statute to protect heritage at the Commonwealth level, addressed 'place,' which it defined as 'a site, area or region; a building or other structure ... and a group of buildings or other structures' (s. 3 (1)). 'Value' is not discussed in the earlier act.

35   The Canadian SOS comprises three fields in a larger database of more than 30 fields, which provide data on location, formal recognition, theme, function, designer and builder, and additional information. Certain historical facts (e.g., location and date) are often found only in the other fields. The three SOS fields are each limited to 4,000 characters.

36   The singular is 'criterion' and the plural is 'criteria,' reflecting the derivation of the word from the Greek 'kriterion'—a means of judging. Many people incorrectly use 'criteria' as a singular noun.

37   Adapted by the author from Russell and Winkworth (2009: 39). That study addresses significance for museum objects and collections, but is largely applicable to historic places as well.

38   This begs some challenging questions: Are 'representative' and 'typical' the same as 'ordinary'? (Logically, 'not extraordinary' should mean 'ordinary.') Is 'ordinary' the same as 'vernacular,' 'common,' and

'everyday'? And if we value the ordinary—we do value the vernacular—what do we not value? American landscape specialist Arnold Alanen ponders 'considering the ordinary' in vernacular landscapes and concludes that 'once a landscape is protected, it no longer is "ordinary"' (2000: 140).

39   The Australian states have their own systems for determining significance. See also Kerr (2013: 70).

40   A National Register criterion; note here that two thresholds must be reached: the place must be associated 'importantly' with a person, and the person must be 'nationally' significant.

41   One other combination would reach 20: one A plus five Cs, and perhaps that should also be admitted over the threshold; alternatively it could be argued that a grade of C ('good') is insufficient to meet any threshold, in which case perhaps C should be worth only 1 or 0.

42   Throsby made this suggestion earlier in Throsby (2001: 86). The concept of cultural value within the context of cultural capital was introduced in Section 2.2.

5. Managing Change

1   'Regeneration' is often called 'revitalization' in the Americas.

2   'Strategic' is, to some minds, a redundant modifier, since all planning should be strategically grounded. The definitions in this section are by no means universal. Sometimes 'goals' and 'objectives' are reversed; in other cases 'goals' and 'objectives' are expressed as 'objectives' and 'strategies'; see, for example, LeClair (2001: 26–7). Many other permutations are found in the literature. The reader should adopt the terminology in general use in her/his jurisdiction.

3   The author is indebted to architect Donald Leung King Hong for articulating the idea of good, better, and best practice. He and his fellow students at the University of Hong Kong pointed out that 'compromise' has a negative connotation in Chinese, whereas in English it is neutral. Preferred words with Chinese-speakers were 'negotiation' and 'mediation.' Compromise conservation treatments—dismissed by some authorities as not being conservation at all—were discussed in Section 3.2.

4   These and additional steps are presented as 'The Recycling Game: An ABC Checklist' in Kalman et al. (1980: 210–15). The book provides case studies of many Canadian adaptations to that date, including some that probably should never have proceeded. An example is Presentation House in North Vancouver, BC, previously a school and then a city hall. It was repurposed to accommodate an arts centre with a studio theatre, community museum, and photography gallery—all of them inadequately. Re-accommodating the occupant organizations remains a community issue nearly 40 years later.

5   This is the title of Cantacuzino (1975), and the expression has been widely used.

6   Redundant churches—particularly Anglican ones—have been a particular issue in the UK, where they are now called 'closed' churches. The *Redundant Churches and other Religious Buildings Act, 1969*, set out a three-stage process for reaching a 'redundancy scheme,' which might recommend demolition, reuse, or retention as an underused building, in which case financial support would be provided by both the Church of England and the government.

7   Or vice versa: the choice of conservation treatment may also inform the choice of use.

8   Most of these factors are named in Parks Canada (2013: 3.4.1.4).

9   The four approaches are described in Buggey and Mitchell (2008); Hohmann (2008); Mason (2008); Rottle (2008). Further methods for managing cultural landscapes and biodiversity protection, many set within an Asia-Pacific context and most focusing on the culture–nature relationship, are found in the contributions to Taylor and Lennon (2012). A pioneering anthology is Alanen and Melnick (2000).

10   With the encouragement of UNESCO, other nations are also moving towards removing financial disincentives, on the premise that the 'uncompetitive' position of heritage is more artificial than intrinsic, and can be addressed with corrective measures.

11   The significance to heritage planning of the Fifth Amendment is discussed in Section 2.1.

12   For a good anthology describing tools and incentives see Schuster et al. (1997). Some of the information that follows is contained in British Columbia Ministry of Small Business, Tourism and Culture (1995), although the book is restricted to the wide range of tools and incentives enabled in that Canadian province.

13   Québec, *Cultural Property Act (Loi des biens culturels)*, R.S.Q., chapter B-4, Sections 47, 89. The Québec legislation calls a building a 'monument.' It derives from the statutes that protect objects of cultural merit. The concept of a protected perimeter derives from a French law of 1943, which enabled the state to protect a perimeter of 500 meters (547 yards) or further. See Rodwell (2007: 42).

14   A '"listed building" means a building … and … any object or structure within the curtilage of the building which, although not fixed to the building, forms part of the land and has done so since before 1st July 1948' *Planning (Listed Buildings and Conservation Areas) Act 1990*, Section 1 (5).

15   Various international perspectives are available in McManamon and Hatton (2000) and Messenger and Smith (2010).

16   An easement is similar to a right of way; the two differ only in technical details.

17   By contrast, Netzer notes that the US Tax Court has found that giving away a façade easement reduces the market value of a property by 11 percent.

18   The provisions are contained in the *Halifax Peninsula Land Use Bylaw*. The regulation has been challenged and modified from time to time, but remains in force after four decades.

19   Construction costs and property values were discussed in Section 2.2.

20   *Historical Resources Act*, R.S.A. 2000, chap. H-9, 28(1).

21   *Local Government Act*, R.S.B.C. 1996, chap. 323, Part 27, 969(1). This is an improvement over earlier legislation, which left the amount of compensation open-ended.

22   The UK's generosity with grants partially compensates for its reluctance to provide tax incentives for conservation.

23   Rising construction and property-acquisition costs over the years have made the incentives less effective than formerly. Recommendations for increasing the incentives were proposed in Coriolis Consulting Corp. et al. (2007).

24   The Historic Savannah Foundation claims to have saved only about 350 buildings; the figure of 800 buildings by 1975, saved at a cost of more than $40 million, is from Ziegler et al. (1975: 72). Since 1979 the work of the Foundation has been complemented by that of the Savannah College of Art and Design (SCAD), which has acquired and rehabilitated—and uses—around 70 historic buildings; see Pinkerton and Burke (2004). Some buildings had been rehabilitated a generation or two earlier but once again fell into disrepair, a poignant reminder of the need to incorporate ongoing maintenance into conservation planning and agreements.

25   For a summary overview, see Pickard and Pickerill (2007); Pickard (2009).

26   The largest tax credit available in the US in 2012 was 20 percent; in 1976 it was 25 percent. Smaller tax credits are available for 'non-certified' historic buildings. Some states supplement this amount with their own tax credit programs (White and Roddewig 1994: 16).

27   Many of the incentives are described in Hlavach 2004: 141–9.

28   The legality of density transfer in the US was upheld by the Supreme Court (1978) in *Penn Central Transportation Co. v. City of New York (Grand Central Terminal)*; see Section 2.1 for a discussion of this 'landmark' case. See also Roddewig and Ingram (1987).

29   Not until 1975 did the City have the power to protect property. The idea of applying a density transfer to resolve the threat to Christ Church Cathedral was first suggested by the present author. See Purden (1973: 9–14); Kalman and Ward (2012: 156–7). In 2002 Christ Church Cathedral received additional density (created *ex nihilo*) to be transferred off-site as an incentive to agree to the designation of the historic interior. Vancouver has used density transfers many times and has adopted extensive program guidelines; they are described at City of Vancouver (n.d.).

30   The discussion draws on numerous sources, principally Stovel 1998; Riddett 2002; Smith 2002; and Federal Emergency Management Agency (US) (2005).

31   This might be accompanied by graphic material, such as a map of risks that illustrates likely areas of impact for specific hazards.

32   In Hong Kong, for example, the *Environmental Impact Assessment Ordinance* (1997) requires an Environmental Impact Assessment (EIA) for a wide range of projects, and a Cultural Heritage Impact Assessment (CHIA) is required as part of all EIAs. Separately from this, certain proposed capital works projects undertaken by government require a Heritage Impact Assessment (HIA), pursuant to the Development Bureau's Technical Circular (Works) No. 6/2009. Separate guidelines are in place for the two kinds of assessments.

33   At least three Australian states have issued similar guidelines for heritage impact statements: see Department of Planning, New South Wales (1991); Heritage Council of Victoria (Australia) (2004); and Heritage Council of Western Australia (n.d.). The SOHI (HIA) is a requirement in some places and is only recommended in others.

34   Development Bureau Technical Circular (Works) No. 6/2009, 'Heritage Impact Assessment Mechanism for Capital Works Projects.' The prescribed process comprises a baseline study, impact assessment, mitigation measures, and conservation proposals, similar to the method described above.

35   The Gantt chart was developed by American management consultant Henry L. Gantt in the early twentieth century.

36   Kerr adopted this definition in 1982, in the first edition of his book. In his (and the *Burra Charter*'s) usage, common in Australia, 'policy' means much the same as 'strategy' or 'recommendation.'

37   The 'macro' conservation plan is the community conservation plan introduced in Section 2.1. As mentioned there, the most effective conservation plans are integrated within the larger comprehensive community plan. The 'macro' conservation plan corresponds somewhat in scale to a 'macro' HIA, and the 'micro' conservation plan to a 'micro' HIA (see Section 5.6). 'Macro' and 'micro' are placed within quotation marks because the use of these terms to describe conservation plans (and heritage impact assessments) is restricted to the present text.

38   The list of topics has been drawn from numerous sources, among them Kerr's method, the 'Burra Charter Process' (Australia ICOMOS 2013b: 10), to which Kerr contributed, and the methods used by the author in conservation planning assignments over the years. Kerr uses the term 'conservation policy' rather than 'managing change'; we prefer the latter because 'policy' in Kerr's context may be confused with official government policy (especially in North America), rather than as a proponent's strategic recommendations. See also Clark (1998), who cites the 'Sheffield template' for a model conservation plan, developed at a seminar in Sheffield convened by English Heritage in 1997. The reader is reminded of Clark's words, cited at the beginning of this section: 'Conservation Plans incorporate a logical development progressing from the understanding of the history and fabric of the site, into an explicit assessment of the significance, and from there, directly into the formulation of policies for retaining that significance. That is all.'

39   Biallas attributes the innovation to legendary American preservation specialist Charles E. Peterson.

40   For a description of a model HSR prepared for the Canadian government, see Drolet et al. (1997).

41   The adjectives 'financial' and 'economic' are often confused. 'Financial' analysis examines the finances—the revenues and expenditures—of a particular entity or group of entities. 'Economic' analysis looks at the larger economy of the city, region, or nation, and is in part an aggregation of the effects of individual financial situations.

42   Noted by Sean Fraser, Director, Heritage Programs and Operations, Ontario Heritage Trust (2013).

43   The risk-preparedness plan (Section 5.5) will have mitigated some of these threats.

44   See, for example, National Trust of Australia WA (2011). North Americans will recall Honda's television commercial for automobile maintenance, in which a mechanic says, with a devilish grin, 'see me now … or see me later!'

References

Aboriginal Affairs and Northern Development Canada (1998) 'The Tr'ondëk Hwëch'in Final Agreement,' (amended 2009) <http://www.aadnc-aandc.gc.ca/eng/1297209099174/1297209186151>.

Abraham, Carolyn (2012), 'Unnatural selection,' *The Globe and Mail*, January 7, F1, F5–7.

Advisory Council on Historic Preservation (US) (2010), *Protecting Historic Properties: A Citizen's Guide to Section 106 Review* (2nd edn.; Washington: Advisory Council on Historic Preservation).

Alanen, Arnold R. (2000), 'Considering the Ordinary: Vernacular Landscapes in Small Towns and Rural Areas,' in Arnold R. Alanen and Robert Z. Melnick (eds.), *Preserving Cultural Landscapes in America* (Baltimore: Johns Hopkins University Press), 112–42.

Alanen, Arnold R. and Melnick, Robert Z. (eds.) (2000), *Preserving Cultural Landscapes in America* (Baltimore: Johns Hopkins University Press).

Allen Consulting Group (2005), 'Valuing the Priceless: The Value of Historic Heritage in Australia,' *Research Report 2* (Sydney: Allen Consulting Group).

Allom Lovell & Associates and Urban Consulting Group (1995), *Economic Effects of Heritage Listing* (North Melbourne: Urban Consulting Group in conjunction with Allom Lovell & Associates).

Anonymous (2007), 'Public History Redux,' *Public History News*, September.

Aplin, Graeme (2002), *Heritage: Identification, Conservation, and Management* (Melbourne: Oxford University Press).

Appleyard, Donald (ed.), (1979), *The Conservation of European Cities* (Cambridge, MA: MIT Press).

Arbogast, David (2010), *How to Write a Historic Structure Report* (New York: W.W. Norton).

Armitage, Lynne (2005), 'Managing Cultural Heritage: Heritage Listing and Property Value,' *European Real Estate Society Conference* (Dublin).

Arrow, Kenneth, Solow, Robert, Portney, Paul R., Leamer, Edward E., Radner, Roy, and Schuman, Howard (1993), 'Report of the NOAA Panel on Contingent Valuation,' *Federal Register*, 58 (10), 4602–14.

Asabere, Paul K. and Huffman, Forrest (1994), 'Historic designation and residential market values,' *Appraisal Journal*, 62, 396–401.

Australia ICOMOS (2000), *The Burra Charter: The Australia ICOMOS Charter for Places of Cultural Significance* (1999 edn.: Australia ICOMOS) (first published 1979; latest revision 2013).

—— (2013a), 'The Burra Charter and Indigenous Cultural Heritage Management,' *Practice Notes* (Australia ICOMOS).

—— (2013b), *The Burra Charter: The Australia ICOMOS Charter for Places of Cultural Significance* (2013 edn.: Australia ICOMOS).

—— (2013c), 'Burra Charter Article 22—New Work' (updated November 2013) <http://australia.icomos.org/wp-content/uploads/Practice-Note_Burra-Charter-Article-22-New-Work.pdf>.

Australian Government (1994), 'Cultural Tourism,' *Creative Nation: Commonwealth Cultural Policy* <http://pandora.nla.gov.au/pan/21336/20031011-0000/www.nla.gov.au/creative.nation/contents.html>.

Australian Government, Department of the Environment (2007), 'The Economics of Heritage,' <http://www.environment.gov.au/heritage/publications/strategy/economics-workshop.html>.

—— (n.d.), 'National Heritage List Criteria,' <http://www.environment.gov.au/topics/heritage/about-australias-heritage/national-heritage/national-heritage-list-criteria>.

Australian Government, Director of National Parks and Uluṟu–Kata Tjuṯa Board of Management (2010), *Uluṟu–Kata Tjuṯa National Park: Management Plan 2010–2020* (Canberra: Director of National Parks).

Australian Government Productivity Commission (2006), 'Conservation of Historic Heritage Places' (Melbourne: Australian Government Productivity Commission).

Australian Heritage Commission (2002), *Australian Natural Heritage Charter for the Conservation of Places of Natural Heritage Significance* (2nd edn.; Canberra: Australian Heritage Commission).

Australian Policy Online (1994), 'Creative Nation: Commonwealth Cultural Policy, October 1994,' <http://apo.org.au/research/creative-nation-commonwealth-cultural-policy-october-1994>.

Baker, Paul (2011), 'U-values and traditional buildings: In situ measurements and their comparisons to calculated values,' *Historic Scotland Technical Paper 10* (Edinburgh: Historic Scotland).

Baker, Paul, Curtis, Roger, Kennedy, Craig, and Wood, Chris (2010), 'Thermal performance of traditional windows and low-cost energy-saving retrofits', *Bulletin of the Association for Preservation Technology*, 41 (1), 29–36.

Bandarin, Francesco (1979), 'The Bologna Experience: Planning and Historic Renovation in a Communist City,' in Donald Appleyard (ed.), *The Conservation of European Cities* (Cambridge, MA: MIT Press), 178–202.

Bandarin, Francesco and Van Oers, Ron (2012), *The Historic Urban Landscape: Managing Heritage in an Urban Century* (Chichester: Wiley-Blackwell).

Barrett, Scott and Dutil, Patrice (2012), 'Social learning, feedback loops, and public spheres: Implementing a values-based management model in heritage conservation,' *Architecture in Canada*, 37 (1), 17–26.

Beeby, Dean (2014), 'More than half of Parks Canada assets in 'poor' shape,' *The Globe and Mail*, February 12.

Bennett, Jeff (2007), 'Cost Benefit Analysis and the Value of Heritage,' *The Economics of Heritage* (Canberra: Australian National University).

Berger, Thomas R. (1977), 'Mackenzie Valley Pipeline Inquiry: Synopsis of Volume Two' (Ottawa).

Biallas, Randall J. (1990), 'The evolution of historic structure reports,' *Cultural Resource Management Bulletin*, 13 (4).

Bigham, D. Alastair (1973), *The Law and Administration Relating to Protection of the Environment* (London: Oyez).

Birnbaum, Charles A. and Peters, Christine Capelle (eds.) (1996), *The Secretary of the Interior's Standards for the Treatment of Historic Properties with Guidelines for the Treatment of Cultural Landscapes* (Washington: US Department of the Interior, National Park Service).

Blackman, Christabel (2011), 'Cleaning the Dirt off Money in Conservation: Ethics and Economics,' *e-conservation magazine*, (20), 7–11. <http://www.e-conservationline.com/content/view/1005>.

Boer, Ben and Wiffen, Graeme (2006), *Heritage Law in Australia* (Melbourne: Oxford University Press).

Boito, Camillo (1883), *Resolutions of the III Congress of Engineers and Architects* (Rome).

Booth, Philip (1996), *Controlling Development: Certainty and Discretion in Europe, the USA and Hong Kong* (London and Bristol, PA: UCL Press).

Box, Paul (1999), *GIS and Cultural Resource Management: A Manual for Heritage Managers* (Bangkok: UNESCO).

Brenneman, Russell L. (1971), 'Techniques for controlling the surroundings of historic sites,' *Law and Contemporary Problems*, 36 (3), 416–22.

Bristol, Katharine G. (2004), 'The Pruitt-Igoe Myth,' in Keith Eggener (ed.), *American Architectural History: A Contemporary Reader* (New York: Routledge), 352–64.

British Columbia Ministry of Small Business, Tourism and Culture (1995), *Heritage Conservation: A Community Guide* (Victoria: Province of British Columbia, Ministry of Small Business, Tourism and Culture).

Brochu, Lisa and Merriman, Tim (2002), *Personal Interpretation: Connecting Your Audience to Heritage Resources* (Fort Collins, CO: National Association for Interpretation).

Bryan, Paul (2010), 'Metric survey for preservation uses: Past, present, and future,' *Bulletin of the Association for Preservation Technology*, 41 (4), 25–9.

Buggey, Susan and Mitchell, Nora (2008), 'Cultural Landscapes: Venues for Community-based Conservation,' in Richard Longstreth (ed.), *Cultural Landscapes: Balancing Nature and Heritage in Preservation Practice* (Minneapolis: University of Minnesota Press), 164–79.

Burns, John A. (ed.), (2004), *Recording Historic Structures* (2nd edn., Hoboken, NJ: John Wiley).

Byrne, Denis (2008), 'Heritage as Social Action,' in G. Fairclough, R. Harrison, J. H. Jameson Jnr., and J. Schofield (eds.), *The Heritage Reader* (London: Routledge), 149–73.

Byrne, Denis, Brayshaw, Helen, and Ireland, Tracy (2003), *Social Significance: A Discussion Paper* (2nd edn.; Hurstville: New South Wales National Parks and Wildlife Service).

Cameron, Christina (1993), 'Cultural tourism: Gold mine or land mine?,' *CRM: The Journal of Heritage Stewardship*, 17 (3), 28–31.

—— (2009), 'The Evolution of the Concept of Outstanding Universal Value,' in Nicholas Stanley-Price and Joseph King (eds.), *Conserving the Authentic: Essays in Honour of Jukka Jokilehto* (Rome: ICCROM), 127–42.

Cameron, Christina and Boucher, Christine (eds.) (2007), *Tangible and Intangible Heritage: Two UNESCO Conventions*

(Round Table organized by the Canada Research Chair on Built Heritage, Faculty of Environmental Design, University of Montreal, Montreal: University of Montreal).

Cameron, Christina and Rössler, Mechtild (2013), *Many Voices, One Vision: The Early Years of the World Heritage Convention* (Burlington, VT: Ashgate).

Canadian Association of Heritage Professionals (n.d.), 'Code of Professional Conduct and Ethics' (Ottawa: CAHP).

Canadian Register of Historic Places (2011) *Writing Statements of Significance* [online text], Parks Canada http://www.historicplaces.ca/media/21054/sos_guide_final_e_new_design.pdf.

Cane, Simon (2009), 'Why Do We Conserve? Developing Understanding of Conservation as a Cultural Construct,' in Alison Richmond and Alison Bracker (eds.), *Conservation: Principles, Dilemmas and Uncomfortable Truths* (Oxford: Butterworth-Heinemann), 163–76.

Cantacuzino, Sherban (1975), *New Uses for Old Buildings* (London: Architectural Press).

Carman, John and Sorensen, Marie Louise Stig (2009), 'Heritage Studies: An Outline,' in Marie Louise Stig Sorensen and John Carman (eds.), *Heritage Studies: Methods and Approaches* (London: Routledge), 11–28.

Carroon, Jean (2010), *Sustainable Preservation: Greening Existing Buildings* (Hoboken, NJ: John Wiley).

Carter, Margaret (1983), *Researching Historic Buildings* (1987 reprint edn.; Ottawa: Environment Canada, Parks Service).

Catling, Christopher (2013), *Constructive Conservation: Sustainable Growth for Historic Places* (London: English Heritage).

Cave, Claire (2013), 'World Heritage: Cooperation, communication and capacity building,' *World Heritage*, (67), 4–13.

Chalana, Manish and Wiser, Jeana C. (2013), 'Integrating preservation and hazard mitigation for unreinforced masonry buildings in Seattle,' *Bulletin of the Association for Preservation Technology*, 44 (2–3), 43–51.

Chambers, J. Henry (1976), *Cyclical Maintenance for Historic Buildings* (Washington: National Park Service, US Department of the Interior).

Chapman, Bruce K. (1976), 'The Growing Public Stake in Urban Conservation,' in Joyce E. Latham (ed.), *Economic Benefits of Preserving Old Buildings* (Washington: National Trust for Historic Preservation), 9–13.

Checkoway, Barry (1994), 'Paul Davidoff and advocacy planning in retrospect,' *Journal of the American Planning Association*, 60 (2), 139–43.

China ICOMOS (2002), *Principles for the Conservation of Heritage Sites in China* (Los Angeles: Getty Conservation Institute).

Chung, Seung-Jin (2005), 'East Asian Values in Historic Conservation,' *Journal of Architectural Conservation*, 11 (1), 55–70.

Chusid, Jeffrey M. (2010), 'Teaching sustainability to preservation students,' *Bulletin of the Association for Preservation Technology*, 41 (1), 43–9.

City of Markham (2012) 'The Markham Heritage Estates Subdivision,' <http://www.markham.ca/wps/portal/Markham/AboutMarkham/Heritage/HeritageSectionStaff/markhamheritageestatessubdivision/>.

City of Vancouver (n.d.), 'Incentives for developers: transferable heritage density bonuses,' <http://vancouver.ca/home-property-development/density-incentives-for-developers.aspx>.

City of Victoria (2013), 'Tax Incentive Program Fact Sheet' (Victoria: City of Victoria).

Civic Trust (dir.), (c. 1960), *The Story of Magdalen Street*.

—— (1972), *Forming a Buildings Preservation Trust* (London: Civic Trust).

Clark, Kate (1998), 'Conservation plans: A guide for the perplexed,' *Context*, (57).

—— (2000), 'Conservation Plans ... a Benefit or a Burden?,' <www.buildingconservation.com>.

—— (2001), *Informed Conservation: Understanding Historic Buildings and their Landscapes for Conservation* (London: English Heritage).

—— (ed.), (2006), *Capturing the Public Value of Heritage: The Proceedings of the London Conference, 25–26 January 2006* (London: English Heritage).

—— (2010), 'Informed conservation: The place of research and documentation in preservation,' *APT Bulletin*, 41 (4), 5–10.

Coles, Susan (Team Leader) (2010), 'Building Codes and Historic Places: Making Connections – Summary Report 2009–2010' (Ottawa: Public Works and Government Services Canada, Heritage Conservation Directorate).

Commonwealth Historic Resource Management Limited (2006), 'A Heritage Strategic Plan for the District of West Vancouver' (Vancouver).

—— (2008), 'Kinsol Trestle Restoration Feasibility Study. Phase 1: Final Report,' (Vancouver).

Commonwealth Historic Resource Management Ltd. and Fowler Bauld & Mitchell Ltd. (1994), 'Saint George's Church National Historic Site, Halifax, Nova Scotia: Conservation Report' (Halifax).

Commonwealth of Australia (1999), 'Environment Protection and Biodiversity Conservation Act 1999' (Commonwealth of Australia).

Coriolis Consulting Corp., Busby Perkins + Will, and TBKG (2007), 'Downtown Victoria Heritage Building Economic Study' (Draft edn.; Victoria, BC: City of Victoria).

Costonis, John J. (1972), 'The Chicago Plan: Incentive zoning and the preservation of urban landmarks,' *Harvard Law Review*, 85 (3), 574–634.

—— (1974), *Space Adrift: Landmark Preservation and the Marketplace* (Urbana: University of Illinois Press).

—— (1977), 'The disparity issue: A context for the Grand Central Terminal decision,' *Harvard Law Review*, 91 (2), 402–26.

—— (1997), 'The Redefinition of Property Rights as a Tool for Historic Preservation,' in J. Mark Schuster, John de Monchaux, and Charles A. Riley, II (eds.), *Preserving the Built Heritage: Tools for Implementation* (Salzburg Seminar; Hanover, NH: University Press of New England), 81–99.

Coterill, David (2007), 'Value of Heritage to the City of Ballarat: Case Study,' *The Economics of Heritage* (Canberra: Australian National University).

Cotter, Holland (2012), 'A tribute to Islam, earthen but transcendent,' *The New York Times*, April 18.

Council of Europe (1975), 'European Charter of the Architectural Heritage,' <http://www.icomos.org/en/charters-and-texts/179-articles-en-francais/ressources/charters-and-standards/170-european-charter-of-the-architectural-heritage>.

—— (1985), 'Convention for the Protection of the Architectural Heritage of Europe' (Granada Convention), <http://conventions.coe.int/treaty/en/treaties/html/121.htm>.

—— (1992), 'European Convention on the Protection of the Archaeological Heritage (Revised)' (Valetta Convention), <http://conventions.coe.int/Treaty/en/Treaties/html/143.htm>.

—— (2000), 'European Landscape Convention' (Florence Convention) (Strasbourg: Council of Europe).

Cox, Jo (1996), 'Assessment and Recording: A Practioner's View,' in Stephen Marks (ed.), *Concerning Buildings: Studies in Honour of Sir Bernard Feilden* (Oxford: Butterworth-Heinemann), 119–57.

Crissman, Richard (1976), 'Giving Lenders What They Need,' in Joyce E. Latham (ed.), *Economic Benefits of Preserving Old Buildings* (Washington: National Trust for Historic Preservation), 126–9.

Cryderman, Kelly (2013), 'Scenic swath of Alberta to be preserved,' *Globe and Mail*, September 12, p. A4.

Cullen, Gordon (c. 1961), *Townscape* (London: Architectural Press).

Cullingworth, Barry and Nadin, Vincent (2002), *Town and Country Planning in the UK* (13th edn.; London: Routledge).

Cullingworth, Barry and Caves, Roger W. (2009), *Planning in the USA: Policies, Issues, and Processes* (3rd edn.; Abingdon: Routledge).

Curtis, Roger (2012), 'Energy efficiency in traditional buildings: Initiatives by Historic Scotland,' *Bulletin of the Association for Preservation Technology*, 43 (2–3), 13–20.

Davidoff, Paul (1965), 'Advocacy and pluralism in planning,' *Journal of the American Institute of Planners*, 31 (4), 331–8.

Davidson-Hunt, Iain (2012), *Pimachiowin Aki Cultural Landscape Atlas: Land That Gives Life* (Winnipeg: Pimachiowin Aki Corporation).

Davidson-Hunt, Iain, Peters, Paddy, and Burlando, Catie (2010), 'Beekahncheekahmeeng Ahneesheenahbay Ohtahkeem (Pikangikum Cultural Landscape): Challenging the Traditional Concept of Cultural Landscape from an Aboriginal Perspective,' in Kristen Walker Painemilla, Alisa Woofter, and Cassie Hughes (eds.), *Indigenous Peoples and Conservation: From Rights to Resource Management* (Arlington, VA: Conservation International), 137–44.

Davis, Howard (2012), *Living Over the Store: Architecture and Local Urban Life* (London: Routledge).

Davison, Graeme and McConville, Chris (1991), *A Heritage Handbook* (Melbourne: Allen and Unwin).

de la Torre, Marta and Mason, Randall (2002), 'Introduction,' in Marta de la Torre (ed.), *Assessing the Values of Cultural Heritage* (Los Angeles: Getty Conservation Institute), 3–4.

Deacon, Jeanette (2010), 'Heritage Resource Management in South Africa,' in Phyllis Mauch Messenger and George S. Smith (eds.), *Cultural Heritage Management: A Global Perspective* (Gainesville: University Press of Florida), 162–75.

Delafons, John (1997), *Politics and Preservation: A Policy History of the Built Heritage 1882–1996* (London: E & FN Spon).

Denhez, Marc (1978a), *Protecting the Built Environment (Part I)* (2nd edn.; Ottawa: Heritage Canada).

—— (1978b), *Heritage Fights Back* (Toronto: Fitzhenry & Whiteside).

—— (1994), *The Canadian Home: From Cave to Electronic Cocoon* (Toronto: Dundurn Press).

—— (1997), *The Heritage Strategy Planning Handbook: An International Primer* (Toronto: Dundurn Press).

Department for Communities and Local Government (UK) (ed.) (2010), *Planning Policy Statement 5: Planning for the Historic Environment* (London: Her Majesty's Stationery Office).

—— (2012), *National Planning Policy Framework* (London: Department for Communities and Local Government).

Department of Planning, New South Wales (1991), *Statements of Heritage Impact* (Sydney: Department of Planning, New South Wales).

Derda, Colleen C. and Moriarity, Lyn (2006), *Preservation Revolving Funds* (Washington: National Trust for Historic Preservation).

Dingle, Peter (2009), *Is Your Home Making you Sick? Chemicals, Contaminants and Toxins in Your Home and What You Can Do to Avoid Them* (Melbourne: P. Dingle).

Dobrowolsky, Helene (2003), *Hammerstones: A History of the Tr'ondëk Hwëch'in* (Dawson City: Tr'ondëk Hwëch'in).

Dower, Michael (1974), 'Tourism and conservation: Working together,' *Architects' Journal*, 166, 941–63.

Drolet, Georges, Gersovitz, Julia, and Fortin, Lyette (1997), 'The West Block of Parliament, Ottawa: An HSR case study,' *Bulletin of the Association for Preservation Technology*, 28 (1), 5–12.

Edelstein, Ludwig (1943), 'The Hippocratic Oath: Text, translation and interpretation,' *Bulletin of the History of Medicine* (Supplement).

EDO NSW (Australian Network of Environmental Defenders Offices, New South Wales) (n.d.), 'Commonwealth Environmental Laws (Fact Sheet 3),' <http://www.edo.org.au/edonsw/site/factsheets.php >.

Engelhardt, Richard (2011), 'Draft Consensus Statement, Mini-conference on Cultural Heritage Impact Assessment' (Hong Kong: University of Hong Kong, Architectural Conservation Programme).

Engelhardt, Richard A. and Rogers, Pamela Rumball (2009), *Hoi An Protocols for Best Conservation Practice in Asia* (Bangkok: UNESCO Bangkok).

English Heritage (1998), *Conservation-led Regeneration: The Work of English Heritage* (London: English Heritage).

—— (2000), *Power of Place: The Future of the Historic Environment* (London: Power of Place Office).

—— (2008a), 'Climate Change & Your Home,' <http://www.climatechangeandyourhome.org.uk/live/>.

—— (2008b), *Conservation Principles, Policies and Guidance for the Sustainable Management of the Historic Environment* (London: English Heritage).

—— (2010), *Understanding Place: Historic Area Assessments: Principles and Practice* (Swindon: Engish Heritage).

—— (n.d.-a), 'Equality and Diversity,' <http://www.english-heritage.org.uk/professional/advice/advice-by-topic/equality-and-diversity/>.

—— (n.d.-b), 'Grants Given,' <http://www.english-heritage.org.uk/professional/funding/grants/grants-given/>.

—— (n.d.-c), 'The National Heritage List for England,' <http://www.english-heritage.org.uk/professional/protection/process/national-heritage-list-for-england/>.

Enright, Robert (ed.), (2010), *Body Heat: The Story of the Woodward's Redevelopment* (Vancouver: Blueimprint).

Eppich, Rand and Chabbi, Amel (eds.), (2007), *Recording, Documentation, and Information Management for the Conservation of Historic Places: Illustrated Examples* (Los Angeles: Getty Conservation Institute).

Erder, Cevat (1986), *Our Architectural Heritage: From Consciousness to Conservation*, trans. Ayfer Bakkakioglu (Museums and Monuments; Paris: UNESO).

Evans, Damian (2013), '2012 LiDAR survey over Angkor, Phnom Kulen and Koh Ker,' *World Heritage*, (68), 60–3.

Evans, M. (2000), *Principles of Environmental and Heritage Law* (Sydney: Prospect Media).

Federal Emergency Management Agency (US) (2005), *Integrating Historic Property and Cultural Resource Considerations into Hazard Mitigation Planning* (State and Local Mitigation Planning How-To Guide; Washington: Federal Emergency Management Agency (FEMA)).

Feilden, Bernard M. (1982), *Conservation of Historic Buildings*, ed. Gillian Lewis and Derek Linstrum (Technical Studies in the Arts, Archaeology and Architecture; London: Butterworth Scientific).

FindLaw 'Penn Central Transp. Co. v. New York City, 438 US 104 (1978),' <http://caselaw.lp.findlaw.com/scripts/getcase.pl?navby=CASE&court=US&vol=438&page=104>.

Finke, Gunnar (2013), 'Cultural landscapes and protected areas: Unfolding the linkages and synergies,' *World Heritage*, (70), 16–25.

Finley, David E. (1963), *History of the National Trust for Historic Preservation 1947–1963* (Washington: National Trust for Historic Preservation).

First International Congress of Architects and Technicians of Historic Monuments (1931), 'The Athens Charter for the Restoration of Historic Monuments' (The Athens Charter).

Fitch, James Marston (1982), *Historic Preservation: Curatorial Management of the Built World* (New York: McGraw-Hill).

Forsyth, Ann and Kudva, Neema (eds.) (2010), *Transforming Planning: 75 Years of City and Regional Planning at Cornell* (Ithaca, NY: Cornell University).

Foster, Jeremy (2012), 'The Wilds and the Township,' *Journal of the Society of Architectural Historians*, 71 (1), 42–59.

Foxe, David M. (2010), 'Building information modeling for constructing the past and its future,' *APT Bulletin*, 41 (4), 39–45.

Fulton, Gordon W. (1999), 'Policy issues and their impact on practice: Heritage conservation in Canada,' *Bulletin of the Association for Preservation Technology*, 29 (3–4), 13–16.

Galbreath, Carol J. (1975), 'Criteria for Defining the Historic and Cultural Landscape,' *Selected Papers: Conference on Conserving the Historic and Cultural Landscape, Denver, May 1975* (Washington: Preservation Press), 1–9.

Garrett, Billy G. (1990), 'Historic structure reports: A redefinition,' *Cultural Resource Management Bulletin*, 13 (4).

Garrod, Brian (2002), 'Managing Visitor Impacts,' in A. Fyall, B. Garrod, and A. Leask (eds.), *Managing Visitor Attractions: New Directions* (Oxford: Butterworth-Heinemann), 124–39.

Gensheimer, Thomas and Guichard, Celeste Lovette (eds.) (2014), *World Heritage and National Registers: Stewardship in Perspective* (New Brunswick, NJ: Transaction Publishers).

Gerousi, Eugenia and Brouskari, Ersi (2013), 'Medieval City of Rhodes: From impregnable fortress to living city,' *World Heritage*, (67), 30–7.

Getty Conservation Institute (2004), *Incentives for the Preservation and Rehabilitation of Historic Homes in the City of Los Angeles: A Guidebook for Homeowners* (Los Angeles: Getty Conservation Institute).

Gilbert, Frank B. (1970), 'Saving landmarks: The transfer of development rights,' *Historic Preservation*, 22 (3), 13–15.

Glendinning, Miles (2013), *The Conservation Movement: A History of Architectural Preservation, Antiquity to Modernity* (London: Routledge).

Global Heritage Fund (2010), *Saving our Vanishing Heritage: Safeguarding Endangered Cultural Heritage Sites in the Developing World* (Palo Alto, CA: Global Heritage Fund).

Gold, Kerry (2013), 'City's architecture gets a shot in the arm,' *The Globe and Mail*, March 30, p. S8.

Government of Canada (1862), 'Documents Relating to the Construction of the Parliamentary and Departmental Buildings at Ottawa' (Quebec).

Green, Howard L. (1998), 'The Social Construction of Historical Significance,' in Michael A. Tomlan (ed.), *Preservation of What, for Whom? A Critical Look at Historical Significance* (Ithaca, NY: National Council for Preservation Education), 85–94.

Greenlivingpedia (2009), 'Hawthorn West House,' <http://www.greenlivingpedia.org/Hawthorn_West_house>.

Grenville, Jane (2007), 'Conservation as psychology: Ontological security and the built environment,' *International Journal of Heritage Studies*, 13 (6), 447–61.

Grubin, David (dir.) (2009), *The Trials of J. Robert Oppenheimer: Complete Program Transcript*.

Gunn, Cynthia (2001), *Exploring the Connection between Built and Natural Heritage: Research Report* (Ottawa: Heritage Canada Foundation).

—— (2002), *Built Heritage: Assessing a Tourism Resource: Research Report*, ed. Veronica Vaillancourt (Ottawa: Heritage Canada Foundation).

Gurran, Nicole (2011), *Australian Urban Land Use Planning: Principles, Systems and Practice* (2nd edn.; Sydney: Sydney University Press).

Hall, Jennifer (1999), 'Consuming the past at a suburban heritage site: Markham Heritage Estates, Ontario,' *Canadian Geographer*, 43 (4), 433–55.

Harris, Donna Ann (2007), *New Solutions for House Museums: Ensuring the Long-Term Preservation of America's Historic Houses* (Lanham, MD: AltaMira Press).

Harrison, Rodney (2013), *Heritage: Critical Approaches* (London: Routledge).

Heritage BC (2010a), 'Annual Report 2009,' (Victoria: Heritage BC).

—— (2010b), 'Persistence Pays Off! Homeowner Protection Act,' *Heritage BC Quarterly*, (Summer), 4. <http://www.heritagebc.ca/blog?articleid=78>.

—— (2010c), 'Victoria Must Pay For Designation,' *Heritage at Risk* <http://www.heritagebc.ca/blog/victoria-must-pay-for-designation>.

Heritage Branch, New South Wales (n.d.), 'What is movable heritage and why is it important?' <http://www.heritage.nsw.gov.au/06_subnav_04.htm>.

Heritage Council of Victoria (Australia) (2004), *Heritage Impact Statements: Guidelines* (Heritage Information Series; Melbourne: Heritage Council of Victoria).

Heritage Council of Western Australia (n.d.), *Heritage Impact Statement: A Guide* (East Perth: Heritage Council of Western Australia).

Heritage Lottery Fund (2008), 'Conservation Management Planning: Integrated Plans for Conservation, New Work, Physical Access, Management and Maintenance at Heritage Sites' (London: Heritage Lottery Fund).

—— (2010), *Investing in Success: Heritage and the UK Tourism Economy* (London: Heritage Lottery Fund).

—— (n.d.) 'About Us,' <http://www.hlf.org.uk/aboutus/Pages/AboutUs.aspx#.Us75H7SnzQo>.

Hewison, Robert (1987), *The Heritage Industry: Britain in a Climate of Decline* (London: Methuen).

Hill, G. (1936), Treasure Trove Law and Practice from the Earliest Time to the Present Day (Oxford: Oxford University Press).

Historic Royal Palaces (n.d.), 'Tower of London: History and Stories,' <http://www.hrp.org.uk/TowerOfLondon/stories>.

Historic Scotland (2002), *Passed to the Future: Historic Scotland's Policy for the Sustainable Management of the Historic Environment* (Edinburgh: Historic Scotland).

—— (2009), *Scottish Historic Environment Policy* (Edinburgh: Historic Scotland).

—— (2012), *A Climate Change Action Plan for Historic Scotland 2012–2017* (Edinburgh: Historic Scotland).

—— (n.d.) 'What Is Listing?,' <http://www.historic-scotland.gov.uk/index/heritage/historicandlistedbuildings/listing.htm>.

Hlavach, Jeannette (2004), 'Heritage Planning in Vancouver,' in Antiquities and Monuments Office (ed.), *Conference Papers on International Conference: 'Heritage and Education'* (Hong Kong: Leisure and Cultural Services Department), 141–9.

Hoffmann, Ben, Roeger, Steve, Stolton, Sue, and Wise, Phil (2012), 'Australia: Dhimurru, Looking After Our Land and Sea,' in Nigel Dudley and Sue Stolton (eds.), *Protected Landscapes and Wild Biodiversity* (Values of Protected Landscapes and Seascapes; Gland, Switzerland: IUCN), 61–70.

Hohmann, Heidi (2008), 'Mediating Ecology and History: Rehabilitation of Vegetation in Oklahoma's Platt Historic District,' in Richard Longstreth (ed.), *Cultural Landscapes: Balancing Nature and Heritage in Preservation Practice* (Minneapolis: University of Minnesota Press), 109–28.

Holdsworth, Deryck (ed.) (1985), *Reviving Main Street* (Toronto: University of Toronto Press).

Hollier, Steve (2011), 'Turning Back the Hands of Time: Historical Reconstructions,' January 26. <http://stevehollier.wordpress.com/2011/01/26/turning-back-the-hands-of-time-historical-reconstructions/>.

Hollis, Edward (2009), *The Secret Lives of Buildings* (New York: Picador).

Hosmer, Charles B., Jr. (1965), *Presence of the Past: A History of the Preservation Movement in the United States before Williamsburg* (New York: G.P. Putnam's).

—— (1981), *Preservation Comes of Age: From Williamsburg to the National Trust, 1926–1949*, 2 vols. (Charlottesville: University Press of Virginia).

Howe, Barbara J. (1989), 'Reflections on an idea: NCPH's first decade,' *Public History*, 11 (3), 68–85.

Howett, Catherine (2000), 'Integrity as a Value in Cultural Landscape Preservation,' in Arnold R. Alanen and Robert Z. Melnick (eds.), *Preserving Cultural Landscapes in America* (Baltimore: Johns Hopkins University Press), 186–207.

Hunter, John and Ralston, Ian (eds.) (1993), *Archaeological Resource Management in the UK: An Introduction* (Dover: Alan Sutton and Institute of Field Archaeologists).

Hutt, Sherry, Blanco, Caroline M., and Varmer, Ole (1999), *Heritage Resources Law: Protecting the Archaeological and Cultural Environment* (New York: John Wiley).

Ibelings, Hans (2013), 'Mies en valeur,' *Canadian Architect*, 58 (8), 26–30.

ICOMOS (1964), 'International Charter for the Conservation and Restoration of Monuments and Sites' (Venice Charter) (Paris: ICOMOS).

—— (1982), 'The Florence Charter for Historic Gardens' (Paris: ICOMOS).

—— (1987), 'Charter for the Conservation of Historic Towns and Urban Areas' (Washington Charter) (Paris: ICOMOS).

—— (1994), 'The Nara Document on Authenticity' (Paris: ICOMOS).

—— (1998), 'Declaration of ICOMOS Marking the 50th Anniversary of the Universal Declaration of Human Rights' (Stockholm Declaration) (Paris: ICOMOS).

—— (1999), 'International Cultural Tourism Charter: Managing Tourism at Places of Heritage Significance' (Paris: ICOMOS).

—— (2002), 'Ethical Commitment Statement for ICOMOS Members' (Revision, November; ICOMOS).

—— (2011), 'The Paris Declaration: On Heritage as a Driver of Development' (Paris: ICOMOS).

ICOMOS National Committees of the Americas (1996), 'The Declaration of San Antonio' (Paris: ICOMOS).

IHBC (n.d.), 'IHBC: The Institute for Historic Building Conservation,' <http://www.ihbc.org.uk/>.

Imon, Sharif Shams (2013), 'Issues of Sustainable Tourism at Heritage Sites in Asia,' in Kapila D. Silva and Neel Kamal Chapagain (eds.), *Asian Heritage Management: Contexts, Concerns, and Prospects* (Oxford: Routledge), 253–68.

Institute of Historic Building Conservation (n.d.), 'Valuing Historic Places' (Tisbury, Wilts.: IHBC).

Iyer-Raniga, Usha and Wong, James P.C. (2012), 'Everlasting shelters: Life cycle energy assessment for heritage buildings,' *Historic Environment*, 24 (2), 25–30.

Jackson, Mike (2005), 'Embodied energy and historic preservation: A needed reassessment,' *Bulletin of the Association for Preservation Technology*, 36 (4), 47–52.

—— (2010), 'Green Home-Rating Systems: A Preservation Perspective,' *Bulletin of the Association for Preservation Technology*, 41 (1), 13–18.

Jacobs, Jane (1961), *The Death and Life of Great American Cities* (New York: Random House).

Jester, Thomas C. and Park, Sharon C. (1993), 'Making Historic Properties Accessible' (Preservation Brief 32; Washington: National Park Service, Technical Preservation Services).

JISC infoNet (2010), 'Managing Project Risks,' *HUT Introduction to Project Management*, <http://www.pmhut.com/managing-project-risks>.

Jokilehto, Jukka (1996), 'International Standards, Principles and Charters of Conservation,' in Stephen Marks (ed.), *Concerning Buildings: Studies in Honour of Sir Bernard Feilden* (Oxford: Butterworth-Heinemann), 55–81.

—— (1999), *A History of Architectural Conservation*, eds. Andrew Oddy and Derek Linstrum (Butterworth-Heinemann Series in Conservation and Museology; Oxford: Elsevier).

—— (2005), 'Definition of Cultural Heritage: References to Documents in History' (Revised. Originally for ICCROM, 1990; Rome). http://cif.icomos.org/pdf_docs/Documents%20on%20line/Heritage%20definitions.pdf.

—— (2009), 'Conservation Principles in the International Context,' in Alison Richmond and Alison Bracker (eds.), *Conservation: Principles, Dilemmas and Uncomfortable Truths* (Oxford: Butterworth-Heinemann), 73–83.

Kalman, Harold (1976), 'An evaluation system for architectural surveys,' *Bulletin of the Association for Preservation Technology*, 8 (3), 3–27.

—— (1979), *The Sensible Rehabilitation of Older Houses* (Ottawa: Canada Mortgage and Housing Corporation).

—— (1980), *The Evaluation of Historic Buildings* (2nd edn.; Ottawa: Government of Canada).

—— (1994), *A History of Canadian Architecture*, 2 vols. (Toronto: Oxford University Press).

Kalman, Harold and Ward, Robin (2012), *Exploring Vancouver: The Architectural Guide* (4th edn.; Vancouver: Douglas & McIntyre).

Kalman, Harold, Wagland, Keith, and Bailey, Robert (1980), *Encore: Recycling Public Buildings for the Arts* (Toronto: Corpus).

Kamin, Blair (2010), 'Historic Preservation and Green Architecture: Friends or Foes?,' *Preservation*, March/April.

Kaufman, Ned (2009), *Place, Race, and Story: Essays on the Past and Future of Historic Preservation* (New York: Routledge).

Keller, Genevieve P. and Keller, J. Timothy (2003), 'Preserving Important Landscapes,' in Robert E. Stipe (ed.), *A Richer Heritage* (Chapel Hill: University of North Carolina Press), 187–222.

Kelley, Stephen J. and Look, David W. (2005), 'A philosophy for preservation engineers,' *Bulletin of the Association for Preservation Technology*, 36 (1), 8–11.

Kennet, Wayland (1972), *Preservation* (London: Temple Smith).

Kerr, Alastair (1999), 'Public participation in cultural resource management: A Canadian perspective,' *ICOMOS General Assembly* (Mexico City).

Kerr, James Semple (2013), *Conservation Plan: A Guide to the Preparation of Conservation Plans for Places of European Cultural Significance* (7th edn.; Burwood, Victoria: Australia ICOMOS. First published 1982).

King, Thomas F. (2004), *Cultural Resource Laws and Practice: An Introductory Guide* (2nd edn.; Walnut Creek, CA: Left Coast Press).

—— (2009), *Our Unprotected Heritage: Whitewashing the Destruction of Our Natural and Cultural Environment* (Walnut Creek, CA: Left Coast Press).

Klamer, Arjo and Zuidhof, Peter-Wim (1999), 'The Values of Cultural Heritage: Merging Economic and Cultural Appraisals,' *Economics and Heritage Conservation* (Los Angeles: Getty Conservation Institute), 23–61.

Kong, Yuk Foon Doreen (2013), 'The inadequacy of Hong Kong's conservation legislation,' *Hong Kong Lawyer*, August, 44–9.

Labine, Clem (1979), 'Preservationists are Un-American,' *Historic Preservation*, March, 18.

Lambert, Phyllis (2013), *Building Seagram* (New Haven, CT: Yale University Press).

Larsen, Knut Einar (1994) *Nara Conference on Authenticity/Conférence de Nara sur l'authenticité* [online text], UNESCO.

LeClair, Christopher (2001), *The Guide to Strategic Planning for Directors of Non-profit Organizations* (Toronto: Canadian Society of Association Executives).

Lee, Ho-Yin and DiStefano, Lynne (n.d.), 'What Governs Conservation?' (Hong Kong: University of Hong Kong).

Letellier, Robin (2007), *Recording, Documentation, and Information Management for the Conservation of Historic Places: Guiding Principles* (Los Angeles: Getty Conservation Institute).

Leung, Yvonne (2012), 'Hong Kong's inadequate heritage preservation law needs updating,' *South China Morning Post*, February 3.

Levy, John M. (2011), *Contemporary Urban Planning* (9th edn.; Boston: Longman).

Lindgren, James M. (2004), '"A Spirit that Fires the Imagination": Historic Preservation and Cultural Regeneration in Virginia and New England, 1850–1950,' in Max Page and Randall Mason (eds.), *Giving Preservation a History: History of Historic Preservation in the United States* (New York: Routledge), 107–29.

Little, Barbara J. (2009), 'Public Archaeology in the United States in the Early Twenty-first Century,' in Marie Louise Stig Sorensen and John Carman (eds.), *Heritage Studies: Methods and Approaches* (London: Routledge), 29–51.

Lloyd, David (ed.), (1976), *Save the City: A Conservation Study of the City of London* (London: Society for the Protection of Ancient Buildings et al.).

Logan, John R. and Molotch, Harvey L. (1987), *Urban Fortunes: The Political Economy of Place* (Berkeley: University of California Press).

Longstreth, Richard (ed.) (2008), *Cultural Landscapes: Balancing Nature and Heritage in Preservation Practice* (Minneapolis: University of Minnesota Press).

Lottman, Herbert R. (1976), *How Cities are Saved* (New York: Universe Books).

Lowenthal, David (1981), 'Dilemmas of Preservation,' in David Lowenthal and Marcus Binney (eds.), *Our Past Before Us: Why Do We Save It?* (London: Temple Smith), 213–37.

—— (1985), *The Past is a Foreign Country* (Cambridge: Cambridge University Press).

Lowenthal, David and Binney, Marcus (eds.) (1981), *Our Past Before Us: Why do we Save it?* (London: Temple Smith).

Lynch, Kevin (1972), *What Time Is This Place?* (Cambridge, MA: MIT Press).

McClelland, Linda Flint, Keller, J. Timothy, Keller, Genevieve P., and Melnick, Robert Z. (1999), 'Guidelines for evaluating and documenting rural historic landscapes,' *National Register Bulletin*, 30 (Washington: US Department of the Interior).

McKean, Charles (ed.), (1976), *Living Over The Shop* (Eastern Region, Royal Institute of British Architects).

Mackintosh, Barry (2004), 'National Park Service Reconstruction Policy and Practice,' in John H. Jameson Jr. (ed.), *The Reconstructed Past: Reconstructions in the Public Interpretation* (Walnut Creek, CA: AltaMira Press), 65–74.

McManamon, Francis P. and Hatton, Alf (eds.) (2000), *Cultural Resource Management in Contemporary Society: Perspectives on Managing and Presenting the Past*, ed. P.J. Ucko (One World Archaeology, London: Routledge).

Manco, Jean (2009), 'History of Building Regulations,' *Researching Historic Buildings in the British Isles* <http://www.buildinghistory.org/regulations.shtml>.

Manogue Architects and Soltys:Brewster Consulting (c. 2006), *Guidelines for the Assessment of Architectural Heritage Impacts of National Road Schemes* (Dublin: National Roads Authority).

Margaret Gowen & Co. (c. 2006), *Guidelines for the Assessment of Archaeological Heritage Impacts of National Road Schemes* (Dublin: National Roads Authority).

Marris, Peter (1994), 'Advocacy planning as a bridge between the professional and the political,' *Journal of the American Planning Association*, 60 (2), 143–6.

Mason, Randall (2002), 'Assessing Values in Conservation Planning: Methodological Issues and Choices,' in Marta de la Torre (ed.), *Assessing the Values of Cultural Heritage* (Los Angeles: Getty Conservation Institute), 5–30.

—— (2006), 'Theoretical and practical arguments for values-centered preservation,' *CRM: The Journal of Heritage Stewardship*, 3 (2), 21–48.

—— (2008), 'Management for Cultural Landscape Preservation: Insights from Australia,' in Richard Longstreth (ed.), *Cultural Landscapes: Balancing Nature and Heritage in Preservation Practice* (Minneapolis: University of Minnesota Press), 180–96.

Mason, Randy (1999), *Economics and Heritage Conservation* (Los Angeles: Getty Conservation Institute).

Mattinson, Deborah (2006), 'The Value of Heritage—What Does the Public Think?' in Kate Clark (ed.), *Capturing the Public Value of Heritage: The Proceedings of the London Conference, 25–26 January 2006* (London: English Heritage), 86–91.

Mayes, Thompson (2003), 'Preservation Law and Public Policy: Balancing Priorities and Building an Ethic,' in Robert E. Stipe (ed.), *A Richer Heritage* (Chapel Hill: University of North Carolina Press), 157–84.

Menuge, Adam (2010), *Understanding Place: Historic Area Assessments: Principles and Practice* (Swindon: English Heritage).

Messenger, Phyllis Mauch and Smith, George S. (eds.), (2010), *Cultural Heritage Management: A Global Perspective* (Gainesville: University Press of Florida).

Miner, Ralph W. (1969), *Conservation of Historic and Cultural Resources* (Chicago: American Society of Planning Officials).

Morris, William (1889), 'Address to the Annual General Meeting of SPAB,' <http://www.spab.org.uk/supporting-the-spab/legacies/>.

Morris, William, et al. (1877), 'Manifesto,' <http://www.spab.org.uk/what-is-spab-/the-manifesto/>.

Morrison, Jacob H. (1965), *Historic Preservation Law* (2nd edn.; Washington: National Trust for Historic Preservation).

Morton, W. Brown, III (2003), *The Secretary of the Interior's Standards for Historic Preservation Projects: Ethics in Action* (Ethics in Preservation, Indianapolis, Indiana: National Council for Preservation Education).

Mourato, Susana and Mazzanti, Massimiliano (2002), 'Economic Valuation of Cultural Heritage: Evidence and Prospects,' in Marta de la Torre (ed.), *Assessing the Values of Cultural Heritage* (Los Angeles: Getty Conservation Institute), 51–76.

Mulloy, Elizabeth D. (1976), *The History of the National Trust for Historic Preservation 1963–1973* (Washington: Preservation Press).

Murtagh, William J. (1988), *Keeping Time: The History and Theory of Preservation in America* (Pittstown, NJ: Main Street Press).

National Main Street Center (1981), *National Main Street Program Training Program* (Washington: National Trust for Historic Preservation).

—— (c. 1981), *Main Street Means Business: National Main Street Center* (Washington: National Trust for Historic Preservation).

National Park Service (1983), 'Archaeology and Historic Preservation: Secretary of the Interior's Standards and Guidelines [As Amended and Annotated],' <http://www.cr.nps.gov/local-law/arch_stnds_0.htm>.

—— (1983), *Secretary of the Interior's Standards for Architectural and Engineering Documentation* (revised edn., Washington: National Park Service).

—— (1992), 'The Secretary of the Interior's Standards for the Treatment of Historic Properties and Guidelines for the Treatment of Cultural Landscapes,' <http://www.nps.gov/tps/standards/four-treatments/landscape-guidelines/>.

—— (1997), 'How to Apply the National Register Criteria for Evaluation' (revised edn., *National Register Bulletin*; Washington: US Department of the Interior).

—— (n.d.-a), 'Introduction to Standards and Guidelines,' <http://www.nps.gov/history/hps/tps/standguide/overview/using_standguide.htm>.

—— (n.d.-b), 'Ebey's Landing National Historical Reserve, Washington,' <http://www.nps.gov/ebla/index.htm>.

—— (n.d.-c), 'Moving the Cape Hatteras Lighthouse,' <http://www.nps.gov/caha/historyculture/movingthelighthouse.htm>.

—— (n.d.-d), 'National Register of Historic Places,' <http://www.nps.gov/nr/>.

National Park Service, Technical Preservation Services (1995), 'The Secretary of the Interior's Standards for the Treatment of Historic Properties,' <http://www.nps.gov/tps/standards.htm>.

—— (n.d.), 'Tax Incentives for Preserving Historic Properties,' <http://www.nps.gov/tps/tax-incentives.htm>.

National Trust for Historic Preservation (1956), 'Criteria for Evaluating Historic Sites and Buildings,' (2nd edn.; Washington: National Trust for Historic Preservation).

—— (2008), 'Actions to Further the Pocantico Principles on Sustainability and Historic Preservation' (Washington: NTHP).

—— (n.d.), 'Preservation Easements,' <http://www.preservationnation.org/information-center/law-and-policy/legal-resources/easements/#.UulOzfuwSgk>.

National Trust for Historic Preservation and National Center for Preservation Technology and Training (2009), *Pocantico Proclamation on Sustainability and Historic Preservation* (Natchitoches, LA: NCPTT).

National Trust for Scotland (n.d.), 'Little Houses Improvement Scheme,' <http://www.nts.org.uk/Buildings/LHIS/>.

National Trust of Australia, Western Australia (2011), *Maintenance Business Case for Public Places Managed by the National Trust* (Perth: National Trust of Australia (WA)).

Nelson, T. (1994), *The Surveyor's Factbook* (London: Gee Publications).

Netzer, Dick (2006), 'Cultural Policy: An American View,' in Vicktor A. Ginsburgh and David Throsby (eds.), *Handbook of the Economics of Art and Culture* (Handbooks in Economics, 1; Amsterdam: North-Holland), 1223–51.

New South Wales Treasury (2004), *Heritage Asset Management Guideline* (Total Asset Management; Sydney: New South Wales Treasury).

New World Encyclopedia (n.d.), 'Edward Coke,' <www.newworldencyclopedia.org/entry/Edward_Coke>.

New York Preservation Archive Project, The (2010), 'Audubon Ballroom,' <http://www.nypap.org/content/audubon-ballroom>.

Nicholson, Adam (1997), *Restoration: The Rebuilding of Windsor Castle* (London: Michael Joseph).

Nissley, Claudia and King, Thomas F. (2014), *Consultation and Cultural Heritage: Let Us Reason Together* (Walnut Creek, CA: Left Coast Press).

O'Donnell, Patricia and Melnick, Robert Z. (1987), 'Toward a preservation ethic,' *Landscape Architecture*, 77 (4), 136.

Oberlander, Judy, Kalman, Harold, and Lemon, Robert (1989), *Principles of Heritage Conservation*, ed. Mary McKinnon (Technical Paper Series 9; Victoria: Province of British Columbia, Ministry of Municipal Affairs, Recreation and Culture).

Ochsendorf, John (2013), 'Toward a philosophy of preservation engineering,' *Bulletin of the Association for Preservation Technology*, 44 (1), 6–7.

Office of the Auditor General of Canada (2003), 'Protection of Cultural Heritage in the Federal Government,' *Report of the Auditor General of Canada* (Ottawa: Government of Canada).

Omkar (n.d.), 'Architectural Guidance: Reichstag Berlin, Germany,' August 15.

Otis, Daniel (2013), 'Mapping a 1,200-year-old mystery,' *The Globe and Mail*, August 17.

Oxford Economics (2009), *Economic Impact of the UK Heritage Tourism Economy* (London: Heritage Lottery Fund).

Page, Robert R., Gilbert, Cathy A., and Dolan, Susan A. (1998), *A Guide to Cultural Landscape Reports: Contents, Process, and Techniques* (Washington: US Department of the Interior, National Park Service).

Pannekoek, Frits (1998), 'The Rise of a Heritage Priesthood,' in Michael A. Tomlan (ed.), *Preservation of What, for Whom? A Critical Look at Historical Significance* (Ithaca, NY: National Council for Preservation Education), 29–36.

Parker, Patricia L. and King, Thomas F. (1990, rev. 1992, 1998), 'Guidelines for Evaluating and Documenting Traditional Cultural Properties,' *National Register Bulletin*, 38 (Washington: US Department of the Interior).

Parks Canada (2009), 'Formative Evaluation of the Historic Places Initiative,' <http://www.pc.gc.ca/docs/pc/rpts/rve-par/21/3_e.asp#top>.

—— (2010), *Standards and Guidelines for the Conservation of Historic Places in Canada* (2nd edn.; Ottawa: Parks Canada. First published 2003).

—— (2013), 'Cultural Resources Management Policy,' *Guiding Principles and Operational Policies* <http://www.pc.gc.ca/docs/pc/poli/princip/sec3.aspx>.

—— (n.d.), 'Fortress of Louisbourg National Historic Site of Canada,' <http://www.pc.gc.ca/eng/lhn-nhs/ns/louisbourg/index.aspx>.

Pawlowska, Agnieszka (2012), 'Canada: Reconceptualising Wildlife Conservation at Poplar River First Nation, Manitoba,' in Nigel Dudley and Sue Stolton (eds.), *Protected Landscapes and Wild Biodiversity* (Values of Protected Landscapes and Seascapes; Gland, Switzerland: IUCN), 91–8.

Pendlebury, John (2001), 'United Kingdom,' in Robert Pickard (ed.), *Policy and Law in Heritage Conservation* (Conservation of the European Built Heritage; London: Spon Press), 289–314.

Pharr, Clyde (1952), *The Theodosian Code and Novels and the Sirmondian Constitutions* (Princeton, NJ: Princeton University Press).

Phillips, Morgan W. (1971), 'The philosophy of total preservation,' *Bulletin of the Association for Preservation Technology*, 3 (1), 38–43.

Pickard, Robert (1996), *Conservation in the Built Environment* (Harlow: Longman).

—— (2009), *Funding the Architectural Heritage: A Guide to Policies and Examples* (Strasbourg: Council of Europe).

Pickard, Robert and Pickerill, Tracy (2007), 'A Review of Fiscal Measures to Benefit Heritage Conservation' (London: Royal Institution of Chartered Surveyors).

Pilzer, David (2005), *Performance Based Building Regulations: PeBBu Domain 7 Final Report* (Rotterdam: Performance Based Building Thematic Network).

Pinkerton, Connie Capozzola and Burke, Maureen (2004), *The Savannah College of Art and Design: Restoration of an Architectural Heritage* (Charleston: Arcadia Publishing).

Pokotylo, David and Mason, Andrew R. (2010), 'Archaeological Heritage Resource Protection in Canada,' in Phyllis Mauch Messenger and George S. Smith (eds.), *Cultural Heritage Management: A Global Perspective* (Gainesville: University Press of Florida), 48–69.

Powter, Andrew and Ross, Susan (2005), 'Integrating environmental and cultural sustainability for heritage properties,' *Bulletin of the Association for Preservation Technology*, 36 (4), 5–11.

Prism Economics and Analysis and Barry Padolsky Associates (n.d.), *Human Resources in Canada's Built Heritage Sector: Mapping the Work Force and Setting Strategic Priorities* (Ottawa: Cultural Human Resources Council).

Providence City Plan Commission (1967), *College Hill: A Demonstration Study of Historic Area Renewal* (2nd edn.; Providence, RI: City Plan Commission).

Punter, John (2003), *The Vancouver Achievement: Urban Planning and Design* (Vancouver: UBC Press).

Purden, Carolyn (1973), 'Crisis in the Cathedral,' *Canadian Churchman*, October 1073, 9–14.

Quinn, Carolyn and Weibe, Christopher (2012), 'Heritage redux: New directions for the movement,' *Heritage*, 15 (3), 4–10.

Rappoport, Paul (2012), 'Counteracting anti-heritage thinking in Australia's planning policy frameworks,' *Historic Environment*, 24 (2), 47–51.

Reiner, Laurence E. (1979), *How to Recycle Buildings* (New York: McGraw-Hill).

Richardson, Boyce (1972), *The Future of Canadian Cities* (Toronto: New Press).

Riddett, Robyn (2002), 'Risk preparedness and cultural heritage,' *Historic Environment*, 16 (1), 6–11.

Riegl, Alois (1903), 'The modern cult of monuments: Its character and its origin.'

Riesenweber, Julie (2008), 'Landscape Preservation and Cultural Geography,' in Richard Longstreth (ed.), *Cultural Landscapes: Balancing Nature and Heritage in Preservation Practice* (Minneapolis: University of Minnesota Press), 23–34.

Rizzo, Ilde and Throsby, David (2006), 'Cultural Heritage: Economic Analysis and Public Policy,' in Vicktor A. Ginsburgh and David Throsby (eds.), *Handbook of the Economics of Art and Culture* (Handbooks in Economics, 1; Amsterdam: North-Holland), 983–1016.

Robertson, B.M. (1996), *Oral History Handbook* (Oral History Association of Australia (South Australian Branch)).

Roddewig, Richard (1983), *Preparing a Historic Preservation Ordinance* (Planning Advisory Service Report; Chicago: American Planning Association).

Roddewig, Richard J. and Ingram, Cheryl (1987), *Transferable Development Rights Programs: TDRs and the Real Estate Marketplace* (Planning Advisory Report series; Chicago: American Planning Association).

Rodwell, Dennis (2007), *Conservation and Sustainability in Historic Cities* (Oxford: Blackwell).

—— (2011), 'Urban Conservation and Sustainability,' in John H. Stubbs and Emily G. Makaš (eds.), *Architectural Conservation in Europe and the Americas: National Experiences and Practice* (Hoboken, NJ: John Wiley), 45–6.

Roe, Maggie and Taylor, Ken (eds.) (2014), *New Cultural Landscapes* (London: Routledge).

Ross, Michael (1996), *Planning and the Heritage: Policy and Procedures* (2nd edn.; London: E & FN Spon).

Rottle, Nancy D. (2008), 'A Continuum and Process Framework for Rural Historic Landscape Preservation: Revisiting Ebey's Landing on Whidbey Island, Washington,' in Richard Longstreth (ed.), *Cultural Landscapes: Balancing Nature and Heritage in Preservation Practice* (Minneapolis: University of Minnesota Press), 129–49.

Ruskin, John (1849), *The Seven Lamps of Architecture* (Noonday Press edn.).

Russell, Roslyn and Winkworth, Kylie (2009), *Significance 2.0: A Guide to Assessing the Significance of Collections* (2nd edn.; Rundle Mall, SA: Collections Council of Australia).

Rydin, Yvonne (2003), *Urban and Environmental Planning in the UK* (2nd edn.; Basingstoke: Palgrave Macmillan).

Rypkema, Donovan (2002), 'The (economic) value of National Register Listing,' *CRM: The Journal of Heritage Stewardship*, 25 (1), 6–7.

—— (2005), *The Economics of Historic Preservation: A Community Leader's Guide* (2nd edn.; Washington: National Trust for Historic Preservation).

—— (2007), 'Historic Preservation and Sustainable Development,' in Dennis Rodwell (ed.), *Conservation and Sustainability in Historic Cities* (Oxford: Blackwell).

—— (2011), 'Historic Preservation and Sustainable Development,' in John H. Stubbs and Emily G. Makaš (eds.), *Architectural Conservation in Europe and the Americas: National Experiences and Practice* (Hoboken, NJ: John Wiley), 473–4.

Rypkema, Donovan, Cheong, Caroline, and Mason, Randall (2011), 'Measuring Economic Impacts of Historic Preservation: A Report to the Advisory Council on Historic Preservation' (Washington: Advisory Council on Historic Preservation).

Salmon, Ryan (2012), 'Preservation Engineering,' <http://www.pvnworks.com/blog/preservation_engineering/>.

Samuel, Raphael (1994), *Theatres of Memory*, 2 vols. (I: Past and Present in Contemporary Culture; London: Verso).

Sandwith, Hermione and Stainton, Sheila (1985), *The National Trust Manual of Housekeeping* (Harmondsworth: Penguin Books).

Sanoff, Henry (2000), *Community Participation Methods in Design and Planning* (New York: John Wiley).

Saunders, Matthew (1996), 'The Conservation of Buildings in Britain since the Second World War,' in Stephen Marks (ed.), *Concerning Buildings: Studies in Honour of Sir Bernard Feilden* (Oxford: Butterworth-Heinemann), 5–33.

Scheffler, Nils (2009), 'Cultural Heritage Integrated Management Plans,' (Thematic Report 2.0, HerO (Heritage as Opportunity) and UrbAct).

Schmitter, Michelle A. (1995), 'Preservation ethics,' *ASHP Journal*, 7 (3), 1, 3.

Schofield, A.J. (2000), 'Now We Know: The Role of Research in Archaeological Conservation Practices in England,' in Francis P. McManamon and Alf Hatton (eds.), *Cultural Resource Management in Contemporary Society: Perspectives on Managing and Presenting the Past* (London: Routledge), 76–92.

Schuster, J. Mark, de Monchaux, John, and Riley, Charles A., II (eds.) (1997), *Preserving the Built Heritage: Tools for Implementation* (Salzburg Seminar, Hanover, NH: University Press of New England).

Selling, Gösta (1964), 'Legal and Administrative Organisation in Sweden for the Protection of Archaeological Sites and Historic Buildings,' *The Monument for the Man: Records of the II International Congress of Restoration* (Venice).

Shipley, Robert (2000), 'Heritage designation and property values: Is there an effect?,' *International Journal of Heritage Studies*, 6 (1), 83–100.

Shipley, Robert and McKernan, Nicole (2011), 'A shocking degree of ignorance threatens Canada's architectural heritage,' *Architecture in Canada*, 36 (1), 83–91.

Shull, Carold D. (2011), 'The National Register of Historic Places of the United States,' in John H. Stubbs and Emily G. Makaš (eds.), *Architectural Conservation in Europe and the Americas: National Experiences and Practice* (Hoboken, NJ: John Wiley), 449–51.

Silman, Robert (2007), 'Is preservation technology neutral?' *Bulletin of the Association for Preservation Technology*, 38 (4), 3–10.

Sinclair Knight Merz (2007), 'Analysis of the Value of Heritage to the City of Ballarat' (Malvern, Victoria: Sinclair Knight Merz).

Slaton, Deborah (2005), 'The Preparation and Use of Historic Structure Reports,' (Preservation Briefs; Washington: National Park Service Technical Preservation Services, US Department of the Interior).

Smechov, Aleksandr (2011), 'The future of real estate zoning in SoHo,' *The Ticker*, 2. <http://www.baruch.cuny.edu/realestate/pdf/baruch-ticker-article.pdf>.

Smith, Chris (2002), 'Heritage conservation risk assessment,' *Historic Environment*, 16 (1), 21–3.

Smith, Graham (n.d.) 'The Making of Oral History,' *Making History (UK)*, <http://www.history.ac.uk/makinghistory/resources/articles/oral_history.html#theory>.

Smith, Laurajane (2006), *Uses of Heritage* (Abingdon: Routledge).

Sobchak, Andrew (2012), 'Let's Talk,' *Building*, (February/March), 14–17.

Sprinkle, John H., Jr. (2003), 'Uncertain Destiny: The Changing Role of Archaeology in Historic Preservation,' in Robert E. Stipe (ed.), *A Richer Heritage* (Chapel Hill: University of North Carolina Press), 253–78.

Stanley-Price, Nicholas (2009), 'The Reconstruction of Ruins: Principles and Practice,' in Alison Richmond and Alison

Bracker (eds.), *Conservation: Principles, Dilemmas and Uncomfortable Truths* (Oxford: Butterworth-Heinemann), 32–46.

Stapp, Carol and Turino, Ken (2004), 'Does America need another house museum?' *History News*, 59 (3), 7–11.

Stella, Frank (ed.), (1978), *Business and Preservation: A Survey of Business Conservation of Buildings and Neighborhoods* (New York: Inform).

Stiftung Frauenkirche Dresden (n.d.), 'Frauenkirche Dresden: Cross of Peace' (updated current) <http://www.frauen-kirche-dresden.de/alansmith+M5d637b1e38d.html>.

Stipe, Robert E. (2003), 'Some Preservation Fundamentals,' in Robert E. Stipe (ed.), *A Richer Heritage* (Chapel Hill: University of North Carolina Press), 23–34.

Stokes, Samuel N., Watson, A. Elizabeth, and Mastran, Shelley S. (1997), *Saving America's Countryside: A Guide to Rural Conservation* (2nd edn.; Baltimore: Johns Hopkins University Press).

Stovel, Herb (1994), 'Foreword: Working towards the Nara Document,' in Knut Einar Larsen (ed.), *Nara Conference on Authenticity/Conférence de Nara sur l'authenticité* (Paris: UNESCO).

—— (1998), *Risk Preparedness: A Management Manual for World Cultural Heritage* (Rome: ICCROM).

Strange, Ian and Whitney, David (2003), 'The changing roles and purposes of heritage conservation in the UK,' *Planning Practice & Research*, 18 (2–3), 219–29.

Street, Broderick (2012), 'Improving water and energy efficiency: Case study of an 1890s cottage,' *Historic Environment*, 24 (2), 31–5.

Striner, Richard (2003), 'Historic Preservation and the Challenge of Ethical Coherence,' *Ethics in Preservation* (Indianapolis, Indiana: National Council for Preservation Education), 2–13.

Stubbs, John H. and Makaš, Emily G. (2011), *Architectural Conservation in Europe and the Americas: National Experiences and Practice* (Hoboken, NJ: John Wiley).

Sullivan, Sharon and Mackay, Richard (eds.) (2013), *Archaeological Sites: Conservation and Management* (Readings in Conservation, Los Angeles: Getty Conservation Institute).

Swanke Hayden Connell Architects (2000), *Historic Preservation: Project Planning & Estimating* (Kingston, MA: RSMeans).

Swanwick, Carys (2002), *Landscape Character Assessment: Guidance for England and Scotland* (Cheltenham and Edinburgh: The Countryside Agency and Scottish Natural Heritage).

Sykes, Meredith H. (1984), *Manual on Systems of Inventorying Immovable Cultural Property* (Museums and Monuments; Paris: UNESCO).

Symons, Thomas H.B. (ed.), (1997), *The Place of History: Commemorating Canada's Past* (Ottawa: Royal Society of Canada).

Taylor, C.J. (1990), *Negotiating the Past: The Making of Canada's National Historic Parks and Sites* (Montreal and Kingston: McGill-Queen's University Press).

Taylor, Ken and Lennon, Jane L. (eds.) (2012), *Managing Cultural Landscapes*, eds. William Logan and Laurajane Smith (Key Issues in Cultural Heritage, London: Routledge).

Teutonico, Jeanne Marie and Matero, Frank (eds.) (2003), *Managing Change: Sustainable Approaches to the Conservation of the Built Environment* (Los Angeles: Getty Conservation Institute).

The Oval Partnership Limited and Commonwealth Historic Resource Management Limited (2008), 'Heritage Impact Assessment Report on the Nurses' Quarters (Block A) of Queen Mary Hospital' (Hong Kong).

Thornes, Robin and Bold, John (1998), *Documenting the Cultural Heritage* (Los Angeles: Getty Information Institute).

Throsby, David (2001), *Economics and Culture* (Cambridge: Cambridge University Press).

—— (2002), 'Cultural Capital and Sustainability Concepts in the Economics of Cultural Heritage,' in Marta de la Torre (ed.), *Assessing the Values of Cultural Heritage* (Los Angeles: Getty Conservation Institute), 101–17.

Tilden, Freeman (1977), *Interpreting Our Heritage* (3rd edn.; Chapel Hill: University of North Carolina Press. First published 1957).

TimberhArt Woodworks (n.d.), 'Historical Timber Frame Restoration: St. George's Anglican Round Church,' <http://www.timberhart.com/pages/timberframersstgeorgesanglican.html>.

Tr'ondëk Hwëch'in (2007), 'Tr'ochëk Heritage Site: Management Plan' (Dawson City: Tr'ondëk Hwëch'in).

Tschudi-Madsen, Stephan (1976), *Restoration and Anti-Restoration: A Study in English Restoration Philosophy* (2nd edn.; Oslo: Universitetsforlaget).

Tung, Anthony M. (2001), *Preserving the World's Great Cities: The Destruction and Renewal of the Historic Metropolis* (New York: Clarkson Potter).

Tyler, Norman and Ward, Robert M. (2011), *Planning and Community Development: A Guide for the 21st Century* (New York: W.W. Norton).

Tyler, Norman, Ligibel, Ted J., and Tyler, Ilene R. (2009), *Historic Preservation: An Introduction to its History, Principles, and Practice* (New York: W.W. Norton).

UK Parliament (n.d.), 'Managing and owning the landscape,' <http://www.parliament.uk/about/living-heritage/transformingsociety/towncountry/landscape/overview/>.

US Department of the Interior, National Park Service (1999), 'How to Prepare National Historic Landmark Nominations,' *National Register Bulletin* (Washington: US Department of the Interior).

UCLG (n.d.), 'Culture 21: Agenda 21 for Culture,' <http://www.agenda21culture.net/index.php>.

UNESCO (1954), 'Convention for the Protection of Cultural Property in the Event of Armed Conflict' (The Hague: UNESCO).

—— (1972), 'Convention concerning the Protection of the World Cultural and Natural Heritage' (Paris: UNESCO).

—— (2003), 'Convention for the Safeguarding of Intangible Cultural Heritage' (Paris: UNESCO).

—— (2005), 'Vienna Memorandum on World Heritage and Contemporary Architecture—Managing the Historic Landscape' (Paris: UNESCO).

—— (n.d.), 'What is Intangible Cultural Heritage?' <http://www.unesco.org/culture/ich/index.php?lg=en&pg=00002>.

UNESCO World Heritage Centre (1994), *Operational Guidelines for the Implementation of the World Heritage Convention* (Paris: UNESCO).

—— (2013), *Operational Guidelines for the Implementation of the World Heritage Convention* (Paris: UNESCO).

—— (n.d.-a), 'Historic Centre of Warsaw,' <http://whc.unesco.org/en/list/30>.

—— (n.d.-b), 'The Criteria for Selection,' <http://whc.unesco.org/en/criteria>.

UNESCO World Heritage Committee (2009), 'Committee Decisions: 35COM 7B.64, Historic Centre of Macao (China) (C 1110).' http://whc.unesco.org/en/decisions/4472/

United Nations Environment Program and World Tourism Organization (2005), 'Making Tourism More Sustainable: A Guide for Policy Makers,' (Paris and Madrid: UNEP/WTO).

United States Conference of Mayors, Special Committee on Historic Preservation (1966), *With Heritage So Rich* (New York: Random House).

University of British Columbia (n.d.), 'UBC Renew,' <http://sustain.ubc.ca/campus-initiatives/green-buildings/ubc-renew>.

Victoria Civic Heritage Trust (2012), '1990–2012 Grant Summary' (Victoria: Victoria Civic Heritage Trust).

Viollet-le-Duc, E.E. (1854–68), *Dictionnaire raisonné de l'architecture française du XIe au XVIe siècle*, 9 vols. (Paris: A.Morel).

Ward, Robert M. and Tyler, Norman (2005), 'Integrating historic preservation plans with comprehensive plans,' *Planning Magazine* (October).

Warner, Raynor W., et al (1978), *Business and Preservation: A Survey of Business Conservation of Buildings and Neighborhoods* (New York: Inform).

Warren, John (1996), 'Principles and Problems: Ethics and Aesthetics,' in Stephen Marks (ed.), *Concerning Buildings: Studies in Honour of Sir Bernard Feilden* (Oxford: Butterworth-Heinemann), 34–54.

Watt, David and Swallow, Peter (1996), *Surveying Historic Buildings* (Shaftesbury: Donhead).

Weaver, Martin E. (1997), *Conserving Buildings: Guide to Techniques and Materials* (revised edn.; New York: John Wiley).

Wells, Jeremy C. (2007), 'The plurality of truth in culture, context, and heritage: A (mostly) post-structuralist analysis of urban conservation charters,' *City & Time*, 3 (2), 1–13.

Weyeneth, Robert R. (2004), 'Ancestral Architecture: The Early Preservation Movement in Charleston,' in Max Page and Randall Mason (eds.), *Giving Preservation a History: History of Historic Preservation in the United States* (New York: Routledge), 257–81.

White, Bradford J. and Roddewig, Richard J. (1994), *Preparing a Historic Preservation Plan* (Planning Advisory Service Reports; Washington: American Planning Association).

Wikipedia (n.d.-a), 'Audubon Ballroom,' <http://en.wikipedia.org/wiki/Audubon_Ballroom>.

—— (n.d.-b), 'Ise Grand Shrine,' <http://en.wikipedia.org/wiki/Ise_Grand_Shrine>.

—— (n.d.-c), 'Hippocratic Oath,' <http://en.wikipedia.org/wiki/Hippocratic_Oath>.

—— (n.d.-d), 'Mackenzie Valley Pipeline Inquiry,' <http://en.wikipedia.org/wiki/Mackenzie_Valley_Pipeline_Inquiry>.

—— (n.d.-e), 'Public History,' <http://en.wikipedia.org/wiki/Public_history>.

—— (n.d.-f), 'Pruitt-Igoe,' <http://en.wikipedia.org/wiki/Pruitt_Igoe>.

Wolloch, Richard (1977), 'Penn Central v. City of New York: A Landmark Landmark Case,' *Fordham Urban Law Journal*, 6 (3), 665–85.

World Commission on Environment and Development (WCED) (1987), *Our Common Future* [Brundtland Report] (Oxford: Oxford University Press).

World Tourism Organization (n.d.), 'World Tourism Organization UNWTO,' <http://www2.unwto.org/>.

Wright, Russell (1976), *A Guide to Delineating Edges of Historic Districts* (Washington: Preservation Press).

Yeomans, David (1996), 'Understanding Historic Structures,' in Stephen Marks (ed.), *Concerning Buildings: Studies in Honour of Sir Bernard Feilden* (Oxford: Butterworth-Heinemann), 214–38.

Ziegler, Arthur P., Jr., Adler, Leopold, II, and Kidney, Walter C. (1975), *Revolving Funds for Historic Preservation: A Manual of Practice* (Pittsburgh: Ober Park Associates).

Index